Wonder Foods

CALIFORNIA STUDIES IN FOOD AND CULTURE

Darra Goldstein, Editor

Wonder Foods

THE SCIENCE AND COMMERCE
OF NUTRITION

Lisa Haushofer

UNIVERSITY OF CALIFORNIA PRESS

University of California Press
Oakland, California

© 2023 by Lisa Haushofer

Library of Congress Cataloging-in-Publication Data

Names: Haushofer, Lisa, author.
Title: Wonder foods : the science and commerce of nutrition / Lisa
    Haushofer.
Other titles: California studies in food and culture ; 80.
Description: Oakland, California : University of California Press, [2022] |
    Series: California studies in food and culture ; 80 | Includes bibliographical
    references and index.
Identifiers: LCCN 2022024990 (print) | LCCN 2022024991 (ebook) |
    ISBN 9780520390386 (cloth) | ISBN 9780520390393 (paperback) |
    ISBN 9780520390409 (epub)
Subjects: LCSH: Nutrition—Economic aspects. | Food industry and trade—
    Economic aspects. | Food—Technological innovations—History.
Classification: LCC TX353 .H334 2022 (print) | LCC TX353 (ebook) |
    DDC 338.4/7664—dc23/eng/20220803
LC record available at https://lccn.loc.gov/2022024990
LC ebook record available at https://lccn.loc.gov/2022024991

Manufactured in the United States of America

32 31 30 29 28 27 26 25 24 23
10 9 8 7 6 5 4 3 2 1

Publication supported by a grant from
The Community Foundation for Greater New Haven
as part of the Urban Haven Project.

To my family

CONTENTS

ILLUSTRATIONS

Introduction

BALLOONS OVER INDIANAPOLIS

THE YEAR WAS 1921, and the afternoon sky over Indianapolis was filled with balloons. Like bloated Easter eggs, they moved between mountains of clouds and formed ever-changing clusters of color against the white horizon. A gentle breeze blew in from the southeast, defying predictions from the night before that had threatened to thwart the spectacle with strong winds. From all across town, over forty thousand people had come to witness the balloons' takeoff for the international balloon race, crowding nearby streets, roofs, and even treetops, in order to catch a glimpse of these wonders of modern technology. An eerie quiet had descended upon the rest of the city, as businesses and industries were forced to shut down for the day. As the announcers barked out the names and state affiliations of each departing balloon, the crowds cheered and waved at the crews, who busily fired their vessels' burners and proudly descended American flags from the rims of their ascending baskets. The crowd lingered long after the last balloon had been waved off and the last patriotic tune of the military band booked for the occasion had faded into the evening's silence. They stood and watched as the flames became smaller and smaller, and finally disappeared, "like big fireflies chasing each other over the edge of eternity."[1]

Elmer Cline was in the crowd that day. For the rest of his life, he would recall the floating balloons in the air, and the sense of awe he felt at their sight. He especially remembered their vivid primary colors. Cline was a rational man, a businessman, not easily moved by spectacle. In fact, his profession often required him to look beyond the kinds of displays that might dazzle others. He was deputy manager of merchandising development of the Taggart Baking Company, and as such, he had constructed many advertising campaigns designed to produce fascination and curiosity in his consumers. In 1915, for example, he had come up with the concept of a "tickler," a series of advertisements that created suspense by not naming the product.[2] A number of advertising trade journals had reported on the tactic, praising Cline's knack for innovation.[3] At the same time, Cline was a stickler for accuracy and authenticity; he had played a significant role in bringing about the Indiana Bakery Law of 1919, the first law in the country to regulate the weight and measure of bread sold to consumers.[4] He was, in short, a man not naturally prone to sentimentality.

But on that afternoon in 1921, Elmer Cline was inspired. Watching the International Balloon Race take off from his hometown, he had felt a sense of wonder. There was no better way to describe the feeling that had overcome him: a mixture of admiration, surprise, and disbelief; amazement at the technical and scientific achievement evident in the display; astonishment at the quasi-miraculous powers at work in overcoming seemingly unchangeable laws of nature. He allowed his mind to conjure up images of a world transformed through the ability to traverse ever greater distances at ever greater speed, unimpeded by the ballast of terrain or exhaustible animal power. If gravity could be overcome so effectively, who knew what other earthly forces could be outmaneuvered.

Ever the pragmatist, Cline applied the profound impressions of that afternoon to a work problem he had been mulling over for some time. He was charged with finding a catchy name for his baking company's newest loaf of bread. While attending the balloon race in 1921, Elmer Cline had found the solution: he would name it Wonder Bread. Over several days, the word *wonder* appeared in a series of newspaper advertisements, in the same "tickler" fashion Cline was known for, leaving consumers to "wonder" what the product might be.[5] On May 23, 1921, the mystery was finally resolved when Taggart's Wonder Bread was launched.[6]

To this day, the red, blue, and yellow balloons of that afternoon's Indianapolis sky, immortalized on the bread's iconic wrapper, form an integral part of Wonder Bread's advertising lore. So does Cline's moment of wonder: again and again, the story of inspiration striking as the balloons rose into the sky has been rehearsed in company literature, magazine stories, and popular histories.[7] The "official Wonder Bread historical reference and cookbook" recalls the 1921 Indianapolis Speedway balloon race with a mixture of pride and pathos, describing how Cline was "filled with wonder" and "struck" by "inspiration" watching "the scene of hundreds of balloons creating a

FIGURE 1. Balloon race, Indianapolis Motor Speedway, 1909. Bass Photo Co. Collection, Indiana Historical Society.

kaleidoscope of color as they floated across the Midwestern sky."[8] It is a captivating origin story, laced with serendipity, awe, and ingenuity, attributes so often associated with scientific discovery and progress.

But as with a well-yeasted loaf of bread, there are holes in the story. For one, there was no international balloon race at the Indianapolis Motor Speedway in 1921. International balloon races had been organized in different locations around the world since 1906, including in the United States, but the 1921 race took place some four thousand miles away in Brussels, Belgium, and Wonder Bread was launched before it took place.[9] There was also a series of national races organized by the Aero Club of America, but in 1921, the national race was held in Birmingham, Alabama. Indianapolis had been the site of national balloon races over a decade earlier, in 1909 and 1910, and the details in the story above are taken from newspaper accounts of the 1909 race.[10] It is not unlikely that Cline had visited either or both of those races, and still remembered the scenes in 1921. But if this was the case, his Eureka moment was not exactly the one evoked in the promotional tales.

A more likely explanation is that Cline and his baking company had intended to tie the launch of Wonder Bread to an international balloon race that was indeed scheduled to take place at the Indianapolis Speedway on October 13, 1920, roughly half a year before the appearance of the first "tickler." Only, the race never took place. It was canceled due, rather mundanely, to a lack of gas.[11] On August 6, 1920, the general manager of Citizens Gas Company had notified the management of the Indianapolis Motor Speedway in an undiplomatic letter that his company was "unwilling to furnish even 1,000 cubic feet of gas for the race under the present condition of fuel shortage."[12] He even declared that there was "no city in the United States that should, under present conditions, undertake to provide gas for this purpose"; such a use of natural resources would, in his mind, be "criminal."

Regardless of how the story emerged, this mythical start to life befits a product that would remain suspended between fact and fiction, between science and superstition, between substance and spectacle, throughout the course of its eventful career. If advertisements of Wonder Bread were to be believed, the loaf was not just another ordinary staple, but a kind of miracle food, a magic bullet that would solve deeply rooted issues in US dietary culture and in US society more broadly. The Chicago World's Fair of 1934 celebrated Wonder Bread as an object of scientific and technological ingenuity, a promising commercial venture, and a potential solution to broader public health challenges.[13] Advertisements emphasized the "intensive research" that had gone into developing it and had produced a "scientifically perfect" national loaf with "remarkable nutritive and dietetic qualities."[14] Wonder Bread was also touted as a marvel of modern convenience, being one of the first breads to be sold in presliced form and linking Wonder Bread's story with the legendary phrase, "the best thing since sliced bread."[15] During World War II, the bread was at the center of a national bread fortification campaign, supported by nutrition scientists, government agencies, and food businesses, which sought to improve the supposedly defective American diet resulting from nutrient-deprived, industrially processed foods.[16] By promising to nourish better, to contain superior nutritional value, and to be more digestible, Wonder Bread proposed a convenient way out of seemingly immutable and difficult social and natural realities. Here, in short, was a hero to save the day (and we do like our heroes to come with unusual origin stories, like Jesus, or Hebe, or Superman).

But there was a dark side to the white loaf. Wonder Bread's vision of a better dietary future was highly selective, and it built on (and perpetuated) transgressions of the past. Advertisements of the bread matched the 'whiteness' of the loaf with images of almost exclusively white, middle-class young women, men, and children.[17] Wonder Bread's racist nutritional vision extended all the way to the production line, where racialized and classed hierarchies were mapped onto a scale of labor tasks according to their proximity to nourishment: only white workers were allowed to handle the dough, whereas workers of color were restricted to mechanical and menial tasks far away from the edible substance.[18] Advertisements also reinforced gendered notions of healthy eating and well-nourished bodies, displaying slender, sexualized women whose Wonder Bread–heavy diet allegedly supplied them with the digestive capacity and "energy" needed to become the kind of "vital women" that "fascinate men."[19] Through its emphasis on the nutritional benefits of wheat, Wonder Bread was also heir to a long history of extractive agricultural practices and indigenous land dispossession.[20] And while the bread fortification campaign may have supplied sections of the population with much needed vitamins, it only responded to dietary challenges that products like Wonder Bread, through their encouragement of industrial and monoculture agriculture, had been complicit in creating in the first place.[21]

Such instances of myopia were a feature, not a bug, of the peculiar alliance at the heart of products like Wonder Bread, a bond that had linked the nutrition sciences and the emerging world of nutritional entrepreneurship since the nineteenth century, which produced many generations of supposedly miraculous food products. Since the 1840s, a growing squad of experts and entrepreneurs in Western imperialist and industrializing nations had begun to mobilize nutritional knowledge in a quest to expand imperial territories, safeguard national food supplies, dominate natural resources, and ensure commercial profit. They hoped to measure, multiply, and monetize the nutritional properties of meat, wheat, and other edibles, and create new commercial articles of food based on their findings. They articulated nutritional theories within decidedly imperialist, extractivist, and white supremacist frameworks of thought and fed them into their marketable nutritional commodities. In the process, they appropriated Native food knowledge and contributed to indigenous displacement and genocide for the sake of creating enough nourishment for white settlers. They exploited colonized people's food resources and laid the basis for a permanent restructuring of global ecologies, agriculture, and trade routes. They advocated for an efficiency overhaul of poor people's diets and digestions in order to turn them into more "productive" and "thrifty" members of society. And they embraced eugenic thought and allowed it to infuse their nutritional theories and products for the sake of "race betterment." Nutritional progress and products, in short, have long served some people and places at the expense of others.

In the century between 1840 and 1940, products like Wonder Bread came to shape our modern relationship to food. This book explores their history. It tells the story of how Western science and the market simultaneously turned their gaze to the contents of the stomach, and experts as well as eaters came to think of food through products, and of the body through food. This was a time of rapid change in how knowledge about nutrition was produced. It was the beginning of the field we call nutrition science, and while we know much about the people, places, and politics involved in its early history, we have not yet fully realized the role of commercial interests and marketable products in shaping the scientific priorities and claims of this field. Nor have we accounted for the exploitative power structures within which nutritional scientific ideas were articulated. There is no doubt that people's relationships to food were, and are, varied and complex, shaped by religion, class, affect, and taste. But at a time when political economy played an ever more central role, not only in specialist circles, but in large areas of political and social life, food and nutrition became increasingly bound up with economic ways of reasoning.

The material result of these developments was a growing number of *wonder foods*—from a concentrated "meat biscuit" to John Harvey Kellogg's famous breakfast cereals. Wonder foods promised marvelous solutions to pressing problems that were at once individual and social, at once nutritional and economical. Their tangible nature made them good tools to think with. Nutrition scientists as well as economic experts converged around these products to articulate new ideas about how food should be produced, consumed, and distributed, and who should eat what, how, and how much. This book examines wonder foods and the ideas they embodied. It argues that the trajectory of modern food was not merely an innocuous artifact of technological innovation and scientific advancement, but the consequence of systemic intellectual commitments in Western industrialized nations to capitalism, empire, resource extraction, and white supremacy. Wonder foods might have dazzled with visions of modernity, efficiency, and scientific progress, but they came with exclusionary views about who deserved to eat, live, and thrive.

WONDER FOODS

Even though Elmer Cline named his bread Wonder Bread, he would not have thought of it as a *wonder food*. Though this phrase might be legible to many readers as designating foods with additional, extraordinary powers, the term is neither a historical nor a contemporary regulatory, medical, or marketing category. Instead, I adopt it here from its vernacular context as an analytical term. Partly, this is to avoid teleology or anachronism. Contemporary words like *superfood*, *nutraceutical*, *functional food*, or *dietary supplement* have no consistent historical equivalent, and they don't map neatly onto historical categories such as protective foods, health foods, medicinal foods, or special foods.[22] Some contemporary terms like *nutraceutical* (a contraction of nutrition and pharmaceutical) have also been designed to convey explicit promotional messages, suggesting the existence of a nutritional-pharmaceutical in-between space populated by products that combine the benefits of both domains, without the disadvantages of either.[23] Adopting such marketing vocabulary is therefore not only imprecise but risks reifying the very ideas such vocabulary is meant to evoke.

The noun *wonder* is rooted in the Old English *wundor* and related to the German *Wunder*, meaning "miracle" or "marvel." It describes anything that exceeds expected occurrences. The wonder foods discussed in this book promised, above all, to transgress norms. They claimed to go beyond, to nourish more efficiently, more naturally, more completely, than ordinary foods. Faced with new food challenges (brought on by empire, industrialization, and a growing consumer society), experts began to ask different questions of nourishment and of eating bodies. They became interested in maximizing the nutritional efficiency of foods, stretching the supply of edible resources, and optimizing eating and digesting bodies. The result was a nutritional growth mentality that differed fundamentally from the emphasis on moderation and balance that had dominated nutritional thinking until the eighteenth century.[24] Concentrated meat extracts, digestion-optimizing gruels, and similar products were the result of this larger shift. They brought with them new ways of describing, and thinking of, foods as "more than": more nutritious, more digestible, more stimulating.

The transgressive character of past wonder foods was also evident in their existence between various realms of expertise and belief. The word *wonder* implies not only an augmented mechanism of action against an imagined baseline but also a miraculous quality that resists conventional ways of achieving truth. By their very definition, miracles are supernatural phenomena that defy rational explanations and thereby rely on "alternative" interpretations, faith, imagination, intuition, and superstition. Foods like Wonder Bread straddled their consumers' needs to understand and rationalize, to comprehend products' precise mode of therapeutic action on bodily inadequacies, on the one hand, and be mystified, surprised, and enchanted, on the other. During a historical period of growing secularization, such products accommodated remnants of religious, spiritual, and magical thinking. At a time of increasingly professionalized scientific authority, they invited (and constructed) the performance of unorthodox expertise and non-expert ways of knowing. Wonder Bread's advertisements, for instance (like those of other products discussed in this book) introduced a fictional female character who also authored a significant number of cookbooks and advice columns around the bread.[25] Female food knowledge, real or not, was a regular feature of many wonder foods, offsetting their male creators' elite scientific authority with a more personable, practically oriented, and experiential perspective.

Wonder foods were also foods to *wonder with*. By making, discussing, and circulating nutritional products, experts wrestled with long-standing questions about the essence of matter, the hierarchy of species, the nature of metabolism, and the purpose of taste and pleasure in eating.[26] According to historians Katharine Park and Lorraine Daston, the investigation of wonders and the sensation of wonder were integral parts of early modern knowledge production that led scientific investigators to "the outermost limits of what they knew, who they were, or what they might become."[27] Even though they were devised during a later period, supposedly at the height of scientific rationality, the wonder foods in this book functioned similarly as projections of what was known about nourishment and what more could be made of it. Rather than simply commercial applications of preexisting nutritional knowledge, wonder foods were means of imagining the eating and digesting body, framing nutritional disease, grasping the natural through the artificial, and interpreting the physiological and chemical effects of foods on eaters. To their makers, wonder foods could stretch the limits of what was deemed natural or possible and intervene in challenges that went far beyond the optimization of individual diets. Toasted breakfast cereal could improve digestion and contribute to "race betterment," while nutritional yeast could clear skin and lead a declining empire to more industrial self-sufficiency. Wonder foods, in short, inhabited imaginative worlds at the intersection of commerce and science. By unraveling their imaginative fabric, this book reveals how economic imperatives and scientific knowledge production around food shaped one another.

Finally, the term *wonder foods* links the products in this book with their pharmaceutical cousins—wonder drugs—and the notion of "magic bullets."

As historians of pharmaceuticals and biomedicine have shown, magic bullets tend to reconfigure complex societal and medical challenges as easily fixable technical problems, and in the process, narrow the range of solutions considered.[28] Like many twentieth-century pharmaceuticals, wonder foods were hailed as simple interventions for the entrenched ills of industrial societies. So-called artificially digested foods, for instance, seemed to offer a practicable solution to food shortages and malnutrition, while saving their inventors and champions from having to reimagine food inequality, wage labor, and poverty on a deeper level. Examining the history of wonder foods can help us understand how we have come to prize certain food solutions at the expense of others.

THE SCIENCE AND COMMERCE OF NUTRITION

By focusing on specific wonder foods and their historical contexts, this book provides a new perspective on the development of the nutrition sciences and their intensifying relationship to the world of nutritional entrepreneurship during the nineteenth and early twentieth centuries. Ever since (and even long before) the publication of Andrew Cunningham and Harmke Cumminga's influential edited collection *The Science and Culture of Nutrition* (which the title of this book references) in the mid-1990s, historians have explored how the nutrition sciences were informed by, and shaped, the broader social, political, and cultural contexts in which they were embedded.[29] Some of this work also examined the role of commercial products in disseminating and popularizing nutritional scientific concepts and vocabulary to an ever-growing consuming public.[30]

But the emergence of food as a commodity—packaged, branded, advertised, and widely distributed—was also intimately linked to the rise of industrial and commercial modes of thinking about food.[31] In what Steven Kaplan and Sophus Reinert have termed the "economic turn" in the mid-eighteenth century, economic ways of reasoning became central, not only to what we might think of as economic matters, but to matters of statecraft, society, and culture.[32] Growing rivalries among the major imperial players, the astounding rise of Britain to its place as a world power (which was interpreted as enabled largely by economic factors), and the recognition that the most urgent problems of the time (such as famine, the food supply, imperial governance) were, first and foremost, economic issues all ushered in the "economic century."[33] The language of economy pervaded politics, science, and everyday life. "Economic man" who worked to accumulate wealth replaced "sinful man" who worked to achieve redemption.[34]

Economic reasoning also came to pervade the realm of food. The commercial contexts in which nutrition was increasingly probed in the course of the nineteenth and early twentieth centuries forced attention on particular questions about food's transportability and durability; the relationship between its content, mass, and function; the ratio between useful and 'wasted' food components; the economizing potential of digestion and taste; and the taste preferences of consumers. These questions came to shape the very core of nutritional knowledge production. Important nutritional scientific milestones, such as the articulation of nutrients and food groups, the unraveling of the physiology of digestion, the role of digestive enzymes, and the discovery of vitamins, were all bound up with theories of political economy, resource extraction, welfare spending, and economic development.[35]

The alliance of nutritional and economic thought had profound consequences for how food was understood to relate to humans and the natural world. This period saw the transition from a nutritional knowledge system based on sensual perception and foods' qualitative properties to one based on foods' content of nourishing constituents.[36] Historian and philosopher of science Gyorgy Scrinis has coined the term *nutritionism* to describe this growing identification of a food's nourishing power with its quantifiable content of nutrients.[37] While the advent of nutritionism is often associated with the growing influence of modern science on matters of food and diet, it was the nutrition sciences' strong economic orientation, this book seeks to show, that gave it shape. In nutrition as in commerce, eighteenth-century equations of economical digestions and balanced humors slowly gave way to nineteenth-century calculations of digestive maximization and nutritional surplus value. Similar developments affected understandings of digestion and taste: digestibility ceased to be a qualitative agreement between aliment and eater and became instead a quantitative capacity of foods and bodies, to be counted and enhanced. Taste no longer indicated the suitability of certain foods for certain constitutions, but a treacherous enticement to follow the path toward conspicuous consumption for all eaters. Rather than simply "scientized" or "medicalized," then, the "modern" diet became, above all, economized.

Along with new understandings of nutrition, digestion, and taste came new ways of telling the story of aliment. Parables of food's divine purpose, perfect design, and geographical specificity were replaced by narratives of nutritional progress, tales of culinary development, and bold speculations about the possibility of bending nature and manipulating nourishment. Such ideas were articulated by new networks of nutritional expertise, brought together by a common commitment to food as a matter of both commercial and scientific importance. As imperial economies gave way to consumer markets in the course of the late nineteenth and twentieth centuries, the production of ideas about wonder foods increasingly relied on the social sciences alongside the natural sciences. By the 1940s, these developments propelled wonder foods on divergent paths: toward high-end consumer products for the rich and healthy in Western industrialized countries, on the one hand, and emergency public health interventions for the poor and sick in low-income countries, on the other.

While visions of nourishment were often articulated with the aim of nourishing some bodies better, they also relied on the nutritional exploitation of other people and places. Wonder foods were not simply ingenious creations of a free-market society; they were products of what Cedric Robinson has termed "racial capitalism," a systematic extraction of value and knowledge from racialized and economically dispossessed groups.[38] The makers of wonder foods routinely appropriated indigenous knowledge, female expertise, and colonial resources under the guise of rendering them simultaneously more scientific and more productive. They reimagined imperial maps and racial hierarchies to further exclude those deemed inferior. Rather than bridging the gap between the kitchen and the laboratory, between distant parts of empire, or between classes of people, wonder foods accentuated these divisions. Rather than ensuring a fair and responsibly produced supply of healthy food to all, they contributed to making nutrition the exclusive province of wealth, whiteness, and willpower, of private responsibility and personal pocketbooks.

ROAD MAP

As quirky and outlandish as they might seem to us today, the particular wonder foods whose stories I will tell in this book—the meat biscuit, the self-digestive gruel, the breakfast cereal, and the yeast cube—all reflect larger historical trends in the history of nutrition science and commerce. Each product represents a group of nutritional consumables that gained particular traction during a certain time period: concentrated foods like the meat biscuit were all the rage from the 1840s to the 1860s; self-digestive or artificially digested foods excited experts and consumers alike from the 1870s to the 1890s; the turn of the century was the moment of the breakfast cereal and all kinds of "health foods"; and everyone, including individual consumers, imperial trade associations, and the earliest international health organizations, was excited about yeast supplements from the 1920s to the 1940s. Designations such as "special foods," "medicinal foods," "health foods," or "protective foods," used by historical actors to refer to these products, suggest that these were foods considered extraordinary even at the time of their making. That each of these products was also exhibited in a public display space or exhibition (just like Wonder Bread at the Chicago World's Fair) indicates that they were deemed worthy of attention, not only by scientific or economic experts, but among a broader public. All of these wonder foods engendered an outpouring of opinions, claims, and ideas, immortalized in published texts and archival documents, which expose their grand nutritional and economic promises, but also the trail of racial oppression and ecological exploitation left in their wake.

The story of wonder foods was written by Western scientists, economic thinkers, and imperialists; it therefore takes place primarily in Britain and the United States, the epicenters of empire, racial capitalism, and nutritional science at the time. Similar products were made in other Western countries such as France and Germany, and the British and American actors in this book drew on nutritional and economic knowledge from those places. But the scale of British and US imperial influence, scientific infrastructure, and economic ambition was extensive during the period in question, and wonder foods took off here to an unparalleled degree. While wonder foods were imagined, made, and described by the privileged, their story also sheds light on the influence and knowledge of those marginalized and exploited by Western imperialism and racial capitalism. Understanding how their contributions to wonder foods were erased while their lives were being threatened by the very racist, extractivist, and sexist philosophies that undergirded many nutritional products is crucial to appreciating the enduring violent legacies of the history of nutrition.

The first section of the book situates the emergence of wonder foods within the history of nineteenth-century nutritional, imperial, and economic thought in Britain and the United States. Chapter 1 focuses on Gail Borden's meat biscuit, an American concentrated extract of beef baked with flour.

It was created by Texan surveyor, entrepreneur, imperialist, and creator of Borden's condensed milk, Gail Borden, and his partner Ashbel Smith, in the late 1840s. The meat biscuit's production was rooted in long-standing concerns over how to make food portable for military campaigns, exploratory travel, and territorial conquest. It also built on older notions of enhancing the nutritiousness of foods by intensifying or concentrating their nourishing "essence." At the same time, the biscuit crystallized a new approach to nutritional knowledge production that was seeking to locate the nourishing capacity of foods in their extractable subcomponents and understand the relationship of such "nutrients" to the size, weight, and transportability of food products. Though poorly executed, the biscuit managed to raise considerable hopes among influential individuals within the US military-imperial network for its potential to transform large cows into small, portable cakes and thereby enable imperial conquest, expand the white imperial settler project, and facilitate the genocide of Native peoples. The chapter argues that the advent of nutritional scientific concepts such as nutrients and food groups was not a neutral scientific advancement that enabled the invention of new nutritional scientific products like the meat biscuit. Rather, imperialist impulses to dominate new territories and appropriate new resources played a crucial role in inspiring new nutritional questions and driving new visions of nourishment and nutritional products.

While the meat biscuit was ultimately a commercial failure in the United States, it had a second wind in Britain, where it resonated with British imperial and economic projects. Chapter 2 situates the meat biscuit within the profound transformations brought about by industrialization, urbanization, colonization, population growth, land use, rising inequality, and access to food that had converged to produce a food crisis of unprecedented urgency and political visibility in Britain. The chapter uncovers the networks of scientific and economic expertise connected by the Great Exhibition that considered products like the meat biscuit promising solutions to the food crisis. The meat biscuit, to British experts, was a means of using "wasted" imperial resources and simultaneously augmenting the nourishing capacity of food at the microscopical level. Together, chapters 1 and 2 argue that imperialist-economic impulses to know food through its functional subcomponents preceded nutritional scientific consensus on food's "nutrients" and methods to reliably extract them.

While the debates about the meat biscuit were largely concerned with food production, nutritional chemistry, and the creation of more cost-nutritious food products, the focus turned in the 1870s and 1880s toward food consumption, digestive physiology, and the optimization of food uptake through individual digestive systems. These are examined in the book's second section. Chapters 3 and 4 analyze a new group of nutritional consumer products enriched with digestive enzymes that claimed to improve digestion and thereby make more efficient use of scarce resources. Whereas in Britain (analyzed in chapter 3), such products were linked to the thrift movement and calculations of the economic burden of sickness, their significance in the United States, where they took off in the 1890s and early 1900s, was rooted in growing concerns about dependence, welfare, and the injurious effects of consumption (chapter 4).

Chapter 3 analyzes Benger's Food, one of several British consumer products enriched with digestive enzymes and marketed for relief of digestive troubles and illness more generally in the 1870s and 1880s. The chapter brings to light the intellectual and institutional ties between the marketers of products like Benger's Food, digestive physiologists, and advocates of the thrift movement. It shows how products like Benger's Food allowed them to imagine a world in which enhanced digestive systems and more digestible foods would lead to a more stable food supply and to a more securely nourished nation. With artificially digested products like Benger's Food, experts reimagined the functioning of the digestive apparatus, the mechanism of digestive disease, as well as the role of the individual in the economic health of the nation.

The flood of enzyme-enriched, "predigested" products that had gripped Britain soon reached the United States, where it incited fears that such products would soon turn the entire country into an army of weak, dependent, "pre-digested Tommies." In response, American physicians and entrepreneurs, including the famous John Harvey Kellogg, reinvented enzyme-enriched foods as nutritive products that merely stimulated (rather than substituted) the natural digestive capacities of individuals during the 1890s and 1910s. Chapter 4 analyzes the creation of Kellogg's health foods, including Kellogg's famous flaked cereal and a range of so-called peptogenic foods. Rather than the result of Kellogg's lone genius or eccentricity, the chapter suggests, these products must be understood within the context of enzyme physiology, eugenics, US imperialism, and the formation of a consumer culture in the early twentieth century. The chapter exposes the links of Kellogg's health foods with Kellogg's studies of Native peoples and their food customs. It argues that Kellogg's reinvention of predigested foods as flaked cereal and peptogenic foods was rooted in a growing concern with "race betterment," eugenic critiques of welfare and health care, and a desire to appropriate Native knowledge and techniques.

The final chapter turns to the growing focus on social science research rather than natural science research in the production of wonder foods and to the use of commercial nutritional products in public and global health campaigns. Chapter 5 examines two diverging uses of yeast. The first is the so-called "Yeast for Health" campaign of the 1920s and 1930s, which advertised Fleischmann's Yeast as a health food to be taken for a variety of conditions. Fleischmann's Yeast and similar vitamin products marked a shift in the relationship between science and business. In response to more stringent scientific oversight over consumer products in the aftermath of the Pure Food and Drug Act of 1906, marketers of products increasingly turned to consumer research and began to invite alternative forms of "expertise" in the evaluation of wonder foods. The second part of the chapter follows the invention of "food yeast" in the context of the British Empire and in the emerging infrastructure of international health. It argues that food yeast was developed as a reaction to an imperial crisis but resonated with the agendas of international health organizations to find cheap, effective interventions for malnutrition. By following these two different stories about yeast, the chapter illustrates the divergent trajectories of wonder foods in the twentieth and twenty-first centuries: toward high-end consumer products marketed to mostly well-nourished, affluent consumers as lifestyle products, on the one hand, and toward emergency medicinal interventions into acute malnutrition in the context of global health campaigns, on the other.

By the end of the 1940s, wonder foods had established their place in individual diets as well as in product-centric approaches to public and global health challenges. Marketers of products could now choose from an established catalog of nutritional physiological mechanisms and nutritional marketing strategies alike. Products at the intersection of the science and commerce of nutrition had become well accepted by consumers, prized by global health campaigners, and infinitely adaptable to changing nutritional fashions. Wonder foods emerged through the interplay of contingent economic, scientific, and white supremacist forces, and the products examined in the following pages make this interplay visible and concrete. But wonder foods are only an extreme manifestation of a much deeper transformation, one that concerns the very essence of our relationship to food and the natural world. It is above all this profound change that the book seeks to lay bare.

ONE

————

"Focussed Flesh"

INTRODUCTION

Hartman Venable was looking forward to this evening with a near perfect mixture of dread and delight. Since he had arrived in St. Jerome (an important Southwestern city where Mr. Venable had been sent as a minister), he had crossed paths with Ezra Micajah Parsons a few times—in the street, at a mutual acquaintance's house, at church. Each time, the encounter had left Mr. Venable curious, bewildered, and a little speechless. Curious because Mr. Parsons had been described to him as the originator of "dozens of inventions"—an amphibious ("terraqueous") machine, a paddle-free steamboat ("a dead failure"), and a preparation of concentrated meat ("Focussed Flesh"). Bewildered because the encounters had all been ended rather abruptly—and rather one-sidedly—by Mr. Parsons. And speechless because it had been nearly impossible to get a word in, as Mr. Parsons had talked incessantly, without pause or pity for his listener. At some point, in between one rapid succession of sentences and the next, Mr. Parsons had gleaned enough presence of mind to finally ask Mr. Venable to dinner.

Mr. Parsons' house lay quite a walk away in the suburbs of St. Jerome, but Mr. Venable could spy it from a distance, with its observatory and flagstaff towering over the roof. The house was surrounded by a good ten acres of land enclosed with a high fence. As soon as Mr. Venable reached the gate, Mr. Parsons stormed out, greeted his visitor, and ushered him inside. Mr. Venable had barely been introduced to Mrs. Parsons ("my second wife") and their daughter Alice ("our owny one") when Mr. Parsons handed him a plate of soup. "It is a fat hen which I condensed with my own hands not three months ago," Mr. Parsons declared; "more nutritive food never was eaten." Mr. Venable dutifully ate what he quickly identified as chicken soup, though his assertions that this was "good soup, excellent soup" were insincerely given. There was nothing inherently wrong with the meal except "a hazy sort of doubt which seemed to rest, like a fog, upon the taste thereof." Besides, he had never cared much for chicken soup and had always known it as invalids' food. Mr. Parsons' wife and daughter seemed to share Mr. Venable's sentiments: "Our little Owny here and I never touch it," Mrs. Parsons assured him. "We don't believe in his inventions, sir,—not one bit." She did, however, hasten to add that she had faith in his motives.

After dinner, Mr. Parsons invited Mr. Venable to take a stroll around the gardens. Mrs. Parsons waved them off with a stern warning to Mr. Venable not to go on her husband's machine, "as you value your life." Mr. Venable thanked her for the meal and followed his host who had already departed for the grounds. The two men walked for a long while, passing a fig orchard, a banana grove, and various groups of lemon, orange, and almond trees. They finally reached a sort of warehouse, and Mr. Parsons begged his guest to step inside. A large baker's oven stood in the middle of the dark, humid room, surrounded by tables and heaps of boxes. Mr. Parsons then picked up a small cracker from a pan on one of the tables and showed it to his visitor. "What do you suppose this is?" he asked Mr. Venable. Puzzled, Mr. Venable guessed that it was a soda cracker. "No, sir," Mr. Parsons triumphantly cried, "That is a spring chicken!" In detail, Mr. Parsons proceeded to describe the process by which he had turned a chicken into a cracker. "I boil the chicken in a vacuum, extract every atom of bone and fibre, leaving the essential chicken itself," he explained. The extracted chicken would then be baked in a pan, expelling all superfluous water. "What is left is intensely and exclusively *chicken*," Mr. Parsons exclaimed proudly. Dropping the chicken in a pot of boiling water would transform it into a nourishing soup, just like the one Mr. Parsons had served for tonight's dinner. "One chicken to a cracker" and "exactly twelve chickens to a pan," Mr. Parsons explained, was the precise ratio of concentration.

Not only chicken but beef, "a calf, and a fat one," and "a whole barnyard of pigs" had been boiled down and put into boxes by Mr. Parsons. "And what do you think that is?" Mr. Parsons asked, picking up another fragment from a slightly bigger pot. "Bite it, and see," he coaxed Mr. Venable. Unable to await Mr. Venable's guess, Mr. Parsons solved the tasting riddle. "That is a turkey," he proclaimed; "a whole drove of turkeys in those pans." Mr. Venable dutifully expressed his astonishment, and in return, was treated to a full exposition of the inventor's ambitions. "In a few years the armies and especially the navies of the world will be fed upon my food," Mr. Parsons prophesied. "It will be by reason of my invention that the North Pole and the South will be discovered." Everything, simply everything the inventor could get his hands on—"a potato into a pill-box, a pumpkin into a table-spoon, the biggest sort of watermelon into a saucer"—would be condensed by Mr. Parsons. "The day will come," he promised, "when a distiller will have learned from me to put a whole vineyard into a barrel." He then paused briefly, an act so uncharacteristic for Mr. Parsons that it startled Mr. Venable. But it had its desired effect, for Mr. Venable found himself listening closely to Mr. Parsons triumphant conclusion: "What I want to say is this: The world is changing. In the direction of condensing."[1]

· · ·

The story above is taken from a semi-fictional account by William Mumford Baker, a Presbyterian minister who, in 1849, spent a year at Galveston, Texas, as assistant pastor to the local church. The protagonist, Mr. Venable, was likely modeled after Baker himself, while the local inventor, Mr. Parsons, was almost certainly based on Texan surveyor, newspaper editor, and inventor Gail Borden (1801–1874), who is perhaps best known today as the creator of condensed milk. Though unique in its explicitly fictional orientation, it was not the first account of Gail Borden and his condensed foods, nor would it be the last.[2] Over time, the reasons for telling Borden's story shifted. At the height of the US-American consumer revolution in the 1950s, biographers turned to condensed milk as an iconic American brand and to Borden as a personification of the American dream, symbolizing "the log-cabin-to-mansion quality which nineteenth-century Americans believed was their peculiar belonging."[3] More recent writers saw in Gail Borden's condensed milk a symbol of the origins of industrialized food and the decline of the American diet. Convenient, processed, and opaque, canned milk stood for a growing lack of transparency, an increasing focus on consumer advertising, and a proliferation of unhealthy eating habits.[4]

Common to most accounts, including Baker's semi-fictional tale, is a de-piction of Borden somewhere between admiration and ridicule: a sincere innovator on the one hand, "consumed with a passion for research, and a desire to improve daily life"; a hopeless tinkerer, on the other, who got lucky once (with condensed milk), while his other ideas were a series of "ludicrous failures," the meat biscuit chief among them.[5] A concoction that not only sounded rather distasteful to modern ears but was ultimately a commercial failure, the biscuit fitted awkwardly into tales of American entrepreneurial success and histories of tasty but innutritious convenience foods alike. But the meat biscuit was not just a harmless if eccentric precursor of condensed milk, nor was Borden merely a well-meaning, pipe-dreaming tinkerer with his head in the clouds and his heart in the right place.

The meat biscuit was, above all, a technology of empire, and its inventor a willing participant in the US imperial project. Together with his business partner, Ashbel Smith, a physician, soldier, and politician, Borden designed and promoted the biscuit specifically to serve the needs of Manifest Destiny, to advance American economic development, and to facilitate the displacement and extermination of the North American continent's Native inhabitants. The need to provide traveling armies and ships with portable and durable rations had long inspired the search for portable foods.[6] But the meat biscuit promised an entirely new approach to nourishment that would enable military mobility and nutritive concentration on a previously unprecedented scale. Through products like the meat biscuit (of which there were many), food experts and entrepreneurs were grasping for a way to locate the nourishing function of food in its subcomponents and create highly nourishing consumables of significantly lesser weight and bulk. This shift toward a constituent-based approach to nourishment, a crucial aspect of our contemporary understanding of nutrients and food groups, did not develop in a vacuum, nor was it advanced with a dispassionate eye toward improving health or advancing scientific nutritional knowledge. Instead, those ideas arose in part to serve imperial and economic ends that were specific to the historical context in which the meat biscuit and similar products were developed.

Crucial to the initial success of the meat biscuit (and responsible for its ultimate failure) was the imperial-military economy that had emerged in conjunction with US expansion across the continent and functioned as an important market for the biscuit. Borden and Smith cultivated ties to important military figures and bartered for a supply contract for their invention. The resulting military correspondence reveals that the biscuit's imperial profile was not merely a promotional strategy devised by Smith and Borden but an idea that resonated with military and political officials at the highest levels of empire and government. At the same time, the biscuit embodied a vision of civilizational progress and a promise of economic development.

The biscuit's processed character and its potential to be manufactured on a grand scale accorded it a place in debates about the relationship between resource abundance and national prosperity (as well as renown beyond the United States, which will be discussed in chapter 2).

GAIL BORDEN, IMPERIAL ENTREPRENEUR

In April 1850, Gail Borden boarded a steamship from Galveston to New Orleans, and from there traveled up the Mississippi River to St. Louis. As his boat joined the line of ships that curved around the river's bend waiting to dock, he had time to observe the city's impressive outline against the gray April sky.[7] The city rose from the river in two soft plateaus of limestone, first abruptly, then gradually, until it reached a modest height of sixty feet above the water. Borden had seen the first houses of the suburbs emerge from the city's deforested surroundings ahead of their approach. But now he observed—with the keen eye of the surveyor—that most of the brick-and-wood dwellings of the city center were crammed into a thickly settled space of two and a half by one and a quarter miles. Clearly, the city had not been built in full anticipation of its rapid expansion. In a mere forty years, the population had grown from 1,400 in 1810, to 77,850 in 1850. This proliferation of St. Louis reflected its place as the "imperial capital of the 'white man's country' of the West" and the linchpin of its export-driven military-agricultural economy.[8] Below, on the landing, dock workers hauled large quantities of molasses, lead, and fur from wagons onto steamships and barrels of wheat, corn, oats, pork, beef, and cheese from steamships onto wagons. St. Louis was the gateway that connected the raw abundance of the American continent to markets, empire, and prosperity.

Borden had come here precisely to profit from this connection. He wished to put the biscuit into the hands (and mouths) of influential military men who might secure its future as a technology of empire. Borden himself, in one capacity or another, had spent much of his life contributing to the territorial expansion of white settler America. Born in 1801 in Norwich, New York, Borden passed a considerable portion of his youth moving ever westward. In 1829, he was granted over four thousand acres of land from the Mexican government in Texas and moved there with his family. In Texas, Borden farmed, kept livestock, and worked as a surveyor. His surveying skills earned him several important positions, including an appointment by

Stephen F. Austin to conduct an official survey of the Texan colony. Borden also worked in the land grant business. He was put in charge of the General Land Office at San Felipe under Austin and later worked for the Galveston City Company. In the port city of Galveston, for which he provided the first map, Borden ultimately settled down and built his meat biscuit business.[9]

Mexico's liberal settlement policy, from which Borden profited, was rooted in a desire to secure what was perceived to be an unstable border region between the republics of the United States and Mexico. It sought to encourage white population growth and thereby dilute the existing Native population to the West. But incoming white US settlers preferred the East for its closeness to important trade routes and to the cotton planting states. They also came in ever greater numbers, so that Mexico finally prohibited Anglo-American settlers from entering Texas in 1830.[10] This caused consternation among the settlers. Many white settlers also brought the people they had enslaved with them, and Borden was no exception.[11] The abolition of slavery in Mexico in 1829 further enraged white US settlers, and they began to organize rebellious activities against the Mexican government, culminating in a proclamation of Texan independence from Mexico in 1836.[12] The conflict over Texas escalated when the United States announced its intention to annex the Texan territory and followed up with a declaration of war on Mexico in 1848.

The result of the Mexican-American War was the so-called Mexican Cession, the second largest acquisition of land by the United States at that time after the Louisiana Purchase. Populated with an ethnically and religiously diverse set of inhabitants, this territory frightened US imperialists as much as it excited them; it offered land but also seemed to threaten the cohesion and stability of the republic. While the decision to go to war over such heterogeneous territories had been contested, the need to settle them now with white Americans seemed indisputable.[13]

Borden's own biography was inextricably linked to these developments of US imperialism. Borden was a delegate to the 1833 convention in San Felipe which petitioned the Mexican government for a repeal of the settlement prohibition.[14] During the armed conflict resulting in the declaration of Texan Independence, Borden published the region's only newspaper, a mouthpiece for resistance against the Mexican government.[15] Letters from this period attest to Borden's continuous shortage of money and the financial difficulties under which he ran his printing business. Even so, he eagerly insisted that any refusal on his part to accept more free printing before payment did not imply that he was "less attached to the cause in which Texas has been engaged," or that he "would withhold any aid which it would be in my power to render my country."[16]

Borden's business partner, Ashbel Smith (1805–1886), played an even more prominent role in the political and imperial aspirations of the mid-nineteenth-century United States.[17] A physician, statesman, and soldier, Smith had studied medicine at Yale University, and had afterward toured the scientific hubs of Europe for three years (as one did in those days in order to become a successful doctor).[18] Upon his return in 1836, he joined the Texan insurgence as surgeon general of the Texan Army. Like Borden, he held government posts in the early Texan Republic after the fighting; he served as the Republic's ambassador to Britain from 1841 to 1845 and as secretary of state in 1845. In this capacity, he secured a treaty of amity and commerce between Texas and Britain.[19] During the Mexican-American War, Smith served again as surgeon general of the US Army. A close friend of Sam Houston, he was selected to represent Texas during the 1851 Great Exhibition in London, where the meat biscuit would be exhibited (chapter 2).

Smith was also an outspoken white supremacist. He repeatedly declared that the "Anglo-Saxon race" was "the most vigorous offshoot of the whole human family," and "genius, moral and intellectual power" were its prerogative alone.[20] The Mexican-American War, in Smith's opinion, was only the inevitable fate of that race to "overrun and possess in perpetuity the vast region extending from our southern boundary to the Isthmus of Panama" in order to "civilize" and "Americanize" "degenerate Mexico."[21] These beliefs were not merely private opinions but firmly held convictions that informed his political and commercial activities. In 1844, for instance, he vocally defended the institution of slavery against British abolitionist voices to the British foreign secretary, expressing in no uncertain terms "the explicit disapproval by the Texan government of all proceedings having for their object the abolition of slavery in Texas."[22]

Borden probably approached Smith strategically for Smith's intellectual and personal connections to medicine and to the US military. Smith maintained a medical practice in Galveston and wrote a widely cited account of the 1839 yellow fever epidemic.[23] He was a member of the American Society for the Advancement of Science and of the New York Academy of Medicine. His plantation home boasted a private medical library, which Borden allegedly visited regularly according to one biographer.[24] As surgeon general during the Mexican-American War, Smith would have come into contact with influential figures in the US Army. All of this made him a formidable ally for Borden's meat biscuit venture. As did his capital: Smith likely invested the considerable sum of five hundred dollars in the meat biscuit business.[25]

Borden and Smith shared an interest in food and agricultural experimentation. On his plantation, Smith raised chickens and grew corn and sugar (a crop he believed would be more profitable to Texas than cotton).[26] Food was of vital importance to the American economic and white supremacist project, and Southern planters like Smith were acutely concerned with the food supply. During the 1840s and 1850s, they imported large quantities of food from the Midwestern United States to avoid sacrificing valuable acreage of potential cotton fields to the production of meat and other food. But lack of food, in the minds of planters, also carried the risk of revolt by enslaved people—easily the most dreaded specter for many nineteenth-century American enslavers.[27] As a result, the search for more efficient means of food production and procurement became a primary concern for planters.[28]

Long before the production of the meat biscuit, Borden and Smith were engaged in experimental agricultural activity with the explicit aim of maximizing the availability of nourishment in a limited space. One of their joint ventures involved the Rohan potato, a crop famed for its high yield and "productiveness" among European and US farmers.[29] According to the *Gardiner's Magazine*, the Rohan promised "much from the bulk produced in feeding cattle." It was unclear, however, whether "more nutritive matter per acre" might not be produced from less "bulky" varieties," and so the Rohan joined a long list of crops and animals tested for their nutritive potential against their spatial requirements in the mid-nineteenth century.[30]

Food was also crucial to realizing American imperialist ambitions and achieving the Jeffersonian Dream. Creating a nation of incorrupt, self-sufficient men required spatially expanding white settlement areas and freezing economic development at the stage of yeomanry.[31] This involved transforming vast stretches of cultivated, inhabited territory into "virgin soil" and "the West" by emptying it of its peoples and fortifying it with costly and bulky military operations. Such operations, in turn, depended on a light, portable, heat-resistant, and above all, highly nourishing food supply. It was this goal that had brought Borden to St. Louis in April 1850. With the meat biscuit, Smith and Borden responded to the military and imperial demand for concentrated nourishment. In so doing, they raised questions about how precisely the nourishing function of a food related to its size and weight.

Today, we understand the nourishing power of foods mostly through what they *contain*. We think of proteins and fats and carbohydrates and vitamins and minerals. We think of food as made up of subcomponents, nourishing constituents, which, through their quantity, determine the nutritiousness and healthfulness of a food. Nutrition labels help us select foods that contain more of a particularly desirable nutrient, such as high-fiber cereal, omega-3-fortified margarine, or orange juice rich in vitamin C. All of these products suggest that determining a food's nutritiousness is best done by analyzing its content of "nutrients" and measuring their quantity. Gyorgy Scrinis has coined the term *nutritionism* to describe this nutrient-centric understanding of foods' nourishing effect, which also allows for easy commercialization.[32] Nutritionism, according to journalist and food writer Michael Pollan, has become a quintessential characteristic of modern nutritional thinking, an indication of the degree to which scientific vocabulary and commercial interests have permeated, and perhaps corrupted, our relationship to food.[33]

There is no doubt that food contains distinct biochemical components and that these biochemical components play an important role in nourishing human bodies. Scientists have developed more and more reliable methods for measuring vitamins, minerals, and proteins, and have linked a lack of these components to nutritional deficiency diseases such as scurvy, beriberi, or rickets. But while humans require a minimum of essential nutrients, there is no evidence that exceeding the required amount of most food components leads to better health. On the contrary, excessive quantities of many nutrients such as vitamin D or protein are likely to do more harm than good.[34] The notion that nourishment can be thought of on a scale, a quantifiable measure that corresponds directly to degree of nutritiousness, is a relatively new idea, not fully articulated until the nineteenth century, and it is rooted in culture as it is in science. Borden and Smith's meat biscuit and other concentrated foods were a part of this development.

Until the eighteenth century, the nutritiousness of food was understood primarily as a function of its *kind* rather than its *content*.[35] Whether a food was animal or vegetable, fresh or ripe, sweet or sour, watery or dry, determined its nature, its quality, its *essence*, and therefore its effect on the bodies of eaters. Rather than an assemblage of distinct nutrients, nourishment was thought to consist of a single nourishing matter.[36] All foods contained it, whether they were vegetables or fruits or meat or bread or cheese. This nourishing matter circulated through the natural world in a grand cosmological cycle: plants would take their nourishment from the earth, animals fed on plants, and humans fed on animals. As nourishing matter thus circulated through the hierarchy of beings, it would undergo a continuous process of change, rendering it more and more nourishing.

At the heart of this notion of gradual, qualitative change of a single nourishing substance lay long-standing ideas about the transformation of matter as a process of "refinement," or "elaboration." Everyday transformative processes that could be observed in practices like distillation, fermentation, or cooking provided models for imagining the alteration of edible matter in the body. Similarly, chemical examination techniques, most importantly distillation analysis, offered ways of grasping (both materially and metaphorically) the nature of substance transformation. For centuries the primary method for investigating the properties of matter, distillation analysis involved the application of heat, a known transformative agent, to produce a progressive change in the substance analyzed.[37] Over successive stages of distillation, a single material would be transformed into an ever more refined substance. In the process, the transformed substance would yield distinct products of distillation—water, spirits, oils, salts, and earth—that would be captured and analyzed. These products, however, were not considered the component parts of a particular substance so much as the "elementary principles of all matter."[38] Since there were four known elements or essences that could be stripped away from any examined substance during distillation, the final distilled substance was also referred to as the fifth element or fifth essence.[39] Our contemporary word "quintessence" still echoes this original meaning. Accordingly, the process of transformation was not one of disassemblage, an isolation of preexisting ingredients from a composite mix. Rather, it was a gradual metamorphosis of a substance into the purest, most "essential," most characteristic version of itself.

Culinary techniques mirrored this understanding of substance transformation. The application of heat in cooking gradually delivered food from its coarse and earthy nature, releasing its essence, its nutritive core. Eighteenth-century cooks produced versions of elaborated and concentrated nourishment, such as broths, soups, gravies, reductions, so-called "restaurants," and even "quintessences."[40] Historian Emma Spary has coined the term *hyper-nourishment* to refer to such foods consisting of rich versions of themselves.[41] "Unearthing" the nutritive essence of food in this manner did not necessarily lead to a quantitative reduction of its weight or bulk; instead, it was embedded in a logic of qualitative transformation, with the aim of developing, intensifying, refining, and transubstantiating food's substance and flavor.[42]

Cookery, in turn, anticipated and imitated what happened to food inside bodies. It functioned as an extension of the digestive process, and the digestive process was governed by the same logic of distillation analysis as cooking itself. In digestion, distant natures—of mineral, plant, and animal origin—were converted into the essence of the eater in a process of gradual elaboration. It was an operation toward achieving refinement, purity, complexity, and above all, similarity of matter—a process of *assimilation*.[43] In this cosmology, what counted as nourishing was determined by a food's degree of similarity in *kind* to the eater. Similar substances required less "elaboration" to be made into human bodily tissue; animal food was believed to be more easily digestible, and therefore more nourishing, than plant food. Eighteenth-century dietetic manuals and chemical texts on foodstuffs tended to be arranged by categories of *kind*: a typical table of contents would distinguish animal from vegetable food, liquid from solid food, and different kinds of meats and vegetables from one another.[44] Taste, because it signaled the similarity of edible substances with the constitution of the eater, was regarded as a sign of the nourishing potential of certain foods for the individual ingester. Rather than an antithesis to nutritional value, taste was an indicator of it. The development and intensification of flavor in cooking practices was therefore an integral part of rendering food more nutritious.[45]

But from the late eighteenth century, a profound change in how nourishment was understood and examined was underway, one that located nourishment in distinct food components. Historians of food and science have described several developments that contributed to this shift in understanding. A broader process of scientific secularization, the growing dominance of chemistry in the sciences and in public life, and new chemical techniques of analysis certainly "opened up organic substances, like food, to the gaze of the chemist," and a scientific "discourse on nutrition" subsumed and secularized moral and religious notions of food.[46] At the same time, food had long been probed within modern chemistry's predecessor, chymistry (or alchemy), which was by no means an occult or fringe practice, but a mainstream scientific enterprise. In order to understand the shift toward content-centric theories of nutrition, we therefore must also look to changes within the discipline of chemistry itself, as well as to the broader historical context in which these changes occurred.[47]

For one, animal and plant chemistry were increasingly practiced within the professional contexts of pharmacy and medicine, and animal and vegetable substances were probed more and more for their medicinal and pharmaceutical purposes.[48] Added to that was the challenge posed by plant materials bioprospected from Europe's expanding empires. A growing number of such substances, previously unknown to European scientists, had to be incorporated into European pharmaceutical and botanical systems, a task for which European colonists often relied on indigenous knowledge of a substance's uses.[49] These professional and material changes were paralleled by a growing concern with existing methods of analysis. Whereas previously, chemists had overwhelmingly relied on their senses to determine a substance's essence, they now began to privilege the role of *function* or *virtue* in revealing a substance's nature.[50] As sensory analysis thus gave way to an emphasis on use, distillation analysis came under attack for destroying, rather than revealing, the essence of matter.[51] Instead, chemists relied more and more on solvent extraction, a method of analysis they regarded as a less radical transformation of a plant's virtues. Solvent extraction consisted in the use of water or alcohol to separate the so-called proximate principles of plant matter, those components that plants would yield upon being subjected to solvent analysis. Whether the extracted substances were the ultimate components of plant matter or were themselves composed of even smaller particles was a matter of debate. But either way, solvent extraction relied on, and reinforced, the notion that a plant contained distinct components, and that chemical extraction was merely a process of separation.[52]

"Extracts" of matter therefore came to displace "essences" in the epistemic logic of matter analysis, and the products of extraction were systematically examined for their respective subcomponents and possible functions. The domain of food and nutrition was no exception. From the early nineteenth century, chemists probed foods for their components, and components for their physiological role in nutrition. In 1827, chemist William Prout categorized the proximate principles found in animals and plants into three major "alimentary principles"—the saccharine, the oily, and the albuminous—and declared that all were equally necessary to human nutrition.[53] Others homed in on single constituents as the primary seat of nourishment. French physiologist François Magendie examined the role of the chemical element nitrogen in 1816 by feeding dogs solely on sugar, a substance considered nutritious at the time, but that contained no nitrogen. The dogs soon developed symptoms of disease, and some even died. Magendie concluded that sugar alone was incapable of nourishing dogs, and that nitrogen played a central role in nourishment.[54] German chemist Justus von Liebig also emphasized the role of nitrogen in the human diet and asserted that nitrogen was the chemical substance responsible for the true nourishing function, the building up of the body's tissues (which we no longer believe is true). Liebig also described an extraction method for meat—essentially a solvent analysis—that supposedly yielded the nourishing constituents of meat more reliably than previous methods of cooking.[55] But it would soon come under attack precisely because it did not contain enough of the very substance Liebig had identified as the seat of nourishment, nitrogen.[56]

By the time Gail Borden began working on his meat biscuit, then, the possibility of identifying nourishing constituents was a widespread hope. But how exactly the nourishment-carrying subcomponents of food could reliably be extracted, or how those subcomponents carried out their nourishing function, was far from resolved. No sooner were nutritious subcomponents raised as a possibility, however, than the idea of concentrating them into a single food and thereby producing a highly nourishing yet light form of nourishment took shape. It materialized and drove nutritional knowledge production even before the precise seat of nourishment had been agreed on. Understanding the transition toward a constituent-based conception of nourishment therefore also requires asking why the idea of compact nourishment gained such traction during this period. The view toward chemistry might reveal *what* happened en route to a constituent-based approach to food. But it is the imperial and economic contexts of products like the meat biscuit that indicate *why* content-centric questions about nourishment were asked so insistently in the first place.

"THE ORIGINAL INVENTOR OF FOCUSSED FLESH"

Although all Borden's surviving claims about the meat biscuit suggest that he alone was the "original inventor of Focussed Flesh," crucial knowledge and inspiration for the product likely came from a different source.[57] According to historian Joe B. Frantz, one "not altogether reliable version" of the origin of the biscuit involved a Comanche food called *pinole*.[58] A Dutch merchant friend of Borden had apparently gifted Borden some of the food, supplied by the merchant's frontier trader from San Saba, Texas. Pinole consisted of "powdered, pulverized, dried buffalo meat, dried crushed hominy and mesquite beans." It could be "eaten dry or moistened and pre-pared as a cake." It could also serve as a travel food, "compound into a buffalo gut" and "worn as a belt." Unfortunately, Frantz does not cite any evidence for his claim, nor does the archival record hold any sources confirming a Native genealogy of the meat biscuit. But the use of a food by the name of "pinole" (from the Aztec word *pinolli*) made from ground grain or maize and used for travel was well-documented among Native peoples in the nineteenth-century Southwest, particularly those with a nomadic way of life.[59] The Comanche peoples were also famous for their knowledge of curing meat, a skill practiced in particular by the women of the tribe.[60] Portable buffalo meat preparations like Pemmican were widely traded and well-known by the 1840s, though the high fat content of Pemmican rendered that Northern preparation of lesser use in the warm climates of the South, where it spoiled easily.[61] Given all this, it is not unlikely that a portable Native food combining meat and ground corn or grain flour found its way into Borden's hands and mouth. It is also not difficult to imagine that, if this was the case, Borden would have thought it unnecessary to credit the Native knowledge he had drawn on for his "invention."

Instead, Borden credited a combination of serendipity and ingenuity (that clichéd mechanism of innovation) for the creation of the meat biscuit. He declared that in July 1849 he had been "attempting to prepare some portable food for a few friends going to California," and in the process, had "made an important discovery, to wit."[62] Having "set up a large kettle and evaporating pan," he had reduced "one hundred and twenty pounds of veal" to "ten pounds of the extract" in the space of two days. But the consistence of the condensed product was that of "melted glue and molasses," and the weather being "warm and rainy" in the middle of July, he had trouble drying it. It then "occurred" to him to "mix the article with good flour and bake it." To his "great satisfaction," the resulting product contained "all the primary principles of the meat."

Borden never indicated precisely what he meant by "the primary principles of the meat," nor did he mention how (or if) he went about measuring them. To an extent, his conception of nourishment seems to have been rooted in the qualitative tradition of eighteenth-century hyper-nourishing essences. Borden's method of applying heat and boiling animal flesh over a long period of time echoed the production of pre-nineteenth-century broths, reductions, and quintessences. Even his ambitions to improve his method through "the employment of suitable apparatus" by which "the

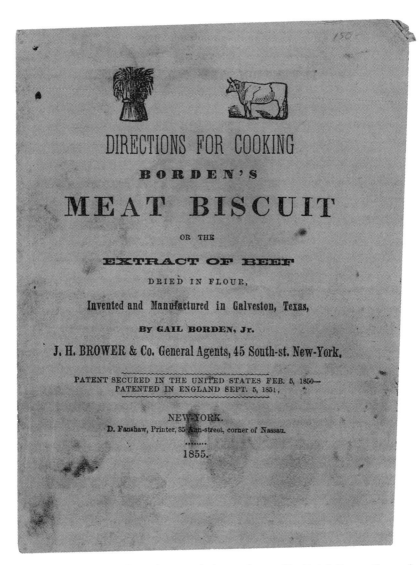

FIGURE 2. Directions for cooking Borden's meat biscuit. The Dolph Briscoe Center for American History, The University of Texas at Austin.

nutritious properties of the meat" would be "separated from the corporeous parts by steam" merely copied older culinary techniques and theories of transformation in the form of the eighteenth-century "digester," a sort of pressure cooker used to prepare flavorful, nutritious essences of meat and bone.[63] Borden also acknowledged Samuel Frederick Gray's 1828 *The*

Operative Chemist, in which Gray described a method for preparing "French portable soup" or gelatin according to French culinary methods of creating hypernourishment.[64] Similarly, Borden's conception of nourishment also still considered the kind and age of animal used. Aside from veal, he had experimented with "pork, fowl, fish, and oysters," and "a tortoise from Aransas bay," but he vastly preferred beef, in particular in comparison to veal.[65] "Young meats," Borden found, "are like unripe fruits, they are tender and palatable, but not so nutritious nor so easily digested as those which are matured." He also insisted that the meat biscuit be made with "fat and well-conditioned animals, for it is only in such that the nutritive and alimentary properties of meat are contained."[66]

At the same time, Borden was grasping for a way to capture, concentrate, and capitalize meat's nourishing subcomponents, ridding it of its bulky non-nourishing matrix. He insisted that he was "extracting the nutritious parts" of animals in order to make a product that contained "a large amount of the most important alimentary substances, in a very small bulk, and a convenient form."[67] One pound of this bread, he boasted, contained "the essence, or extract, of more than *five* pounds of meat." Borden's partner, Ashbel Smith, also emphasized the meat biscuit's unprecedented concentration of nourishing components in such compact form. "I believe there does not exist in nature or art the same amount of nutriment in as small bulk or weight, and as well adapted to support, efficiently and permanently, mental and physical vigor, as is concentrated in the meat biscuit in question," Smith gushed.[68] While Borden referred to Gray's portable soups, he also acknowledged Justus von Liebig and his meat extract. How much he really knew of Liebig's work before making the meat biscuit is unclear. Liebig's name may only have been pointed out to Borden by Ashbel Smith or the patent agency he employed, and Borden's method of long boiling was precisely what Liebig had criticized as being unconducive to producing the nourishing components of meat. But however much Borden knew about Liebig, and however much he held on to a somewhat antiquated notion of nutritiousness, he (and Smith) clung to the idea of having created a smaller, lighter, and nutritionally selective preparation, containing only the nourishing components of meat in previously unheard of quantities.

The patent agency Borden consulted picked up on this ambivalence in his claims. Patent agencies had developed in the aftermath of the Patent Act of 1836. The Act had established a central agency staffed by scientifically trained examiners who took a much greater role in scrutinizing the precise language and content of applications. In response, patent writing became an increasingly specialized practice, and the processes of inventing and authoring patents became more and more separated.[69] Munn and Company, the company Borden employed, was one of the most successful companies that authored applications for patents on behalf of inventors. The agency publicized this work through its mouthpiece, *Scientific American* magazine. A self-proclaimed "advocate of industry," *Scientific American* reported on the activities of the Patent Office and showcased the wider landscape of American "scientific, mechanical and other improvements."[70]

Borden had sent a specimen of the meat biscuit to representatives of Munn & Company some time in 1849. Shortly afterward, *Scientific American* announced Borden's product and reported on the tasting experience: after "seasoning it properly," they had found the biscuit "both palatable and nourishing."[71] But they also advised Borden that "the mode of preparing the concentrated liquid, or paste beef, has been long known to the world," and was described in chemical texts such as those of Gray or Liebig.[72] What was novel about the biscuit, in the eyes of the agency, was its combination with flour and its portable cake form. Munn and Company clearly understood the meat biscuit as part of a longer history of meat concentrates and dried soups. It was perhaps because of this that they suggested the invention be referred to as "Portable Desiccated Soup-Bread" in the patent.[73]

But Borden seems to have pushed back. While the final patent contained a caveat that Borden was not claiming "the extract of flesh made into what is known as 'portable soup'" as his invention, it still included the process of "extracting the nutritious parts of flesh or animal meat of every description" as a crucial part of the patentable process. The final product, so the patent claimed, would thus contain "a large amount of the most important alimentary substance in a very small bulk and convenient form." Describing the process of making the meat biscuit in the patent, Borden doubled down. "I take the flesh of a fat animal or of any kind of good eatable fowl, fish, &c.," he declared, "and extract all the nutricious [*sic*] parts out of it for the purpose of mixing it with the meal or vegetable flour." His method of extracting nutritiousness consisted of "mascerat[ing] [flesh] with heat or steam until its nutritious or alimentary properties are completely separated from the bony and fleshy parts, and are contained in the broth or soup." Borden thus regarded the process of extracting nutritiousness as central to his discovery and promised to have found a way of doing so that would ensure an unusually high concentration of nourishment in easily portable form.

While Munn and Company were clearly aware of the weaknesses in Borden's line of argumentation, they still supported the product and defended Borden against claims that his meat biscuit was perhaps not novel enough. At once a referee and a cheerleader, the company established a link between Borden and scientific circles. By sharpening Borden's claims about how the biscuit worked, the agency played a crucial role in shaping the product as an innovative and promising new form of nourishment with great dietetic and economic potential. Munn and Company also perpetuated Borden's origin story about the biscuit's creation and affirmed his role as the preparation's sole inventor, albeit standing on the shoulders of other white Western inventors. As an agency concerned with claims of innovation and scientific priority, the company might have acknowledged Borden's debt to past portable Native food preparations, like pinole, pemmican, and similar such foods. Instead, it aligned Borden and his biscuit firmly and exclusively with the past and future of Western nutritional science.

EMPIRE AND ECONOMICS

Once the place of the biscuit in the trajectory of Western nutritional science had been adequately negotiated and all traces of its likely Native provenance erased, Smith and Borden went about promoting the meat biscuit to the military-imperial market of Manifest Destiny. They crafted a narrative for the biscuit as a technology of empire and rapid military movement with a targeted and precise nourishing function. In a pamphlet composed specifically for marketing purposes—which they placed into the hands of important military and medical figures—they situated the meat biscuit firmly within the context of American imperial expansion and economic development that occupied military men at that very moment.[74] They declared that the "settlement of Oregon, and the incorporation of the Californias into our Union" rendered "a direct communication overland with those distant territories, one of the most urgent political and industrial wants of our country."[75] According to the pamphlet, it was "more and more imperative" for "our people" to have "direct intercourse with the Pacific regions, and with the vast intervening districts, for the purpose of making settlements." The meat biscuit, so Borden and Smith claimed, hastened the project of Manifest Destiny by collapsing the geographical space to the West. Its ability to withstand high temperatures and humidity made it superior to other "meat glues" for the hot and humid climates of the Western continent. The biscuit also recommended itself for the peculiar character of travel across the North American continent because of its dryness. "It may be carried in sacks, suspended from one's saddle bow, for weeks or months over the prairies, or through the desert, without the risk of spoiling," Smith insisted.[76] Above all, the biscuit's high nutritiousness-to-weight-and-bulk-ratio would facilitate the long expeditions required to secure imperial territories. "One ounce of the meat biscuit makes a pint of rich nutritious soup," Smith and Borden claimed, and calculated that "five ounces a day," or "a pound for three days," would be enough to nourish one man.[77] Such a light and economical source of nourishment would be of immense value to "the iron men of the frontier," who usually had to rely "for subsistence on their rifles."

Armed with the meat biscuit, the pamphlet promised, the US military would be able to prevent the disastrous fates suffered by previous expeditions, whose men were "reduced to eat their mules," forced to "return," or worse, "perished miserably" on their way to settlements. Even if the consequences were not quite so extreme in some cases, the calculus of company size, nourishment quantity, and weight loaded onto mules was of crucial importance to the success of expeditions. The larger the group, the safer the operation, but the more food would also have to be carried and loaded onto mules. The heavier the weight carried by the animals, the more quickly they would become exhausted and the more often they would need to be watered, which in turn could lead to unnecessary detours and a longer route—requiring yet more nourishment. To underscore the potential of their invention in this context, Borden and Smith calculated the "mule load" of the meat biscuit. A regular mule load was considered to be 300 pounds; the biscuit would nourish seven men for up to two months and still amount to a mere 150 pounds of mule load, halving the burden on the animals. The meat biscuit, they concluded, was "the bridge across the wilderness."

The meat biscuit would also facilitate the detection and elimination of the coveted territories of Native inhabitants. "Our frontier, it is to be feared, will long be subject to Indian depredations," they lamented in the pamphlet, but "Mr. Borden's discovery greatly adds to our means of prompt and efficient pursuit and protection."[78] Aside from allowing faster movement and saving the troops from having to barter with (or steal) the food stores of Native peoples they encountered on their route, the biscuit would accomplish this feat through the "advantage of a small and momentary flame" required for its preparation. "The fire for cooking is one of the greatest dangers in the

Indian country, as it betrays the situation of the camp to the hostile Indian," they warned. The meat biscuit's short cooking time would thus "not lightly be estimated by persons whose path has been among hostile Indians."[79] Smith and Borden were confident that before long the meat biscuit would "form a part of the indispensable supplies of every expedition into our western wilds, and of every military corps on our frontier."[80]

These services to imperial expansion were linked to economic advantages. Playing on the link between the food supply and the plantation economy, Smith and Borden advertised the biscuit as a cheap meat transportation technology that might be attractive to planters and slaveholders everywhere, even in that "natural appendage of the United States," Cuba.[81] "Without mentioning more particularly our plantations," Smith suggested unsubtly, "I will barely allude to the fact, that immense quantities of jerked beef are annually imported from South America into Cuba, for the sugar and coffee plantations of that Island; with equal freedom to import the meat biscuit, the latter would drive the jerked beef from the market."[82] The biscuit would achieve this, Borden and Smith insisted, through its extremely economical conditions of production; it was prepared "at a very low price, in countries where, as in Texas, beeves on foot are extremely cheap."[83] It was also extremely economical with regard to transportation. "Putting it up in tin cases or casks," they insisted, "costs less than barreling a like amount of beef; being much smaller in bulk, and dry, its transportation is less."[84] The biscuit, its makers teased, might just be the missing variable in the complex equation linking food, space, empire, and capital.

Finally, the biscuit would contribute to the economic development of the United States by providing a means of processing the abundant resources of Texas and similar territories locally. The relationship between resource abundance and economic development had long been a hotly debated issue among political economists and naturalists. In the eighteenth century, French philosopher Montesquieu had claimed that natural abundance predestined the inhabitants of a country to unproductivity, while his contemporaries David Hume and Adam Smith faulted the indirect influence of poor institutions for depressing the economy of resource-rich countries.[85] The issue was later studied in great detail by naturalist Alexander von Humboldt during his travels to South America and Mexico in the first decade of the nineteenth century, where he accused Spanish institutions of impeding the natural economic progression of the region.[86] But he also believed in a causal relationship between high fertility, raw material abundance, and economic stagnation. What we today call the "natural resource curse"—the seemingly underwhelming economic development of resource-rich nations—greatly puzzled eighteenth- and early nineteenth-century thinkers.

The question of economic progress, natural resources, and wealth formed part of what literary studies scholar Kyla Wazana Tomkins has called a "broad comparative landscape" of imperial-economic thought during the nineteenth century.[87] Imperial powers looked back with anguish to the fate of past empires, and with apprehension to the future of their own. The United States, in particular, still wrestled with its colonial past while simultaneously harboring future imperial ambitions. In 1851, American economist Henry Charles Carey articulated the anxiety over American resources as a critique of the United States' continuing dependent relationship with its former colonizer, Britain. Britain, according to Carey, had secured for itself a "monopoly of machinery for the conversion of the products of the farm and the plantation into cloth and iron."[88] While British political economists had assigned Britain the role of "workshop of the world," other nations were reduced to the status of mere producers, and were exploited for their raw materials, Carey charged.[89] But civilizing societies naturally tended toward a less monopolistic distribution of production and consumption, according to Carey. By allowing Britain to extract American raw materials and exploit American soils, the United States was effectively complicit in halting its own economic development. Rather than serve as a raw materials supplier to British processing facilities, Carey concluded, the United States should look to developing its own manufacturing capabilities.[90]

According to Borden and Smith, the meat biscuit would bring about American imperial ambitions not only by collapsing continental space but also by accelerating American economic development. Manifest Destiny was not merely a geographical orientation but also a chronological project, an inevitable civilizational path that nations must either follow or risk being left behind. The recent Mexican-American war had demonstrated, in Smith's view, what happened to a country that failed to develop its resources and thwarted the development of its commerce and industry through bad economic stewardship. Mexico's "all pervading military despotism" had "made industry hopeless and deadened the energy of that people."[91] In addition, Mexico's rich natural resources, instead of helping it flourish, had "gone to enrich the merchants of the British Isles."[92] Military aggression was not merely a necessary means but in fact the only solution, "the predestined fate of degenerate Mexico," in Smith's cosmology. "No nation once degenerate," he opined, "has ever been regenerated but by foreign conquest." Only "the sword" could intervene successfully in the economic degradation of a resource-rich country; it was "the great civilizer," and it "clears the way for commerce, education, religion, and all the harmonizing influences of morality and humanity."[93]

The subtext was clear: in order to keep up with the civilizational race of nations, the United States, and the South in particular, had to develop its natural resources shrewdly or else risk being plunged back into despotism, losing its right to self-governance. In a letter to James De Bow, editor of the pro-South, pro-manufacture, pro-slavery magazine *De Bow's Review*, Smith laid out the link between the meat biscuit and the imperial-economic development of the South.[94] Smith had approached De Bow precisely because De Bow's vision of American economic progress closely aligned with his own. In the pages of the *Review*, De Bow had been championing an integrated economic development of Southern communities similar to the vision articulated by Carey in which agriculture and manufacture worked closely together in one place. The meat biscuit, Smith insisted, deserved to be recognized by the *Review* precisely because it was an "important manufacture" located "in our section of the confederacy" that was "specially adapted to the grazing and grain-growing regions of the South and West."[95] While planting would remain "the chief occupation of the South," the money made through agricultural production went elsewhere; "it soon finds its way abroad for the fabrics and manufactures of the northern states and of the Old World," Smith complained. To "increase the amount of those large sums, and to keep a portion of them at home," Smith believed it was necessary to "establish and foster those manufactures suited to our climate and productions."

But this was not merely a matter of business acumen. To their makers, products like the biscuit were intertwined with the future of US-American civilization and prosperity. Echoing the comparative debates of political economists on resources and imperial progress, Smith asserted that "no purely agricultural country has ever vied in wealth, and its numerous and high appliances, with those other countries where, without neglecting the soil, manufactures and commerce have flourished."[96] In order to prohibit the descent of the American nation into a state of economic backwardness, Smith argued, the products of the American earth needed to be transformed into wealth by processing them. Smith described in great detail the large-scale, advanced production facilities of Borden's meat biscuit factory that turned Texan natural resources into a highly manufactured product. The cleanliness of the premises, the sophisticated machinery, the huge capital (about ten thousand dollars) it had already swallowed up, all worked toward the single goal of turning the production of the meat biscuit into an "extensive establishment" and "manufacturing it on a large scale."[97] As we shall see, the meat biscuit in Britain was perceived as a raw material that could seamlessly be integrated into the British imperial model of "specialized internationalism." In the United States, however, it symbolized the potential of American manufacture and industry to redraw the imperial-commercial map, to take back control of American industry and manufacture, and to escape the resource curse.

MILITARY MARKETS

The pamphlet in hand, a few canisters of pulverized meat biscuit tucked under his arm, and a myriad of ideas about the biscuit's bright imperial future in his head, Borden made his way through the streets of St. Louis. He was headed to see Brevet Major A. B. Eaton, a military officer and assistant commissary of the St. Louis subsistence office. At the subsistence office, the nation's food production was joined to its imperial ambitions and economic future. Created in 1821, and expanded during the Mexican-American War, it was the arbiter of military supply contracts and provided attractive business opportunities for entrepreneurs like Borden.[98] The United States military played a decisive role in the imperial conquest and economic development of regions like Texas and New Mexico.[99] By displacing, killing, or controlling the local population, building transport routes, and establishing settlements, it created demand for supplies and sustenance and thereby drove up the production of commodities. Imperial conquest relied on food technologies like the meat biscuit, and at the same time shaped the food-producing landscape in decisive ways.

At the office of Major Eaton, Borden opted for a blunt strategy. He handed Eaton the pamphlet, offered him a taste of his product, and told the Major outright that he wanted the merits of the meat biscuit to receive an army test.[100] Whether through the pamphlet's rhetoric, Borden's (undoubtedly) persistent salesmanship, or the qualities and taste of the biscuit itself, Eaton was convinced. He echoed the pamphlet's hope that the biscuit might render the troops more flexible and nimbler in Indian territory. "It is very evident that we shall be under the necessity of having many mounted troops on our far-Western frontiers among the Indians," he asserted, "and that every discovery or invention that will aid in rapid movements is important."[101] He ordered "a canister of a few pounds of the pulverized biscuit" to be sent to Colonel E. V. Sumner, at the time the commander of Fort Leavenworth (and later military governor of New Mexico). Sumner had himself been an assistant commissary of the army (according to Eaton "one of the best"). He was now about to embark on a lengthy march with his troops and was therefore "the proper officer to whom to commit the trial."

Sumner rose to Eaton's challenge with great enthusiasm and a considerable degree of confidence in his own authority over the matter. The biscuit, Sumner wrote to Eaton, had been "all, and more than the inventor thinks it is."[102] For several days, Sumner had lived on it entirely and had not needed any other food. He provided commentary on dosage ("the inventor thinks that five ounces a day will support a man . . . I could not use four ounces a day") and on how he had customized the biscuit for his own use ("made into soup, with nothing added, but salt and pepper"). He even observed "a great advantage which had not been enumerated," that the biscuit allowed him to "dispense entirely with tea and coffee." Above all, Sumner felt the biscuit opened enormous possibilities to increase the scale, speed, and efficiency of military operations. "I have long thought," he contemplated, "that the compression of wholesome food into smaller compass was one of the most important things that remained to be discovered, in this age of inventions." Mastering such compression, he hoped, would increase the mobility, and reduce the cost, of military operations. "Think," he enthused, "of a Regiment of 500 men cutting loose from all magazines for two months with no other baggage train than 50 or 60 pack mules." He calculated that the amount of biscuit needed to supply such a company would amount to a mere 9,375 pounds, which could be carried "easily" by 45 mules. Sumner concluded by proposing that the inventor "had better send" him a few dozen canisters of meat biscuit for his "march upon the plains" in the summer. It would be a good opportunity, he believed, "to put this discovery to a thorough test."

Sumner's eager letter spurred Eaton into action. He recommended that Borden "be at once requested to forward through the proper channel . . . the 300 lbs. of the Meat Biscuit [Colonel Sumner] suggests in his letter."[103] The matter was then bumped up to the secretary of war himself, Charles Magill Conrad. In October 1850, Conrad received a letter from John G. Tod, an old acquaintance of Gail Borden's, who had served as a naval inspector at

Galveston naval station, examining supply purchases, during the time Borden was customs collector there. During the Mexican-American War, Tod had functioned as an agent of the US Army quartermaster general. He also acted as a lobbyist for the political and commercial prosperity of Texas in Washington and was sent as Texas delegate to the Great Exhibition in London in 1851, along with Ashbel Smith.[104]

In his letter to Conrad, Tod spelled out the direct link he saw between a new kind of concentrated nourishment and the white supremacist objectives of the imperial project.[105] While a "mode of preparing Beef gelatine" had been "long known to the world," Tod argued, the possibility of "concentrating in the same substance the nutritious properties both of animal and vegetable food" and thereby achieving "a combination absolutely necessary to the healthful sustenance of Man" was entirely novel. In addition to its nutritional completeness, the biscuit stood out to Tod for its high concentration of nourishing substance in relation to its bulk. "One pound of these Biscuit [sic]," he enthused, "affords more nutriment than five or six pounds, of ordinary food." For these reasons, the biscuit would be found of "incalculable value" to "all Mounted Men on our Indian frontier, where rapid movements are of vital importance in protecting our settlements, and checking the incursions of the savages," Tod insisted. By doing away with the present "burdensome rations," then, the biscuit would achieve nothing short of "ensur[ing] the active operations, so impossible at present." It was impossible, for Tod, to overstate the role of the biscuit in the United States' white imperial-military future: "Its introduction into the Army," he concluded grandly, "will contribute more to the suppression of the nomade [sic] tribes of the South West, than the sword or carbine."

To support his advocacy, Tod also forwarded Sumner's report and included a specimen of the biscuit itself, "prepared in Texas over 13 months since."[106] Conrad gave in to Tod's persuasion. On October 31, he ordered "a sufficient quantity of the meat biscuit to be purchased and issued at some convenient point to give the article a fair trial."[107] Tod immediately related the good news to Borden. "We have some strong and fast friends at Washington," Borden wrote to Smith.[108]

It was not until May of the following year, however, that the biscuit would be tested. Tod had to send another entreating letter to the secretary of war in February. In it, he doubled down on his hopes for the biscuit's ability to transform the army's battle against Native peoples. "The cumbersome ration is a serious evil in rapid movements," he declared, "and it is only by light and rapid movements, of our frontier Troops, that we may ever expect to chastise marauding Savages, or protect our borders."[109] The delay may also have been due to manufacturing difficulties on Borden's part; Borden's fresh beef supply was unreliable, a drought messed with the water supply (crucial to condensing beef through steam or boiling), and the oven failed to reach the high temperatures required to preserve the biscuit.[110] The Secretary of War finally delivered specific instructions for the biscuit to be purchased for testing in March 1851.[111] A scouting party to Fort Graham, Texas, in June that same year was identified to serve as a live experiment, and a board of six, consisting of officers, lieutenants, and one army surgeon, was assembled to serve as examiners.

The examining committee hoped that the tests would ascertain the biscuit's preservability, palatability, dosage, and nutritious capacity. The captain of the scouting exhibition instructed the board to "number the ounces of Meat Biscuit required for a ration per day," to investigate "its capability of sustaining life in health and vigor for a number of consecutive days under circumstances requiring great bodily exertion," to examine "its nutritive and other qualities, and its general effect upon the System when eaten exclusively or in part."[112] The Board was also to advise whether the biscuit could replace the current Army ration in its entirety or in part. The form of the test consisted simply of "personal experiments with the Meat Biscuit on the march" conducted by the soldiers and the board members, which, according to the commanding captain, would enable the board to "give a correct and enlightened opinion upon the subject."

Only six weeks later, the board returned with a devastating report. After a month-long march, "whilst undergoing great fatigue and bodily exertion," the board was "perfectly satisfied" that the meat biscuit, "in whole or in part," could "not be substituted for the ordinary ration of the army."[113] The biscuit, the board felt, did not "possess the qualities requisite to sustain life in health and vigor," not only when administered in the recommended dosage, but also if increased "to the amount of 12 ounces per ration." While the ordinary ration could be eaten "with relish and satisfaction" by the soldiers, the meat biscuit was "not only unpalatable," but also failed to "appease the cravings of hunger." It caused "head-ache, nausea, and great muscular depression." On this latter point, the examiners expanded in more detail. The Biscuit, according to Merrill and his colleagues, impaired "the capacity of the healthy human-system to sustain as much mental or bodily labor as it can be legitimately called upon to perform." It diminished the men's power "of resisting the extremes of heat & cold," a charge directly challenging the biscuit's claim to suitability for hot climates. The biscuit was thus neither suited to the extreme activity nor to the extreme temperatures of "frontier" life, in the eyes of the board. But more devastatingly, it failed in its most basic nourishing function. The biscuit, the officers concluded, did not "impart to the system the power to carry on its normal action, with that energy and regularity which constitute health."

We can only speculate why the board produced such an annihilating verdict of the biscuit. It is possible that, as Borden himself thought, the board had corrupt motives when condemning the meat biscuit and defending the existing ration. In this context of close military-commercial collaboration, it is not unlikely that board members had ties to existing ration suppliers. Another possible explanation, uttered by Borden's most thorough biographer, is that the meat biscuit simply did not taste good. Like several other commentators, the board members, after all, declared the biscuit "unpalatable." As Frantz suggests, "people did not like it, which is always the best reason for not buying any food."[114] But in the surviving sources about the meat biscuit, we find as many voices raving about the biscuit's taste as we find tasters turning up their noses.

Whether the board differed in their evaluation from that of other military officers or not, what is important for our purposes is that both the biscuit's champions and the nay-sayers were united in considering the meat biscuit a potentially important tool for their imperial enterprise. Even as they condemned Borden's biscuit as unable to fulfill its promises, the board members declared that they had "most earnestly hoped to have found in this Biscuit" a new ration that was "so easily transported" and that could be used precisely to address "the exigencies so frequently arising in our operations upon this extensive frontier."[115] Those who had wanted the biscuit to be tested had done so with explicit reference to its potential role in hastening frontier operations and Indian removal, with little proof of its nutritional soundness. Contrary to the nourishing richness of eighteenth-century concentrated "hypernourishing" essences, the biscuit represented a kind of nutritional "lightness" achieved through targeted extraction and accumulation of nourishing constituents and the elimination of non-nourishing bulk. In the imperial-military context of its production and promotion, the biscuit's promise of nutritional lightness was connected explicitly to the operational lightness of frontier activities that, in the minds of its military champions, would be indispensable in the fight against the Native inhabitants of coveted imperial lands.

Even in the absence of a final answer to the question of the seat of nourishment, even without a convincing method of measuring the nourishing constituents, and even with all the resemblance the biscuit still bore to older preparations, military consumers were eager to find in the meat biscuit a wonder food that would facilitate the expansionist and white supremacist project of the United States. The imperial impulse to develop portable, highly concentrated nourishing products, in other words, was not the natural consequence of advances in nutrition science and chemistry. Rather, imperial imperatives preceded and drove the search for a convincing resolution of the nourishment problem. The salient question is therefore not why the meat biscuit failed. It is rather why such a poorly executed and scientifically ambiguous preparation came so close to being so successful.

CONCLUSION

The story of Gail Borden and his "invention" is not merely an entrepreneurial failure on the path to condensed milk or an amusing footnote in the history of marginal nutritional curiosities. Nor is it a morally neutral story of US-American ingenuity, technological advance, or nutritional scientific progress. Gail Borden's meat biscuit was an imperial technology, designed to facilitate the establishment of American empire and ensure the persistence of white supremacy. It was produced and promoted by a network of military-imperial agents who controlled the intersection of science and commerce, mobilizing it for their imperial-economic projects.

The biscuit marks a moment of transition between ways of knowing food, and between mechanisms for creating "more-than" foods. On the one hand, the biscuit was still understood—by employees of the patent agency as well as by Borden himself—within the tradition of soups, broths, and quintessences, characterized by an intensification of flavor and essence as markers of enhanced nutritiousness. At the same time, the meat biscuit reflected its makers' desire to produce superior nutritiousness by extracting and accumulating the specific nourishing constituents of food while minimizing its bulk.

Explaining the emergence and enduring appeal of this new approach to nourishment requires that we look beyond the growing power of science and chemistry over food. Instead, clues are found in the commercial and imperial contexts in which the nutrition sciences developed and in which wonder foods, such as the meat biscuit, were built. Imperial concerns about distance, whiteness, and prosperity played a crucial role in shifting scientific interest toward a reduction in weight paired with a multiplication of nutritiousness. The biscuit's enthusiastic reception by many military officials was not the result of its proven superior nutrient content. Rather, the biscuit was explicitly designed as a technology of light transportation, vast empire, and rapid movement, and it was praised by judges and eaters on the basis of its ability to facilitate conquest, realize Manifest Destiny, and sustain white supremacy— whether it could ultimately deliver on this claim or not. Like a true magic bullet, it promised to transform the complex challenge of colonization into an engineering problem solvable through a technical-nutritional fix.

As such, the meat biscuit was also a food to wonder with. Makers and champions of concentrated food products imagined a food future of less bulk, less burden, more efficiency, and more specificity. The meat biscuit was one of many such food products designed to concentrate the nutritious essence of food and turn nourishment into a better version of itself. At the same time, the meat biscuit concretized economic visions of how the production, consumption, and distribution of food ought to be organized. Born of a specific set of economic, imperial, and dietetic anxieties, the biscuit reveals the degree to which economic, imperial, and dietetic philosophies mutually constituted one another. Historians of US imperialism and capitalism have shown that economic visions of the United States were inseparable from aspirations for empire and Native genocide. The meat biscuit provides further evidence of a common intellectual and interpersonal infrastructure linking cuisine, capital, colonization, and conquest.

TWO

The Raw and the Civilized

INTRODUCTION

Ashbel Smith would come to know the inside of 21 Regent Street, London, extremely well. The sand-colored three-story building usually housed the Royal Horticultural Society, but during the Great Exhibition of 1851 it had become the meeting place for the Jury on Substances Used as Food.[1] Over several weeks, Smith and his fellow jurors spent up to six hours each day examining specimens, deliberating the value of this or that food, and making decisions about which submissions to reward with prizes.[2] The committee kept Smith so busy that he might not have even seen the famous Crystal Palace, the exhibition's main venue, were it not for the regular meetings with the other juries of their joint category, "raw materials," in the India Tent.[3] Surrounded by crimson velvet wall hangings and towered over by an ivory throne gifted by the Rajah of Travancore to the Queen, Smith listened to recitations of examinations and evaluations of resources from the empire, and mused on his own nation's place in this spectacle.[4]

Overall, Smith found the United States "poorly represented" at the exhibition, as he confessed in a letter to Sam Houston.[5] It would have been better to send nothing at all, he lamented, rather than be subjected to "the disparaging sneers so liberally cast on American skill and industry and I may add, American civilization." Indeed, British commentary on the exhibition emphasized the largely agrarian character of American contributions and dismissed the nation's ingenuity as being largely devoted to "improvements in agriculture" ("as might be expected").[6]

All of Smith's hopes were now on the meat biscuit. Problems at the factory had delayed Borden himself, and he had asked Smith to "represent the importance of the new article of diet at the great Industrial Exposition of the World" in his place.[7] He had also authorized Smith to "make contracts or engagements for the manufacture or supply of the Meat Biscuit." Aside from his representative and judicial functions, promoting the meat biscuit was therefore Smith's main objective in coming to the exhibition.

In Smith's mind, the biscuit was a manufactured good, a processed improvement on a raw material that had the potential to propel the United States further on the path toward economic development (chapter 1). But the British men of science, commerce, and empire he would seek to interest in the biscuit had something else in mind. They saw in the meat biscuit a means of mobilizing what they considered imprudently used, "wasted" raw materials all across the empire. As such, the biscuit would be part of a broader solution to a long-brewing crisis.

At the time of the exhibition, Britain was facing a wide range of challenges brought about by its rapid industrialization, urbanization, and imperial expansion. This included a food crisis of unprecedented proportions, caused by profound agricultural and commercial transformations during the eighteenth and nineteenth centuries and exacerbated by bad harvests, famines, and food riots. The Great Exhibition was, in part, an intervention in this crisis. While it was certainly intended to showcase Britain's industrial and imperial power, it was also designed, in the words of Jeffrey Auerbach, to "identify and rectify Britain's manufacturing deficiencies."[8] The exhibition brought together a group of "Experts" (capitalized and in quotes in the jurors' report), including "various eminent merchants" and "and other persons having the confidence of the public and of the Jury" who weighed in on the nation's most pressing challenges, including the food problem.[9]

Despite their heterogeneous set of skills and knowledge in matters of science, commerce, and empire, this network of experts approached the food problem through a common comprehensive philosophy. Whether they discussed colonial resources, the dietaries of institutions, or the chemical constituents of individual foods, they called for the elimination of *waste* in all things. Waste, to them, was at once a justification for resource extraction, a doctrine of economic development, and a theory of taste and nutrition. Minimizing wasteful practices and products, in their minds, would lead to a more stable food supply, a more successful empire, and a more civilized humankind.

The meat biscuit, and other products like it, played an important role in their waste-free vision. Much like their military counterparts across the Atlantic, British experts appreciated such products for their potential to provide nourishment in a more efficient, targeted, and less voluminous manner. But, unlike their US colleagues, British experts saw in products like Gail Borden's Meat Biscuit not so much a vehicle for making local food travel as a means of bringing distant food closer. Their interest was less about nourishing specific groups—soldiers, sailors, surveyors—more effectively during short periods of time than in transforming the nourishment of entire populations indefinitely. In what historian Chris Otter has called a "radical shift to outsourcing," they mobilized what they regarded as the "wasted" resources of Britain's (former) colonies.[10] In doing so, they hoped to maneuver Britain out of its food crisis, while at the same time cementing its imperial, racial, and culinary hierarchies.

A NETWORK OF EXPERTS

In 1837, Charles Dickens published a series of short satirical stories relating the proceedings of a fictional society called "The Mudfog Society for the Advancement of Everything." The tales described the meetings of the society in which members read papers, presented inventions, and discussed ideas. A Mr. Wigsby, for instance, produced "a cauliflower somewhat larger than a chaise-umbrella" which had been "raised by no other artificial means than the simple application of highly carbonated soda-water as manure." Mr. Wigsby further explained that "by scooping out the head" (which he assured the assembled members would "afford a new and delicious species of nourishment for the poor") he was able to create a "parachute" whose flying power he intended to demonstrate by making "a descent from a height of not less than three miles and a quarter." Another paper on the "wonderful efficacy of the system of infinitesimal doses"—the theory that "the very minutest amount of any given drug, properly dispersed through the human frame, would be productive of precisely the same result as a very large dose administered in the usual manner"—prompted a question from a member about whether "it would be possible to administer—say, the twentieth part of a grain of bread and cheese to all grown-up paupers, and the fortieth part to children, with the same satisfying effect as their present allowance." The presenter (Professor Muff) replied that he was "willing to stake his professional reputation on the perfect adequacy of such a quantity of food to the support of human life—in workhouses, the addition of the fifteenth part of a grain of pudding twice a week would render it a high diet."[11]

Dickens's tone was humorous, yet it reflected a cruel reality. Since the Napoleonic Wars at the beginning of the century, Britain had gradually been gliding into a social crisis that pressured a new set of technical, economic, and scientific experts (not unlike the Mr. Wigsbys and Professor Muffs of the Mudfog Society) to find new solutions for poverty, food shortages, and economic decline. Britain's rapid industrialization during the late eighteenth and early nineteenth centuries had brought about profound changes in land use, urbanization, and population growth with lasting consequences for access to food and rising inequality. This deeper transformation was exacerbated sporadically by a number of acute crises. Bad harvests struck Britain in the years between 1839 and 1842, accompanied by a significant economic depression beginning in 1839. The potato blight aggravated existing food shortages and inadequate food management; periods of scarcity followed in Scotland and England, and recurring famines haunted Ireland between 1845 and 1852. These domestic struggles took place amid growing imperial expansion abroad. Long-standing rivalries between European empires rekindled with renewed vigor. As a result, European channels of supply on which British merchants had already heavily relied, became an increasingly unstable source of nourishment. The abolition of slavery and the development of European substitution goods (like beet sugar for cane sugar) further threatened to undercut British colonial planters' competitiveness in the global food market.[12]

The food crisis hit with political urgency. The French Revolution, which had after all evolved around issues of food management, still loomed large in the minds of British politicians, and animated those charged with finding solutions for the food problem. A series of food riots on British soil in the early decades of the nineteenth century kept the memory of French events alive. Anxieties about food were also sustained by the lasting impact of economist Thomas Malthus. His calculations of population growth and resources carried great weight with mid-nineteenth-century experts and gave them reason to fear that Britain's population might soon outstrip its food supply. Moreover, British citizens were kept abreast of the food situation daily through the country's flourishing print culture and the rise of political activism around food-related issues such as the New Poor Law (the "Starvation Act"), the Great Famine, the Corn Laws, and the Sugar Duties Act. Newspapers and pamphlets increased the political visibility of food inequality and rendered hunger, in the words of James Vernon, a "newsworthy item." The food question, in short, crystallized issues of political stability, inequality, and economic development.[13]

The food crisis galvanized a group of diverse experts, linked by a number of institutional and intellectual ties, around the nexus of food, science, and empire. Many came from humble, Nonconformist (non-Anglican) backgrounds whose professional prospects had altered since the establishment of Nonconformist universities in Britain, such as University College London and Edinburgh, where a majority of them obtained their education. Some went on to hold posts in the burgeoning field of sanitary science, which, together with the empire, constituted an important field of professional opportunity for educated men who did not form part of the nobility.[14] They shared a belief in addressing the challenges facing the nation through scientific and technocratic knowledge, and seized upon the matter of the food supply, among other topics, as a ripe opportunity to assert their expertise over the most pressing political and social issues of the time. The Great Exhibition of 1851 strengthened existing ties between experts and provided opportunities to forge new connections. It gave experts formal roles in organizing, judging, and promoting the products on display, and allowed them to publicize their ideas in the exhibition's voluminous educational literature. Experts connected to the exhibition also played crucial roles in carrying forward the spirit and substance of the exhibition and argued for the continued display of the exhibition's specimens after its closure in collections such as the Food Collection, the Animal Products Collection, and the Waste Products Collection.

Among them were physician and naturalist Edwin Lankester (1814–1874) as well as his teacher John Lindley (1799–1865). Lankester was a lecturer on Materia Medica and had published a number of books on food. He also gave a series of public lectures on the subject of food in the aftermath of the Great Exhibition and served as superintendent of the South Kensington Museum in 1858, which first housed certain remains of the exhibition's displays after its close, including the Food Collection and the Animal Products Collection. Lindley was a botanist who had written a report on the potato crop failure and food scarcity in Ireland.[15] Both Lankester and Lindley were jurors at the Great Exhibition; Lankester in the category "Manufactures from animal and vegetable substances," and Lindley in the category "Substances used as Food," alongside Ashbel Smith.[16]

Lindley's co-investigator of the famine in Ireland was Lyon Playfair (1818–1898), who was also responsible for appointing Ashbel Smith to the food jury. A chemist, physician, and member of parliament, Playfair was special commissioner of the exhibition, devised the exhibition's classification

FIGURE 3. The Food Museum and Animal Products. *The Leisure Hour*, Vol. 8, April 14 1859, p. 232.

scheme, and played a crucial role in promoting its vision.[17] He was also Lankester's predecessor as superintendent of the South Kensington Museum and was pivotal in assembling the collection of animal products housed within it. Playfair's collaborator on the Animal Products Collection was Peter Lund Simmonds (1814–1897), a publisher, colonial planter, and empire enthusiast.[18] Having spent his youth traveling as a midshipman and working as a bookkeeper in Jamaica, he began promoting the interests of the colonies in Britain by publishing the *Colonial Magazine* and drawing extensively on a network of colonial correspondence in which he was immersed. He was also a prolific writer on the subjects of waste materials and empire, and he gave a number of speeches on waste product utilization.[19]

Learned societies, and in particular the Society for the Encouragement of Arts, Commerce and Manufacture, provided a further institutional link between experts and connected them to a wider network of interest in food, empire, and economic policy. Founded in London in 1754 in the Enlightenment spirit of patriotism and improvement, the society promoted "useful" knowledge to benefit an imagined "public" and sought to bring together broader economic and imperial interests through local technological and commercial innovation.[20] In its mid-nineteenth century incarnation, the society was corresponding with a number of agricultural and commercial societies throughout the empire, and was engaged in formalizing those ties (often forged during the Great Exhibition) into a standing network for circulation of information and specimens. This exchange of knowledge as well as 'stuff' became so important that the society campaigned for a "colonial penny postage" to facilitate exchange. Food items were among those discussed and exchanged, with a particular emphasis on ways to stretch their quantity and optimize their process of production. To this aim, the society offered an extensive list of premiums: prizes were awarded, for instance, for "the best, simplest, and most economic Flourmill," for "the importation of not less than half a ton of well-dried Plantains, or Bananas from the West Indies," and for "the importation from China, India, or elsewhere, of any new Vegetable Oils or Fatty Substances, which can be used as food."[21]

Animating these experts and connecting their diverse interests was a common intellectual commitment to eliminating waste of all kinds. Britain's current predicament, they agreed, could be alleviated if sources of waste were identified and minimized. They saw waste in everything—from the organization of industrial production and the agricultural practices of the colonies to the configuration of institutional dietaries at home and even the composition of foods themselves. They also saw enormous profit in the prudent utilization of what they considered otherwise wasted materials. The meat biscuit fit within this framework. Whereas to Borden and Smith the biscuit signified the promise of manufacture and economic development, to British experts it represented the salvage of raw materials that had previously been at risk of being wasted.

WASTE AND WEALTH

In King's Cross, London, next to Battle Bridge and the Smallpox Hospital, stood a large hill. It rose against the sky like an eclipse over the sun, shading the neighboring suburban houses in a cloud of darkness, even on warm days. Small knots of grass, thistles, and groundsel broke up the monotony of the hill's gray surface in places where it had been left undisturbed for a while. Every now and then a flock of sparrows punctured its towering silence

FIGURE 4. *King's Cross, London: The Great Dust-Heap, Next to Battle Bridge and the Smallpox Hospital.* Watercolor painting by E. H. Dixon, 1837, Wellcome Collection.

in predatory descent while crows patrolled its circumference. This was the "great Dust-heap," the tallest of London's infamous "mounds of cinders, ashes, and other emptyings from dust-holes and bins."[22] A worthless heap of rubble to the untrained eye, the great dust heap was in fact "worth thousands of pounds" to those who knew how to use it.

In the foreground of the mountain stretched a long ditch surrounded by a broken-down fence on which laborers were busy digging and scavenging new deposits of fresh rubbish. Known as the "Searchers and Sorters," they were divided into highly specialized departments. One group picked out pieces of unburnt coal big enough to fuel another fire; another was responsible for gathering the best of the cinders and selling them to laundresses. Two further departments called the "soft-ware" (staffed mostly by women) and "hard-ware" specialized in the gathering of animal and vegetable matter for the creation of manure, and in the collection of broken pottery, to be converted into new roads, respectively. The soft-ware department included the subdivision of the dead-cat department, dedicated (unsurprisingly) to the collection and resale of cat skins ("sixpence for a white cat, fourpence for a coloured cat, and for a black one according to her quality").[23] To these seekers, a day on the dust-heap could result in a respectable income.

Waste loomed large in the mid-nineteenth-century British imagination. This particular dust heap was represented in Richard Henry Horne's serialized story "Dust; or Ugliness Redeemed," which appeared in Charles Dickens's literary magazine *Household Words*.[24] The dust heaps and their workers marked London's urban landscape, visible reminders of both Britain's deep social crisis and the enormous economic potential ascribed to accumulated rubbish. London's waste workers, the so-called dust collectors, were depicted by Henry Mayhew in his 1851 report on *London Labour and the London Poor*.[25] They were also immortalized by Dickens himself in *Our Mutual Friend*. But waste was not merely an urban sanitary problem or an occasional source of income for those whom the nation's engine of progress had left behind. It was a unifying intellectual and practical commitment by Britain's technical and scientific elite, a belief that the country's most pressing problems could be solved by mobilizing previously wasted resources.

The nineteenth-century ideology of waste utilization had broader political and moral connotations than our contemporary idea of "refuse."[26] It built on eighteenth-century domestic practices of recycling and tinkering as well as religious notions of perfect design and purpose. As historian Simon Werrett has shown, the eighteenth-century "household economy" encompassed a natural cycle of metamorphosis in which objects shifted use by moving from one context to another, or from one temporal stage to the next (not unlike ideas about the essence of nourishment discussed in chapter 1).[27] Economy in the house demanded a careful balancing between the preservation of old things and the acquisition of new ones. Nineteenth-century writers incorporated these ideas into their thinking by contrasting waste with function, suggesting that to devise uses for otherwise wasted substances was to reveal their God-given purpose.[28] To Lankester, uncovering that "the refuse of bone manufactures, the offal of slaughter-houses, and the refuse of our large towns" were, on closer inspection "not refuse" at all, meant realizing "that God has made no waste in the world."[29]

But the nineteenth-century philosophy of waste elimination also went beyond eighteenth-century notions of repurposing. For one, there was a shift in scale from domestic recycling to industrial reuse.[30] Early iterations of waste elimination were articulated within treatises of economic thought on the optimization of industrial production. In his classical text *On the Economy of Machinery and Manufactures* (1832), often represented today as a pioneering work in industrial operations research, mathematician and mechanical engineer Charles Babbage suggested that the creation of value through machinery and manufacture had three principal causes. The first was the extension of human labor power; the second was the minimization of time; and the third was "the conversion of substances apparently common and worthless into valuable products."[31] He elaborated on the third point by enumerating a number of commonly discarded substances used in the manufacture of valuable materials. The source of goldbeater's skin, a flexible material used in the production of gold leaf, was the offal of animals; old tin kettles could be converted into black dye used by calico printers.[32] Babbage expanded the idea of waste utilization to labor, time, and the logistics of production. Identifying uneconomical practices in these areas, he believed, was key to optimizing industrial manufacture and maximizing profit.

Along with a greater focus on manufacture came a different algebraic frame of mind, away from the equations of the eighteenth century and toward the multiplications of the nineteenth. In the fourth edition of *The Economy of Machinery*, Babbage added detailed calculations of the gain in value created by utilizing every part of a horse in a manufacturing purpose.[33] Whereas eighteenth-century repurposing had implied a shift in use within a balanced economy, nineteenth-century waste elimination was thus aimed at an overall *increase*: of usable material, of productivity, of wealth. Minimizing waste meant maximizing output. Bringing into circulation the totality of undervalued "unappreciated" substances, in the words of Simmonds, had the potential of creating *additional* value.[34] Nineteenth-century waste thinking thus mirrored a larger shift in economic thought from the balance-centric input-output models of mercantilism to the preoccupation with investment, growth, and surplus value of nineteenth-century capitalists.

Nineteenth-century experts also differed in their conceptions of waste from their predecessors by naturalizing the ability to utilize waste efficiently as an evolutionary trait of higher beings and advanced societies. Playfair claimed that the efficient use of time, labor and resources separated highly evolved from less evolved beings and manifested in the natural organization of animals.[35] In particular, the configuration of the digestive (waste-processing) apparatus could indicate an animal's evolutionary stage. Higher animals, he argued, had optimized the process of digestion by using only one stomach, whereas lower animals had to rely on several organs for the same process, making their labor more intensive and their results less efficient. Avoiding waste was thus an accomplishment of both economic and evolutionary development.

The principle of waste utilization was applied across a number of contexts and disciplines, from metaphorical forms of waste in public spending or social organization to material waste in agriculture. In their professional societies, experts discussed, side by side, prudent strategies of "wasted" capital reinvestment and schemes to apply the literal wastes of urban excrement for the benefit of rural agricultural development. In a speech given to the Society of Arts, an experimental farmer petitioned that "the surplusage of our town and city profits should find useful employment on the land."[36] "Surplusage" referred to unused monetary capital as well as human shit, both capable of producing additional value. Britain's cities possessed financial capital in "superabundance," the farmer argued; this capital should be used to make agriculture "profitable." Similarly, the "waste" of town sewage could be turned into manure and increase agricultural yields and profits. He even calculated "the extent to which our food might be increased by the application of town sewage," concluding that Britain's urban excrement would "fertilize 500,000 additional acres" of land.

Science would be crucial in realizing this vision of wealth through waste, according to the experts brought together at the Great Exhibition. In a speech on the results of the exhibition, Playfair suggested that the field of chemistry, in particular, could contribute to the economization of the production process by devising "methods of utilizing products apparently worthless, or of endowing bodies with properties which render them of increased value to industry."[37] Lankester also called attention to the ability of chemistry to find new profitable uses for industrial waste materials in a series of lectures given at the South Kensington Museum.[38] As the chemical properties of substances were becoming more and more known, Lankester suggested, it was possible to repurpose previously wasted materials by extracting their valuable chemical substances, such as the fat and oil from skin waste accumulated during the tanning process, which could be made into soap and other fatty products.

Experts concretized their obsession with waste in the display spaces and literature of the Great Exhibition and argued for the establishment of permanent collections that would promote the value of waste.[39] Their ambition was to expand the existing specimen of the Great Exhibition into a large and comprehensive "economic museum" or "trade museum," "a centre in which science should lead on to the industrial applications, to the useful purposes of life."[40] To this aim, the Society of Arts teamed up with the Commissioners of the exhibition and built a number of collections based on the specimens of the Great Exhibition to be housed, first, in the newly formed South Kensington

Museum and later in the Bethnal Green Museum.[41] Under the supervision of Playfair and Lankester, the Museum included an animal products collection, which contained a category on the "Application of Waste Matter" showing "the various shapes in which those hitherto waste[ed] products were again brought into the useful purposes of life so that nothing was in fact waste."[42] Joining the Animal Products Collection were the Waste Products Collection, assembled by Simmonds, and the Food Collection, designed to illustrate "the nature and sources of the food which rich and poor alike need for the maintenance of their daily life."[43] The close kinship between waste, food, and the utilization of natural and industrial by-products suggested in these displays would also inform experts' engagement with food and nutrition.

ANALYSIS AND SYNTHESIS

In response to the food crisis, the experts connected by the Great Exhibition were keen to reduce waste in nourishment. They grasped for previously un- or underutilized sources of nourishment and methods to streamline existing eating patterns according to more economical principles. They debated the potential productivity of agricultural planting practices and high-yielding crops, and they searched for a better scientific mechanism to distinguish useful from useless, efficient from inefficient, cost-nutritious from nutritionally wasteful foods. These economic, agricultural, and scientific efforts were not separable to our experts, but intertwined.

Already in the first edition of his 1832 treatise *Vegetable Substances Used for the Food of Man,* Lankester sought to "trace the progress of our own country towards one of the chief objects and indications of civilization,— that of obtaining an abundance and a variety of wholesome and agreeable vegetable food, at the cheapest rate, and with unfailing regularity, for increasing inhabitants."[44] He surveyed the food plants of the world using an approach that combined natural history and materia medica, arranged by plant groups, with a description of their morphology, growing conditions, use, and preparation. He also wrestled with the question of how to determine the nourishing potential of foods and compare crops according to their nourishment-yielding profile.

Attempts to quantify the relative nourishing potential of different food-stuffs when planted in the same area of soil had a long history. Lankester looked to the past for instances when foods had been compared as to their yields of nourishing substance. An oft-cited example, according to Lankester, was a calculation of Alexander von Humboldt in his *Essai politique sur le royaume de la Nouvelle-Espagne*. Humboldt had contrasted the amount of nourishment per one hundred square meters of soil when planted with banana trees with the same amount of soil when planted with wheat for one year. The banana field, Humboldt had concluded, would yield two thousand kilograms of "nourishing substance," while wheat only yielded fifteen kilograms of nourishment. This meant that the same sized territory could nourish twenty-five people if it was planted with bananas compared to one person if it was planted with wheat.[45] Lankester also engaged with a passage from a collection of tracts on the Corn Laws that grappled with the question of whether wheat or potatoes would yield more nourishment, if both were grown on "an acre of land, with the same degree of labour bestowed upon it, and the same portion of manure applied to it."[46] Wheat would yield considerably more weight per acre than potatoes, the tract concluded. But it also cautioned that the key was to ascertain "the quantity of nutrition in a given quantity of either wheat or potatoes."

The crucial question, Lankester rightly suggested, was how exactly the nourishing power of a given food could be measured. In the 1832 and 1840 editions of his treatise, Lankester still relied on an eighteenth-century conception of nourishment as uniform matter (chapter 1).[47] The subcomponents of plants identified by chemical analysis—such as gluten, mucilage, and saccharine matter—were all nourishing, he believed, though different in their nutritive quality and refinement. When determining the nourishing powers of plant foods, then, one simply had to add up the quantity of all these nourishing principles. For each vegetable food, Lankester noted the content of total nutritious substances as a percentage of its overall weight or bulk. Carrots contained 10 percent of nutritive matter, oats boasted 75 percent, while wheat contained a staggering 95.5 percent of nutritious substance. Plants thus identified as yielding a high percentage of nourishment per weight could contribute to a less wasteful utilization of the world's food resources. Salep, for instance, a flour made from orchid tubers, contained "a greater quantity of nutriment in the same bulk than any other vegetable body," Lankester announced, and had therefore been discussed as a standard provision on any ship undertaking a long voyage.[48]

But how did the different types of extracted nourishing matter compare in their nutritiousness? Gluten, mucilage, and saccharine matter certainly all had a nourishing function, and adding them up might give an adequate quantity of overall nourishing materials. But was there a difference in nourishing potential between a vegetable that contained a certain amount of gluten and one that contained the same amount of saccharine matter? Like many of his contemporaries, Lankester was searching for a comparative mechanism to rank the nourishing power of distinct food components. In the 1832 edition of his book, Lankester relied on a ranking method based on the animal or vegetable nature of substances that had been articulated by agricultural chemist Humphry Davy in 1813.[49] According to Davy, gluten was "the most nutritive" of isolated substances, because it "approaches nearest in its nature to animal matter."[50] Gluten was known to be present in wheat, which, according to Davy, made it a superior nourishing grain to others. Continuing his hierarchy of nourishment, Davy asserted that "next in order as to nourishing power, is sugar, then farina; and last of all gelatinous and extractive matters."[51] But the exact effect of these substances on the body remained unclear. "The difficulty of estimating the nutritive power of the raw substances is not wholly removed by this appeal to chemistry," Lankester quoted Davy, "because we are still ignorant of the effect which the combination of the saccharine matter with the mucilage and gluten may produce when used as aliment."[52]

In the 1846 version of his treatise on vegetable food, Lankester found a more promising solution. Like Gail Borden himself (chapter 1), he began to rely on Liebig's chemical theories, which made a particularly compelling case for how the constituents of nourishment might relate to their function in the body. Playfair, who had been a student of Liebig's in Giessen, had popularized and translated Liebig's works into English, while also conducting his own research on the constituent properties of food.[53] According to Liebig, the chemical elements found in food correlated to specific tissues of the human body and therefore served two distinct purposes. Providing the body with heat and strength was the task of the so-called respiratory or non-nitrogenous principles (those which contained primarily carbon, oxygen, and hydrogen). Building the tissues of the body fell to the so-called flesh-forming, or nitrogenous principles (those which contained primarily nitrogen). Since Liebig regarded tissue formation as the true purpose of nourishment, he singled out nitrogen as the most important element of nutrition.[54]

The appeal of Liebig's constituent-based, nitrogen-centric theory consisted above all in the extent to which it troubled existing conceptions of nourishment. The presence of more or less nitrogen did not seem to reflect the distinction between animal and vegetable food; contrary to expectation, some vegetable foods seemed to contain a higher amount of nitrogen than animal foods.[55] Nitrogen could also not be linked to a specific taste. Neither natural laws nor subjective experience, it seemed, could be trusted to indicate foods' nourishing function. But this also meant that neither natural laws nor tastes were ongoing limitations to what food could be, or what could be food. The notion that each food nourished in exactly the same way also suggested that reflections on foods' kind, including previously assumed geographic limitations of foods' nourishing power, could be disregarded, leaving the globe open to food extraction from afar. As a result, the nitrogen theory provided food experts with a unique opportunity to radically rethink the current food system and extend their economizing impulses of the food supply to the molecular level.

Constituent-based theories also allowed food experts to measure the nourishment content of a food and relate it to the food's cost. Using such calculations of cost-nutritiousness, experts investigated the nutritional efficiency of individual foods and institutional dietaries. One of the most influential assessments was carried out by Playfair's teacher, Jonathan Pereira, who assembled the dietary tables of Britain's prisons, poorhouses, hospitals, and the military. He analyzed each food item according to its nitrogen and carbon content as well as its cost and compared its nutritive value to other foods.[56] This was followed by an official report in 1864 by physician and medical officer of the Poor Law Board Edward Smith on institutional dietaries, particularly those of prisons. The guiding principle of Smith's report was to "show in which way the largest amount of nutriment can be gained by those who have money to spend in private dietaries and upon how little cost those may be supported who are fed by public dietaries."[57] Foods that were nutritious (high in nitrogen) but expensive could simply be replaced by foods that were equally high in nitrogen but cheaper, whether they were animal or vegetable foods, local or imported, tasty or revolting.

Aside from reorganizing institutional dietaries, experts connected to the Great Exhibition sought to identify new and previously unused sources of nourishment, based on their belief in the nourishing constituents. The exhibition (as well as the Society of Arts) served as a hub for this enterprise. Just like Lankester's suggestion to extract chemicals from waste materials and turn them into valuable industrial products, experts adopted a constituent-centric gaze with which they examined possible new sources of nourishment in waste matter. The blood of abattoirs, for example, attracted the attention of the jurors. Since blood was by necessity the reservoir from which nourishing constituents were absorbed, experts credited blood with a particularly rich concentration of nutrients. But quite a lot of blood was daily wasted as a by-product in slaughtering. The planned construction of several new slaughterhouses in London prompted the jurors to wonder "whether the blood of the numerous animals killed there can be utilized or not." The question was answered favorably by the makers of "Brocchieri's Blood Cakes," a preparation that promised to "utilize the nutritious principles of the blood of animals killed for food."[58] Even though the jurors found the name of the preparation "unfortunate" and its taste "perfectly insipid," they still praised the principle upon which it was designed.[59]

They also lauded the blood cakes' high concentration of nutritious matter. The focus on constituents and nitrogen supplied experts not only with a mechanism to identify new sources of nourishment, but to quantify the nutritious content of different foods and compare them. During the course of the exhibition, Playfair conducted detailed chemical analyses of food specimen. He found that Gail Borden's Meat Biscuit contained an astounding "32 per cent of flesh-forming principles" or "4.9 percent of nitrogen" per unit, while Warriner's Osmazome measured only a respectable "14 per cent of flesh-forming principle" or 2.1 per cent of nitrogen."[60] The unappetizing blood cakes by Brocchieri contained the most nourishment, beating even the much-praised meat biscuit. With "43 per cent of flesh forming principles" or "6.6 per cent of nitrogen," they provided "double the nutritive value of ordinary butcher meat."

From measuring and comparing, it was only a small step to intervening and optimizing. The meat biscuit (and similar foods) promised not only to reproduce the nutritious elements of meat, but to *augment* them. Borden's creation claimed to supply the "essence of five pounds of good meat" in the form of only "one pound of biscuit."[61] Nutritiousness, as understood through nutritive constituents, had become an amplifiable value where more nutritious substance nourished better. In a letter to the Society of Arts titled "What is Food?" a railway engineer pushed this sentiment to the extreme, speculating that "as our analysis grows into synthesis, many new varieties of food will be produced artificially."[62] Whereas in previous times, "food consisted only of the productions of nature," he suggested, present-day food increasingly consisted of "artificial preparations, or the productions of nature chemically altered." Such foods had been called "adulterated," but who was to say what would be subsumed in the category of food in the future? "There is danger of people being poisoned by quacks," he conceded, "but there is also danger of stopping progress."

While sources of domestic waste and institutional dietaries at home were important areas of intervention for mid-century food experts, their core focus lay beyond. They sought to locate previously wasted nourishing matter in Britain's current and former colonies. The empire, in their minds, was a "vast treasure-trove of untapped wealth and resources," which it was their task to unearth.[63] The displays and texts of the exhibition doubled as a detection exercise to identify previously unknown, unused, and unvalued substances. Like nourishing matter itself, the empire could be analyzed for parts that were useful and parts that were currently going to waste.

Experts' vision of the world involved a bountiful, inexhaustible empire that offered ever new sources of sustenance and wealth to those ingenious enough to recognize and utilize them. To Simmonds, Britain's manifold challenges, such as "the increase of population, the extension of colonization, the greater demands made by manufacturers, and the continual waste occurring," had created "urgent wants" for "New Materials of Commerce" as well as "a larger supply of old staples than are at present available." Drawing on his experience as a "Colonial planter" and the extensive colonial correspondence network with "cultivators, producers, and scientific men in all parts of the world" he had forged, Simmonds presented a panoply of "Undeveloped and Unappreciated Articles" that could be brought within Britain's reach through skillful waste utilization.[64] In an encyclopedic exposition, he enumerated a range of potential products, from animal and vegetable substances to insects, minerals, chemical products, and pharmaceutical substances. He emphasized "the value of the dead carcases [*sic*] of horses, and the numerous purposes to which offal is applied." He lamented "how little attention" had been paid "to the trade in succades, Sweetmeats and jellies." And he boasted that "the soil of tropical countries" was "almost overrun" with medicinal and other useful plants.[65]

Nothing was considered out of bounds in the search for new and previously underutilized sources of nourishment, from more durable, cheaper, transportable varieties of well-known staple foods, such as wheat or potatoes, to substances previously not even belonging to the category of "food." Lindley's official jury report on the food category at the exhibition reflected this broad outlook but took care to assess each exhibited specimen for its potential usefulness as a new source of nourishment. Overly unusual specimens such as "sea-slugs, and birds-nests, and other curious matters," were

FIGURE 5. Colonial produce. *Dickinsons' Comprehensive Pictures of the Great Exhibition of 1851* (London: Dickinson Brothers, 1852).

dismissed by Lindley because, "whatever may be their value," they belonged "to countries so far removed from us that we cannot feel their importance."[66] Overall, however, he felt that the exhibition had revealed an encouraging number of "new preparations" and "new sources of supply" and had pointed Britain's experts to "new countries" from which "manifest improvements in alimentary substances" could be obtained.[67] Among substances "previously unknown or scarcely attended to," Lindley presented two new sources of fecula (a starchy plant extract) from two species of arrowroot, one from Santo Domingo and one from Western Australia.[68] From Scinde and New Zealand came two cakes made from "Typha Bread," a species of aquatic plant pollen, which were considered a nutritious food by both local populations, and which chemical examinations in Britain had confirmed to contain a high amount of nutritious matter.[69]

The meat biscuit made use of another kind of wasted nourishment, in the minds of experts. It captured the large quantities of cattle herds on the plains of Australia and North America. Since meat cultivation required large areas of land, its production had become increasingly impractical in a small, populated, rapidly industrializing island nation like Britain. Many of the colonies, by contrast, contained a bounty of "cheap and abundant" animal food.[70] In

Australia, meat was "absolutely wasted in extraordinary quantities"; entire flocks of cattle were "slaughtered for the tallow alone, and whole herds for their bones and hides." And Borden and Smith had boasted about the "abundant pasturage on the broad prairies" of Texas, which made beef cattle one of Texas's "staple productions."[71] For the jurors at the exhibition, the meat biscuit represented a method by which this wasted abundance might be "imported into England and sold at a cheaper rate than fresh meat in our metropolitan markets, to the great benefit of all classes."[72] Lindley therefore considered it "one of the most important substances which this exhibition has brought to our knowledge."[73] Through products like the meat biscuit, Lindley raved, it would be possible to convert animals from far-away places that were there "of little or no value" into a substance "of such durability that it may be preserved with greatest ease, and sent to distant countries." It was as if "a new means of subsistence was actually offered to us."

But the meat biscuit and similar products resonated with the spirit of waste optimization not only for their ability to collapse *distance* but also for their potential to collapse *mass*. The scale of the mid-nineteenth-century British food crisis required nourishment to travel in greater quantities over larger distances at lower weight and cost and greater nutritiousness than previously thought possible. The meat biscuit's high content of nutritious matter and its process of manufacture were hailed in the catalog of the Great Exhibition as saving an "immense expense in the transportation of useless bulk and weight of meat."[74] The search for the wasted resources of the empire, and the attempt to maximize them through global extraction and transportation, thus further forced attention on the nutritive power of food in relation to its physical properties—its mass, its weight—properties that would determine its economic potential on the imperial map.

The equation of edible products from foreign territories with "waste" required resources be defined as "raw" materials. British experts repeatedly contrasted the manufactured nature of domestic goods with the supposedly under-manipulated and under-experimented character of global products, whether they were agricultural or industrial. Today, "processed food" is regarded with suspicion by many people. But nineteenth-century British food experts saw a clear hierarchy in the stages of manufacture, from raw material to finished manufactured product. This was reflected in the classification scheme of the Great Exhibition devised by Playfair and Prince Albert. With its four divisions—raw materials, machines, manufactures, and fine arts—the classification was meant to reproduce and emphasize the production process.[75]

The displays, too, foregrounded processing. The multivolume *Official and Descriptive Catalogue* of the exhibition contained lengthy descriptions of manufacturing processes, and even the entries in the abridged one-volume catalog, a very popular item of sale at the exhibition, often showcased exhibitors' attempts to illustrate the process of production through their displays.

The division between raw substance and manufactured good was then mapped onto a spatial configuration of empire. In their writings, experts cast the empire's periphery as the supplier of raw materials and the metropolis as their processor. This mapping reflected a prominent Free Trade vision of "specialized internationalism" and of the empire as a "cog" in the global manufacturing process.[76] In his survey of commercial products of the vegetable kingdom, Simmonds insisted that the majority of substances imported to Britain were "raw" materials; "very few of these products," he claimed, speaking of vegetable staples like grains, fruits, roots, and sugar, "come to us in any other than an unmanufactured state; they are shipped to this country as the chief emporium and factory of the world."[77] British ingenuity could improve these unaltered, unprofitable substances by identifying them as useful in the first place, and by applying a certain experimental spirit. The increasingly difficult access to sugar, for example, could be alleviated by identifying and testing the "variety of plants furnishing saccharine juices," Simmonds claimed, while the failure of the potato crop might be mitigated by "experimentalizing on new tuberous roots."[78]

The meat biscuit and similar preparations were lumped together with the list of animal and vegetable substances whose raw state could potentially be processed to full potential. Simmonds placed the meat biscuit and similar preparations at the end of a long enumeration of "undeveloped and unappreciated articles of raw produce from different parts of the world."[79] He declared that not enough use had been made of the "many species of concentrated and portable nutritious food," such as "Du Liscoet's biscuit beef for soup," "Warriner's osmazone[*sic*]," and the "meat biscuit." Just like vegetable fibers, rubber trees, and insects, such products were part of a "bountiful Nature" that satisfied every demand once "diligent investigation and inquiry" had been "set on foot."[80] Natural abundance, in turn, came with an obligation to yield. Since Britain was now "more than ever dependent upon our colonies," remarked a discussant of Simmonds's paper, it was "our duty to encourage the inhabitants of those countries to supply us with the produce with which nature had so bountifully provided them."[81]

Beyond the utility of helping Britain stock up on its supplies and raw materials for manufacture, the extractive enterprise championed by Simmonds and his colleagues would act as a draw "towards general civilisation" across the entire globe.[82] Even those territories not under Britain's formal imperial or military control could thus be brought within reach. The supposed civilizing force of commerce had, in the eyes of Simmonds, already incited "the petty monarchs of Africa" to abandon the trade in human beings for the trade of palm oil and induced "the Zulu and Kaffir tribes" to settle down "more readily into the peaceful pursuits of stock-breeding and cultivating the soil," instead of "waging exterminating wars with each other." The project of 'taming the peoples of the world' into engaging in trade and tending to their land and resources would, in turn, unlock bountiful resources for British needs, Simmonds believed. "When we perceive the new and vast fields which are laid open to investigation and enterprise," Simmonds suggested, from "the empires of China and Japan being no longer sealed countries" to "the interiors of the vast continents of Australia, Africa, and America, being ransacked by Commerce" and "the island groups of the Pacific and Eastern Archipelago . . . being now fast peopled by Europeans," who, he asked, "shall set a limit to the new and useful products which may be there developed and brought in to the aid of the merchant and the manufacturer?"

THE RAW AND THE CIVILIZED

Simmonds was not alone in connecting the appropriation of "wasted" resources to civilization. Experts justified their hunt for other places' resources by declaring it a path to progress. They projected the geographic configuration of metropolis versus periphery, of raw material versus refined product, onto a temporal axis of economic development. As historian Pratik Chakrabarti has shown, nineteenth-century "deep" historical imaginations of nature and the colonial appropriation of natural resources were closely intertwined.[83] In the writings of food experts connected to the exhibition, spatial and temporal hierarchies of nourishment formed an elaborate justification for imperial expansion, resource extraction, and the superiority of the British palate.

To Lankester, resource extraction (both agriculturally from the soil and commercially from other nations) followed a natural course of evolution, from a state of primitivism to a state of development, that paralleled that of civilization. In the "rudest state of society," Lankester argued, man depended on the "spontaneous products of uncultivated wilds" for food. The sign of an economically advanced nation, by contrast, was its ability to accumulate resources from elsewhere. "When a nation has commercial intercourse with the uttermost ends of the earth," he claimed, "it soon makes all the valuable products of other places its own."[84] Reliance on a single food was thus a mark of primitivity. A society that supplemented its local food resources through a variety of foods from elsewhere, by contrast, was more advanced on the scale of development.

Such an advanced state of society was also characterized by a taste for a greater variety of things. "In the infancy of societies," Lankester observed, people were "necessarily satisfied with the enjoyment of such indigenous productions as fall most naturally within their reach." More advanced societies, however, "naturalized" articles of food which had at one time been "introduced as luxuries" so that they formed part of "the sustenance of the common people." In so doing, they had something to "fall back" on so that "what would otherwise be famine is at worst changed into privation."[85]

The acquisition of new "civilized" tastes was therefore not only a sign of an advanced stage of civilization, but a way of reinforcing progress by guarding against famine. New appetites could be acquired, and once acquired, they attested to the resourcefulness of eating subjects in a world of scarce resources. In this context, Lankester's anecdote of a gentleman "from a remote part of Scotland" who had cultivated "such a fondness for some weed thrown up by the sea, and which through poverty of the inhabitant was made to form part of their sustenance, that in after-life, when he had returned from a protracted residence abroad, he procured a supply of his favourite weed to be regularly sent to him to London," was less an exposition of the man's eccentric palate, than a comment on the degree to which any civilized man's palate could be developed for the purpose of avoiding dependence on a single crop.[86]

Lankester's insistence on taste and resourcefulness in procuring food as a mark of civilization was echoed by Playfair. In a lecture at the exhibition dedicated to the use of chemistry in manufacture, Playfair contrasted the willingness of civilized nations to procure food with the naïve content of less civilized nations. "European nations," he observed, "as they increase in wants, examine every material, to see if it be adapted to their ministration; they do not, like the African Dokos, bury their heads in the ground, and shaking their legs in the air, thank the Supreme Being that they are content with snakes, ants, and mice, for their food."[87] The ability to annex new soils, appropriate new foodstuffs, and acquire new tastes, in Playfair's view, distinguished the resourceful and industrious European white man from his complacent colonial subjects.

Misplaced contentment with one's lot and lack of appetite for different foodstuffs also affected the economic output of a nation, in Lankester's opinion. It decreased productivity and kept labor prices low. The inhabitants of India, he reported, had no gusto for anything but the most basic needs, and consequently did not aspire to great industry. "Having few artificial wants," he said of them, "they are without those habitual incentives to exertion which actuate so powerfully and so beneficially people of the same rank in countries like our own. If they can acquire a meal for themselves and their families they have little thought about higher comforts; the price of labour in such countries is, in fact, equal to very little beyond the purchase of the lowest description of food."[88] Experts conjured up a vision of a *homo economicus*, whose "habitual incentives" prompted him to trade and be productive.[89] But this vision worked to enforce, not erase, a racial distinction between the civilized colonizers and the uncivilized colonized.

"Uncultivated" places, in the double sense of the word, were also vulnerable to the unmitigated impact of extremes, such as famines and the climate. Reliance on a single food exposed their inhabitants to severe food shortages in times of crop failure, untempered by the moderating influence of varied supplementary foodstuffs. Quoting economist David Ricardo, Lankester warned that there was "no refuge from calamity" for societies in their infancy; "dearth to them is attended with almost all the evils of famine."[90] Similarly, uncultivated soil exposed its population to the harshness of intemperate climate. Without cultivation, Lankester argued, the effects of climate would be allowed to damage the earth so that it would "speedily become uninhabitable." Vegetable cultivation thus had a beneficial effect on climate, and "no vegetable productions tend so much to bring about this beneficial result as those which are cultivated for human food."[91] Lankester asked the reader to consider that in "countries which are uncultivated the weather is mostly in extremes," like in parts of India or South Africa. By contrast, in countries that had recently intensified and expanded their agricultural production, the climate had become milder. Scotland was a prime example, a country that had only recently benefitted from "the introduction of agricultural improvements," and a change in climate had been the consequence.[92]

The picture painted by Lankester and Playfair pinned a raw, wild, famine-ridden, climatically extreme and gustatorily unadventurous periphery against a refined, civilized, well-supplied, moderate and sensorially adept metropolis. This convenient dichotomy rationalized the development of foreign soils while promoting commercial and agricultural extraction of resources from the periphery supposedly to benefit "civilization." It also worked to cement the distinction between colonial raw materials and domestic manufactured goods by erasing the labor of producing these resources in the first place as well as drawing a link between resource scarcity and industriousness. "The industry of the European," Lankester claimed, "surrounds him with a much greater amount of blessings than the almost spontaneous bounty of Nature to the Indian who lives upon his patch of bananas." By contrast, a person who lived amid a wealth of resources so that "the produce of two or three [breadfruit] trees" would " suffice for a man's yearly supply," was "not likely to call forth the faculties of his mind which wait upon a constant course of assiduous labour."[93] Abundance, in short, led to laziness, and laziness prevented natural resources from being utilized to their fullest, resulting in waste.

Products like the meat biscuit symbolized more than a new means of preserving or transporting food. In the imagination of British food experts, the biscuit would convey notably nourishing substances from places of abundance to places of scarcity, and at low cost. It would diversify the British palate and increase British resilience against dietary dearth. It would contribute to the economic, agricultural, and climatic development of "less advanced" nations. And it would create a more industrious, peaceful, civilized, and well-nourished global population. "A more simple, economical, and efficient form of portable concentrated food than the American Meat Biscuit of Gail Borden has never been brought before the public," concluded the jurors' report.[94]

CONCLUSION

The meat biscuit never became a bestseller, even in Britain. Despite the praise bestowed upon it at the Great Exhibition, the product failed to attract the interest of corporate buyers. Borden himself moved on to producing condensed milk, which proved an infinitely more successful venture. Its launch coincided with improvements in canning technology and the beginnings of the US Civil War. Borden finally achieved his ambition to secure a military contract, and condensed milk became a sensation practically overnight. But the drive toward concentration discussed in this and the previous chapter long preceded the technical and commercial developments that propelled condensed milk and must be taken into account to explain its appeal. The end of the biscuit's career may have been caused by Borden's wandering attention. It may have been due to the fact that Borden held on to a model of consumption—corporate consumption—that was already largely displaced in Britain. Issues of taste may have played a role. Competitor products (especially Liebig's meat extract) were perhaps too successful and pushed the biscuit out of the market.

But it is not so much the biscuit's failure as its persistent success that requires explanation. At the Great Exhibition, the meat biscuit was met with resounding enthusiasm. It was awarded the Gold Medal of the jury for food and showered with praise in the jury's report. Borden himself was granted an honorary membership of the Society of Arts. Smith's involvement might partly explain this initial favoritism of the jury toward the product, but the biscuit continued to capture the imagination of Britain's food experts. It resonated with experts' concerns over Britain's food crisis and satisfied their taste for scientific-technical, commercial, and imperial solutions. To Lankester, Playfair, Simmonds, and their network, the biscuit was more than food. It promised to overcome existing limits of nourishment, turn previously wasted resources into profitable commodities, secure a stable supply of raw materials, and contribute to the economic advancement of the world.

As in the United States, discussions about the biscuit in British circles continued to focus on mechanisms of nourishment. Experts' imperial perspective on the food supply and their concern with eliminating unnecessary bulk of any kind intensified the search for the functional constituents of foods and their role in the human body. Liebig's nitrogen theory offered one compelling answer to these questions and provided an easy mechanism of measurement, satisfying experts' demand for tools of assessment and comparison. It also disrupted older ways of understanding nourishment, thereby paving the way for a radical rethinking of food. That Liebig turned out to be completely wrong about the specialized physiological functions of nitrogenous versus non-nitrogenous food constituents did not prevent his theory from gaining traction. The success of Liebig's theory, then, cannot be put down simply to its superior accuracy. Instead, it must be understood within a longer history of entangled nutritional, imperial, and economic thought. The nutritional scientific ideas and products discussed here certainly reflected genuine scientific lines of inquiry, as well as cultural, religious, and social preoccupations of their times. But they also evolved through interaction with commercial imperatives, imperial aspirations, and racist impulses.

The focus on waste and waste-optimizing products like the meat biscuit forced attention on particular aspects of the British food crisis. It configured food shortage as a problem of underrealized production, procurement, and trade. It divided a profound social crisis into distinct, bite-sized engineering problems and offered bespoke scientific-technical solutions. It launched a flurry of experimental activity and investigative spirit toward a narrow set of questions. Like the members of the Mudfog Society, experts neglected to consider the larger structural factors underlying the food crisis—poverty, social inequality, land privatization—even as they zealously discussed ever more ambitious and—to a present-day eye—morally dubious nutritional strategies. Thanks to the expanding alliance of nutrition science and commerce, experts were able to rationalize the global implications of their extractivist enterprise.

THREE

Digestive Economies

INTRODUCTION

In the small town of Liskeard in the South of Britain, Louisa Down's mother was considered a "living wonder."[1] At nearly seventy-three years of age, Margaret had existed in splendid health for over a decade, despite having been declared practically dead thirteen years ago. At the time, she had suddenly been taken ill with a bad stomach complaint: as soon as she ate anything, even the lightest morsel of food, she brought it back up again, sometimes even with blood. She had been unable to do her chores around the house or dress herself, and she needed help with the simplest of tasks. After a while she had been afraid to eat. As the months passed, she became "nothing but skin and bone," as her daughter would often say.

Six doctors had been called to Margaret's aid, none of them able to help. In hushed tones, they had all confirmed the hopelessness of the situation, and gently prepared the family for the worst. The announcement, though painful, had not come as a great surprise to Louisa; Margaret's declining condition was plain for all to see. To make matters worse, the expense of the illness was beginning to weigh on the poor family. They knew they could not afford any further treatments.

But just as they had begun to accept their mother's fate, a new doctor arrived in town. He went by the name of Dr. Chipperfield and was as cheerful in his demeanor as might be expected from one so called. His head filled with the latest medical ideas and social ideals (both acquired in far-away London), he agreed to treat Margaret free of charge. The therapy was simple: it consisted solely in the application of a new food product, called Benger's Food. A wine glass at a time, the product had slowly shown effect. Margaret's health improved, she felt stronger, gained weight, and was even able to take up light work again. By night, she threaded her needle by lamp light, as she had always done. Having adopted a diet of Benger's Food, she never went back, and had lived on the preparation ever since. As far as Louisa and her family were concerned, this "wonderful woman" owed her life, entirely, to this "wonderful food."

This story about Margaret and her miraculous cure through Benger's Food was related by her daughter Louisa in a letter addressed to the company producing Benger's Food. It is one of many such communications written by a user of the food to the company. Carefully preserved in the company's archives, such letters attest to the genuine enthusiasm surrounding products like Benger's Food as well as to the increasingly consumer-oriented approach of nutritional entrepreneurs seeking to market new wonder foods. Benger's Food was the brainchild of Frederick Baden Benger, a pharmaceutical chemist, and William Roberts, a physician and physiologist. It consisted of a mix of wheat flour, sugar, and what was at the time referred to as "digestive ferments" (today called digestive enzymes). According to the preparation instructions, Benger's Food should be dissolved in cold water and added to warm milk (not unlike today's method of preparing pudding or custard from a mix). Once added to the milk and left to rest for a specified period of time, the ferments contained in the product would supposedly become active and "predigest" the food, making it easier for it to be absorbed in the gut. Benger and Roberts developed the product, drawing heavily on the work of a "female relative" of Roberts's, as part of Roberts's research into the physiology of digestion. With Roberts's help, Benger then went on to promote the product commercially. He marketed it to people with weak digestive systems, and in particular to "infants, invalids, and the aged." First designed in 1880, Benger's Food became a popular and widely sold product by the end of the century, exported from the United Kingdom as far as Australia.

Benger's Food was not a singular, marginal phenomenon but belonged to a larger group of similar products based on the digestive ferments in Britain, the United States, and other Western industrializing countries. Preparations of the ferments pepsin, trypsin, and diastase as well as enzyme-enriched, "predigested" or "artificially digested" foods filled the shelves of grocers, the windows of pharmacies, and the advertising pages of magazines between the 1880s and the 1910s. They went by such imaginative names as Nutrimentive Powder, Liquor Pepticus, Liquor Pancreaticus, Peptenzyme, Peptocolos, Peptodyn, Darby's Fluid Meat, Liquid Bread, and Malted Milk. The remnants

FIGURE 6. Can of Benger's Food. From the Museum of Healthcare, Kingston. Used with permission.

of this trend are still with us: many of our modern breakfast cereals and products such as Ovomaltine (Ovaltine) and Horlick's started out as predigested foods, while Pepsi-Cola once contained pepsin.[2]

These products were bound up with new ways of understanding digestion and new methods for investigating the digestive system and its diseases. Pharmacists, physiologists, and physicians saw in digestive ferments not only the key to understanding digestive function but the possibility to launch an entirely new therapeutic approach, a means of controlling the digestive process in specific and powerful ways. By cracking digestion, they hoped to elevate dietetics to a science with broad applicability. The research method of "artificial digestion," which combined the preparation of artificial digestive agents with a simulation of digestive processes outside the body played a crucial role in this transformation. It suggested that the digestive process occurred through the work of distinct, identifiable physiological agents— ferments—that could be extracted from the digestive organs of other animals and administered to humans to restore, or even enhance, digestive function. An important initial market of Benger's ferment products was therefore the scientific and medical community who engaged in debates about digestion and sought to use ferment products in their experiments as well as in their medical and nursing practice.

The scientific questions raised by artificially digested foods were inseparable from the economic contexts in which they were produced. The common link was the British thrift movement from the 1870s and 1880s which extended the mid-century obsession with repurposing waste efficiently. The call to thrift resounded at a time when British researchers, sanitary scientists, and political economists were searching for more practicable solutions to a whole host of national problems, many of which, such as the food question, had persisted since mid-century. But whereas the 1850s ideology of waste had focused largely on the production and procurement of food, the 1880s thrift movement was concerned with food consumption and usage by individuals. The creation of Benger's Food and similar products represented perhaps one of the most extreme manifestations of the thrift spirit. It allowed its makers and users to fantasize about economizing the food supply by controlling the uptake of food through individual digestive systems and improving the digestibility of foods.

The imagined addressees of this vision were not primarily rich middle-class or upper-class consumers, but people like Margaret: poor, sick, elderly, working-class people, especially those who couldn't work (of course including infants). Their health, food choices, and digestive capability came under close scrutiny as British sanitary scientists and political economists grew increasingly concerned about the cost of sickness to the nation and the role of nutrition in maintaining and restoring the working faculties of the British population. They articulated a notion of "National Health" to emphasize the link between Britain's economic well-being and the health of its productive citizenry, and they promoted their vision, once again, at an exhibition, the International Health Exhibition of 1884. In Margaret's case, the success of Benger's Food consisted not only in the disappearance of her symptoms, but also in the restoration of her labor capabilities.

ARTIFICIAL DIGESTION AND THE INVENTION OF DIGESTIVE FERMENTS

René Antoine Ferchault de Réaumur maintained a veritable "living collection" of hens, ducks, geese, and chickens in his yard.[3] With the help of his gardener and a few workers, he kept them in good shape, feeding and watering them and keeping their surroundings clean. Every now and then he would select a vulture or a rooster, bring it into the house, and use it for one of his rather interventionist experiments. Réaumur was an experimental naturalist, and the birds were his "experimental subjects."[4] One particular investigation involved a buzzard, which Réaumur had selected particularly for its regurgitating abilities. Taking a small, open-ended metal tube, Réaumur inserted a small piece of beef. He placed the tube with the beef into the beak of the buzzard and forced the bird to swallow it. Once the buzzard had regurgitated the tube, Réaumur examined the tube's contents. He found the meat reduced in size and weight as well as altered in color, consistency, and taste. The meat had clearly been partially digested, Réaumur concluded, and he thought he knew how. Since the meat had been protected by the metal tube from the movements of the stomach, it could not have been ground down through mechanical force alone. A chemical solvent must have been at work.[5]

Hoping to collect samples of this solvent, Réaumur inserted a few pieces of sponge into the same open tube and forced another buzzard to swallow it. After the bird had regurgitated the tube, Réaumur squeezed the sponges now soaked with stomach liquid into a container. He then added the liquid as well as the sponges to a piece of meat inside a metal tube and placed the whole in an oven at 23 degrees Celsius to imitate the heat of the stomach. The next day, he inspected the tubes, but did not find the changes he had hoped to see. The meat was not sufficiently dissolved; it smelled very bad and had probably been "corrupted." The sponges, meanwhile, had dried out. Nevertheless, Réaumur refused to consider the experiment a failure. In writing up his course of action for prosperity in 1752, he stressed how easy it had been to obtain stomach liquid by the method he had outlined. He also gave detailed instructions to future researchers on how to apply his method and avoid the mistakes he had made.[6] One failed experiment was not grounds for Réaumur to dismiss the possibility of examining digestion outside the bodies of living beings.

Though Réaumur did not succeed in cracking the mechanism of digestion (even by his own account), his experiments shaped future investigations about digestive physiology and chemistry. At stake was not only the precise mechanism of digestion—whether it was primarily a mechanical or a chemical phenomenon, or perhaps the result of some other yet unknown mechanism—but also the degree to which it would be possible to investigate life processes such as digestion using ordinary chemical or mechanical methods in the first place.[7] Réaumur had devised a method for obtaining stomach liquid and demonstrated how to test this liquid as a digestive agent outside the animal body. He had also raised important new questions about the digestive process: What was the nature of the chemical solvent likely involved in digestion? How did it produce digestive changes? And could it be captured and used to reproduce digestion outside of living bodies? Together, these questions and Réaumur's approach would come to inform the nineteenth-century research enterprise of artificial digestion.

Artificial digestion was at once concerned with identifying and isolating a digestive agent, such as a chemical solvent, and using it in order to imitate and investigate digestion outside the bodies of animals. Contrary to eighteenth-century attempts to duplicate animal digestion in automata, such as Jacques de Vaucanson's defecating duck, nineteenth century artificial digestion experiments were not performed to demonstrate the limits of equating live phenomena with mechanical or chemical processes.[8] Instead, nineteenth-century experimenters truly believed that artificial digestion could reproduce the digestive process as it occurred in living beings. They argued that artificial digestion was closer to digestion in living beings than anatomical studies made with the dead bodies of animals. They also suggested that it was a more practicable approach than gastric fistulas, abnormal openings in the stomach wall through which the contents of the stomach could become accessible to an investigator. A gastric fistula allowed US army surgeon William Beaumont to conduct digestive experiments on a live patient in the 1820s, observing and measuring the speed at which certain pieces of food would undergo change in the stomach.[9] But fistulas were rare occurrences and could not possibly be produced deliberately.

The practical requirements for the kind of research Réaumur performed were also considerable. Not every researcher had access to a flock of fowl in their backyard, and the upkeep and subsequent slaughtering of non-regurgitating animals to assess their stomach contents was no breeze either. It was not until the 1830s that a more feasible method was found to isolate a substance believed to possess digestive capabilities and convincingly demonstrate its role in digestive transformation. In 1836, German physiologist Johann Eberle observed that the contents of animal stomachs seemed to fill with a mucus-like substance after feeding.[10] Because the walls of the animals' stomachs were uninjured, he believed that this mucus was secreted from the stomach walls. Using calf stomachs, he created a solvent extract of the stomach's innermost layer, the mucus membrane, which he referred to as "artificial mucus." He proceeded to compare the effect of this artificial mucus on different foods to that of the "natural" mucus in the stomachs of animals he killed and dissected immediately after feeding. The "artificial" mucus, he concluded, "behaved, on the whole, like the natural."[11] Eberle's colleagues Johannes Müller and Theodor Schwann recognized the potential of Eberle's insights and continued his experiments. They procured dried calf stomach, cut it into small pieces, subjected them to hydrochloric acid, and filtered the whole through canvas and paper, producing a murky, yellowish extract. They then attempted to "digest" pieces of egg white with this liquid and succeeded to produce decisive changes.[12]

In order to characterize the substance they had extracted, Müller and Schwann demonstrated its physiological behavior against a set of reagents.[13] The resulting profile was different from any other known chemical agent, in their opinion. Until now, chemical changes in organic bodies had been assumed to occur when one substance joined with another and both original substances were changed as a result. These usual chemical processes were characterized by equal proportions between all substances involved. A different kind of transformation was known to occur in inorganic matter. Here, a substance could cause transformation in another without itself undergoing change. Such "contact reactions" were characterized by a disproportionate relationship between the substance causing change and the substance undergoing change. The process of fermentation, familiar from brewing or wine making, stood between those two worlds. A small amount of ferment could alter a relatively large quantity of substrate, but over the course of the process, the ferment would lose its ability to produce change.

Schwann and Müller found that the substance they had extracted did indeed occasion powerful changes in egg white, even in minute quantities. At the same time, it seemed to lose its ability to produce such changes over the course of the experiments. Schwann therefore concluded that, rather than coining a new term, it would be appropriate to "extend the concept of fermentation" to the processes they had observed. The crucial characteristics of both processes were sufficiently similar to merit the name.[14] Schwann coined the term *digestive ferments* to refer to the new type of chemical agent producing the changes he had observed. He also believed that the specific substance Müller and he had characterized "truly effects the digestion of the most important animal foods," not just egg whites, and accordingly gave it the name *pepsin* (from the Greek *pepsis* meaning 'digestion')."[15]

The research of Eberle, Schwann, and Müller did not settle the debate about the nature of the digestive process. But it did suggest a method of producing the digestive principle from animal organs that could be much more easily obtained and handled than live animals. While the chosen name "ferments" stressed continuity to known chemical processes, Schwann's and Müller's experiments also strengthened the idea that these were entirely new kinds of physiological agents.

These two factors—a method for obtaining pepsin and the as yet undetermined nature of digestive ferments and therefore of digestion—propelled further experiments with artificial digestion and, at the same time, spurred digestive product development. Over the coming decades, physiologists, physicians, and pharmacists continued to probe the material correlates of digestion and their potential role in digestive changes. They applied Schwann's and Müller's method for procuring digestive ferments but also developed their own versions of digesting substances to use in their experiments. And even before the precise nature and mechanism of digestive ferments could be settled, they envisioned therapeutic uses for ferments in digestive disease.

As early as a year after Eberle's, Schwann's, and Müller's research, pepsin was tested by other researchers. They tried it on different foods, measured its effect against hydrochloric acid, and compared it to substances extracted from other animals, such as horses, cows, and pigs. Despite inconclusive results from this research overall, one observer of the experiments hoped "that digesting liquid may very soon be applied at the sick bed and studied with regard to its healing properties."[16] Even those who doubted pepsin's central role in digestion were eager to see it used as a remedy. Pepsin, one German chemist argued, merely "predisposed the previously un-dissolvable to solvability," while hydrochloric acid was the true dissolving agent. Nevertheless, he declared that "the thought very much suggests itself if it might not be possible to find an indication for pepsin for certain disturbances of digestion, dyspepsia etc."[17] Initial hopes of finding a therapeutic use for pepsin were soon followed by the first tentative experiments to put its role in digestive disease to the test. Physicians tried the drug on themselves and on their patients with limited degrees of success.[18] When the drug did not perform as hoped, they tended to fault the quality of pepsin preparations rather than doubt pepsin's efficacy. Pepsins made "in a pharmacy" elicited physicians' and chemists' particular disapproval, having been insufficiently examined for their "purity and composition."[19]

One reason physicians were so eager to cement the role of pepsin in digestion and digestive disease was the imprecise nature of existing diagnostic categories used to describe digestive troubles. Medicine, said one chemist, had reached the point where "the very general designations of disordered digestion, weak stomach et cetera, with which it is impossible to connect a clear definition, could no longer be sufficient."[20] Digestive ferments, by contrast, promised to order the digestive process. French physician Lucien Corvisart, who collaborated with pharmacist Charles-Pierre Boudault to produce one of the first commercial pepsin products, called "nutrimentive powder," conceptualized digestive pathology around a "lack of the digestive principle."[21] Digestive disease, he specified, could be divided into defects of trituration (too little muscle movement), defects of retention (too much muscle movement), and defects of secretion (not enough digestive ferments). Digestive ferments were the choice remedy in defects of secretion but could also be tried as a supportive therapy in conditions with inadequate contracting activity of the stomach.[22] If digestive ferments cured the patient, in turn, the underlying condition must necessarily be a defect of secretion. Digestive ferments, Corvisart concluded, were thus also a "precious diagnostic tool."[23]

Physicians' enthusiasm for a potential novel approach to digestive disease quickly fell on receptive ears. By 1857, "nutrimentive powder" as well as a number of imitator preparations were advertised to medical professionals for use in their experiments as well as in their patient care. In Britain, a

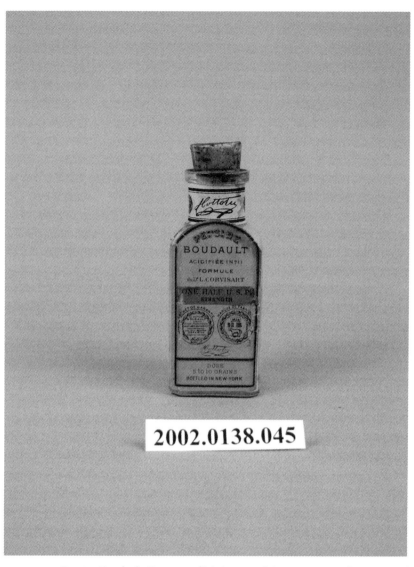

FIGURE 7. Pepsine Boudault. Division of Medicine and Science, National Museum of American History, Smithsonian Institution.

"Boudault's pepsine" was advertised by pharmacist Peter Squire and his son William Stevens Squire, who had translated Boudault's work into English and published it for an English-speaking audience. The Squires, who prided themselves on having been appointed the "sole agents" for Boudault's pepsine in Britain, had to contend with another "Boudault's Pepsine" imported by pharmaceutical chemist Twinberrow, one made by Howard Hopley in his "Pharmacy Française," and a Liquor Pepsinae by pharmacists Savory and Moore.[24]

Despite the proliferation of pepsin products, their therapeutic value in disease remained as uncertain as the role of digestive ferments in the digestive process. A German pharmacist declared in 1860 that "a myriad of unanswered questions about the nature of the so-called pepsin, its physiological significance, and its (yet to be proved) lack in dyspepsia" needed to be clarified before its practical application could be sanctioned.[25] The mismatch between inconclusive research and therapeutic enthusiasm placed ferments in a peculiar position by the 1860s and early 1870s. The digestive ferments, according to the German pharmacist, had become a matter of "mercantile speculation" and had to be regarded as "suspect" as a result.[26] Another German pharmacist predicted that pepsin would "fashion itself as a lucky over-the-counter sales article of apothecaries," and urged his colleagues to "take hold of it soon before the merchants take possession of it."[27] Time was of the essence, however, since its preparation was "not the most difficult, and could easily be executed by anyone else who is not an apothecary, eventually even pass into the hands of [female] cooks."[28]

What was a nightmare to some was music to the ears of the makers of Benger's Food. Frederick Baden Benger and William Roberts's collaboration began precisely in the fraught commercial-pharmaceutical, culinary-medicinal space occupied by ferment products. But unlike German pharmacists, they wished to enlarge not constrict it. Together, they seized upon digestive ferments and their liminal status as a professional opportunity with wide-reaching scientific, professional, and social implications. Digestive ferments, to them, signified an entirely new science of digestion and dietetics, the promise of career advancement, and the possibility of altering the prospects of the working classes and of the whole nation.

A SCIENTIFIC-COMMERCIAL COLLABORATION

If the meals at the Angus Hotel in Norwich had been less renowned for their excellence, several members of the Lancashire and Cheshire branch of the British Medical Association might have lost their appetite before the post-meeting dinner there even began. This night's list of speeches at the local meeting included an address by William Roberts on the digestive ferments and their therapeutic uses. The practical orientation of the speech, with its demonstrations of "predigestion" on a number of articles of food, might have left even the sturdiest physician's stomach a little queasy. Roberts was leaning over a table with various specimen of digestive ferment products—including a "pepsin elixir" by Symes and Company, "Pepsin Essenz" by Corbyn, Stacey, and Co., and "various kinds of pancreatic preparations" by Mottershead Company, the company owned by Benger.[29] Roberts's voice was animated as he talked through the wondrous scientific and therapeutic possibilities these articles opened up. To him, it was clear that the digestive processes inside the body "could be imitated successfully in the laboratory, and even in the sickroom and nursery."[30] Considering the many unanswered questions that still existed about digestive ferments, and that Roberts himself would attempt to settle over the coming years, this utterance was perhaps more of a wishful declaration than a substantiated conclusion.

Roberts and Benger had met a few years prior in Manchester, but Benger had long been eager to collaborate with physicians. Since the Pharmacy Act of 1868, pharmaceutical chemists like Benger had been in a bind. The Act had set up a registration system that required at least the Pharmaceutical Society's minor exam to carry the title chemist and druggist and to dispense poisons. In theory, this would draw a firmer boundary between the dispensing of medicines and the sale of other commercial articles, which had been a major source of income for unlicensed chemists and druggists. But in practice, dispensing medicines was often not enough to sustain registered pharmacists' business, especially since their numbers had grown after the Act and they continued the sale of nonpharmaceutical articles. This, in turn, increased physicians' distrust of what they perceived as an overly entrepreneurial-minded pharmaceutical profession. In response, many physicians chose to dispense their own medicines, which only exacerbated the prescription crisis.[31] Ever the pragmatist, Benger was eager to collaborate closely with medical professionals. But he was also under no illusion that even if physicians were to relinquish all prescribing habits, most pharmacists "would be still compelled to depend on other sources of income."[32]

The Pharmacy Act had also created the class of pharmaceutical chemists, who, like Benger, had passed the Society's major exam. The title was rather perfunctory; it did not entitle its holder to more dispensing than those who had graduated with the minor exam. But it signaled a certain academic interest in the field of pharmacy, and Benger had that in abundance.

Throughout his pharmaceutical practice, Benger had not been content with simply preparing medicines according to predetermined formulas. Instead, his interest was in experimental pharmacy and in advancing pharmaceutical knowledge. Even as a young assistant at John Bell's pharmacy in London, where he worked immediately after passing his exams, Benger had relished experimental activity and thrown himself into studying glycerine, a pharmaceutical solvent.[33] At Bell's, he had met Standen Paine, a similarly minded pharmaceutical chemist. When Paine relocated to Manchester to take up the management of Mottershead, a pharmaceutical firm specializing in laboratory supplies, Benger followed him, and both men worked side by side as joint owners of the company for many years.

It was at Mottershead that Benger began experimenting on the digestive ferments. While physiological and chemical research into digestion was booming in the second half of the nineteenth century, Benger's passion for the digestive ferments stemmed from a pharmaceutical perspective. He began with a study of so-called anti-ferments, substances considered capable of preventing the spoilage of pharmaceutical preparations.[34] Fermentation, as it was then understood, was considered a major culprit of unintentional pharmaceutical adulteration. There were many potential applications for this line of research, including in the production of food, where "anti-ferments" like salicylic acid, sulfurous acid, and other substances were widely used in preserved foods by the end of the nineteenth century.[35] From anti-ferments, it was only a small step to ferments. During his years in Manchester, Benger devoted much of his time and energy to the study of digestive ferments and contributed new insights to the knowledge about digestive processes. In one series of experiments he examined pepsin and showed (or so he thought) that what had until then been referred to as "pepsin" was in fact a combination of at least two substances, a protein-digesting substance, and a substance that had the power to curdle milk.[36]

Benger's activities with ferments attracted the attention of Roberts, who was keenly interested in the physiology of digestion. Roberts was a medical doctor from Manchester who had trained at University College London. One of his teachers there was physiologist William Sharpey, who seems to have sparked Roberts's interest in physiology. After his medical studies, Roberts worked as a surgeon at the Manchester Royal Infirmary and began lecturing at Manchester University and Owen College in anatomy, medicine, and physiology. Meanwhile, he performed physiological experiments, often using Benger's laboratory facilities at Mottershead Company. Experimental physiology was a booming discipline in the second half of the nineteenth century, and an ideal method of inquiry for someone who, like Roberts, wanted to make their mark in the world of scientific medicine. Diet, digestion, and the digestive ferments, meanwhile, were topics of great scientific but also broader social importance, and Roberts's interest in them was likely not coincidental.

As the joint owner of a laboratory supply company, providing materials for physiological experiments was part of Benger's job description, and he furnished Roberts with a series of digestive ferments made from animal organs: Liquor Pepticus, a preparation of pepsin, the stomach ferment, and Liquor Pancreaticus, which supposedly contained the digestive ferments of the pancreas. But Benger and Roberts's collaboration also went beyond that of an experimenter and a materials supplier. They conducted experiments on the physiology of digestion and on artificially digested foods.[37] Much of their research was focused on the practical applicability of digestive ferments; for example, they attempted to determine the precise quantity of digestive ferment required to digest a certain quantity of food. Roberts publicized the results of their experiments, together with Benger's preparations, in his speeches and writings.

In his speech for the local meeting of the British Medical Association, Roberts drew on much of the research he and Benger had undertaken. He sketched artificial digestion as a promising, fast-paced, research endeavor with considerable clinical implications, but with many gaps still left to be filled. At the time Roberts and Benger had begun their collaboration, the focus on pepsin and the stomach as the agent and seat of digestion had long obscured the role that other organs and their ferments could play in the digestive process. But by the time Roberts addressed his colleagues in 1879, digestion was beginning to be regarded as a collaborative endeavor between many different ferments secreted by different organs of the digestive tract. In a table attached to his printed speech, Roberts listed the various digestive juices and ferments associated with them side by side. Saliva contained diastase; the gastric juice, as Benger's research had suggested, contained not one but two ferments, pepsin and a yet little known "curdling ferment"; the pancreas contained four different kinds of ferments, trypsin, diastase, another curdling ferment, and what Roberts referred to as an "emulsifying ferment"; only the gallbladder and the intestine remained a question mark. Roberts still included them in the table, however, confident that their ferments would yet be found, and their functions determined. The table, then, functioned as both a stock-taking exercise and a vote of confidence in the future of artificial digestion research.

Growing consensus had also emerged around the transformative nature of digestive ferments. In his table, Roberts was able to record the known changes effected by specific ferments on specific substances. The diastase of the saliva and the pancreas transformed starch into sugar or "maltose" and "dextrin"; the gastric and pancreatic ferments pepsin and trypsin acted on "proteids" to produce "peptones" (which Roberts considered the end-product of protein digestion); the curdling ferments curdled the casein of milk; and the emulsifying ferment of the pancreas emulsified fat. It was clear, Roberts stated, that "a complicated series of ferment-actions is required to complete the digestion of our food."

At the same time, much work still needed to be done. "Our information is still imperfect on several points," Roberts conceded.[38] This uncertainty did not prevent Roberts from adding a fourth column to the table, one that detailed the various "medicinal substitutes" of the digestive ferments. In this category belonged the "various preparations of malt, extracts of malt, malt flour, and extracts of pancreas," which could replace the salivary and pancreatic diastase; the "various preparations of pepsin, pepsin-wine, liquor pepsinae, lactopeptin etc.," which substituted a lack of pepsin; "rennet," which stood in for the curdling ferment; and "pancreatine, glycerine extract of pancreas, liquor pancreaticus," and "pancreatic rennet," which could assume all the functions of the various pancreatic ferments.[39] Together, these products constituted "the equivalents or substitutes available for administration to patients in whom this or that digestive juice may be supposed to require artificial assistance." Here was a (nearly) complete roadmap of the digestive tract with various points of possible intervention through digestive ferment products. These myriad preparations reflected a shift from an emphasis on pepsin as the "digestive principle" toward an interrelated system of multiple digestive agents and transformative steps.[40]

The prospect of an entirely new system of therapeutic intervention into the digestive tract guided Roberts's and Benger's research. Like others before them, they allowed their therapeutic enthusiasm to distract them from such trifling obstacles as the continuing lack of diagnostic categories that corresponded with the remedies at hand. Together, Roberts and Benger pushed their own distinctive approach to ferment remedies, which consisted in an emphasis on the pancreas as the most promising ferment-producing organ. It had "at least four distinct kinds of action on food-stuffs," Roberts explained:

converting proteins into peptones, curdling the casein of milk, transforming starch into sugar, and emulsifying fats.[41] Roberts also emphasized the supposedly superior strength of the pancreatic ferments as digestive agents. Measuring the weight and volume of pancreatic diastase required to transform a specified amount of starch in a given period of time, Roberts arrived at the "astounding result that pancreatic diastase is able to transform into sugar and dextrin no less than forty thousand times its own weight of starch."[42] Such a result, especially "considering its infinitesimally minute mass," appeared "marvellous" to Roberts. "Extracts of pancreas," he concluded, "are destined . . . to play a considerable part in the dietetic therapeutics of the future."

If pancreas ferments were paragons of potency, the pancreas extract of Mr. Benger was the most wondrous of them all. "Liquor Pancreaticus" (a name Roberts had coined) was a "limpid, straw-colored fluid" of "very little taste or smell of its own," but despite being so "pale and bland," it was "an elixir of really remarkable powers," Roberts exclaimed.[43] A true multitasker, it supposedly curdled milk "like rennet," changed "starch into sugar with unrivaled energy," transformed "albuminous substances into peptones" with only the "aid of a little alkali," and emulsified "fats more perfectly than any other known agent." While Roberts thus evaluated and recommended Benger's preparations, Benger disseminated Roberts's research with his products and their promotion. In advertisements geared to the medical and pharmaceutical profession, Benger emphasized that the two Liquors were "used by Dr. Wm. Roberts" and "described by him in recent papers on 'The Digestive Ferments and their Therapeutic Uses.'"[44] He also excerpted passages of Roberts's speeches that mentioned the extracts favorably.[45]

But as much as he had faith in pancreatic ferments as medicinal preparations, Roberts had a more ambitious vision for digestive ferments. "However useful pancreatic extracts may prove to be for administration by the mouth," he announced, "I anticipate far more important results from their employment in the preparation of peptones or peptonised aliments."[46] The artificial imitation of digestive processes in the laboratory had progressed to a sophisticated level, Roberts believed, but similar advances had not been achieved with artificially digested aliments; such a scheme had barely "passed beyond the tentative stage."[47] Yet Roberts was convinced that this was an enterprise worth pursuing. "There cannot be a doubt," he asserted, "that, if we had at our disposal an available supply of artificially digested (or peptonised) proteids in a state fit for human food, we should find numerous conditions in which such a resource would offer promise of important advantage."

FIGURE 8. Liquor Pancreaticus. From the Museum of Healthcare, Kingston. Used with permission.

Roberts's vision to extend the application of digestive ferments to the realm of food would resonate with a generation of British sanitary reformers who were seeking new solutions to the old problem of the nation's food supply. The wide reach and cultural currency of artificial digestion and digestive ferment products was linked to changing ideas around food and economic life that emerged during this period. Once again, reformers, scientists, and public health advocates scrutinized the issue of food. But unlike mid-century efforts to reduce "waste" in food production, procurement, and institutional usage, their ambitions to optimize the food supply and improve the health and nutrition of the population on a large scale converged around the notion of thrift. Thrift united a growing emphasis on individual responsibility for health and nutrition, an increasing awareness of the cost of sickness, a shift away from food production to food consumption and from chemical to physiological approaches to nutrition, and an increasing focus on digestion as a variable in the food economy.

THE THRIFT MOVEMENT

In 1880, Benjamin Ward Richardson, a physician, physiologist, and sanitary reformer, addressed the assembled members of the Society of Arts, Commerce, and Manufacture in a speech titled "Thrift in Relation to Food."[48] To illustrate the choices that lay before those who governed England to solve its food problem, he used the metaphor of a family of twenty-five whose head was trying to decide among many strategies to feed his family. That there still was a food problem, there could be no doubt. "All in England have cause, I think, to admit that England cannot, under existing conditions, find sufficient food from her own soil for her own children." Disagreement existed, however, as to what strategy was most promising for solving the food crisis. There were those who believed that "safety may always be ensured by food supply from abroad, from our colonies, and from other nations." Others preferred instead to rely on "increased cultivation at home" through the "utilization of all so-called waste products." Both strategies were criticized by Richardson as too unreliable and not sufficient. Food should be cultivated at home and procured from abroad, to be sure, but to effectively solve England's food problem, a third strategy was needed: thrift. "Our family of twenty-five," Richardson declared, "must become a thrifty family. . . . From the all potent twenty-fifth man down to the infinite helpless man through all the ranks, thrift must be the order of the day."

A few years later, Richardson would be even more explicit about which of these measures he favored. In a text aptly titled "The Skeleton in the National Cupboard," he prophesied that if there were a hostile invasion of England, there might not be immediate starvation, but England "would in a short time be convulsed politically, not from actual deficiency of supply, but from the difference of ability on the part of consumers to lay by stores of supply."[49] According to Richardson, the political fate of the nation lay, more than ever before, not in the hands, but in the stomachs, of individuals. What Britons chose to consume would have a decisive influence on Britain's ability to economize its food supply, more so, in Richardson's opinion, than costly measures to produce and procure more food from the empire and at home. In his speech to the Society of Arts in 1880, he outlined several options that were available to thrifty families to make economic food choices.[50] They could learn to live on less food altogether and avoid excess, which, in Richardson's opinion, was still a common problem especially in cities. Or they could select foods that were highly nourishing at little expense. This meant forgoing alcohol, which, according to Richardson, contained no nourishment at great cost, or choosing certain nourishing vegetable foods over meat. As chemical investigations had demonstrated, many vegetables, like peas, beans, rice, oats, barley, and wheat, contained more nourishing, "flesh-forming" substance in relation to their weight than meat; "weight by weight," Richardson suggested, "vegetable substances, when they are carefully selected, possess the most striking advantages over animal in nutritive value."

There was just one problem. Vegetable foods, unfortunately, were often much less digestible than meat. Indeed, pure vegetable substances provided a challenge for the digestive system of many humans, Richardson believed. "Many persons will always be found," Richardson suggested, who ... will digest vegetable food that has been prepared for them by passing through the system of other animals better than when they themselves take it first hand from the plant." In other words, vegetable food was much more digestible once it had been converted into the flesh of animals through their digestive system and become meat. If it were not for the small matter of their digestibility, vegetable foods would constitute an economic means of nourishment, and a "condensed vegetable diet" might even be adapted universally. These "difficulties," however, were "not insurmountable," according to Richardson.

What was needed was "an inquiry" into "whether the transmutation of vegetable food, which now is obtained by the digestion and passage of the blood into the tissues of lower herbivorous animals, may not be effected by chemical processes, apart from the intermediate animal altogether."

Such a prospect might have been unimaginable in premodern times. But "there should be no difficulty," Richardson believed, "except the labour of research, in so modifying food taken from its prime source as to make it applicable to every necessity without the assistance of any intermediate animal at all." The first steps toward this had already been accomplished by physiologists, Richardson argued. "Changes quite as difficult have been accomplished by scientific labour in the laboratory," he suggested, "and if men of science will . . . follow up the artificial digestion and condensation of vegetable foods by synthetical imitations, assuredly perfect production of perfect food from the vegetable kingdom, without the aid of the intermediate lower animal, will be another triumph of science over nature."[51] Food, in short, would be "so under the control of man, that new races of men, constructed on better food than has ever yet been prepared, would rise up to demonstrate the greatness of the triumph by their improved physical endowments, and their freedom from certain disease."[52]

Richardson's speech reflected a broader change in sentiment among British sanitary and social reformers since mid-century. Whereas mid-century experts with an interest in the food supply had looked to chemical analyses of foods' nourishing constituents in order to optimize food production and procurement, reformers of the 1870s and 1880s were increasingly concerned with the selection, preparation, and digestion of food through consumers. Instead of minimizing "waste" in the system, they sought to promote "thrift" in individuals, and artificially digested foods like Benger's Food would play an important role in their vision. Like its mid-century counterpart, "waste," "thrift" was a multidimensional ideology that merged sanitary and social reform impulses, economic philosophies of how to maximize national wealth, and medical and scientific theories about nutrition and digestion. With its own society (the National Thrift Society), its own journal (*Thrift*), and an extensive popular literary output in the form of pamphlets, tracts, and lectures, thrift reached a considerable degree of visibility during the 1870s and 1880s.

The thrift movement had its roots in long-standing efforts to establish savings schemes and promote the habit of thrift, especially in the working classes. From the late eighteenth century, a number of savings organizations, such as the Friendly Societies, provided financial support to sick workers and offered safeguards for the poor.[53] During the nineteenth century, advocates of self-help increasingly called for the cultivation of thrifty habits and suggested various insurance schemes as solutions to the unpopular Poor Law and its supposed perpetuation of "pauperism." The writings of Samuel Smiles, a Scottish reformer and Chartist, became particularly influential in this respect, perhaps also because his national heritage played into English stereotypes of Scottish thriftiness. He argued that poverty and pauperism persisted despite the introduction of higher wages in many professions and suggested that adopting thrifty habits could help the poor on their path to self-liberation.[54] In this context, thrift became one of several strategies, proposed alongside others such as higher wages or compulsory insurance, to solve the complex problem of poverty.

A recurring theme in the thrift literature was that its object was deemed to be a quintessentially un-English habit. "Thrift is not among the good qualities of the English people," declared the introduction of the National Thrift Society in *Chambers's* magazine, and lauded the society for thriving to make a "national habit" of thrift, as it was "in France, Belgium, Germany, and Austria."[55] The unthriftiness of the English was contrasted with the thrifty habits of the French, in particular. As Linda Colley has argued, the construction of the Catholic, "superstitious, militarist, decadent and unfree" French "Other" was crucial in forging a common British national identity during the eighteenth century.[56] Such eighteenth-century constructions of un-French British identity had relied heavily on notions of Britain as a prosperous and commercially healthy nation. Nineteenth-century thrift discourse, by contrast, exposed anxieties over the finite nature of British material resources. "British wealth, is, alas! like a garden without a wall, whence the very subsoil is falling away, or like a laden vessel, the rich cargo of which is falling out," lamented political economist Leone Levi in the *Thrift* journal.[57] Fixing Britain's economic decline vis à vis other nations required correcting its inhabitants' unthrifty habits. "Large economies," Levi proclaimed, "depend upon little economies."[58]

But the thrift movement went beyond efforts to inspire pecuniary frugality. According to the editor of the *Thrift* journal, thrift heralded the conservation of everything from energy to expenditure; any waste of "opportunities, privileges, power, learning, time, food, abilities, or wealth" was to be rebuked.[59] Instilling the habit of thrift in the nation's citizens was not only an economic advantage but also a civilizational one, Levi insisted. The virtues that enabled saving—"prudence, wisdom, moderation, and intelligence"—were nothing but the "offspring of civilization and moral," Levi claimed.[60] "Savages," he drove home the racist point, "are not thrifty."

Within this broad definition of thrift, health and nutrition were deemed of particular importance. Data gathered by the Friendly Societies had thrown the cost of sickness into sharp relief. In an address given at the International Health Exhibition, surgeon, physiologist, and vice-chancellor of the exhibition James Paget calculated that a total of twenty million weeks of work or eleven million pounds was lost to the nation through sickness each year.[61] Additional losses occurred through diseases of childhood, which often required the attention of a working parent and left children "deformed," "feeble," or "invalid," and therefore less able to work.[62] Such losses were all the more tragic because "a very large proportion of the sickness and the loss of work" was preventable, Paget insisted.[63] But thrift reformers of the 1880s took a very different approach to prevention than earlier generations of sanitary scientists. They articulated the notion of an economically oriented "National Health" focused on individual health behavior. National Health was thrift reformers' response to "National Insurance" and to the ambitious structural and legislative measures proposed by previous sanitary scientists. Richardson captured this former ideal in his utopian depiction *Hygeia— a City of Health*.[64] Hygeia was a model of what state spending, regulatory oversight, and urban planning could do. It boasted a perfect sewage system, well-spaced houses, meticulously kept records of disease, and medical supervision of slaughterhouses and food adulteration. But to thrift reformers, a "City of Hygeia" was "hard to attain and would involve immense expenditure and endless watching."[65] A more practicable approach would be if individuals took care of their own health. Since the "sick and afflicted" were "a trouble and an expense" to the nation, it was the "highest duty of every individual" to "keep himself healthy."[66]

Reformers promoted thrift to the working classes in particular as a practicable means of improving their lot and contributing to the National Health. "Sanitary houses and healthy occupations may at present be almost beyond their reach," a reformer proclaimed of the poor, "but, as they can choose their own food, if we can only teach them to adopt what will nourish the body most completely at the least cost, there will be a chance of their resisting the injurious influences constantly surrounding them."[67] Since "health" was "their sole capital," gaining an understanding of the "economy of food" was imperative to the working classes.[68] Popular thrift writings reminded workers to tend to their bodies as they would to a machine in need of maintenance. Adequate nutrition, according to one writer, was a means of providing the body with "fuel" and enabled laborers to perform "the greatest amount of work . . . with the least wear and tear."[69] Thrift meant outsourcing the externalities of industrial work—the bodily wear and tear of manual labor—to the laborers themselves.

Thrift advocacy was soon followed by thrift accounting. Reformers assembled records of what the poor bought and ate to estimate potential sources of saving. Leone Levi's printed lectures on *Work and Pay* assembled a number of tables from a variety of sources detailing the expenditures of working families in different parts of Britain and the world. Levi concluded that "a considerable economy may be effected in our every-day expenditure without abridging in the slightest manner our means of subsistence and comfort."[70] He identified several sources of "waste" that could be economized, including "a very considerable portion of what is spent in drink," but also "waste in our cooking" and "in many of our household arrangements."[71]

Efforts to educate individuals in thrifty food consumption built on mid-century chemical investigations of foods' nourishing content. But thrift also involved a new concern. From the 1860s, food experts had expressed doubts that simple calculations of cost-nutritiousness could guarantee the most economical use of food. Edward Smith's investigations of workhouse dietaries (chapter 2) had already drawn attention to the inadequacy of equating the quantity of chemical food constituents with their nourishing power in the body. "The principle which must guide us," he urged, was "not simply the least cost of food," nor was it "cheapness combined with nutritive elements," because "nutritive elements vary greatly in digestibility, and the more digestible are cheaper at a greater cost than the less digestible at a less cost."[72] Aside from "low monetary value," "high nutritive material," and "acceptability to the appetite," calculations of cost-nutritiousness needed to pay attention to "digestibility." It was insufficient to determine "how much material [food] offers at a given price," Smith cautioned; instead, the question was "how much nourishment the body can obtain from it at that price."

To determine digestibility, scientists would have to go beyond "the well-known observations upon a man who had an artificial opening into his stomach" (an unsubtle reference to William Beaumont's experiments on Alexis St. Martin), Smith believed.[73] Those investigations had shown only "the rapidity of the process" but said nothing about the efficiency with which foods were extracted during the digestive process. What was needed instead, according to Smith, was an understanding of "what proportion of a given food passes off by the bowel unused, and therefore what proportion is applied to the nourishment of the body, and what is cast out as useless." Investigations of this kind had already shown that animal food was more digestible than vegetable food, and that certain parts of vegetable foods (the farina) were more digestible than others (the husk and the skin). Such insights confirmed Smith's larger point: "that the value of different foods cannot be taken upon their chemical qualities alone."

Artificial digestion and its products would provide a compelling answer to Smith's concerns. His critique of food economization measures based solely on their chemical constituent quantities was reflected in the thrift movement through an emphasis on cooking (as an aide to efficient nutrient uptake), on digestive physiology (as the process during which food's efficient uptake into the body was determined), and on artificially digested foods such as Benger's Food (as means through which the newly recognized problem of digestibility could be bypassed). Thrift of food, in short, took place in the kitchen, in the bodies of eaters, and in the laboratories of digestive physiologists. Nowhere would this vision of National Health and thrifty digestion be better crystallized than at the International Health Exhibition of 1884.

THE INTERNATIONAL HEALTH EXHIBITION

In its galleries, lectures, and publications, the International Health Exhibition of 1884 placed cooking, digestion, and digestive ferments front and center of its display of an individualized National Health. Food formed the first category of the exhibition's Health Division, and together with cooking, it occupied the largest section on the exhibition floor.[74] Displays reflected the proliferation of cooking tools, schools, and instructional texts across the country. A section dedicated to "Cookery Practically Demonstrated, Economical Cooking, Workmen's and other Kitchens, Cheap Restaurants, Bakeries, Cafes, Foreign Cookery Etc." showcased energy-conserving cooking stoves, "self-acting cooking pots," and a model bakery "fitted with the latest improvements in ovens and machinery."[75] The London National Training School of Cookery provided practical demonstrations, lectures, and "cheap dinners" in a spacious side-wing of the exhibition building. The recipes for these cheap dinners could be purchased as a collection edited by the superintendent of the National Training School of Cookery.[76] Economic cooking

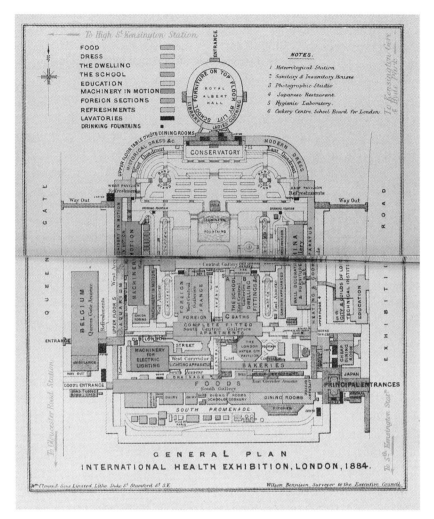

FIGURE 9. Plan of the International Health Exhibition. *Illustrated London News*, September 9, 1884, p. 263.

was combined with accountability in a Dining Room using "Duval's system." It provided diners with an itemized price list of all items consumed that was "left on the table during the whole of the repast, open to the inspection of the guest."[77] In another dining room, the Vegetarian Society served "six-penny vegetarian dinners."[78] Visitors to the exhibition could see, smell, and taste the idea of preparing meals in an economic manner and take charge of their own health and pocketbook.

Cooking was represented as an economizing activity in two ways: it could balance the household budget and it was preparatory work for adequate digestion. Early modern cookbook authors had long emphasized the continuity between cooking and digestion and even conceptualized the digestive process itself as a form of cooking or 'concoction.'[79] But nineteenth-century scientists and reformers reinterpreted the relationship between digestion and cooking as a continuous process of enzyme activity. William Roberts drew on his work with digestive ferments to argue that cooking was not merely a means of "improving the savour of food" or a process of "mechanical disintegration," but comprised transformations similar to those produced by digestive ferments acting on food. Through cooking, Roberts suggested, foods were rendered "incomparably more susceptible to the action of the digestive ferments than in the uncooked state."[80]

The idea of cooking as preparatory digestive work for the efficient uptake of nutrients sustained a gendered division of labor within a National Health economy. According to the author of the *National Thrift Reader*, every girl should "learn to be a good housekeeper as earnestly as every boy should learn how to be a good book-keeper or money-maker."[81] Urban sanitary issues such as "the building, drainage, ventilation, and water supply" of a home were the domain of the "father or master of the house," whereas the woman held sway "within the home." It was she who "buys and prepares the food of the family," and whose "good or bad administration" was felt by those she cared for. It was therefore "very necessary" that she "be well instructed in domestic Thrift."[82] Richardson sought to naturalize this arrangement of divided spheres within National Health by recalling an ancient economic precedent. In the Socratic text *Oeconomicus*, he pointed out that Ischomacus, "a grand Sanitarian," had taught his wife to spend an income thriftily, to examine corn carefully so to avoid feeding her family bad-quality food, to keep order in the house, and to care for the sick. The example of Ischomacus's wife illustrated that "long before the word Sanitation was heard of, or any other word that conveyed the idea of a science of health, the good, cleanly, thrifty housewife was a practical sanitary reformer."[83]

The shift in emphasis toward food preparation thus came with a growing focus on women as the holders of responsibility over the nation's food choices and economic food usage. It was women who determined that their working husbands would receive all the nutritive benefits of the foods they prepared. Through their cooking, women increased the digestibility of foods and thereby contributed to the economy of the family and, ultimately, of the nation. To Samuel Smiles, the "worthlessness of ill-managing wives" was above all constituted in their inability to be proper cooks, which deprived their husbands of much of the nutrients contained in the foods they had so desperately earned.[84] After a lot of "planting, rearing, and reaping" of different foods by men, they were "handed over to the female half of the human species to be converted into food, for the sustenance of themselves, their husbands, and their families." But many women across the country seemed not to keep up their half of the bargain, Smiles asserted. "Thousands of artisans and laborers are deprived of half of the actual nutriment of their food," he lamented, "and continue half starved, because their wives are utterly ignorant of the art of cooking. They are yet in entire darkness as to the economizing of food, and the means of rendering it palatable and digestible." Ill-cooked meals, he warned, were not only a danger to the husband's stomach but a threat to the family's budget. Bad cooking was simply "waste—waste of money and loss of comfort." Even the stability of marriage was at stake: "Whom God has joined in matrimony," Smiles sighed, "ill-cooked joints and ill-boiled potatoes have very often put asunder."

While the imagined addressees of these teachings on cooking, digestibility, and thrift were mostly women, the knowledge about foods' digestibility would be supplied by male laboratory scientists. The exhibition showcased recent advances in digestive physiology research and encouraged visitors to consider digestibility in an economic composition of their diets.[85] A contribution to the Health Exhibition literature titled "Diet in Relation to Health and Work" drew on research in digestive physiology to portray natural digestion as an imperfect process that could be enhanced. If digestion were perfect, the author suggested, "that which passes away would be a residuum wholly without nutriment," but this was "far from being the case."[86] A thorough knowledge of the "degrees of digestibility" was therefore of the utmost importance. Recent research on the "income and output" of food in the body had illuminated the digestibility of different foods.[87] A table summarized the results of this research, ranking foods according to their degree of digestibility and the amount of "residue" that had passed away unused.[88] These calculations could inform the composition of economical diets. For instance, rice was almost equal to white bread in its digestibility, whereas potatoes produced "nearly 10 per cent. of waste, or substances which pass away without being utilized." Rice was therefore preferable "in point of economy."[89]

The exhibition also offered a detailed exploration of the digestive ferments. A series of lectures followed the digestive process including the physiological changes occasioned through the digestive ferments from the mouth to the intestine. It contained a description of the pancreatic ferments that relied on Roberts and Benger's research and called their method of preparing a "very active solution" of the pancreatic ferments "one of the best."[90] Another lecture was dedicated entirely to the digestive ferments and included practical demonstrations with ferment preparations.[91] In one experiment, the lecturer applied a commercial pepsin and hydrochloric acid to a small amount of fibrin and allowed the audience to marvel at the "considerable quantities of red liquid accumulating in the beaker" in a short time, evidence that "the fibrin is almost instantaneously being dissolved before us."[92] Whereas much of science at the time required the mediation of the microscope, the wondrous rapidity and transformative capacity of digestive ferments was visible to the naked eye.

The research into digestive ferments had not only provided insight into the workings of the digestive system, however, but had also shown methods through which the ferments could be easily procured and used. "The ferments of the alimentary canal," the speaker declared,

> not only reside in their juices, but are to be extracted from the very tissues of the glands which form them. We may, for example, from the salivary glands of an animal which secretes active saliva, obtain a solution which possesses the power of acting on starch; similarly, we can, from the dead stomach of animals, which secrete gastric juice, obtain pepsin. . . . From the sweetbread or pancreas of dead animals, we may similarly obtain gastric juice, and effect the remarkable changes in the alimentary canal to which I have drawn your attention.[93]

Manufacturers had turned these physiological substances into readily available commercial products, the speaker declared, "with which we can artificially digest."[94] All that was needed was to "take certain alimentary constituents, add to them pancreatic preparations, and place them at the temperature of the human body, and digestion will go on as it would in the alimentary canal." As a prime example of the "immense practical importance" of scientific knowledge, the speaker concluded, the insights of digestive ferment research were "immediately applicable to the relief of suffering humanity."[95]

The International Health Exhibition thus showcased not only the theory of digestive ferments but its application. A wide range of ferment products and artificially digested foods were displayed and celebrated, including Benger's Food. From German chemist Stuetz came "Leube-Rosenthal's Improved Meat

Solution" which was prepared by "digest[ing] meat with a strongly acid solution of pepsin."[96] The Kreochyle company supplied samples of "Liquid Meat, "a food containing "the whole of the soluble albumen of the meat in an uncoagulated and easily digestible form."[97] A number of "malted foods" boasted their contents of perfectly digested and instantly absorbable starchy matter. A description of Mellin's Food, for example, highlighted its digestibility achieved by a preparation process in which "the whole of the starch" had been "reduced into dextrin and grape-sugar."[98] To advocates of artificial digestion, artificially digested foods offered a way to bypass the question of digestibility altogether. By applying digestive ferments to food before it even entered the digestive tract of humans, they imagined, perfectly digested versions of important alimentary substances could be produced.

ARTIFICIALLY DIGESTED FOODS

In artificially digested foods, the idea of perfectly thrifty digestive bodies was carried to the extreme. With the help of digestive ferments, Richardson's dream of "synthesized" foods—man-made products that would follow up on the insights of physiological research on artificial digestion—could be realized through the predigestion of foodstuffs with digestive ferments. Artificially digested foods began as implicit (and explicit) critiques of chemical extraction methods and chemical extracts that claimed to have captured the nourishing subcomponents of food. Artificial digestion research had demonstrated, above all else, the almost wondrous transformative power of digestive ferments. Ferments produced a change that went beyond a mere dissolution or disintegration and resulted instead in a new substance with its own physiological characteristics. No chemical extraction method, and therefore no chemical extract, many physiologists believed, could fully reproduce the complex changes that food underwent during digestion, and that artificial digestion had made visible and measurable.

Early preparations of artificially digested foods built on this idea. For French physician Corvisart, the "digestive principle" alone transformed "aliment" into "nutriment." Chemically extracted preparations like "bouillon, osmazome or meat extract, and the "widespread alimentary or convalescent pastilles composed of it" were perhaps slightly more than brute aliments, he conceded, but they were not "perfect nutriments."[99] In his experiments, Corvisart sought to realize ways of nourishing patients "whose stomach, through a fault of secretion, is no longer capable to subject aliments to the necessary modifications to sustain life" by "bypassing their stomach altogether."[100] He therefore tried to "effect the artificial digestion of aliments in vessels and administer them entirely digested by the gastric juice in the form of bouillons, pastes, gels, etc."[101]

Corvisart never followed up these early investigations into artificially digested foods with a commercial product. But the idea of using pepsin to prepare more perfectly digested and therefore more nourishing foods was soon taken up by physicians and pharmacists in Britain. In 1867, William Marcet, a physician and lecturer on chemistry, published a pamphlet in which he described "a new process for preparing meat for weak stomachs" involving the "digestion of roasted meat through pepsin and hydrochloric acid.[102] The object of this process, he explained, was to "extend the preliminary digestion of meat one stage further than is done by cooking, before it is taken into the stomach, thereby relieving this organ from the task of carrying out, unassisted, the digestion of cooked meat."[103] Detailed instructions for the process and even for building an apparatus for digesting encouraged others to copy Marcet's method.

Equally motivated by a frustration with conventional meat extracts, British physician and physiologist William Pavy and pharmacist Stephen Darby developed an artificially digested food by the name of "Darby's Fluid Meat." To Pavy, "beef tea, broths and the extracts of meat prepared in the ordinary way" were all "physiologically a very imperfect representation of an article of nourishment."[104] "Darby's Fluid Meat," by contrast, was based on the assumption that "the same solvent menstruum that is employed by nature for dissolving meat" would produce exactly the nutritive material "which is made use of" in the human body.[105] It was produced by subjecting meat to "the organic digestive principle" and an "appropriate quantity of acid." The result was a liquid containing the constituents of meat "in such a form as to be ready at once for absorption."

But the most successful attempts to create artificially digested foods were undertaken by Benger and Roberts. Like their predecessors, they initially sought to improve on chemically extracted food concentrates of supposedly superior nutritional value. "Everybody knows," Roberts summed up years of accumulating skepticism, "that ordinary beef-tea does not contain in solution any of the fibre of the meat"; its properties were therefore "rather of a stimulating than a dietetic character."[106] But if beef tea was "treated with extract of pancreas," a "large proportion of the beef" would be "digested," he declared. Since the end product of protein digestion through the pancreatic ferments was called "peptone," Roberts proposed to name such a preparation "peptonised beef tea." Only a few culinary steps separated peptonised beef-tea from a "peptonised beef jelly," which could be prepared simply by adding gelatin "after the process of artificial digestion" had been "completed" in the beef tea. Next came "peptonised wheat-jelly," a "partially digested bread, to which is added a little gelatin." It was made by subjecting a "strong wheat-flour gruel" to the "action of pancreatic extract" and stiffening the whole with gelatin. The resulting preparation had the consistency of "soft jelly."[107]

Roberts immediately tested these preparations. A comparative analysis of ordinary beef tea and peptonized beef tea suggested that peptonized beef tea contained more than double the meat solids and almost three times as much organic meat matter as ordinary beef tea. An analysis of peptonized gruel showed that it contained a high amount of "nitrogenized matter" as well as "sugar and dextrine."[108] The peptonized wheat jelly, according to Roberts, brought into play "the double digestive power of the pancreas": having been submitted to pancreatic extract, "the starchy matter" of its flour was converted into "dextrine and sugar," and the "gluten and other albuminoid matter" were transformed into perfectly absorbable "peptones." Artificially digested preparations came with a measurable seal of digestive efficacy.

While Roberts collaborated closely with Benger during the making of these products, he also relied on the expertise of a female member of his family to "give variety to peptonised dishes by preparing soups, jellies, and blancmanges containing peptonised aliments."[109] This unnamed relative developed a number of culinary creations, each "containing a large amount of digested starch and digested proteids," but also "possessing excellent flavour." She prepared soups either by mixing stock with peptonized gruel and peptonized milk-gruel, or by using a watery peptonized gruel to extract "shins of beef and other materials." To make peptonized jellies, she added "a due quantity of gelatine or isinglass to hot peptonised gruel," and "flavour[ed] the mixture according to taste." For a peptonized blancmange, a little cream was added to the peptonized, flavored jellies. Some of these recipes ended up as products in the range of digestive ferment preparations made and sold by the Mottershead Company, such as Benger's Peptonised Beef Jelly, Benger's Peptonised Chicken Jelly, or Benger's Pancreatised Lentil Flour.[110]

The culmination of these culinary variations subjected to pancreatic extract, in Roberts's opinion, was a "self-digestive farinaceous food."[111] This was an "ingeniously conceived preparation" that had been "brought out by Mr. Benger as an improvement upon the malted flour suggested by Liebig." It was made by "heating wheat-flour in an oven" until the starch was "partially dextrinized" (converted to the more digestible form of sugar, dextrine), and then mixing it with liquid extract of pancreas. The result was a "pancreatised flour" that could be prepared into a meal by blending it with cold milk to form a paste, and then stirring in boiling milk or water. The self-digestive process of the food would occur "as soon as the ingredients are mixed together" and could be adjusted in length "according to the degree of pre-digestion required." Here was a perfectly adjustable, outsourced process of digestion within a product. Benger's Food was born.

The female culinary work involved in the creation of Benger's Food and other ferment preparations was essential to the dissemination of digestive ferments among all sections of the population. It propelled the broader public health vision such products embodied. "If artificially digested food is to be employed on the large scale, and among all classes," Roberts insisted, "means must be found to bring the preparation of it within the range of culinary operations and the apparatus of the kitchen and sickroom."[112] Aside from promoting artificially digested foods, Roberts therefore advocated the education of housewives and nurses in peptonizing food in homes and hospitals. Whereas Pavy, in promoting his Fluid Meat, had felt that artificial digestion required "such precision" that it could not be "successfully carried out in the hands of the public," Roberts sided with Pavy's rival Marcet, who had recommended "that the process of preparation should be carried on in the patient's house as the article is wanted."[113] To Roberts, it was "obvious that if articles of this class are to come into general use among the sick, they must be prepared at small cost; and this can only be accomplished when they are prepared at home by the nurse or cook."[114]

In his speeches and publications, Roberts provided detailed instructions for preparing artificially digested foods. He was careful to adjust these directions to the realities of the world beyond the tightly controlled physiological laboratory. The recipe for peptonised milk, for example, suggested that "the degree to which the peptonising change has advanced" could be assessed through tasting. "The point aimed," Roberts explained, was the development of a bitter taste that was "distinctly perceived, but . . . not unpleasantly pronounced."[115] He also specified an easy mechanism for "regulating the peptonizing action" by simply increasing or diminishing either the dose of the pancreatic extract or the amount of time it was allowed to act on the food. At the same time, he acknowledged that it was impossible to obtain pancreatic extract "of absolutely constant strength" and allowed for a "certain latitude" in the interpretation of measures of quantity and time in his instructions. Because precise digestion-friendly temperatures were difficult to obtain outside the laboratory, Roberts developed a method for peptonizing "at a temperature of 60 to 65 Fahr., which may be regarded as the ordinary degree of warmth maintained in rooms occupied by invalids."[116] The advantage of this method was that it could be "regulated with the utmost nicety by occasionally tasting the mixture, and watching the development of the bitter flavour."[117]

Roberts even provided instructions on how to equip one's kitchen so that it would be ready for peptonizing. For the pantry, he recommended "a reliable pancreatic extract" for all peptonizing purposes as well as "a preparation of pepsin or rennet for the production of whey"; a household-proof alkali "of known strength" such as bicarbonate of soda (baking soda); and a supply of various flours (which all varied in the quantity and kind of protein that could be extracted from them) such as "oat, maize, malt, and lentil flours."[118] Useful apparatus included "a thermometer" to "regulate the warmth required in the predigestion of food" as well as a "double-cased saucepan" for the preparation of beef-tea and gruels. Completing the list were "a pair of scales, glass-measures, and a mincing-machine."[119] For the convenience of housewives and home nurses, Benger's company manufactured a "Portable Nursery and Sick-room Kitchen" which contained all the ingredients and equipment recommended by Roberts in a box.[120]

The preparation of artificially digested foods quickly spread through hospitals and household kitchens. Instructions for peptonizing and recipes involving artificially digested ingredients appeared not only in medical journals and textbooks but also in nursing manuals and sickroom cookery books.[121] E. M. Worsnop, a cookery instructor trained at the National Training School for Cookery, gave recipes for peptonized oysters, predigested beef-tea, digestive junket, and "humanized milk" in her *Nurse's Handbook of Cookery*.[122] Peptonized milk, gruels, and beef tea became a standard entry in many instructional nursing and domestic economy texts.[123] Visitors to the International Health Exhibition could even admire a "Peptonizing Apparatus" by the company Savory and Moore by means of which "artificial digestion may be readily carried out at home."[124] Pancreatizing had become mainstream. "At the present day," observed a Bristol physician, the "process of intestinal digestion is imitated almost exactly and easily out of the body, and now daily in our hospitals, and even in private houses."[125]

FIGURE 10. Savory and Moore's Peptonizing Apparatus, *London Medical Record*
September 15, 1883.

With this extension of the reach of digestive ferment products came a
broadening of the products' imagined purpose. In his writings on the experiments with Benger, Roberts increasingly thought of digestion as a series of
processes requiring a considerable amount of work. The matter that formed
ferments, he believed was "no more than the material substratum of a special
kind of energy."[126] This energy performed digestive transformation, but its
capacity was finite, and depended on the amount of ferment. More ferment
meant more work, and vice versa. As Roberts thus reinterpreted the digestive
actions of ferments as energy-intensive processes, he and Benger presented
artificially digested foods as means of saving bodily energy. Advertisements
of Benger's Food emphasized "the ease with which" it could "be digested
and absorbed" and thus afforded "Digestive Rest," even as it supplied all
necessary nourishment.[127]

This profile made Benger's Food an ideal preparation not only for digestive disease, but for sickness in general. Based on the notion of digestive
activity as an energy-intensive process, Roberts suggested that the exter-
nalization of digestion could economize the strength of an individual, and
thereby become a solution to all states of physical weakness, such as infancy,
old age, and most of all, sickness. The idea of sickness as a process of energy
expenditure drew on empirical observations, such as that sick patients often
had no appetite, meaning that their powers of digestion were reduced as
the body's energy resources were otherwise engaged. But it was also part of
a larger shift in the late nineteenth century toward what historian Anson
Rabinbach has called the "fatigued body."[128] As the pathophysiology of sickness was reconceptualized as a process of energy expenditure, energy-saving

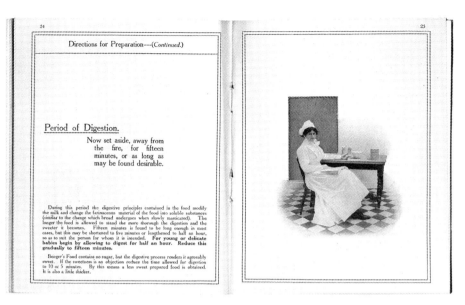

FIGURE 11. "Period of Digestion," in Benger's Food Ltd., *Benger's Food and How to Use It*, ca. 1915 (From the Collection of the Historical Medical Library of the College of Physicians of Philadelphia. The image is used by kind permission of the College of Physicians of Philadelphia. Copyright 2022 by The College of Physicians of Philadelphia).

technologies, like Benger's Food, became interesting therapeutic means to address disease and disability of all kinds. By outsourcing the energetically taxing process of digestion, artificially digested foods promised to provide a solution for all invalids, not just for sufferers of a weak digestion.

The preparation instructions for Benger's Food encouraged users to experience the product as an outsourced, adjustable digestive system. After mixing a tablespoon of Benger's Food with four tablespoons of cold milk and gradually adding half a pint of boiled milk, the mixture then had to be set aside in a third step called the "Period of Digestion."[129] The directions indicated that, "during this period, the digestive principles contained in the food modify the milk and change the farinaceous material of the food into soluble substances." By altering the duration of this stage, the degree of digestion could be adjusted. "The longer the food is allowed to stand the more thorough the digestion and the sweeter it becomes or vice versa." Advertisements connected the food's dose-dependent digestive completeness with the relative strength of the digestive organs. "If the digestive functions, however weak, can do any work at all they should be given work to do *to the extent of their powers,"* one advertisement claimed. It was "in the easy process of its preparation," the ad continued, that "the digestibility of Benger's can be regulated to a degree of extreme nicety."[130]

While Benger's Food began as a specialist medicinal preparation designed to provide a targeted intervention into digestive disease and inefficient food usage, it was soon marketed broadly to "infants, invalids, and the aged," precisely those groups that, like Louisa Down's mother, had lost their capacity for contributing productively to the nation. The broad culinary application Roberts had intended for Benger's Food was not only meant to improve the availability of scarce food resources and turn England into a food-thrifty nation. Instead, it also promised to bridge the gap between productive and less productive sections of society. By outsourcing digestive labor, Benger's Food could do the work that unproductive digestive systems could not. For this, it was amply rewarded by the reformers united by the International Health Exhibition. Two of the three Gold Medals awarded in the category "New Varieties of Food" went to digestive ferment preparations, one of which was Benger's Food.[131]

CONCLUSION

Between 1870 and 1890, much of the world seemed enthralled by the allure of Benger's Food and other ferment-based products. Pepsin pills, pancreas preparations, and peptonised puddings of all kinds gripped the clinical imagination of physicians, the experimenting enthusiasm of physiologists, the professional zeal of pharmacists, and the reformist ambitions of sanitary scientists.

From their beginnings as experimental supplies for research into the mechanism of digestion in the eighteenth century, ferment products served as tools to grasp the digestive process, to reimagine digestive disease, and to rethink digestive therapy. Through ferments, digestion had a material correlate that could be extracted from animal offal in laboratories, pharmacies, and even kitchens and sickrooms. The digestive process could be quantified in its impact, adjusted in its potency, and reproduced outside the body. Digestive pathologies could now be approached as defects of secretion and attacked selectively through the substitution of the offending ferment. The elusive realm of nutrition and digestion, physicians and reformers dreamed, might finally be based on solid scientific footing.

Parallel to their scientific and clinical appeal, digestive ferment products also resonated with the social and economic ambitions of sanitary reformers. Their potential to optimize or even bypass inefficient digestive systems projected the concerns of the thrift movement and its obsession with economizing National Health onto the bodies of Britain's eaters and digesters. Artificially digested foods critiqued mid-century chemistry-centric approaches to the food problem and extended mid-century concerns with food production and procurement into the realm of consumption. The focus on ferment products was part of a series of attempts that sought to turn the unwieldy task of securing the nation's nourishment into a manageable effort of teaching thrift, promoting cooking, and enhancing digestibility in foods and peoples. It was an effort in shifting the economic burden of food and health to individuals, and to women in particular. Like true magic bullets, ferment products reconfigured long-standing social and economic challenges as technical problems solvable through a scientific-commercial fix.

If mid-century concentrated foods had crystallized a racial and geographical hierarchy of dietary customs and eaters, the artificially digested foods of the 1870s and 1880s extended the distinction between superior and inferior eaters to class, ability, and age. To Roberts, dietary preferences had evolved favorably not only among "the more successful races," but also among "the easier classes of a nation."[132] Both had proven the "beneficial tendencies of their food-habits" through their "greater success in the struggle for predominance." Among the winners of the dietary competition were first and foremost the "British races and the other races of Western Europe" who were in "every way, but especially in intellectual power, and in their productiveness of men of originality and eminence, far in advance of all others."[133] But within this geographical, racial, and classed enclave, culinary habits evolved around the productive members of society. It was the "robust and healthy," the "sober and temperate," and those of "mean or average constitution," in other words "those who are bearing the burden of the day, and fighting the battle of life," Roberts insisted, "upon whose bodily and mental efficiency" depended "national progress and ascendancy." Separate eating customs applied for those outside of the productive bulk of the nation; aside from sick individuals, this included "infants and children" and "persons advanced in years." Those groups had a reduced dietary repertoire and exhibited the matching impaired digestive capacities.

Artificially digested foods occupied the economic and physiological chasm between differently productive members of society. In a context preoccupied with the cost of sickness and the potential losses incurred by the nation through inefficient digestive systems, Benger's Food and other similar products addressed not only concerns about the dwindling food supply but also deeper fears about national productivity and Britain's racial and economic place in the world.

FOUR

A Physiology of Consumption

INTRODUCTION

A doctor, a stenographer, an interpreter, and a nun sat on a horse-drawn cart. It was a hot summer's day and they drove through a streetless stretch of land in the southwestern corner of Arizona. Over hills and tree trunks they went, through puddles of water and mud, rocking and jolting as their merciless driver paid no heed to their impassable surroundings nor their incessant cries to slow down. When they finally reached their destination, they shakily descended from the vehicle, brushed off pieces of twigs and leaves that had caught in their hair and clothes, and silently thanked their lucky stars that they had made it this far.[1]

The doctor was John Harvey Kellogg, the infamous health reformer, Sanitarium director, and breakfast cereal magnate. He had come here to examine and exploit what he designated "the last genuine specimen of the primitive aboriginal left in North America."[2] The subject of his "observations" were the Quechan people, whom he referred to as the "Yuma Indians." He had brought along a stenographer to record his impressions and enlisted the help of a Quechan translator and driver. The nun was Sister Alphonse, a member of the Catholic order that ran a school for Quechan children in the former military garrison of Fort Yuma. Kellogg had approached the sisters as soon as he arrived, and they had introduced him to the chief of the Quechan.[3]

At the reservation, Kellogg sought to confirm his belief that the Quechan way of life was the original way of life of the North American continent, simple and unspoiled by the encroachments of civilization. He wished to inspect Quechan people's houses, dress, and customs, but above all, he wished to inspect their diet. He had his stenographer note the major crops, agricultural practices, food preparation methods, and eating habits of the Quechan. Their diet, according to Kellogg, consisted entirely of "the natural productions of the soil, eked out by the products of a scanty agriculture."[4] They grew corn, mesquite beans, potatoes, pumpkins, and a few other crops, and also ate the "seed of certain weeds." These crops, Kellogg emphasized, were raised by the Quechan "without the aid of plows, spades, or other agricultural implements." Kellogg also observed how Quechan women prepared tortillas from corn, using "the most primitive of mills, the *metate*." All of these details the stenographer recorded with great care, and Kellogg published them as an illustrated serial article shortly after.[5]

Kellogg used what he had learned from the Quechan to make and market his health foods. Health foods played an essential role in the "Sanitarium system," a comprehensive philosophy of "biologic living" taught and practiced at Kellogg's famous Sanitarium in Battle Creek, Michigan.[6] The Sanitarium offered paying customers a kind of boot camp to improve their life habits and surroundings. During their stay, they were fed the Sanitarium's custom-made meals as well as a number of prepared "health foods" made in the Sanitarium's kitchens and health food department. Health foods soon became an essential part of Kellogg's business and were shipped to health seekers all across the United States. They incorporated Kellogg's religious beliefs, his medical training, as well as ideas of previous health reformers like Sylvester Graham. They also appropriated Native techniques and Native knowledge. Kellogg's famous flaked cereal, in particular, was informed by his obsession with Native food practices and techniques and relied on Native imagery in promotional materials. His trip to the Quechan may well have been the foundation of our morning bowls of cornflakes today.

Kellogg's health foods and his reliance on the Quechan and other Native peoples were part of a broader ideology of "race betterment." Race betterment was Kellogg's response to late nineteenth-century concerns about "race degeneration" and to skepticism within the eugenics movement toward nonhereditary influences on racial characteristics. Kellogg was himself an ardent eugenicist; he had gradually developed strong eugenic leanings over the course of his career and played an active role in the movement. He also believed that altering a person's lifestyle and environment could have a positive effect on their "racial fitness" (which is perhaps not surprising, given that his entire livelihood was predicated on this idea). A growing number of eugenicists, however, focused primarily on heredity, and dismissed environmental improvements as futile measures that would only prolong the lives of degenerates and further degrade the gene pool. These concerns also came with an economic dimension: To many hereditary-minded eugenicists, social and environmental improvements were nothing but charity, and charity removed the incentive to productivity, further exacerbating degeneration.

Kellogg's philosophy of race betterment constituted a compromise between environmental and hereditary views within eugenics. His position aligned with other environmentally minded social reformers, such as home economist Ellen H. Richards, who had coined the term *euthenics* to mean a "science of better living."[7] Crucial to Kellogg's idea of race betterment was an evolutionary view of society, a classic tale of "civilization as risk," in which a natural but savage mode of life had been displaced by a state of over-civilization.[8] Native peoples like the Quechan symbolized one extreme of this chronology to Kellogg. At the other end was an imagined white, effeminate, chronically ill city dweller whose life had been made too easy by the comforts of modern civilization. The key to beating degeneration, in Kellogg's mind, was a compromise between the two. This could be achieved through a return to natural living mediated through modern science and technology. The health foods devised by Kellogg and his staff embodied this compromise of primitivity and modernity. In the mind of health reformers like Kellogg, health foods would be the means by which a scientifically controlled, technologically managed natural reset of humanity could be achieved.

This chapter examines the development of successive health food product lines by Kellogg and his collaborators from the 1890s to the 1910s as tools of race betterment. The first section shows how Kellogg's earliest health foods merged Native knowledge and techniques with Grahamism, religious reformism, and digestive enzyme physiology into American versions of artificially digested foods. By associating his products with both, primitivity and progress, Kellogg claimed to have created "natural" techniques of predigestion that would restore eating bodies to their full capacity. The second part of the chapter argues that Kellogg's turn to subsequent generations of health foods was rooted in a growing critique of predigestion that reflected eugenic concerns with welfare and dependence. Predigested products increasingly symbolized facile means of substituting gluttony and enabling degeneration. This physiological concern mirrored broader social anxieties over the effects of philanthropy, insurance, and the facile arrangements of modern societies that supposedly had made life too easy for those deemed eugenically inferior. Kellogg's "peptogenic foods" addressed these concerns by promising to incentivize the digestive system to naturally stimulate itself.

Together, Kellogg's health foods and the ideas about digestion and race betterment that they embodied amounted to an elaborate critique of consumer society and, at the same time, an endorsement of consumption. Rather than indulging or abandoning pleasure entirely, Kellogg believed, consumers needed to be taught to consume the right way. Whereas health reformer Sylvester Graham had advocated for a production-centric "physiology of subsistence," in the words of historian Stephan Nissenbaum, Kellogg combined research on digestive secretion, a philosophy of taste and appetite, and central tenets of race betterment into a physiology of consumption.[9]

JOHN HARVEY KELLOGG AND
THE SANITARIUM HEALTH FOODS

John Harvey Kellogg (1852–1943) was born into a heterogeneous religious landscape and a crowded medical marketplace.[10] Michigan, where he spent most of his life, became a hub for religious reform in the second half of the nineteenth century after the Second Great Awakening had virtually depleted the Eastern states of heathens to evangelize. Kellogg's upbringing was shaped by the preaching of evangelical missionaries, most importantly Ellen White, the cofounder of Seventh-day Adventism. White and her followers believed that Christ's second coming was imminent, and that the faithful needed to prepare in body and soul for his arrival. Christian physiology, which comprised an emphasis on bodily care, a vegetarian diet and alcohol abstinence, was a central aspect of Adventist doctrine. White came to Battle Creek (where the Kellogg family had settled) in 1855 and took the young John Harvey under her wing.

Supported by White's religious visions as well as her finances, Kellogg was chosen to obtain a basic medical education in order to bring the gospel of health to the people.[11] A focus on natural therapies united Christian physiologists and sectarian medical practitioners, and Kellogg was sent to attend Trall's Hygeio-Therapeutic College, a popular healing facility founded by hydrotherapist and physician Russell Thacher Trall. Trall's College housed patients, administered a mix of water cures and diet, and provided medical training according to the doctrines of Christian physiology. Kellogg also insisted on attending an orthodox medical college. Having been granted his wish, he completed his medical education at the College of Medicine and Surgery of the University of Michigan and the prestigious Bellevue Hospital, New York.

FIGURE 12. Manufactory of the Battle Creek Sanitarium Health Food Co., *Year Book of the International Medical Missionary and Benevolent Association*, 1897, between pp. 136 and 137).

In one of her visions, Ellen White saw that Adventists were to open their own health reform institution. She was right—in 1866, the Western Health Reform Institute opened its doors in Battle Creek. Kellogg took over the reins of the institution in 1875 and gave it a new name, the Sanitarium. He also attempted to furnish it with a new image as a firmly religious but forward-looking, rational medical facility.[12] Paying guests and a few charity cases came to the Sanitarium for specific illnesses and to improve their general condition. Most guests were white and middle class.[13] The "Sanitarium method" which they underwent at Battle Creek combined careful regulation of diet, exercise, sleep, bowel movement, and one's mental state with Grahamite and Seventh-day Adventist ideas of temperance and sexual continence as well as mainstream scientific and physiological ideas.[14]

Healthy eating was a central component of the regime, and health food products were an integral feature of the Sanitarium dietary system. Shortly after Kellogg took over the reins at the Sanitarium in 1876, he instituted a separate Sanitarium Health Food Department and began to oversee the manufacture and sale of food products under the name "Sanitarium

Foods."[15] The Health Foods Department undertook what they described as "experiments" to create new products or to improve existing ones according to Sanitarium needs.[16] By 1881, nineteen different articles, mostly cereal-based products, were sold by the Sanitarium Food Company, which became a subsidiary of the Sanitarium.[17]

Meals prepared for Sanitarium guests during their stay often featured products created in the Health Foods Department as ingredients.[18] In 1883, home economist, health reformer, and John Harvey Kellogg's wife Ella Eaton Kellogg established an "experimental kitchen" (also referred to as a "culinary laboratory") which played a central role in assembling bills of fare for the Sanitarium dining room.[19] Ella Kellogg devised a plethora of "new methods and original recipes" using existing health foods, and she also invented new products.[20] She published many of her recipes in cookbooks and instructional texts, which often listed Sanitarium products available for purchase.[21] Ella Kellogg's works promoted Sanitarium health foods and likely broadened the market for their consumption.

Product development was closely intertwined with Sanitarium life. To assess their products, Kellogg and his co-experimenters (his brother William Keith Kellogg and his cousin Arthur Kellogg) relied not only on their own judgment but also on the assessments of Sanitarium staff and patients. Ella Kellogg; William Keith's wife, Elmirah; and other Sanitarium staff (especially medical staff) were repeatedly involved in assessing products for their taste and texture. For a meat-free bouillon, for example, Kellogg (while in Paris) demanded that Arthur Kellogg provide samples to Ella Kellogg, Abbie Winegar (a physician and the "medical matron" of the Sanitarium), Elizabeth Stewart (the head of the Sanitarium nursing department), William Keith Kellogg, and Dr. Paulson (either Mamie or David Paulson, both were Sanitarium physicians).[22] Ella Kellogg also gave feedback on how a product fared when used in cooking.[23] She once wrote to William Keith that she and the kitchen staff had been experimenting "with the pea, bean, and split pea product" and had worked out "quite a number of recipes," but that she was "not satisfied with the product itself"; it was "too granular."[24] Patients, too, were asked to gauge the potential of new products or to report criticism of existing products. Speaking of a batch of test soups, for example, William Keith Kellogg announced his intention to "sample some of the patients and see if we can not work up a little business on soups."[25]

But while the creation of health foods relied on considerable input from Sanitarium staff and patients, Kellogg played a dominant role in the development of new products. He gave near daily instructions to Arthur and William Keith Kellogg on how to conduct health food experiments, which products he was envisioning, and which ingredients they were to combine in what quantities and with what methods.[26] He also wrote about products at length in his published works and unpublished notes. His ideas about food and health are therefore particularly pertinent to understanding the Sanitarium's food products.

"A MILD RETURN TO SAVAGERY"

Kellogg's thinking about food evolved over time. His early views on healthy eating were heavily indebted to minister and dietary reformer Sylvester Graham, while eugenic ideas played a growing role in his later approach to nutrition and in subsequent generations of his health foods. But the evolutionary chronology that underpinned Kellogg's nutritional thought was present from the outset and emerged organically from Grahamite doctrine. As historian Daniel Bender has shown, evolutionary narratives were an intellectual and cultural strategy through which US-Americans coped with the rapid industrialization of the late nineteenth century.[27] Like in the case of British imperial and economic thinkers connected to the Great Exhibition, such theories depended on constructions of the "savage" other (chapter 2). They played a central role in the US imperial enterprise and paved the way for full-blown eugenic and euthenics theories and practices.[28]

The flipside of progressive narratives of industrial superiority were cautionary tales of over-civilization and degeneration. The economic development of a nation brought wealth, advanced sanitation, medical progress, and improved transportation, according to industrial enthusiasts, but it also brought the temptations of abundance, the potential for those deemed degenerate to survive in greater numbers, and the means for those of less advanced nations to immigrate to more developed lands, in the eyes of critics.[29] Graham had captured these fears in a theory of economic development similar to that promoted by the British champions of the meat biscuit, but it came with a cyclical and anti-capitalist twist. Nations, according to Graham, moved inexorably from a "state of little more than animal existence" toward an "age of wealth," and with it, an "age of luxury and refined sensuality and excess."[30] But the amenities of a more prosperous nation also came with a "current of indulgence" that gradually made man "incapable of sustaining those social and civil institutions" that usually protected him against "his degenerating luxuries and excesses."[31] The result was a vicious cycle of further degeneration and, as Kellogg put it, the dilution of the "population in civilized countries" with "the less fit elements of the community."[32]

Over-civilization also manifested in overcivilized food preparations and dietary habits. In particular, Graham denounced "stimulating" foods as part of a broader critique of stimulation of all kind. Stimulating foods were those that excited more than they nourished, such as alcohol, tobacco, tea, and coffee, as well as "condiments" such as pepper or mustard. Most disconcerting, in Graham's mind, was the modern trend of hoarding the nourishing properties of aliment in unnatural proportions and seeking to eliminate seemingly unnecessary bulk. To Graham, God's creation was perfect, so there could be no doubt that "bulk, or a due proportion of innutritious matter in our food" had been placed there for a reason and was necessarily "quite as important to health as nourishment."[33] His particular disdain was reserved for modern bread. Whereas the bread of olden times had consisted of moderately ground coarse grain, modern milling techniques had begun to "put asunder what God has joined together" and separated the flour from the bran. The result was a "superfine flour" in which "the farina and gluten and saccharine matter of the wheat" were "almost perfectly concentrated."[34] Such a high concentration of nutritious substance, Graham alleged, was "in direct violation of the laws of constitution" that the Creator had "established in the nature of man" and would act as a "stimulus" to the organism.

Kellogg shared Graham's aversion to stimulating foods. Like Graham, he advocated for a vegetarian, alcohol-free, plain diet and critiqued "superfine wheat flour." But Kellogg's critique of superfine flour focused less on its disproportional concentration of nourishing constituents than on its lack of the right nutrients ("gluten"), removed by the "modern miller" merely to obtain a "white and fine appearance."[35] Modern bread, while appealing to modern tastes, supplied only little nutritious substance. Added to that was the poor digestibility of many modern foods, Kellogg contended. Even the coarse flours produced by Graham and others in order to improve the nutritious content of the grain contained indigestible material that was unsuitable for the digestively inept American stomach. As a result, the entirety of civilized humankind currently lived under conditions of "partial starvation"—a circumstance which was "undoubtedly responsible for a vast amount of disease, decrepitude, and death."[36]

Both Kellogg and Graham emphasized the long-term consequences of modern foods. A vicious cycle perverted the natural sensations of those giving in too easily to modern culinary temptations. Being constantly overfed with the wrong foods, the stomach would gradually become "so adapted to the stimulating properties of those substances" that it would lose its natural hunger for the right kinds of foods, according to Graham.[37] Kellogg maintained that all forms of sensory pleasure mutually reinforced one another. He contended that stimulating foods and beverages such as tea, coffee, tobacco, spices, candies, and meat lead to "unchastity," masturbation, prostitution, and even premature puberty in children.[38] Conversely, masturbating children and prostitutes often exhibited gluttonous tendencies, according to Kellogg; "capricious appetites" in children could be an early warning sign for the equally deviant appetites of the "solitary vice." Gluttony, in Kellogg's mind, was both symptom and cause of unnatural lust.

Graham and Kellogg also connected their dietary philosophy with an economic critique. To Graham, modern unnatural bread was a product of the modern unnatural arrangement of production and consumption. Like the human body, the soil required a perfect balance of input and rest. But the unnatural concentration of populations (just like the unnatural concentration of nutrients) in ever growing cities (those eternal foes of American yeomanry) had upset the natural, balanced distribution of mankind across the land. This development had compelled food producers to artificially increase yields and intensify agricultural production.[39] As a result, Graham found the soil "exhausted by tillage" and "debauched by the means which man uses to enrich and stimulate it."[40] A soil deprived of its natural proportions of nutrient and innutrient matter would fail to produce bread that contained the right balance of nutrients and bulk.

Graham's "physiology of subsistence" doubled as a fantasy of imperial expansion.[41] If over-nutritious bread was the product of over-producing soil, truly perfect bread could only be produced from "pure virgin soil." It was in the "comfortable log houses of our western country" that naturally nutritious bread could be found, that "the new soil, in its virgin purity, produces . . . vegetables appropriate for human aliment in a more perfect and healthy state than any soil, which has been long under cultivation, can be made to do."[42] Graham's food philosophy was the dietetic equivalent of Jefferson's imperial-economic dream, a restoration of the country's economic and dietetic original state.[43] Within this conceptual framework, concentrated stimulating food epitomized precisely what had gone wrong in the nation's culinary and economic development.

Whereas Graham had directed his critique primarily at the producers of food, Kellogg would pivot to food consumers and their digestive systems. And where Graham had advocated imperial expansion, Kellogg was above all concerned with reverting the degeneration of the white race. He proposed an individual reboot of the system toward an imagined original state of life, assisted by modern science and technology. In order to achieve this, he constructed an ideal natural lifestyle by studying and stereotyping Native peoples. Native peoples, in Kellogg's mind, provided a unique opportunity to observe both ideal forms of dress, diet, and social organization, and the detrimental effects of civilization. Kellogg's imagined Native was no longer "a simple child of nature" but had "acquired sufficient of the manners and the vices of civilization" to render "him" a "sophisticated barbarian." While "he" was thus "tamed in his savagery" (a welcome development in Kellogg's mind), "he" was also forever "despoiled of his primitive simplicity and natural instincts."[44]

The Quechan were the exception. In their bodies and habits, Kellogg sought to read what he considered the unspoiled American way of life. On his trip to Fort Yuma, Kellogg tried to ascertain what he considered the civilizational chasm between the Quechan reservation and the boarding school for Quechan children run by the Catholic sisters. Kellogg had gained entry to the school with the help of a local physician. At the school, Kellogg studied both the children as well as a number of Quechan women who worked at the school. The latter, he considered representatives of the "natural" way of life of the Quechan, while the former, in Kellogg's mind, had already been subjected to the damaging influences of civilization.

Kellogg's first interest was the lung capacity of Quechan women working at the school. Recent measurements of lung capacity had shown a difference between men's and women's breathing, but Kellogg believed that this was not an innate difference. Instead, he faulted civilizational habits, in particular the corset. The Quechan women, according to Kellogg, "had never been subjected to the deforming and restraining influences on civilized dress," and his experiment was designed to "compare" the Quechan women's "movements of the chest in the process of breathing" with those of "narrow-waisted civilized women."[45] He set up a pneumograph in the school doctor's office and, one by one, examined the women.

It is unclear to what extent Kellogg used coercion, but given the unequal power dynamics at the school, the women could not possibly have fully consented. What is more, Kellogg praised the help of a sister in the "delicate work" required to "induce" the women to "submit to an examination" and described them as "exceedingly wily and very suspicious of any new or strange-looking instrument."[46] The pneumograph, according to Kellogg's report, inspired fear in the women and was "regarded as some sort of an infernal machine which might go off at any minute." Kellogg's dismissive and condescending tone likely masks the real terror the women must have felt given the long history of violence against Native peoples in the region. The report also gives no indication that Kellogg felt any need to reassure the women, whereas he describes in great detail his efforts to secure the trust and cooperation of one of the Catholic sisters.[47]

As Lundy Braun has shown, lung capacity measurements played an important role in America's long history of scientific racism. They had been used by antebellum plantation physicians to argue that enslaved people were unfit for freedom. The spirometer, in this context, worked to legitimize racial essentialism by supposedly revealing innate breathing shortcomings among Black enslaved people. Kellogg's use of pneumography in Fort Yuma, by contrast, served to establish a control group of pristine, natural bodies against which the deteriorating effects of civilization could be measured. Kellogg found, as he had expected, that "Yuma women breathe like Yuma men, and like civilized men, with the exception of those few brainless fops who wear corsets and part their hair in the middle."[48]

Kellogg's next interest was with the foodways of the Quechan. In addition to examining Quechan crops and cooking at the reservation, Kellogg participated in the brutal history of nutritional experimentation in Aboriginal Communities and Residential Schools for Native children in North America.[49] He used Quechan children who had been forced to attend the school as a natural experiment of the corrupting effects of civilized life. He interrogated Sister Alphonse about the "influence of civilization upon the health of the Indian boys and girls" and was told that the adoption of a "civilized diet" consisting of "corned beef, coffee, white bread, corn-bread, and beans" had led to "indigestion, water-brash, and other troublesome symptoms" among the children.[50] The children themselves, Kellogg reported, continued to crave the diet of their community; nothing, Kellogg insisted, "afforded them so much delight as the Friday afternoon half-holiday, when they were allowed to make *tortillas* for themselves." Even after they had been at the school for several months, this delight did not diminish. The fault, Kellogg concluded, lay entirely with those who had tampered with the children's natural appetites. It was "a pity," he concluded, "that those who had charge of the education and development of these children of nature, should begin by cultivating an unhealthful taste."

While Kellogg thus faulted the effects of civilization for leading to bodily decline, ill health, and perverted tastes, and idealized the pristine customs and foodways of the Quechan, he also hastened to qualify his condemnation of civilized life and commendation of savage existence. "We would not wish to be understood as esteeming the habits of savagery preferable to those of civilization," he clarified, "or as extolling the advantages of savage life."[51] To Kellogg, "neither the savage nor the civilized man" was in a "normal condition"; both represented extremes.[52] What was needed was a combination of the advantages of both ways of life, and a rejection of the disadvantages: the "irregularities and exciting exposures of savage life," on the one hand, and the "enervating and depraving practices of civilization," on the other. What was needed, in short, was a "mild return to savagery."[53] It was in the service of this goal that he envisioned his own rather un-humble role: "The man who will perfectly solve the problem thus involved, or so modify the present mode of civilized life as to eliminate its unnaturalness, will be recognized for all time as the greatest benefactor of the race."[54]

GRANOLA, GRANOSE, AND GOFIO:
NATURALLY PREDIGESTED FOODS

The early health foods devised by Kellogg and his staff at the Sanitarium reflected this goal of creating "civilized" yet "natural" products. Kellogg married his racist-evolutionist ideas of primitive food with Grahamism, theories of nutritive constituents, and the latest insights of modern digestive physiology. He diagnosed the current food situation in the United States as diseased with unnatural, innutritious, indigestible food products combined with unnatural tastes. Modern distorted palates, Kellogg reasoned, craved foods that were poor in nutritious content and hard of digestion. This dire situation had attracted the resourcefulness of a medical and dietetic industry, which Kellogg, true to his health reformist roots, claimed to despise.

While Kellogg embraced the insights of digestive physiology recently gained in Britain by William Roberts and others (chapter 3), he criticized in particular the outpouring of digestive enzyme products it had brought forth. Europe's enzyme craze took the US market by storm in the 1880s and

1890s. Major pharmaceutical manufacturers produced lines of pepsin, diastase, and other enzyme-related products. New York–based company Reed & Carnrick, for instance, produced a composite enzyme product called Peptenzyme; Parke, Davis & Co. marketed multiple enzyme preparations such as Pepsin Cordial and Taka-Diastase; and Sharpe & Dohme as well as Smith, Kline & French each had their lines of pepsin and pancreatin elixirs. Entire companies were founded solely for the purpose of producing enzyme-related products, such as the American Ferment Company, the Maltine Company, and the Malt-Diastase Company; others, like Fairchild Brothers & Foster, specialized in digestive ferment products.[55]

But whereas British producers freely referred to "artificially digested foods," US companies tended to emphasize the naturalness of using a physiological component of the body to restore its original, albeit diseased, digestive function. Reed & Carnrick, for example, claimed that because of the mere mechanical extraction process used to make Peptenzyme, their product contained "a proportional quantity of the enzyme principles of the whole series of digestive organs" and acted "just as the secretions of the natural organs when in life," since they had "not been injured during the process of isolation."[56] US producers also capitalized on American preferences for "natural remedies" by developing "naturally occurring" predigested foods. Particularly popular were also so-called vegetable digestive ferment products, such as products based on the "ferments" of the pineapple and the papaya. Both fruits were investigated by physiological chemist Russell Chittenden for their "digestive principles" which he found to be powerful and little selective (and therefore broadly applicable).[57] Commercial preparations carried such inventive names as Zumo Anana, Dygestif (pineapple), Papayans and Papoid (papaya).[58]

This emphasis on naturalness also stemmed from precisely those US imperial fantasies and evolutionary narratives of progress and decline that Kellogg had sought to locate during his quest for "mild savagery." In products like Zumo Anana and Papoid, marketers of enzyme products pretended to rediscover the natural foods of Native peoples and make available their naturally occurring digestive enzymes through US-American science. A particularly egregious example of this tendency was the Taro Food Company's *Taroena*, a product allegedly derived from the Taro Root.[59] A direct gain from the "coming of the Hawaiian Islands within the domain of the United States," according to one pamphlet, Taroena supposedly contained "its own digestive ferment" and therefore boasted "inherent digestibility."[60] The Taro root, the pamphlet claimed, was a naturally perfect food; it "possessed all the ingredients essential to the support of animal life" and "required little or no effort" by the "gastric secretions" to be digested.[61] The product Taroena supposedly retained all these natural properties but was "more concentrated in strength."[62] Side by side, the pamphlet contrasted images of Hawaiian "natives," "native huts," and Hawaiian scenery with testimonials from US physicians and other "experts." The message was clear: the Taro Root might be a "nature-made food" that had made Hawaiians a "remarkably hardy race," but the expertise to extract its true nutritive value and efficient use pertained to white men of science.[63]

The early Sanitarium health foods were versions of such "naturally" predigested products. By fulfilling the "natural demands of the human digestive organs," they functioned as alternatives to the "artificial means of aiding the feeble American stomach" through the "powerful digestive agents" made from animals like the "pig, the calf, the barnyard fowl, and even the ostrich."[64] Initially, the focus of Kellogg and his colleagues was on cooked cereals and the role of cooking in rendering foods more easily digestible. Granola (still today a breakfast staple) was one of the first such preparations. It was a "combination of the most easily digested grains" prepared in such a way "as to secure to a large extent the advantages of those changes naturally effected by the digestive process.[65] During the manufacturing process, "many hours of the most thorough cooking" rendered it a "thoroughly cooked" and "partially digested" product.[66] In addition, it promised to be truly nourishing. Aside from "persons with weak digestion," "feeble children," and "invalids," it was therefore also (yet another) portable food for "travelers and excursionists": like Gail Borden's Meat Biscuit, it promised to contain "the largest amount of nutriment in the smallest bulk" ("one pound more than equals three pounds of best beef").[67]

Notions of concentrated nourishment, digestive enzyme physiology, Graham's doctrines, and a product called Granula, a baked mixture of Graham flour and water developed by hydropathist and health reformer James Caleb Jackson, all certainly served as inspiration for the development of Granola.[68] But Kellogg also drew on "a staple food of the natives of the Canary Islands," Gofio. Granola, a pamphlet claimed, resembled Gofio "in flavor and mode of preparation."[69] Gofio, according to the pamphlet, was responsible for attracting "hundreds of invalids" to "that out of the way place" due to its "remarkable virtues as a curative agent in various forms of dyspepsia." Gofio so impressed Kellogg that he created his own version

FIGURE 13. Advertisement for Granola, *Good Health* 30 (1895).

of it and marketed it as a health food. Whereas in the case of Granola, he had changed his product's name so as not to risk a lawsuit by the makers of "Granula," he had no such qualms about the intellectual property of the Canary Islanders, and named his product, simply, "Gofio."[70]

Gofio was prepared by placing "whole grain of some sort, wheat, rye, barley, or corn, in an "earthen vessel over a slow fire," and stirring it constantly, until it was "well parched and browned."[71] The grain was then "ground in a mortar" and, with a little water or goats' milk added, was "ready for use." To Kellogg, it was common knowledge that "the peasantry of the Canary Islands" were "among the most robust and vigorous men in the world," and they existed, almost entirely, on this "single article of food." Gofio allowed the Canary Islanders to perform "the hardest labor" while knowing "nothing of the horrors of American dyspepsia, Kellogg insisted. Alluding to his trip to the Quechan, Kellogg also claimed that the "North American Indian" made "a rude kind of Gofio in a similar manner," and that Kellogg himself had witnessed "the women of the primitive Yuma tribe of New Mexico making Gofio from the seeds of a native grass." The Sanitarium Food Company offered a Maize Gofio and a Wheat Gofio at 10 cents per pound each.

The influence of Native knowledge and techniques also informed the creation of what is perhaps the Kelloggs' most famous product: flaked breakfast cereal. Existing accounts of the invention of Granose, the first flaked cereal the Kelloggs made, emphasize Kellogg's 1893 visit to fellow cereal producer Henry Perkins's Shredded Wheat factory in 1893 as a pivotal moment that inspired the Kelloggs to turn away from the existing Grahamite panoply of unchewable and monotonous cereal products, and create instead a more palatable, bite-sized, and altogether more modern product.[72] The Kelloggs attempted to press raw, soaked grain between a pair of steel rollers, but failed to produce the desired result. They then tried cooking the wheat before putting it through the rollers, with no more success. Finally, they left out a batch of soaked, cooked wheat by accident and unwittingly invented tempering. The tempered wheat, when put through the rollers, produced perfectly flaked and easily digestible cereal. Modern breakfast cereal was born.

What gains no mention in accounts of Granose is Kellogg's earlier visit to the Quechan in 1889. During that visit, Kellogg had taken an eager interest in the preparation of tortillas by Quechan women and noted in detail the equipment they had used. He described the *metate* as "a rough stone slightly hollowed out" upon which the corn, soaked overnight, was "rubbed to a paste by the aid of a stone roller." The corn paste was then formed into thin cakes and cooked on stones heated by coals. Kellogg even obtained "a specimen of the tortillas" by bargaining with the Quechan.[73] He watched as the two wives of the chief baked "several rolls of corn paste" into "thin cakes" on a "heated sheet iron." All of this, Kellogg noted in his report published in *Good Health*, complete with an illustration of the "varieties of metate" he had seen used. The Kelloggs' first attempts at making Granose, in which they soaked grain overnight and then tried to press it through rollers, replicated almost precisely Kellogg's description of Quechan tortilla making.

The Kelloggs then used images of Native peoples and tools in their promotional material for Granose. Such depictions associated Granose with romanticized notions of "primitivity" and the wisdom of lost times. In a promotional brochure, Kellogg reprinted the drawing accompanying his report on the Quechan alongside other representations of "ancient millers" and their tools. The stone metate was placed alongside a Syrian hand-mill, a "primitive mill" used by a "Pima Indian woman," and an Indian mortar; Palestine women "in the process of flour-making as anciently practiced" were shown next to "an Indian woman of Arizona, employed, as the writer has seen these simple children of nature, in the doors of their primitive dwellings, grinding the grain for the family meal at sunset."[74] Ella Eaton Kellogg also dedicated a section of her book on scientific cookery to the metate, and

SOME ANCIENT MILLERS.

[7]

FIGURE 14. Racist illustration of "Ancient Millers." Battle Creek Sanitarium, *Battle Creek Sanitarium Health Foods*. From the Collection of the Historical Medical Library of the College of Physicians of Philadelphia. The image is used by kind permission of the College of Physicians of Philadelphia. Copyright 2022 by The College of Physicians of Philadelphia.

displayed images of the device and of women making tortillas.[75] In a Sanitarium brochure titled *Undigested Cereals the Cause of American Dyspepsia*, the images of the Quechan, Syrian, and Indian women had disappeared and were collapsed into a representation of a generic "olden" family shown in what was presumably meant to depict Roman or Palestinian dress, making bread amid antique vases and vessels.[76]

Scholars of Kellogg and his health foods have rightly interpreted the invention of flaked cereal as a moment in which Kellogg turned away from his religious past and from the "natural" foods promoted by Graham and health reformers and moved more fully toward health foods created through modern technological intervention, scientific knowledge, and entrepreneurial ingenuity. According to Nicholas Bauch, both Kellogg and Graham promoted foods that were close to their natural state, but whereas Graham's foods were based on "a mistrust of modified, processed, manufactured, industrially grown, and shipped foods," Kellogg's ideas were "*founded* on the promise that technology could make better foods than nature could."[77] But Kellogg's embrace of modern, technologically assisted natural foods must also be understood within the broader context of imperialism and scientific racism that manifested in Kellogg's (and many of his contemporaries') obsession with "mild savagery." His scientific-technological rhetoric served as a tool of appropriation of Native knowledge and practices. Kellogg's own emphasis on technological ingenuity and his lack of acknowledgment of any intellectual contribution other than that of fellow white US-American cereal producers should not blind us to his indebtedness to the knowledge and techniques of the Native peoples he had studied.

The physiology of digestive ferments, in particular, served Kellogg to convert Native knowledge into his own discovery. He coined the term *heat digestion* to refer to the process of transformation in cereal foods during toasting, which according to Kellogg accomplished what enzymes did: converting one substance (starch) into its digestive subproducts (maltose, dextrin), thereby predigesting or "dextrinizing" the food. But in contrast to flat Quechan tortillas and the crispy bread of "olden times," modern loaf bread was voluminous and therefore prevented much of the starch from undergoing the natural processes of transformation that heat occasioned and that, according to Kellogg, increased bread's digestibility.[78] An accumulation of indigestible material was the result. Granose (and tortillas), by contrast, consisted of small thin flakes and therefore reached the final stage of starch digestion more easily than modern bread or even conventional cereal products. Through its thin shape, it was exposed to such high temperatures that its starch was "thoroughly dextrinized."[79]

In their promotional materials, the Kelloggs juxtaposed the images of "ancient" tools and practices with technical-scientific language and images that validated them to his white consumers. They spoke of "interesting laboratory experiments" that had corroborated "the effect of thorough heat digestion in the conversion of starch."[80] They displayed a series of differently colored vials that represented the stages of starch digestion based on a well-known experimental technique. As starch was gradually converted into sugar, it lost its capacity to color iodine blue, and turned a reddish hue instead, and then finally, became yellow. At the same time, they re-naturalized Granose by associating it with Native food wisdom. In one editorial, the Kelloggs spoke of a "native Mexican woman" whose "acute observation" had taught her that the process of ripening produced similar changes to those taking place in the cooking of food.[81] The starch of the fruit was turned into dextrin and levulose, rendering the fruit "mellow and juicy." A similar conversion, the editorial contended, was at work in the heat digestion of starch. Granose and other Sanitarium foods, the editorial assured readers, were "thoroughly cooked and predigested, like the fruit which has been 'cooked in the sun.'"

Similar rhetorical tactics also allowed the Kelloggs to conjure a notion of natural sweetness that functioned as a marker for digestibility. The "simple processes" of the "ancient miller" rendered bread not only "dark" and "coarse" but "sweet," as Kellogg himself could testify, according to one brochure.[82] "Primitive man," he insisted, "does not rob himself of the Creator's choicest gifts by seeking to improve (?) nature." Scientific vocabulary, once again, served to explain the development of sweetness in toasted cereal and seize it as an integral part of the Kelloggs' own invention. A promotional characterization of Wheat Granola described how, "by the prolonged action of the heat, the starch is . . . largely converted into *dextrine* and *dextrose*, which give to the food qualities that render it readily assimilable, and impart to it a most agreeable, sweet, nutty flavor, equaled by no other food offered to the public."[83]

When creating their health foods, the Kelloggs therefore took care to engineer a sweetness that could be detected by consumers as a marker for digestibility and naturalness. In one in-house note, Kellogg was quoted by his brother as insisting that "the sweetness is an indication of the degree to which the starch has been converted into sugar, and the product must be quite sweet in order to conform with the description made of it, and what

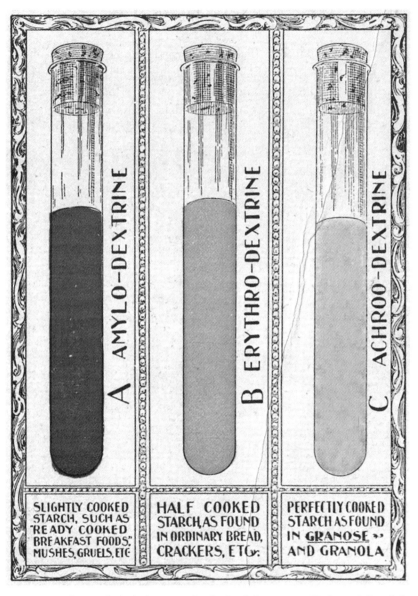

FIGURE 15. Stages of starch digestion. Battle Creek Sanitarium, *Undigested Cereal the Cause of American Dyspepsia*. From the Collection of the Historical Medical Library of the College of Physicians of Philadelphia. The image is used by kind permission of The College of Physicians of Philadelphia. Copyright 2022 by The College of Physicians of Philadelphia.

is claimed for it."[84] In another note, Kellogg requested experiments with "partially malted cereals" and with "partially digesting the flour paste" until "considerable sugar is developed."[85] The Kelloggs also taught their consumers to interpret the sensuous properties of their foods as markers of their digestibility. In textbooks addressed to a lay audience, Kellogg encouraged his readers to draw on their own sensory experiences in order to imaginatively reconstruct the effect of starch transformation. "You have noticed that if you chew a bit of hard bread a few minutes it becomes sweet," Kellogg suggested in an instructional textbook aimed at children. "This is because," he continued, "the saliva changes some of the starch of the food into sugar."[86]

Sweetness as a marker of digestibility and a natural result of the Kelloggs' sophisticated process was codified into the patent for flaked cereal, which Kellogg applied for in 1896. Soaking the grain enabled a preliminary "digestion" of the grain by the aid of the ferment "cerealine," which converted parts of the starch to dextrin and thereby added "to the sweetness and flavor of the product."[87] The preliminary digestion also rendered the grain "somewhat glutinous" and made it possible to apply high pressure during the rolling process, producing "very thin flakes" that were "readily roasted to assume a sweet flavor."[88]

Absent from the patent were any references to the Native foods and methods Kellogg had studied. Elsewhere, Kellogg acknowledged this influence on the development of the Sanitarium health foods. His research to "discover and devise" healthful foods, he claimed, had "included a study of the dietetic habits and the food substances employed by the people of all the principal countries of the world, both civilized and uncivilized."[89] He had collected "specimens of native foods . . . from all parts of the Old and the New World" and studied them with the help of "chemical and food laboratories, and an experimental kitchen." On the basis of this research, he had developed "a few choice preparations possessed of intrinsic and specific merit."

The development and patenting of early Kellogg health foods thus erased the intellectual debt the Kelloggs owed to the Quechan and other Native peoples. They appropriated indigenous techniques and knowledge and used them to authenticate their own products, even as they condescended to the supposed "primitivism" of Native peoples. The racist-chronological mindset that underlay the creation of these early products would also inform the next generation of Kellogg health foods. But more and more, Kellogg's immersion in eugenics and the challenges it posed to environmental reform would drive his nutritional theorizing and shape his nutritional products.

By the turn of the century, predigestion and its products—whether "natural" or not—came into disrepute. Partly, this was the result of a growing hostility toward large corporations in the United States, specifically the meatpackers, who had seized upon the fashion for ferments. Demand for ferments had allowed large meatpacking companies to turn offal by-products into commercial pepsins and other digestive ferment products. Offending vegetarians and anti-monopolists alike, digestive enzyme products thus became entangled with reformist crusades. If doctors could be "duped into prescribing plenty of pepsin and pancreatin," one physician claimed, offal waste could now "be made a source of income to these already gigantic financial concerns."[90] Pharmacists feared that the packinghouses' "unlimited capital and great commercial sagacity" would enable them to "get the kernel" of the production of pepsin and other ferments, while "the manufacturing pharmacists," who had "created the product and bled for it," would "get the empty shell."[91]

Kellogg, too, was appalled by the "great beef and pork packers" who had "gone into the business of making pepsins, beef extracts, peptones, etc."[92] Aside from sympathizing with anti-pharmaceutical sentiments, he also feared that grocers would soon sell digestive ferments "along with the pork and potatoes, beef, bread, beans, etc., that they are supposed to help digest." Digestive ferments, in other words, were simply enabling a gluttonous lifestyle. "Abused stomachs" were "loaded with oysters and pickles, pigs' feet and sardines, night after night, week in and week out," lamented a physician in the *Eclectic Journal,* "and five grains of pepsin are expected to restore such dilapidated old concerns to their original condition."[93] Even advertisements of "natural" vegetable ferment products emphasized digestive enzymes' ability to serve as accomplices to indulgence. A striking and uncharacteristically colorful illustration in the *New York Medical Journal* compared the before and after of the digestive action of papaya extract on a veritable feast of minced pie, roast beef, and fried sausage.[94] While the illustration was intended to demonstrate the strength of a papaya ferment product, such images helped associate self-digestive foods with self-gratification.

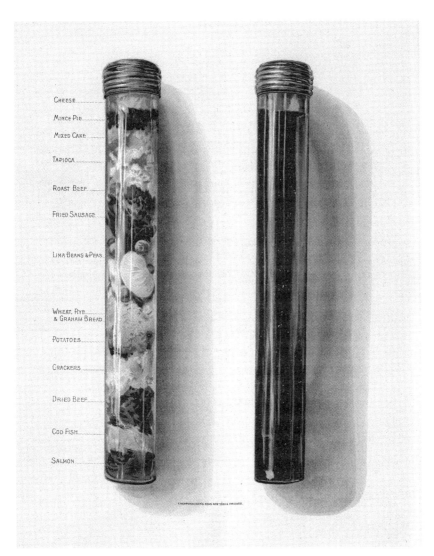

FIGURE 16. Before and after "digestion" with papaya extract. Illustration from Frank Woodbury, "On the Digestive Ferment of the Carica Papaya in Gastro-Intestinal Disorders," *New York Medical Journal* 56 (July 30, 1892): 115–18.

This association was strengthened by the growing number of not strictly medicinal items of consumption that contained digestive enzymes. By the early twentieth century, pepsin could be found in a number of chewing gum preparations, such as Wrigley's Spearmint Pepsin Gum, Adam's Pepsin Tutti Frutti Gum, or Beeman's Pepsin Gum.[95] Pepsin and other enzymes

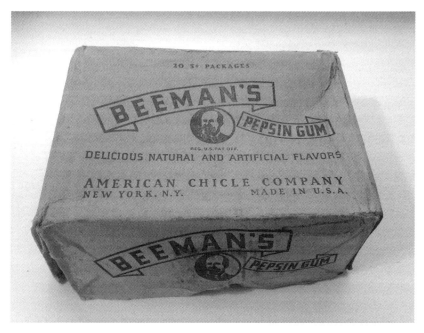

FIGURE 17. Beeman's Pepsin Gum. Author's own collection.

also featured as popular ingredients in health drinks sold in pharmacy soda fountains; one particular recipe would become known as *Pepsi-Cola*.[96] The side-by-side appearance of an announcement for "Pepsin Tonic: A New Soda Drink," and an article pronouncing the "Passing of Pepsin" in the pages of the *Practical Druggist and Spatula* in 1908 illustrates the simultaneous enthusiasm for, and distrust of, enzyme products toward the turn of the century.[97] Digestive enzymes had become, at once, popular consumer products, emblems of capitalist production, and symbols for the indulgences of civilized modernity.

As a result, the entire mechanism of digestive ferment therapy came under attack. The idea of *substituting* a natural process of the body, outsourcing it to spare the body "work," was fundamentally flawed, critics claimed.[98] Such substitution would ultimately un-teach the digestive system how to secrete digestive ferments and perform its own digestive labor. This physiological concern echoed a broader societal discontent with civilizational advances, which had made things *too easy*. In popular culture, the vocabulary of peptonization, enzyme substitution, and related processes was employed as a metaphor to decry the corrupting influences of facile modern arrangements.

An editorial on civilization titled "The Conflict of Modern Society" lamented that all modern contrivances—from easily accumulated capital to effortless travel and communication and even distilled newspaper articles, had been "comminuted, peptonized, and otherwise prepared with a view to the utmost economy of effort in consumption."[99]

Concerns about the excessive outgrowths of modern convenience were personified in "Predigested Tommy," a character in John F. Cowan's 1905 short story of the same title.[100] The story follows the visit of Predigested Tommy and his mother, formerly Tirza Ann Toothaker (but now Mrs. T. Anna Jenkins-Jones since she had married a "Boston banker") to Tommy's grandparents' house (the Toothakers) in the country. It describes how mother and son arrive with a giant box of "Nochew and Swallow's Self-eating foods" in tow, which is dutifully hauled home, eyebrows raised, by Tommy's sturdy grandfather. Over dinner, Tommy's grandmother tries to offer the boy "some fat ham" and "eggs" but is prevented just in time by Tommy's mother, who protests that her son's stomach is "weak," and that he has "never eaten anything but predigested foods." Tommy is also given "predigested education" and "predigested sports"; in both areas, his mother gives him a range of options he might like, rather than forcing him to make up his mind to choose a rigorous mental or physical activity.

The mother's habit of pandering to the boy's likes and dislikes without forcing him to select also plays out in the realm of consumption. Unable to choose between an assortment of neckties, the boy is reassured by his mother not to "cloud one moment" of his "sweet life" trying to make up his mind. "If we take the whole box home," she reassures him, "it may make itself up after awhile without an effort." When Tommy's mother finally hands the boy "three chewless proteid tablets" and "four spoonfuls of the peptonized pabulum," Tommy's grandfather becomes greatly concerned over the boy's unused teeth. "I should think that any self-respectin' set of teeth or slavery glans would want to go out of business in disgust if they wa'n't never recognized or given nothin' to do," he bursts out, and warns his daughter that if she keeps "on feedin' that boy them chewless things," she'll "soon have a new human specimen—a toothless, stomachless man to go along with them there horseless carriages an' wireless telegraphy."[101]

The criticism of effortlessness embodied in peptonized products was linked to a broad spectrum of social and economic thought during the late nineteenth and early twentieth centuries. The story of Predigested Tommy was reprinted in the pages of Lilian Heath's *The Red Telephone*, an

THE PREDIGESTED SHADOW.
"It is better to be strong than have an 'easy' life."
—Page 53.

FIGURE 18. The Predigested Shadow. In Lillian M. Heath, *The Red Telephone* (Chicago: W. R. Vansant, 1905), p. 53.

exposé written against "temptations" or "shadows" that act "from within" and "from without." Among them were the temptations of liquor, wealth ("easy money"), unstrenuous education, and prostitution ("the White Slave trade" or "easy virtue"), all connected through a common tendency to offer facile comfort and ultimately leading to degeneracy.[102] In all cases, the path away from this shadow world led through discipline and self-knowledge. Wealth, for instance, was not condemned wholesale; it was even desirable in an individual who recognized their own thoughts and communion with God as sources of wealth, "one who thus *knows* himself to be at one with all wealth."[103] Reconciling abundance with righteousness required judgment and character, even moral virtue. The crucial question for the preservation or decline of civilization, according to an editorial on the conflict of modern society, was whether a nation's virtue would keep pace with its material development, or whether it would decline "through the very abundance of the enjoyments and facilities of all kinds which it is furnishing." This, the editorial concluded, was "The problem of the Sphinx . . . : how to stand up against the sun of our own prosperity."[104]

A critique of unearned wealth was also articulated by agrarian populists, for whom the riddle of the Sphinx was "agricultural depression in the midst of general prosperity and the lack of a relation between commodity prices and production costs."[105] They identified the figures of the banker or "middle man," alongside the railway monopolist, as the un-laboring, undeserved profiteer of their own hard work (it is surely no coincidence that Predigested Tommy's mother had developed her modern ideas about diet after marrying a "Boston banker"). This "army of useless toilers," wrote N. B. Ashby, a lecturer of the National Farmer's Alliance in *The Riddle of the Sphinx*, had made easy profits through the farmers' dependency on selling their crops right after harvest time, giving "the middle man and the speculator their opportunity to reduce prices to a ruinously low figure."[106]

The discourse about lack of exertion as a marker for undeservedness also increasingly undergirded eugenic debates about charity and the welfare state. Philosopher and Social Darwinist Herbert Spencer, whom Kellogg read and admired (like many of his fellow countrymen), had famously argued that philanthropy delivered to the poor was nothing but an unfair advantage provided to the inferior races in the struggle for life, and hence a damaging influence on racial progress.[107] Inspired by Spencer's developmental views, debates about philanthropy centered on the effects of charity for society at large. Alexander Johnson, president of the National Conference of Charities, articulated a conception of the dependence created by charity suffused with the language of degeneration, and reminiscent of the conception of the pre-digesting stomach, unable to help itself. "Every time a want is supplied by a man's own efforts," Johnson announced, "the faculty which is called into play becomes stronger, and the recurring want is smaller proportionately to the power of meeting it."[108] If wants were supplied by "some one else," however, "the power of meeting it by one's own effort" was "weakened," and the want became only greater. If man followed the former course, he would become "stronger, more independent, a more perfect being," according to Johnson. If he regularly repeated the latter, however he would inevitably become "a pauper, a parasite, as incapable of providing for himself as the insect parasite which has established itself in the body of its victim and has become a mere sac, its sole powers being those of absorbing nutriment prepared by the digestive functions of another creature and propagating its species."[109]

While the debate about charity and race thus retained liberal notions of the self-sufficient individual, it placed them within a social and racial context. As Daniel Bender has shown, self-sufficiency, independence, and resourcefulness were themselves conceptualized as racial traits that could be fostered and passed on to subsequent generations, contributing to the decline or uplift of the race.[110] In agrarian populist rhetoric, the self-sufficient farmer was imagined as descending from a common lineage of hardy, Anglo-Saxon peasants. National Farmer's Alliance lecturer Ashby contended that the "leading agricultural people of to-day" were "descendants of the 'fierce sea-robbers' of the fourth and fifth centuries," and belonged to "the great Germanic race, which has forged to the front in civilization and in all the avenues of progress and material advancement."[111] The progress of civilization had artificially robbed the farmer of his independence and his ability to rely "almost wholly upon the resources of himself and family." Through "changing industrial conditions" and increasing specialization, he had been pressed to "confine his efforts to the field of producing raw products for the market." This had made him into a different being. "The farmer of to-day," Ashby lamented, "is a dependent, linked in the industrial chain; a producer, simply—a manufacturer, if you please, of raw products, which are fashioned by other hands into their final forms for consumption."[112]

In debates about social insurance, philanthropy, and the welfare state, the damaging inbred effect of promoting dependency was fashioned into an argument against providing any form of financial or educational assistance to Black Americans. In 1896, Frederick Ludwig Hoffman, a statistician of the Prudential Insurance Company (who would also give a speech at the Race Betterment Conference held at Kellogg's Battle Creek Sanitarium) wrote a manifesto against welfare published by the American Economic Association, titled *Race Traits and Tendencies of the American Negro*.[113] In it, he portrayed "self-reliance in the Anglo-Saxon race" as the "result of the struggle of ages," as opposed to "easy conditions of life." The "colored population," by contrast, were "gradually parting with the virtues and the moderate degree of economic efficiency developed under the regime of slavery," leaving them increasingly dependent on the white race. To blame were the "easy conditions of life" and "a liberal charity" which permitted the "weak and incapable" to "increase and multiply." This "downward tendency of the colored race" could only be stopped if "the negro should sternly refuse every offer of direct interference in his own evolution," instead of "clamoring for aid and assistance from the white race."[114]

Kellogg was connected to these ideas through his growing interest in eugenics, his missionary work, and his fascination with Native peoples. While he condemned the extreme laissez-faire position advocated by Spencer (though only on the grounds of its immoral effect on the giver), he also insisted on the potential harm of promoting dependence and praised the spirit of self-help as the only path to permanent racial uplift.[115] "Indiscriminate Charity," he wrote in an article on City Medical Missions, "is without doubt highly demoralizing and reprehensible. It encourages shiftlessness and vagrancy."[116] The highest principle of missionary work for "helping dependent persons" was "to help them to help themselves." The incorporation of "Industrial Departments" in many of the missions supervised by Kellogg and the missionary branch of the Seventh-day Adventist Church worked to realize this principle. According to Kellogg, they served to "test the sincerity of those who apply for aid," and gave them the "opportunity to work in return for the assistance given them." Willpower and work, not convenient reliance on outside assistance, were the stimulus to financial and moral betterment.

In his studies of "American Aborigines," Kellogg emphasized self-help and independence as moral traits acquired through hard work and thoughtful reflection. In so doing, he reconciled his fascination with the habits of "primitive peoples" with his concern about racial degeneracy and his unshaken belief in the superiority of the civilized races. The reason the Quechan had been more successful than other tribes, in Kellogg's mind, was that they were "wholly independent of Government."[117] They had "owned and occupied" their lands "for generations." They were "self-sustaining," and lived "as they have done for ages." They received "no rations, or other means of support, from the Government, as do many other Indian tribes," and hence they were "wholly independent." This quality was endangered, not helped, by programs such as the feeding of children in schools. Children taken away from their tribe and their natural eating habits were not only prompted to develop unnatural tastes but contributed to their own decline by giving in to the easy pleasures of civilization.

While Kellogg thus lauded the intuitive rightness of certain culinary practices of independently living Native peoples, he also emphasized their alleged propensity to privilege easy comforts—itself a marker of barbarism according to Kellogg's logic. "As the savage builds his hut of those materials which he finds close at hand, or most accessible with little reference to their durability or stableness," Kellogg explained, "so he builds his body of those foods which are most easily procurable, or which he finds most convenient to his taste for which his appetite clamors, and which produce the most agreeable sensations while slipping by his palate, or momentarily detained in contact with his tongue."[118] Civilized man, by contrast, had learned to forgo convenience by exercising self-discipline, hard work, and study. It was knowledge of food and retraining of one's misguided senses that would lead to an overall improvement of diet. "One tenth of the time given to the study of dietetics which is given to the study of house building, selection of materials with reference to strength, durability, and adaptation to desired ends by most civilized men and women," Kellogg wrote, "would lead to a thorough revolution in prevailing customs and habits in relation to diet." There might have been an intuitive rightness in certain barbaric practices, Kellogg believed, but civilized man had learned to rationally guide his pleasures, tame and control his desires, and work productively with his appetite.

PEPTOGENIC FOODS

Kellogg translated his concerns over economic dependence and racial degeneration into a physiological philosophy of the appetite and a new set of health foods. Central to Kellogg's pivot, aside from his growing immersion in eugenics, was his frustration with enzyme products and the notion of dependence they seemed to embody. He became interested in a current of physiological research that sought to unravel the mechanism by which enzyme secretion was prompted in the first place. "What the stomach requires in cases of inactivity of the gastric glands is not a substitute for the normal product of these glands," he declared, "but an increase of the activity of the glands."[119] Rather than subsidizing the distorted stomach's unnatural cravings with "peptones, peptonoids, or pepsins," what was needed were "peptogens."

The notion of "peptogens" had its origin in physiological research on gastric stimulation. As the processes of digestion and the composition of digestive fluids became more and more disentangled, researchers had begun to examine the source of digestive enzyme secretion. Physiologists such as Moritz Schiff in Germany, Ernest Starling in Britain, and Ivan Pavlov in Russia had debated whether gastric secretion was perhaps stimulated by a mechanical irritation as the food entered the digestive tract, a nerval impulse, a chemical property of the food itself, psychologically, or through previously unrecognized communicating substances in the blood, later identified as hormones. Kellogg's own conception of peptogens and gastric stimulation was informed by this research. He studied the works of Schiff, Starling, and Pavlov and combined them with his own digestive experiments, a religious notion of divine immanence, and a philosophy of consumption.

As early as 1896, Kellogg referred to "peptogens" in his book *The Stomach*. "Certain properties and elements of the food," he contended, "serve to stimulate the action of the glands by which the digestive fluids are produced."[120] Among them were "gluten, albumen, and other proteid substances," as well as dextrin, all capable of stimulating "the glands of the stomach to produce gastric juice."[121] These were, of course, the products of different kinds of digestive processes; but whereas Kellogg had previously lauded them for their ability to counteract his patients' "partial starvation," he now emphasized their ability to stimulate the gastric organs to work. Kellogg also believed that there was a peptogenic power in the "natural flavors of foods." This, he believed, was quite distinct from the action of the classic "stimulants" in the Grahamite sense. Condiments, such as "mustard, pepper, pepper-sauce, and other substances," only "burn and sting as they go down the throat," Kellogg warned; they did "not stimulate the secretion of normal digestive fluid."

Kellogg strengthened these observations with experiments of his own. Using a stomach tube and chemical analysis (a method he had described in detail in his 1893 article on investigations of digestion), he compared the amount of gastric secretion after an ordinary test meal with that after different meals of supposedly peptogenic substances, such as dry water crackers or gluten. He found a significant increase in gastric secretion after the meals consisting of peptogens.[122] Kellogg also ventured to prove the physiological difference between true, naturally stimulating flavors, and the purely irritating "stimulants" such as mustard, pepper, or alcohol. He measured the gastric secretions in a "young man aged nineteen years" and other test subjects after a "usual test breakfast" and after the same breakfast, but with either brandy or claret added. The result was a drastically diminished activity of the gastric glands.[123]

While Kellogg thus studied the peptogenic effects of different food components, he also emphasized the importance of psychic influences on the secretion of gastric enzymes. In particular, he was impressed with Pavlov's experiments demonstrating the enormous importance of the anticipation and the taste of food for copious gastric secretion. Over the years, Kellogg and Pavlov had developed a professional friendship and mutual admiration (perhaps a little stronger on Kellogg's side).[124] The influence of Pavlov's concept of the appetite on Kellogg's thinking is most evident in Kellogg's 1915 chapter, "Eating for Health and Pleasure."[125] In it, Kellogg discussed at length "one of "Professor Pawlow's interesting experiments" which "proved that the amount and efficiency of the gastric juice depend very much upon the enjoyment of the food."[126] Pavlov had divided the esophagus of a dog and connected one part of it with a tube. "When the dog was fed," Kellogg recounted, "the food, instead of passing into the stomach, dropped out through the opening into a dish." Meanwhile, the dog "thought that he was having a good meal, and the gastric juice immediately began to form in the stomach and continued to pour out as long as he kept on eating and enjoying the food."

But this was not an invitation to simply eat what one wanted. Taste, the quintessential discerning faculty, a quality of judgment, was not an intuitive process but had to be learned and trained. The task was to convert one's perverted yearnings into a natural appetite, and this could only happen through education and discipline. A right balance had to be found, for example, between craving many different kinds of flavors, and developing a more focused palate. "A variety of foods is necessary to assist the appetite," Kellogg explained, but "simplicity" was equally "very important for good digestion."[127] The "natural appetite," in fact, was "easily satisfied with a small number of foods." At best, then, the appetite was an inner compass on the path to finding the right nutritious regimen, both qualitatively and quantitatively. If trained right, the appetite would "crave the right kind of food in the right quantities" and would incite the body to "make all the digestive juices needed for the digestion of food."[128] Eating for nutritiousness, digestibility, and pleasure mutually reinforced one another.

The Sanitarium system realized this notion of the healthy appetite as a useful and pleasurable technique acquired through training. Patients at the Sanitarium underwent an exhaustive battery of diagnostic tests that afforded ample opportunity for introspection and dietary learning. Tests included stool examinations and analyses of stomach fluid procured through a tube after a test meal. Kellogg also commanded patients to "make a careful study of [their] nutrition" and learn to carefully observe the rumblings and ruminations of their own stomachs.[129] Studying one's nutrition included measuring one's food intake as well as paying attention to one's likes and dislikes. "The patient is asked to eat what his appetite calls for," Kellogg conceded, but also had to take detailed notes "with reference to quantities and qualities of foodstuffs."[130] The data thus gathered by dietary introspection would result in the creation of a personalized and optimized dietary plan. By perfecting this exercise, patients could learn to restore their natural appetite and put it in service of their nutritional needs. The palate could "become a valuable mentor, even a reliable selector of the food."

The process of developing bodily self-knowledge was ultimately a religious experience through which the workings of the creator were intimately revealed. Kellogg's articulation of a philosophy of appetite coincided with, and was strongly guided by, his growing adherence to the religious doctrine of divine immanence, the idea that God's presence is revealed through the material world.[131] In *The Living Temple*, he interpreted the physiological workings of the body, and of digestion in particular, as evidence of the workings of an intelligent, guiding, controlling presence. "One cannot study the remarkable changes which the food undergoes in the digestive process," Kellogg remarked, "without being fully persuaded of the existence of a presiding intelligence which guides and controls each step of the process by which the commonest food stuffs, such as bread, fruits, and vegetables, are converted into the living, sentient, acting, thinking, substances of the human form divine."[132] In order to capture the precise mechanism by which the divine force acted on the material world, but was not equivalent to it, Kellogg devised a new meaning for the notion of *stimulus,* a term so crucial to the idea of peptogens and the appetite, and one that he had previously so powerfully condemned.[133] He equated the action of taste, peptogens and chewing on the secretion of digestive juices with the creative, stimulating, exciting power of the sun.[134] Sunlight stimulated proliferation and growth, but did not become materially embroiled in the processes of transformation. Similarly, appetite was an intelligent power that activated the desirous faculties of the body to consume wisely and process divine nourishing energy in a purposeful manner. "Appetite," Kellogg declared, was "nothing more than a disposition to draw upon nature's storehouse for a new supply of living substance." Learning to restore the natural appetite and practicing appetite-guided nutrition was thus a process of not only anatomical but spiritual regeneration and reinvigoration.

It was this conception of stimulus that was embedded and materialized in a new range of health foods developed by the Kelloggs referred to as 'peptogenic foods.' Among them was the Sanitarium's "Pure Grape Juice," which promised to possess peptogenic qualities and thereby increase "the capacity of the stomach for receiving and digesting other foods."[135] The two different meanings of stimulation appeared in the same sentence in the advertisement, which explained that physicians were always on the lookout for "unstimulating" substances that at the same time possessed the property of "stimulating the appetite." Another peptogenic product was "Pan-Peptogen," a "liquid dextrinized preparation which aids the formation of both acid and pepsin."[136] A 1902 advertisement of the product claimed that it was the result of a long search "for some reliable beneficial means of helping the worn-out and crippled human stomach to do the work required of it." It was "not in itself a digestive agent," but "enables the stomach to make the gastric juice necessary for the digestion of the food."[137]

Kellogg also rebranded existing Sanitarium food products as peptogenic foods and emphasized their stimulating qualities. Maltol, for example, a "liquid, predigested food," was advertised as containing Maltose, "a powerful peptogenic substance" that "stimulates the secretion of digestive fluids and so aids digestion."[138] Bromose, a fig-nut product, was described as both, "almost completely digested," and as "possessed of powerful peptogenic properties," thereby aiding "in the digestion of other foods."[139] Kellogg also emphasized the peptogenic properties of dry foods. One of the categories of foods in the Sanitarium Diet Lists was that of "Dry Diet," under which foods such as Granola and Bromose were listed. Granose, Kellogg explained, "stimulates the flow of saliva to a greater extent than any other food with which we are acquainted."[140] Another category grouped together the familiar group of "nitrogenous" foods; however, the description specified that the "nitrogenous elements of food are also peptogens; that is, they stimulate the secretion of gastric juice."

In articles, Kellogg reinterpreted the peptonized or predigested qualities of his foods, such as the "diastatic properties of malt," as peptogenic qualities.

In an editorial titled "Fat and Blood," he claimed to have conducted "experiments" with malt that had convinced him that "the valuable properties of malt extract are due to the peptogenic properties of the maltose and the dextrin which it contains."[141] In another editorial, he emphasized the role of dextrin, not as an end-product of starch digestion, and therefore a predigested food, but as a "powerful peptogen." Foods that contained this property included "browned rice and the toasted wheat flakes, well browned zwieback, and granose flakes or granose biscuits."[142]

Kellogg was not alone in making peptogenic foods and rebranding existing preparations according to the idea of peptogenic stimulation. Commercial products claiming to have a stimulating effect on digestive secretion flooded the market at the turn of the century. Reed & Carnrick's Peptenzyme boasted the addition of "*Osmogen* or *Embryo Ferments*," through the action of which "the different organs of digestion are strengthened and stimulated to greater activity."[143] Their Liquid Peptonoids promised to have a "marked influence in stimulating the digestive functions," and could therefore "be considered a Peptogen as well as an Assimilable Food."[144] Other products emphasized their good taste as a stimulation to gastric secretion. Proteinol, for instance, was advertised as possessing "sapidity" which ensured that the product was "taken with pleasure by the patient, stimulating the gustatory nerves, increasing the alimentary secretions, insuring the easy digestion and prompt assimilation of PROTEINOL."[145]

Still other products were based on newly articulated ideas about hormonal stimulation of the digestive process. Carnrick's Secretogen, for example, a preparation based on Bayliss and Starling's description of the hormone secretin, promised to be a "Natural Stimulus to the Outpouring of Digestive Secretions." Not only could it cause "the outpouring of the secretions already formed," according to a promotional brochure, but it was capable of bringing about "the formation of new enzyme material."[146] Hepptine was the name of a preparation that combined Pavlov's notion of a "natural gastric juice" (obtained from the living animal rather than through organ extracts from dead animals) with the principle of a stimulating substance produced by the gastric mucosa (clearly echoing the hormone *secretin*). It promised to consist of nothing but the "pure gastric juice of the living pig," while it acted "as an excito-secretory stimulant," by "increasing the gastric secretion" as opposed to "applying its digesting powers to the nourishment."[147] Even natural "vegetable" ferment products were reinterpreted as peptogenic. Johnson and Johnson claimed that their Papoid "stimulates natural digestion" in addition to providing digestive substitution of three glands. "It is far better to make the stomach do its own work," the advertisement declared.[148]

Educating oneself in the study of dietetics, developing appropriate tastes, and selecting proper foods, would accomplish the paradoxical goal of simultaneously leading patients back to a natural state, but also elevating them from their primal desires through adequate effort. The Kelloggs' peptogenic products provided the means by which such effort could be substituted and symbolized through acts of consumption. With their stimulating nutritional mechanism, the products encapsulated the principle of helping the stomach to do its own work, of inducing the digestive organs to produce appropriate digestive secretions proportional to, and targeted toward, the kinds and amounts of food eaten.

At the same time, the products offered relief from the hard work of rebooting the appetite and promised optimal digestion to Sanitarium patients. The Sanitarium supplied set categories of foods for particular types of conditions as well as individualized "diet lists" and even set menus. By means of these lists, Kellogg declared in an article on the Medical Dietetics in the Sanitarium, "the patient is given the opportunity to select of a large variety of foods which are adapted to his condition, without being obliged to study and ponder the question whether this or that is likely to agree with him."[149] In a rhetorical twist, Kellogg even condemned the same habit of dietary self-study that he so ardently encouraged elsewhere. The "habit of introspection or inquisitive peering almost incessantly into one's stomach," he declared, was "a most pernicious practice, the common prevalence of which among dyspeptics, is one of the greatest obstacles met with in the treatment of disease."[150] Consumer convenience, it seemed, trumped dietary discipline and discernment—at least among those white, affluent patients whom Kellogg and his staff considered "consumers."[151]

CONCLUSION

In 1914, leading eugenicists congregated in Battle Creek to attend a conference on Race Betterment organized by Kellogg. For five days, figures like biologist Charles Davenport, statistician Frederick Hoffman, home economist Annie Dewey, and librarian Melvin Dewey espoused their views on the relative importance of heredity and environment and worked out "constructive suggestions for race betterment."[152] Kellogg himself opened the event with a welcoming address and gave a lecture titled "Needed—A New Human Race."[153] In it, he argued that only by adherence to the laws of both "eugenics and euthenics" would humans be capable of escaping "the destructive influences which have exterminated other races of animals."[154] Whatever natural advantages heredity provided, all would be lost in an unnatural environment. It was imperative, Kellogg suggested, that "man" recognized the importance of preserving "the essential conditions of his primitive life."[155]

Implementing this renaissance of primitivity did not require sacrificing the achievements of civilization. "We need not return to savagery to be healthy," Kellogg suggested, "but we must see that the air we breathe is as clean as that which the savage breathes, that the food we eat is as wholesome and pure as the water we drink."[156] The health foods Kellogg created and exhibited at the Race Betterment conference exhibition simultaneously affirmed the role of the civilizing process in separating the refined from the barbarous races and condemned the perverse outgrowths of civilization as a straight path to debauchery and degeneration. On the one hand, Kellogg believed that the rapid decline of the race was "the natural result of perverted habits and the cultivation of abnormal appetites." On the other hand, he both idealized the simple diet of the "savage," and accused him of consuming foods for "which his appetite clamors."[157] This downward spiral could only be halted through a return to natural taste through hard work and introspection, and, somewhat paradoxically, through the consumption of more health food products. Kellogg's health foods were true wonder foods in that they promised to transcend their nutritional function and bridge the gap between primitivity and progress, between nature and artifice, and between the environmental and economic aspirations of eugenics and euthenics.

The Kelloggs' health foods were also tools to think with. They were immersed in scientific debates about the cause of gastric secretion, religious controversies about divine immanence, and economic feuds about the effects of charitable giving. Through his peptogenic foods, Kellogg articulated a new conception of 'stimulation' that departed from Grahamite notions of "overstimulation" and physiological ideas of digestive substitution. At the same time, peptogenic foods embodied broader cultural critiques of dependence, degeneration, and a number of "predigested" and "peptonized" intellectual, financial, and social practices. They crystalized Kellogg's nostalgia for a lost natural world with an ever more certain commitment to the course of civilization and race betterment. Kellogg's health foods, in other words, neither simply continued older reformist-nutritional ideas nor entirely opposed conventional scientific approaches to food. Instead, they appropriated Native knowledge and merged it with religious, eugenic, and nutritional scientific thought to suit changing economic and cultural pressures.

But the Kelloggs' naturally digested and peptogenic foods embodied not only a physiological and theological system of digestive disease but also a comprehensive consumer philosophy. Through a process of selecting, merging, and filtering religious, scientific and consumerist ideas, Kellogg articulated a notion of the appetite as a stimulus to the digestive process, which, if trained well, could provide direct sensual information about the suitability and palatability of a given food for the individual eater. He embedded this in a philosophy of consumption as a purposeful and rewarding vocation that required training, judgment, and autonomy. This philosophy came complete with a range of consumer products that successfully reconciled the problematic and promising aspects of consumption. They provided pleasure and convenience and simultaneously demanded the eater exercise self-control and follow the path to self-knowledge. This orientation toward consumer preferences displayed by Kellogg and his family would soon reach new heights in the marketing of another wonder food: yeast.

FIVE

The Brewer, the Baker, and the Health Food Maker

INTRODUCTION

The year 1919 was a big one for yeast.

In the first few months of the year, a number of research papers appeared that suggested yeast possessed promising nutritional properties.

It began in January, when physiological chemist Philip B. Hawk published not one but two articles on yeast with a number of colleagues. The first, titled "Baker's Yeast as Food for Man," examined the value of baker's yeast as a source of protein in the human diet.[1] It concluded that baker's yeast formed "a very satisfactory article of diet for man." The other, titled "Compressed Yeast as Food for the Growing Organism," also examined baker's yeast, but the focus was on yeast's content of "so-called accessory food substances or vitamines" and their importance in a "growth-producing diet."[2] Hawk and his colleagues fed rats a diet that was "inadequate for growth" because it lacked "water soluble B," and then added yeast to see if it improved the rats' growth rate. The addition of yeast, they observed, produced "an immediate gain in weight."

In April, four researchers from the Connecticut Agricultural Experiment Station and the Sheffield Laboratory for Physiological Chemistry at Yale University published a study on "The Nutritive Value of Yeast Protein" in the Journal of Biological Chemistry.[3] They, too, were interested in the nutritional properties of yeast, and cited the results obtained by Hawk and his colleagues. But instead of baker's yeast, they examined the effect of two forms of brewer's yeast on the growing capacity of rats. They reported that the rats had survived on a diet in which brewer's yeast was the sole source of protein and the "water-soluble vitamine."

Both research groups acknowledged that yeast had long been known for its "food properties," but credited the recent war for the "renewed emphasis" on the nutritious potential of yeast.[4] With its food shortages, the war had forced attention on the potential "dietary use of products entirely neglected in the past."[5] Yeast had received particular attention as a potential "emergency food for man." Brewer's yeast, according to the Connecticut and Yale researchers, was a "highly nitrogenous by-product of the fermentation industries," which, however, had been "largely wasted" until now. Since 1912, it had also been suspected as a source of vitamins, a term only coined that year to refer to previously undetected nutritious substances that were assumed to be essential to growth and life.[6] Yeast, in short, was a promising candidate for what might become an important food product.

Finally, in July, yeast was the star of an advertisement by the Fleischmann Company, a producer of baker's yeast.[7] Fleischmann's Yeast was the brand of baker's yeast used by Hawk and his colleagues in their experiments on humans and rats. The ad suggested that yeast's "value in breadmaking" was known to "every housewife," but few people had ever thought of it as "health maker." "It's that, too," the ad claimed, and insisted that physicians "all over the country" were "testifying as to its great medicinal value for such annoying complaints as pimples, blackheads, boils, carbuncles, constipation." It was "so simple to take," too; the cakes could be eaten "straight" or "in a 'Yeast cocktail,' dissolved in fruit juice," in the comfort of one's "own home." To learn more, readers were invited to order a booklet on "Fleischmann's Compressed Yeast and Good Health."

All around, it seemed, the feeling was that yeast, in the words of the Fleischmann's Yeast advertisement, was "a wonderful product."[8] In the coming years, the preoccupation with yeast would continue, but what started out as a seemingly uniform research endeavor around a single product in the 1910s had diverged along two very distinct paths by the 1940s. The first launched yeast as a health food marketed to affluent consumers in rich countries. The second turned yeast into a cheap dietary supplement targeted at poor people in the Global South. This chapter tells these two stories about yeast.

According to existing accounts of the first story, vitamins and a cunning advertisement campaign drawing on vitamin science played by far the most important role in yeast's transformation from a baking ingredient into the health food "Fleischmann's Yeast."[9] By the second decade of the twentieth century, vitamins gripped the imagination of scientists and the public alike.[10] Seeking to capitalize on the enthusiasm for vitamins, the Fleischmann

Company supposedly "commissioned" research into the healthful properties of yeast in order to find a new marketing strategy for its product after a decline in home baking had tanked yeast sales.[11] Drawing on this research, it then launched the "yeast for health campaign," one of the most successful campaigns in the history of advertising, persuading a generation of consumers to eat yeast for their health. Although the use of vitamin science and advertisements showcasing scientific expertise were undoubtedly important for the success of the campaign, the first part of this chapter argues that it was instead the use of new consumer-centric advertisement strategies that gave yeast its big break. Rather than just a cautionary tale of unscrupulous marketing or a triumphant story of scientific innovation commercialized, yeast's trajectory as a health food represents deeper changes in the relationship between nutrition science and commerce.

The research of 1919 was taken into a rather different direction by the inventors of "food yeast." Food yeast was a version of brewer's yeast championed by the British Colonial Office and the emerging international health community as a potential source of nourishment for poor people in the colonies. Specifically invented as a low-cost, high-protein, and vitamin-rich supplement, food yeast was envisioned as a cheap and targeted intervention into what was referred to as "tropical" or "colonial malnutrition."[12] At a time when international organizations such as the League of Nations and the Food and Agriculture Organization of the United Nations were increasingly concerned with nutrition, food yeast offered a practicable and scientific solution to a complex humanitarian and social problem. At the same time, British colonial administrators promoted yeast for its potential to modernize the empire by promoting colonial industry and ensuring the growing economic independence of the colonies.

These two diverging paths of yeast, the chapter argues, reflect two major trajectories of wonder foods in the twentieth century. On the one hand, wonder foods were more and more specialized luxury goods straddling the line between food and medicine, marketed to consumers with a relatively high lifestyle and access to an abundance of healthy food. On the other, wonder foods became important humanitarian technologies in the fight against malnutrition supplied to low-income countries by global health agencies, but also marketed by nutraceutical companies to untapped markets at the "bottom of the pyramid."[13] In unraveling the divided fate of yeast, the chapter seeks to locate twentieth-century wonder foods within the longer history of nutrition science, empire, and wonder foods.

Founded in 1868, the Fleischmann Company had a long history of emphasizing health and drawing on scientific expertise to promote their baker's yeast. Prior to the Yeast for Health campaign, the promotion of Fleischmann's Yeast was focused almost entirely on the merits of the bread it would produce. Advertisements stressed the wholesomeness and digestibility of bread that could be obtained from baking it with Fleischmann's Yeast, while tapping into the fashion for economic foods. Promotions of Fleischmann's Yeast in early recipe books and advertisements drew on the celebration of bread and bread making first performed by Sylvester Graham and other health food advocates. To Graham, yeast had been the preferable, "natural" alternative to chemical rising agents. Recipes for Graham bread multiplied in the aftermath of his teachings, and the name Fleischmann's Yeast secured a firm place in recipe collections.[14]

Since the initial marketing goal of the Fleischmann Company was to persuade women to swap homemade yeast for commercially produced, store-bought Fleischmann's compressed yeast cakes, mentions of the product in late nineteenth-century recipe collections emphasized the unreliability and dangers of home-made yeast, while advocating the convenience and safety of Fleischmann's. A late nineteenth-century recipe booklet, composed by writer and women's rights advocate Eleanor Kirk, showcased Fleischmann's Yeast as key to a reliably wholesome bread without the unnecessary and wasteful expenditure of energy required to make dependable yeast in the home. Good bread, in turn, was emphasized as central to a thrifty yet nourishing diet. A member of the Women's Work Association, Kirk was sensitive to both the demands placed on working women and the hardship of domestic labor; at the same time, she ascribed to a traditional view of women's role in supporting their husband's capacity for work by supplying healthy, economical meals. While Kirk's promotion of Fleischmann's Yeast was certainly a financially motivated endeavor for the self-supporting mother, it also conformed to Kirk's wider beliefs in minimizing unnecessary female labor within a traditionally gendered working economy.[15] By 1884, an article in *Good Housekeeping* noted that Fleischmann's Yeast had "nearly superseded home-made" yeast in the larger cities and towns.[16]

In the early decades of the twentieth century, the product's advertisers received new impulses from the teachings of chemist Wilbur Atwater and early domestic economists on the relative cheapness of bread in relation to its nourishing properties. Based on Atwater's calculations of nutrients provided in relation to a substance's quantity and price, Atwater considered bread a particularly economical foodstuff. Not only did it supply a high quantity of nourishing matter at relatively little cost, but there was "no refuse" in bread, meaning there was no indigestible substance, such as bone in meat, that had to be paid for but did not contribute to nourishment.[17] Advertisements for Fleischmann's Yeast emphasized this association of bread with wholesomeness and economy. "Good bread," a 1915 advertisement insisted, "is the most nourishing, most healthful and most economical food. It solves the problem of the high cost of living."[18]

The product also profited from the selective alliance between US businesses and the United States Department of Agriculture in the form of the 1906 Pure Food and Drug Act. The Act had restricted the circulation of adulterated foods and regulated food labeling.[19] Advertisements for Fleischmann's Yeast appeared in the mouthpiece of the National Association of State Food and Dairy Officials, the *American Food Journal*.[20] Though founded in opposition to chemist and pure food advocate Harvey Washington Wiley and his campaign for regulation, the journal quickly began to use food legislation in favor of food producers, for example by pitting honest, complying businesses against greedy, fraudulent, monopolizing manufacturers.[21] The Fleischmann's Yeast Company advertised heavily in the pages of the journal, pitching the product as a model of "Purity and Quality," guaranteeing "perfect bakings."[22]

With the start of World War I, Fleischmann's Yeast advertisements began to echo appeals to the importance of diet at the front and to patriotic food economy at home.[23] "To the support of our nation," one advertisement declared, "our organization as well as our product is pledged."[24] Another emphasized the "alertness" essential to soldiers at war, which according to the advertisement relied on "proper food, right living, and good training," and especially, "good wholesome bread." The same advertisement reminded those at home to "use bread economically. Do not waste it."[25] By the time the Yeast for Health campaign started, then, the company had a robust history of adjusting to important scientific, regulatory, and social developments concerning food, and using them to gain a larger share of the existing market for its product.

PHILIP B. HAWK AND SCIENCE POPULARIZATION

By the closing of the decade, however, the company was in difficulty. The great success of its earlier campaigns, which had largely convinced women and bakers to switch homemade yeast for Fleischmann's, now threatened to become its downfall. Home baking, even if commonly performed with Fleischmann's Yeast, was on the decline. A number of developments converged to exacerbate this trend. With the industrialization of the nineteenth century came a reorientation of life around towns and urban centers, away from rural homes and landed property. Urbanization meant larger numbers of people living in smaller spaces, such as apartments or boarding houses, which often did not have private, spacious kitchens, or any kitchens at all.[26] With the site of economic productivity shifting to factories and cities with longer commutes, eating also increasingly took place outside of the home.[27] For a rising middle class, public eating became an important site of public engagement.[28] The company therefore confronted the challenge of a shrinking market.

In response to these developments, the company's sales promotion department set out to "uncover new markets and stimulate new wants."[29] Crucial for this next phase of its advertising strategy was an article written by Philip B. Hawk in October 1917, two years before his research on yeast, protein, and vitamins discussed in the introduction. The article was titled "The Use of Baker's Yeast in Diseases of the Skin and of the Gastro-Intestinal Tract" and appeared in the *Journal of the American Medical Association*.[30] Together with three medical colleagues from the fields of dermatology and gastroenterology, Hawk reported on a series of cases of various ailments, including skin conditions and digestive disorders, which had been treated with Fleischmann's Yeast. The article played an important role in the Yeast for Health campaign and was quoted repeatedly in the earliest advertisements. Almost exclusively, these advertisements emphasized the health benefits of yeast, appeared in medical journals, and targeted the medical profession.[31]

According to some accounts, Hawk and his colleagues were acting directly at the request of the Fleischmann Company. In his history of the Fleischmann family, anthropologist Paul Christiaan Klieger stated that Hawk "was commissioned by Fleischmann to study the curative health values of baker's yeast," while science journalist Catherine Price in her history of vitamins argued that the company "turned to a professor of physiological chemistry at Jefferson Medical College in Philadelphia and asked him to study the health value of baker's yeast."[32] This version of events is corroborated by a 1921 article in *Advertising & Selling*, an advertising trade publication, which described the Yeast for Health campaign and Hawk's role in it. After the discovery of vitamins, the article claimed, the Fleischmann

Company "felt that because yeast was rich in vitamins, it might be possible that the product would prove of value in the treatment of various diseases," and "commissioned" Hawk to "make an investigation into the therapeutic value of compressed yeast."[33]

There is no direct evidence that Hawk was engaged in a formal way by the Fleischmann company, aside from these sources. Other accounts simply state that the campaign "was given a strong start" by Hawk's article, or that the company reprinted the article, together with other scientific material on yeast, in a booklet distributed to interested customers.[34] While it is difficult to determine the exact nature of the relationship between Hawk and the company, the word *commission* in this context might conjure up notions of biased or even corrupt science. But such an interpretation overlooks the existence of a much broader culture of collaboration between scientists and producers of consumer goods during this period.

Hawk was a respected member of the medical and scientific community, with all the accolades to prove it. His career began at the laboratory of physiological chemistry at Columbia University. From there, Hawk moved on to the Laboratory of Physiological Chemistry of the Department of Medicine at the University of Pennsylvania, and ultimately to the Laboratory of Physiological Chemistry of Jefferson Medical College, where he became professor of Physiological Chemistry and Toxicology. He was also a member of the American Society of Biological Chemists and of the American Physiological Society.

In their 1917 article, Hawk and his colleagues had acknowledged having used Fleischmann's Yeast in their trials. While pecuniary compensation or a direct commissioning of research may or may not have occurred, it is likely that the yeast was supplied, even offered, by the company. By the late nineteenth century, the custom of providing experimenting scientists with samples of products to be used in their work had become widespread. As scientific experiments relied more and more on reproducibility and control of laboratory equipment, it had become good practice to indicate not only the procedure of the experiment, but the precise composition and quantity of laboratory substances used. Companies, in turn, advertised their willingness to assist experimental science through free supply of samples in the pages of medical and pharmaceutical journals (chapter 3).

Physicians and pharmacists had also long been enlisted to evaluate products. The overseeing capacity of medical science over medical and food products was formalized in 1905 through the Council on Pharmacy and

Chemistry of the American Medical Association and the Bureau of Chemistry of the Department of Agriculture, the enforcing arm of the 1906 Pure Food and Drug Act. The Bureau of Chemistry examined and published the composition of proprietary foods and medical products. It was authorized to compel producers to change the composition or labeling of their products. The Council on Pharmacy and Chemistry, by contrast, controlled access to the advertising spaces in medical journals, most importantly the *Journal of the American Medical Association*. Access was granted only if a drug was responsibly advertised and deemed therapeutically beneficial.[35] Quickly, however, producers of proprietary foods and drugs turned this oversight into a promotional advantage and leveraged the authority of the Council and the Bureau as endorsements. Journals prided themselves on presenting only advertisements whose subject had received the Council's seal of approval; the *Texas Medical Journal* even drew attention to the carefully selected nature of their advertisers, all of which had been "endorsed by the Council of Pharmacy and Chemistry," in an editorial.[36] Among the products proudly displayed as an example of an "ethical and meritorious" preparation from a "reliable" house was Fleischmann's Yeast. "No junk here," the editorial concluded.

Hawk's examination of Fleischmann's Yeast in 1917 must be understood in this context. Given the established culture of product evaluation by medical professionals, it is likely that the yeast he used had been provided by the company. Hawk's competencies also made him a logical choice to examine the product, while his inclinations to participate in educational efforts of food consumers made him a likely candidate to say yes. His research focused on metabolism and nutrition, and his work on yeast followed logically from his interest in digestion. Yeast had been crucial to dispensing with a firmly held assumption about the distinction between so-called unorganized ferments (ferments that were not cells like pepsin or diastase) and organized ferments (cellular agents like bacteria or yeast).[37] In 1907, the Nobel Prize in Chemistry was awarded to Eduard Buchner who had isolated a substance he called *zymase*, a noncellular enzyme, from the yeast cell, demonstrating that the fermenting action of yeast was the result of this unorganized ferment, and not of the yeast cell itself.[38] The third edition of Hawk's popular textbook on physiological chemistry began with a summary of this important research.[39]

Hawk's concern with digestive enzymes was part of a broader interest in what happened to food inside the body. Together with colleagues, he had developed a method for measuring the so-called "physiological residue" of digestion—the amount and kind of stomach fluid that remained in the stomach after digestion of a test meal—using a new stomach tube.[40] The method served Hawk to calibrate ranges of normality in digestion, both with regard to the quantity and character of the digestive fluid and with regard to the presence of undigested food after certain periods of time.[41] Unlike previous tubes, the new tube could also be tolerated for longer. This allowed Hawk and his colleague to measure the stomach content at frequent intervals during digestion and thereby map *the entire cycle* of gastric digestion."[42] This "fractional method" was the basis upon which Hawk undertook an extensive study of foods' fate in the digestive tract.

Much of this research stemmed from a renewed anxiety about intestinal "stasis." With the growing influence of bacteriology and the germ theory of disease, older concerns about digestive efficiency merged with new apprehensions about the action of bacterial microorganisms during the digestive process. Improper digestion not only prevented the efficient uptake of nutrients but incited the formation of toxic by-products of bacterial "fermentation." The end result, many physicians believed, was a kind of inner poisoning or 'autointoxication.'[43] The concern with autointoxication reinvigorated physiologists' attempts to trace the digestibility of different foodstuffs and communicate their results to the digesting public. The results of Hawk's analysis of the secret life of foodstuffs inside the body were published in the *Ladies Home Journal* in the form of a series of thirteen articles between November 1916 and October 1918. The magazine devoted a generous amount of space to Hawk's lay-friendly explanations to question such as, "What Does the Stomach Say to Honey," or "Is Frozen Fish Easier or Harder to Digest than Fresh Fish." It also provided "a research fund" through which the investigations had been "made possible."[44]

Hawk was thus in the middle of conducting analyses about the digestibility of hard-boiled versus soft-boiled eggs for his popular articles when he embarked on the research that would lead to the publication of his 1917 article on the therapeutic use of yeast. The article marked a pivotal moment in the advertising of Fleischmann's Yeast, but not because of its emphasis on vitamins. In fact, the article does not mention vitamins. Instead, it referenced older as well as more recent traditions of employing yeast as a therapeutic agent. Yeast had long been used as an empiric remedy to treat skin conditions and digestive troubles, and Hawk added diabetes, anthrax, respiratory diseases, vaginitis, and general infections to the "long list of widely differing disorders."[45] This panacea-like use had turned physicians away from yeast in the nineteenth century, according to Hawk, until interest in yeast's remedial powers had been revived by a French physician in 1899. The physician had conducted clinical observations of yeast in the treatment of furunculosis, a skin condition, with satisfactory results.[46] Over the next decade, more studies on yeast's therapeutic potential had followed. But the majority of this research, Hawk lamented, had been conducted with brewer's yeast. Hawk's purpose for his 1917 study was to see if the results of his predecessors could be replicated using baker's yeast. He and his colleagues administered Fleischmann's Yeast to ninety-one patients with a range of different conditions, including furunculosis, acne, constipation, urethritis, and bronchitis. He also wished to examine the difference between live and dead yeast and ascertain the best mode of administration (with or without food).

On the one hand, this research on yeast was a logical extension of the work Hawk had already been doing on other foodstuffs. With his colleagues, he employed the fractional method and observed "the action of yeast in the stomach when given suspended in water, beef tea or orange juice, with meals or between meals" in healthy subjects.[47] The clinical investigations Hawk undertook, however, clearly exceeded his competencies as a physiological chemist, and were, on the whole, crudely conducted. Even contemporaries noted that the study was "poorly controlled" and consisted mostly in "observations."[48] There was no control group with similar conditions that had not received yeast. The total number of patients per condition ranged from seventeen in the case of furunculosis to three in the case of gastrointestinal catarrh and only one in some groups such as erythema, pruritus, and swollen glands. Patients received widely differing additional treatments and varying doses of yeast. Still, Hawk and his colleagues concluded that baker's yeast was "a useful remedy in the treatment of furunculosis, acne vulgarism, acne rosacea, constipation, and in certain other cutaneous and gastrointestinal conditions."[49]

Hawk's relationship to the marketing campaign of Fleischmann's yeast, then, was perhaps both more and less than a direct commission to produce convenient scientific results. On the whole, the trials with yeast align with his broader research program and engage with existing discussions waged in established scientific circles. But he also formed part of a culture characterized by an increasingly cozy relationship between scientists, producers of consumer goods, and the educational and promotional media that brought them into close proximity. The Fleischmann Company would utilize his research to secure new markets.

A significant difference between Fleischmann's Yeast and earlier wonder foods was the central role played by professional advertising companies. The initial stage of the Yeast for Health campaign was managed by Philadelphia-based advertising agency Donovan and Armstrong. It deliberately replicated medical and scientific practices. In particular, advertisements drew attention to the fact that it was Fleischmann's Yeast that had been used in experiments with baker's yeast. "Used in All Tests" proclaimed a typical advertisement in the *West Virginia Medical Journal* in October, 1918, and quoted the passage in which Hawk had declared his use of Fleischmann's.[50] By drawing physicians' attention to some of the questions pursued in the study, such as the comparative digestibility of living or dead yeast, the ads also suggested avenues for further experimentation.[51] Other ads emphasized the "scientific precision" that could be achieved in prescribing Fleischmann's Yeast, suggesting that its cake form would function as a helpful dosing aid.[52]

Early advertisements also propagated Hawk's favorable clinical results by displaying the names of treated conditions in their titles. Conditions were named exactly as they had appeared in the article (for example acne vulgaris, constipation, or gastro-intestinal catarrh), using the article as a source of inspiration for potential indications for the product, but also drawing physicians' attention to familiar medical matters they might be interested in. The headline "Rich in Vitamins" was only one of many slogans flagging a treatable condition, in this case "an improvement in the general physical condition of the patient quite unassociated with the improvement of the symptoms associated with the particular disease in question" (a quotation taken directly from Hawk's article).[53]

The same journals that featured advertisements of Fleischmann's Yeast also contained seemingly genuine discussions by physicians of the results of Hawk's findings. A 1918 article on constipation mentioned the use of compressed yeast "with marked success in the hands of Hawk and other physicians," while also debating other remedies, including proprietary preparations.[54] Another, in the same journal, mentioned the "strikingly good results" obtained by Hawk and colleagues from using yeast especially "in purulent skin conditions."[55] These writings were likely advertisements disguised as genuine articles: they appeared in identical form in several journals without indicating the pieces' original sources (as was the custom by then for reprinted original articles).[56] No author was named for these articles, but it is possible that they were written by R. E. Lee, a medical doctor whom the Fleischmann Company employed to handle the medical aspects of the yeast business. Throughout the first phase of the campaign, then, the agency took great care to display deference to scientific authority, mimic professional standards, and comply with the unspoken norms of the medical and scientific community.

In September 1919, the notorious J. Walter Thompson Company took over the advertisement of Fleischmann's Yeast. Initially, the agency continued the existing approach of showcasing medical and scientific authority and emphasizing medical conditions. While an increasing number of advertisements now addressed consumers directly, the agency took great care to stress the limits of the product's therapeutic competency. Ads reminded consumers that "Fleischmann's Yeast is a food not a medicine" and asked them to consult their physician in all cases of acute disease.[57] The agency also increasingly grouped all existing medical indications around vitamins. Because the precise mechanism through which vitamins contributed to health remained a matter of debate, the agency drew on familiar therapeutic mechanisms to concretize the illusive effect of vitamins. Advertisements portrayed yeast simultaneously as an essential constituent indispensable to a fully nutritious diet, a substitute for digestive activity relieving the taxed organism from unnecessary expenditure of digestive labor, and as a stimulant to digestive activity. Vitamins tied together a myriad of diverse known empirical effects of yeast into a single but multifaceted therapeutic mechanism.

But after the initial years of extolling the product's scientific virtues, consumer interest began to drop. An analysis for 1922 and 1923 found a decrease in sales between 19 and 27 percent compared to 1921.[58] In a 1924 report on the first years of the Yeast for Health campaign, employees of J. Walter Thompson's Department of Information and Records remarked that by the spring of 1923, it had already become "evident that the news value of this appeal [emphasizing specific ailments] had begun to weaken."[59] Unsolicited testimonials and consumer investigations had indicated that consumers had internalized the main messages and uses for yeast. "We could assume that its merits were generally known and accepted," remarked the report, "and instead of telling the reader everything about it, we could assume that he already knew a great deal." But the testimonials and investigations had also opened up the possibility of "a radically different approach," a move away from appeals to scientific studies and details of the products' physiological mechanisms. The strategy the agency hoped would salvage the product was to "bring intimate consumer evidence to bear in the advertising."

In order to execute this plan, the agency prepared for a prize contest that would solicit testimonials in the thousands. Prize contests as such were not a new idea; they had been popular advertising tools in the first two decades of the twentieth century to generate interest in a product, and above all, to increase sales. Fleischmann itself had already held such a contest in 1916, but it had been focused primarily on increasing sales by incentivizing consumers to purchase.[60] By 1920, such contests seemed on the way out, having been "worked to death," as one advertiser put it.[61] Instead, advertisers reinvented the essay contest as a strategy to "make the buyer sell the product or idea to himself."

The first Yeast for Health prize contest was structured along these lines. According to a retrospective analysis of the contest, its purpose was primarily to "create a lot of new interest and enthusiasm in Fleischmann's Yeast for Health—to get people talking about it, wondering whether it wouldn't be good for *them* too." The second objective was "to find out just *what* people had been eating Fleischmann's Yeast *for*."[62] Prior to the contest, the J. Walter Thompson agency had been gathering preliminary data on this question through a number of consumer investigations, mail questionnaires, and interviews with yeast dealers. Users, it turned out, had been using Fleischmann's Yeast for a variety of ailments, such as "pimples and boils, constipation, indigestion and stomach trouble, blood impurities, thinness, and general run down condition."[63] But the purpose of questionnaires was to confirm the success of advertisement copy and calibrate its target market. A contest, by contrast, would put the range of uses by consumers front and center.

On July 15, 1923, the first announcement of the contest appeared in all magazines and newspapers that had been carrying Fleischmann's Yeast advertisements previously.[64] Titled "The Greatest Health Contest Ever Held," the announcement promised $5,000 in prizes for the best three-hundred-word reports on "What Fleischmann's Yeast has done for you." The text of the announcement briefly recapped the main benefits of the product supposedly shown by science, but it went on to solicit the consumer's take. "Proved by science—popular with millions—we know that," boasted the announcement. "But we want to know *more*. We want to know just what it has done for *you*." Consumers were encouraged to tell "their own story in their own way."[65] Over twenty-five thousand users participated in the contest.

Following the contest, the agency conducted a thorough analysis of the contest itself and the essays submitted. The agency was particularly interested in learning about "all the ailments written about that do not come under consideration under the first 4 headings, namely constipation, skin

THE FLEISCHMANN COMPANY ANNOUNCES

The Greatest
Health Contest ever held

$5000.⁰⁰ in prizes

for the best 3oo-word reports on
What Fleischmann's Yeast has done for you ··

If you have ever eaten Fleisch-mann's Yeast for health, this contest is held for you!

Write the story of your experience—and win one of the 153 cash prizes, offered below. Everyone knows the health value of Fleischmann's Yeast. Millions of cakes are consumed daily.

And now we want a report from *everyone* whom Fleischmann's Yeast has benefited.

During the past six years the Fleischmann research laboratory, with the assistance of many of America's foremost scientists, has worked continually to discover all the facts

Skin trouble are the body's warning that something is wrong. Fleischmann's Yeast helps to correct these cause by keeping stomach and intestints in a natural, healthy state.

Constipation is an almost universal evil, and one of the most difficult to cure. Thousands have found that Fleischmann's Yeast overcomes constipation naturally and permanently.

about Yeast as an aid to better health. Today we know the familiar little yeast cake with the yellow label is a food with a unique power.

It "tones up" the whole system and builds strength and vigor.

It corrects skin and stomach disorders.

It offers a simple and effective way to overcome constipation—permanently and without the help of habit-forming cathartics.

Proved by science—popular with millions—we know that. But we want to know *more*.

We want to know just what it

has done for you. We want every man and every woman whom Fleischmann's Yeast has benefited prior to the first announcement of this contest to write us about it—telling their own story in their own way (employees of the Fleischmann Company alone excepted).

We believe this will be the greatest Health Contest ever held.

It begins today.

It closes August 15th.

A board of impartial judges will award the prizes for the most interesting and convincing reports; and the prize winners will be announced in this paper during September.

This announcement will not appear again. Write us for full details today.

People troubled with loss of appetite and energy, or faulty digestion, have found that these trouble disappear when they eat Fleischmann's Yeast regularly.

Win one of these 153 cash prizes—
First prize $1000 ·· Second prize $500 ·· Third prize $500
— 10 prizes of $100 each — 40 prizes of $25 each
—100 prizes of $10 each

FLEISCHMANN'S YEAST

This contest is open freely to all. Write us at once—we will send you free, and without any obligation on your part, the special folder giving full instructions, together with the sheet on which all contestants' letters must be written.
THE FLEISCHMANN COMPANY
P. O. Box 1251, City Hall Station
New York, N. Y.

FIGURE 19. Announcement for the Yeast for Health essay contest. *New York Tribune,* July 15, 1923.

---

trouble, stomach trouble, general run-down condition."[66] In the instruction to tabulate these ailments, a J. Walter Thompson agent asked his staff to note "that 'ailments' is not all inclusive and that 'uses' is a larger term, as some people used yeast for home brew, for making bread and so on." Agency staff were to keep an open mind about potential other uses previously not considered in the context of yeast. "If, in reading over the letters," the agent instructed," you find any other use of yeast which seems to be very interesting, will you please set aside those letters in a similar pile."

Many essay contestants, it turned out, had used yeast for reasons other than those suggested in previous advertisements for Fleischmann's Yeast. The existence of "supplementary uses," as one report put it, implied that users were not only imaginative but also willing to use yeast for several purposes at once. This indicated a promising strategy for broadening the market for yeast and at the same time committing users to more frequent and long-term use of the product than the limited pattern of consumption a purely medicinal product allowed.

Following the contest, the agency applied the lessons learned to a magazine advertising campaign that centered the consumer and moved away from specific medical indications. Information about Fleischmann's Yeast and its health benefits were reduced to a small column; the rest of the page was filled with users and their stories. Headlines emphasized that these were ordinary people, people every reader might have come across in their daily lives. "You know such people," "People you might know," or "They might be your neighbors," proclaimed the headlines of advertisements.[67] Photographs depicted exclusively white, middle- to upper-class men, women, and children, suggesting that only a particular group of people was meant to identify with the people in the photographs. Headlines such as "What everybody knows," "All around you people know this secret," "A story told by thousands," conveyed the sense of a shared community of users with special knowledge.[68] Together, the ads suggested that yeast was a product consumed by most (affluent, white) people most of the time, and not just by sick people for specific medical conditions.

"IT NEEDS MORE EMOTIONAL APPEAL"
—YEAST MARKETING, DISEASE,
AND SCIENTIFIC KNOWLEDGE

In November 1927, the J. Walter Thompson Company conducted a survey among a group of people who they felt used Fleischmann's Yeast insufficiently—educated people with a strong belief in science.[69] They chose readers of the *New York Times* and the *New York Herald-Tribune* to represent that group. One hundred and two people were asked to comment on the product and on the current advertisement strategy used to sell it. The result confirmed the poor opinions of this group toward the product. The company identified two main reasons for their skepticism, with implications for the marketing of the product more broadly. The first was a strong belief in the orthodox institutions of scientific medicine, paired with a distrust of "homeopathic" cures or home remedies. Lay expertise in the form of consumer testimonials, the agency judged, were therefore useless to convince this group. "The people interviewed," the report insisted, "constitute that part of the public least influenced by the reported experiences of satisfied customers. They constitute the part of the public most opposed to medical treatment at home, the part most susceptible of conviction through scientific data."[70]

The second reason was that they, quite simply, did not need the product. This, the agency reasoned, was partly a result of the first problem. Consumers had been taught so well to accept the sharp demarcation between credible medical practice and quackery that they saw no reason to consult anyone but a doctor, and consume nothing but medicine, in case of illness.[71] This was aggravated by the successful reframing of digestive disease around autotoxins, in which Fleischmann's Yeast had played a role, and from which it had benefitted initially. Thanks, in part, to aggressive advertising, constipation was now widely understood as a potentially grave illness requiring expert attention. People became "frightened at their condition" and rushed to take "strong purgatives" for "quick relief" precisely because they had learned to associate "intestinal stasis" with "intestinal toxesis." This understanding of constipation was at odds with how the agency had represented yeast to consumers. "Fresh Yeast, which we say works mildly, slowly, gently, does not seem to be a very useful remedy to a man who has a splitting headache and who thinks it is because his system is clogged with poisons," the report remarked dryly.

Luckily something could be done about both objections by "working along new and different lines."[72] Yeast, the report insisted, ought not to be lumped together with "homeopathic medicine," nor should it claim to be a medicine. The product, it became clear, would henceforth have to occupy a tight niche. It had to appeal to both science and consumer expertise; it had to be recognized as a health product and simultaneously deny any association with professional medicine. Advertisement copy had to reflect "what yeast for health *is* and *is not*," the report insisted. "Yeast *is* a corrective food. Yeast is not a medicine, whether prescribed at home or by the physician." If people needed a doctor, "let them go to the doctor by all means." The place of yeast, however, was "to prevent chronic conditions from developing and to combat conditions before they become dangerous."

With this new profile, yeast was in the market for a corresponding condition to treat. The need for taking the product (which consumers had indicated they didn't feel) had to match the particular market position agents hoped the product would occupy—adjacent to, but not congruent with, the medical market and the market for healthy eating. Advertising agents reasoned that the condition had to be harmless enough not to require medical treatment, but still distinct enough to provide grounds for intervention. The agency settled on creating a new definition of constipation. "As for the argument 'But I don't need it,'" explained the report, "the task here is to open the understanding of people generally to the fact that constipation is a word with a very wide meaning. It doesn't mean just bowel stoppage. It may mean lateness or incomplete elimination, and its signs and symbols are myriad— headache, dizziness, lassitude, 'blue spells,' coated tongue, loss of appetite."[73]

In order to thus broaden the meaning of constipation, agents suggested relying not only on framing the notion of constipation in a certain light to consumers but encouraging scientific theories that ran contrary to the auto-intoxication theory, and that promised to be most conducive to creating a broad market. "Fortunately for us," the authors of the report explained, "the poison idea is still only a hypothesis, a hypothesis supported by considerable evidence, it is true, but one still vigorously debated, and one challenged by very sane and competent investigators." These "sane and competent investigators" had espoused a view of digestion that considered digestive disease to be mostly a mechanical rather than a chemical pathophysiological process and emphasized the relationship between digestive troubles and "the psychic factor." This view was very favorable to the advertising goals of the company, in the eyes of the agents. "The mechanical explanation," they suggested, "makes it easier to take a wholesome view of the subject."[74]

The agency thus resolved to display "deference to the newer mechanical view," and include language to "emphasize food, not drugs, as the means of handling stasis," in their advertisements in medical journals.[75] Ads continued to feature consumer stories, but these were now focused almost entirely on nonphysical complaints. A writer from New York City, for example, had taken yeast for writer's block, triggered by meeting the subject of the biography he had been working on.[76] A woman from Long Beach, California, "became almost frantic" when her "health began to go back on" her because she could not delegate any of her work to others. According to the advertisements, constipation was to blame for these troubles. "At the root of all these ills," the ads declared, "generally lies an unhealthy condition of the intestinal tract. Fleischmann's Yeast corrects this condition."[77]

By 1928, advertisements were portraying trivial physical complaints and nonphysical symptoms as belonging under the broad umbrella of constipation: unpleasant breath, headaches, depression, lack of energy, bad skin, and indigestion. "Such Symptoms as these are warnings," proclaimed the title of one ad.[78] Irritability, not eating right, lashing out, were all just examples of "what constipation does to people," claimed another.[79] There was no escaping the condition. "We all come to it—sooner or later!" prophesied the ad. The logical consequence of this appeal was that yeast was a food for all.

This new "line of attack," the agency hoped, would bring users' quotidian worries and minor physical complaints firmly under the umbrella of constipation. It was crucial, the report suggested that, to "sympathize with the people in their ailments" and "enter into their unhappy experiences in an understanding way." Ads were to reassure consumers by validating their complaints, "saying that the symptoms are real, because they have a physical cause which can be got at and removed." The "skeleton" of the new tactic, as sketched out in the report, was to be:

> You have headaches.
> There is a physical cause—
> constipation.
> Science now meets constipation
> with a new technique—control of the dietary.
> Your remedy, proper eating—
> with yeast as an accessory food.[80]

By inserting such a "strong emotional element" into the campaign, the agency hoped, the market could be considerably broadened. "Sympathizing with people in their ills and urging them to do one little thing which would make life yield them the joy it ought to," the report concluded, "is calculated to break up inertia and bring in the ones who say 'I don't need it.'"[81]

By encouraging consumers to devise indications and picking and choosing scientific theories of disease that would suit their marketing purposes, the J. Walther Thompson company had turned the relationship between research and business, which had characterized most of the nineteenth century, on its head. Theories of health and disease were now increasingly adjusted to a product's prospective consumer markets rather than the other way around. Figuring out the consumer, in other words, came to take precedence over figuring out the product. While the J. Walther Thompson agency thus set in motion a number of developments that to this day characterize a particular kind of wonder food, a very different kind of product was taking shape in the British Empire and the emerging international health context.

THE INVENTION OF FOOD YEAST

The year was 1940, and the British Empire was in trouble.

The past decade had brought growing unrest in the colonial territories and mounting critiques of Britain's imperial management. A dramatic drop in the price of sugar had played an important role in catapulting these developments.[82] The consequences of Britain's mid-nineteenth-century imperial philosophy of colonial resource extraction now seemed to come back to haunt the imperial power. Imperial experts had fixated so much on the colonies as suppliers of raw materials to Britain's manufacturing interests that they had neglected the development of significant industries in the empire itself. Added to that was the emphasis on waste product optimization and agricultural efficiency that had led to overproduction and price drops, particularly in the sugar industry, by the 1920s.[83] After the Great Depression, sugar prices dropped even further, and fueled widespread protests in the major sugar-producing colonies.[84] Colonial unrest only fed existing critiques of British imperial governance articulated by voices in Germany, the United States, and the British colonies. Britain had to act if it was to save its empire.

Rather than bow to the growing tide of anti-imperialist sentiment, however, Britain dug in its heels. In 1940, Parliament enacted the Colonial Development and Welfare Act. As historian Sabine Clarke has argued in her study of Caribbean science and industrial development in the 1940s and 1950s, the Act was an attempt to modernize the empire and find long-term solutions for Britain's sugar problem. Attempting to open up ever new markets for sugar was a short-sighted strategy, in the eyes of imperial planners; a more promising course of action was to develop new uses for the by-products that could be made from sugar. In order to achieve this goal, the Colonial Office created the "Colonial Products Research Council," which began an extensive research program into possible new industrial products derived from colonial sugar.[85]

"Food yeast" was one such product. In contrast to brewer's or baker's yeast, which had been known and used for a long time, food yeast was cultivated specifically as a cheap source of nourishment and an efficient use of industrial waste in the first half of the twentieth century. Investigations into yeast as nourishment dated back to the nineteenth century, when brewing companies in Europe and the United States searched for ways to dispose of a chief by-product of the brewing process.[86] When chemical analyses of yeast identified it as a source of protein, it was used in animal feeding as a cheap substitute for other protein fodder.[87] The term "food yeast" had been coined by a subcommittee of the British Royal Society's Scientific Committee on Food Policy tasked with exploring the value of yeast in human nutrition.[88] The committee had thought it "helpful to coin a specific name" to signify a "special type of yeast which can be found in human nutrition" conforming to "a certain standard" in "appearance, taste, vitamin content and protein content."

Instrumental in the process of creating food yeast was Aage Christian Thaysen, a Danish microbiologist who worked at the Chemical Laboratories of the British Department for Scientific and Industrial Research. In selecting a yeast strain as the basis for food yeast, Thaysen was less concerned with the different nutritional properties of different strains. He was confident that yeast, on the whole, supplied sufficient amounts of protein and vitamins, and he cited the 1919 studies on brewer's yeast (mentioned in the introduction to this chapter) to support his belief.[89] What mattered, aside from palatability, was that the yeast type had to "give high yields and abundant crops, with the least expenditure of time and plant."[90] If yeast was to nourish "those sections of humanity who were least blessed with worldly riches," Thaysen reasoned, it was "essential" to make a food yeast "at the lowest possible price." This concern with cheap and plentiful production in places with abundant raw materials ultimately swayed Thaysen toward the yeast strain *Torula utilis*.

Torula utilis had been used in Germany during the First World War in an attempt to create cheap sources of protein as animal fodder from sugar and sulphate of ammonia.[91] Because of the shortage of sugar during the war, however, the manufacture of protein through Torula utilis had never been realized on a large scale. Using Torula utilis, Thaysen and his colleagues developed a process that accelerated yeast's rate of production.[92] Ordinary baker's yeast, though perfectly palatable, required a very long time to produce. It took eight to nine hours to grow during which time air had to be constantly pumped into the vats of yeast solution. Between batches of yeast, additional time was required for the cleaning and sterilizing of the vats. And a relatively large portion of yeast had to be reinvested into the production process on a continual basis. As a result, it was currently impossible "to produce more than two batches of yeast in 24 hours," Thaysen explained. On top of all that, baker's yeast was "a very unstable preparation" that "rapidly" underwent "decay" if it was not kept at sufficiently low temperatures. Baker's yeast, with its slow rate of production, was an expensive product, suitable for rich consumers buying from well-equipped grocery stores with excellent storage and refrigeration capacity. But it was entirely useless for feeding the masses of malnourished inhabitants of an empire at little cost and building an industry around a by-product.

Thaysen and his colleagues therefore embarked on a "fundamental study" to identify "ways and means for improvement in rate of output of yeast."[93] By studying the growth stages of Torula utilis and experimenting with different densities of yeast cells, they developed a process that made it possible to multiply yeast by a factor of 64 during a relatively short amount of time, compared to a mere "four-fold increase" in the production of baker's yeast during the same time. Instead of having to be interrupted after eight to nine hours, like baker's yeast, the growth process devised by Thaysen could be run continuously, so that more yeast could be produced while less time and labor was required for cleaning the vats in between batches. Because the growing solution was continuously replaced, there was also a reduced risk of infection, which prevented additional costs arising from unusable batches.

Thaysen proceeded to set up "a small pilot plant" at the research laboratories in Teddington, England, to test the new yeast for scale.[94] The plant was large enough to simulate industrial production and also "supply samples of food yeast for experiments in human and animal nutrition." It produced "some 100 to 150 lb. of food yeast" weekly, an amount that made Thaysen and his colleagues confident that their scheme was feasible. The yeast produced at Teddington was "a light straw-colored flaky powder" with "a pleasant nutty or meaty taste." Upon chemical examination, it yielded an impressive protein content of "between 40 and 45 per cent.," the "whole range of B vitamins in balanced proportions," as well as a number of other vitamins. Samples of food yeast were made available for nutritional experimentation. One study showed that the product was "most beneficial in the rearing of pigs"; another tested food yeast in human workers, with promising results.

The positive experiences at Teddington encouraged the Colonial Office to set up a commercial scale plant using funds from the Colonial Development and Welfare Act.[95] The choice of location was crucial. The food yeast project required "easy access to a cheap supply" of sugar or other carbohydrates. "Fortunately," Thaysen wrote, "the British Empire offered a choice of several such places." The "West Indies" and "India" had "molasses"; the "African continent" offered "maize and other grains"; the "Middle East" was abundant in "waste citrus fruit" and "carob beans"; and even "Canada and Newfoundland" were considered for their supply of "waste sulphite liquor from paper manufacture."[96] The choice fell on Jamaica. The Colonial Office set up a food yeast production facility in Frome, using the West Indies Sugar Company as manufacturing agents. Known as the Colonial Food Yeast Company, it produced ten thousand tons of food yeast per year.[97] Similar plants were expected for other parts of the Caribbean.[98] At the same time, the Indian Central Government decided to construct a food yeast plant in India, while the South African, Australian, and New Zealand governments also took "preliminary steps" to produce food yeast.[99] By the late 1940s, food yeast had emerged as a product of, and for, empire.

FOOD YEAST AND INTERNATIONAL HEALTH

Interest in food yeast came not only from the Colonial Office but also from the burgeoning field of international health. Established in 1923, the League of Nations Health Organization (LNHO) quickly turned to nutrition as one of its priorities by the 1930s. The widespread hunger and poverty after the Great Depression, a growing concern for the social determinants of health, a larger shift away from infectious and toward chronic illness, and scientific developments in vitamin research (the so-called "newer knowledge of nutrition") all contributed to cementing the LNHO's commitment to issues of food and diet.[100] Like other activities of the League, the nutrition work of the Health Organization was limited by strong national interests and the LNHO's ambivalent stance toward two different approaches to international health: a broad emphasis on social medicine and the social and economic factors determining health and disease, on the one hand, and a narrower focus on health statistics, microorganisms, biomedical technologies, and specific diseases.[101] At the same time, through its data collection work, the LNHO was instrumental in highlighting the issue of nutrition as an international and colonial problem.

In 1931, the LNHO appointed Irish physician and nutrition scientist Wallace R. Aykroyd as its first nutritionist.[102] Aykroyd had begun his career studying vitamin deficiencies in Newfoundland and then worked at the Lister Institute in London, which was renowned for its vitamin research. During his tenure as the League's nutritionist, Aykroyd copublished a report on the relationship between nutrition and public health, which highlighted the dietary deficiency diseases but also called out the relationship between nutrition, poverty, and the food supply.[103] The report was largely focused on European nations but also contained a short section on nutritional challenges in the colonies, where it reported widespread malnutrition.

In 1935, the LNHO appointed a "Mixed Committee" to investigate the "relation of nutrition to health, agriculture, and economic policy."[104] It was composed of representatives of the LNHO, the International Labor Organization, and the International Institute of Agriculture, including biochemist and champion of the "newer knowledge of nutrition" Elmer McCollum as well as Edward Mellanby, the secretary general of the British Medical Research Council. Once again focused on Europe, the committee highlighted the progress that had already been achieved in recognizing nutrition as an important determinant of health and a matter of national and economic importance. The final report contained sections on the relation of income and education to nutrition, on food prices, on agriculture, as well as food habits. Like Aykroyd's report on the relationship between public health and nutrition, the Mixed Committee report contained a chapter on "evidence of malnutrition in certain countries," including in the "colonial areas." It also contained a table ranking various "protective foods" according to their content of protein, minerals, and vitamins.[105] Yeast was included among "protective foods" or "those chiefly valuable for providing minerals, vitamins, and 'good' protein."

The LNHO's efforts on behalf of nutrition were closely intertwined with attempts of the British Colonial Office to manage the crisis in its colonies. Both League reports highlighted the need to investigate nutrition in the colonies. Accordingly, in 1937, the Assembly of the League of Nations tasked the Technical Commission on Nutrition to conduct a study of "the diet of the populations of Asia and of tropical countries generally."[106] To complete the task, the Technical Committee appointed a special committee under the direction of Edward Mellanby that also included Aykroyd. By now, Aykroyd was the director of the Nutrition Research Laboratories in Coonoor, India, illustrating the close institutional and personal ties between colonial science and international health during this period.[107] According to the special committee, the "diets of the vast majority of the populations of Eastern and tropical countries" were so "grossly deficient" that reaching Western standards was unrealistic. Instead, the special committee declared it necessary to "set up some attainable goal." While the special committee acknowledged that in general, "it should be the aim of nutrition policy to rely on natural" and "locally produced foodstuffs," it also conceded that "circumstances may . . . arise in which certain groups may benefit from the distribution of vitamins in pure and concentrated form," provided that such concentrates could be obtained "cheaply in large quantities."

Yeast fit this description. According to the subcommittee, it was "rich in nitrogenous elements and in the B group vitamins" and was therefore "of particular value in correcting deficiencies in the diets of tropical and Eastern peoples." The special committee therefore recommended that "methods by which yeast rich in water-soluble vitamins can be produced cheaply on a large scale in such countries should be investigated." For this purpose, and for other nutritional inquiries concerning specifically the diets of "such countries," the special committee proposed a close collaboration with Aykroyd's new place of work, the Coonoor laboratories. The laboratories, the special committee imagined, would "act as a centre of liaison" with the Technical Committee and also "between Far-Eastern countries."[108]

While food yeast was thus firmly rooted in early international health efforts as well as in British colonial policy and its attempt to rescue the empire, it was also embedded in anti-imperialist critiques of British colonial management. As James Vernon has shown, malnutrition in the colonies became a focal point of critique launched against colonial administration, and modern nutrition science became "an important means for imagining a modern and scientifically planned nationalist future for India."[109] The Coonoor laboratories played an important role in this vision. Aykroyd's predecessor at Coonoor had exposed the extent of malnutrition in India under colonial rule, and Aykroyd continued his work.[110] Given the ubiquity of malnutrition, Aykroyd believed, only a sophisticated nutritional science would deliver Indians from chronic hunger. The growing emphasis on nutrition resulted in the establishment of the Indian Food Department in 1942. Among the research the Department funded were a number of "consumer trials" with food yeast.

Interest in nutrition and food yeast also came from the newly established Food and Agricultural Organization of the United Nations (FAO). In 1943, representatives of the governments of forty-four nations had met in Hot Springs, Virginia, to declare their commitment to a permanent organization dedicated to food and agriculture and to outline the chief aims and principles of such an organization.[111] The ultimate goal of the organization, according to the final report of the conference, would be to achieve "freedom from want," one of the four freedoms defined by US president Franklin Roosevelt in his 1941 State of the Union address. Freedom from want required freedom from hunger, and this was to be achieved by dealing "with the various problems of food and agriculture, not in isolation, but together." Section 1 of the conference was dedicated specifically to issues of nutrition and diet. Delegates in this section felt that recent nutritional scientific insights had firmly established "the kind of diet which man requires for health," but that in many parts of the world, diets remained unsatisfactory. Accordingly, the principal tasks of the FAO would be, first, to "complete the picture" of global malnutrition "in dismal detail," and second, "to replace it with a brighter one."[112]

To achieve these goals, the FAO set out to continue the LNHO's work providing detailed accounts of the nutritional state of individual countries and to identify strategies for improving hunger worldwide. Crucial to this aim was the assumption that although diets varied widely across the world, a healthy diet differed little "in its fundamental composition" from country to country.[113] Comparable and measurable dietary components, including calories, macronutrients like proteins, fats, and carbohydrates, and micronutrients such as vitamins, would enable the FAO to implement its idea of an international nutrition program, in which existing dietary deficiency would be measured and translated into nutritional requirements.[114] The strategies imagined by the planners of FAO in 1943 included broad structural interventions such as education, agricultural reform, and the training of specialist personnel. But the nutrient-focused international program outlined at the conference also steered the organization toward narrower measures focused on the specific substitution of nutrient deficiencies through nutrient-dense products like "yeast, wheat germ, and rice polishings."[115] Though the report warned that the "indiscriminate distribution of synthetic vitamins is not to be recommended as a public-health procedure," it still recommended that the "possibility of producing dried yeast on a large scale in countries in which abundant supplies of sugarcane molasses, and other cheap sources of fermentable carbohydrates, are available" ought to "receive careful consideration."

Through their enthusiasm for food yeast, international organizations, the British Colonial Office, and local colonial administrations reimagined hunger and poverty in the colonies as a geographically and biochemically distinct condition best targeted with specific nutritional interventions. While the nutritional programs of the LNHO and the FAO had been articulated as broadly international schemes, a distinct approach soon crystallized around what the organizations referred to as "tropical countries," a term often used to mean the colonial territories of European imperial powers. As historian Michael Worboys has shown, the conception of "colonial malnutrition" emerged in the interwar period and captured a growing tendency by colonial administrators and international organizations to consider causes other than infectious diseases as reasons for economic underdevelopment in colonial and former colonial territories.[116] Already in 1936, the British Economic Advisory Council had appointed a special committee to conduct an investigation on "Nutrition in the Colonial Empire."[117] In its final report, the committee attempted to define the "general character of colonial dietaries." Colonial dietaries, the report stated, were largely vegetarian, with few animal products (and almost no milk), with a high proportion of caloric intake derived from carbohydrates. Often based on a single crop and insufficient in quantity, the colonial diet was above all low in proteins and vitamins. The result of this dietary pattern was a high prevalence of deficiency diseases like beriberi and pellagra, but also "a great deal of ill-health, lowered resistance to other diseases, and a general impairment of well-being and efficiency."[118] While the committee emphasized the degree to which "the problem of malnutrition" in the colonies was chiefly "a problem of economic development" and therefore required above all economic and largescale structural measures, it also suggested that in the interim, particularly affected groups might "benefit from the distribution of highly protective foodstuffs in concentrated form, provided that these can be obtained cheaply in large quantities."[119]

An instrumental figure in preparing the report was physiologist Benjamin S. Platt (1903–1969). Platt served as a nutrition advisor to the British Colonial Office and was later appointed to the Advisory Committee on Nutrition by the FAO. On recommendation of the Economic Advisory Council on Nutrition in the Colonial Empire, Platt carried out a number of nutritional surveys in the British Empire. In 1939, he led a nutritional investigation in Nyasaland (present-day Malawi), followed by an extensive survey of nutrition in the British West Indies from 1944 to 1945.[120] He documented the extent of malnutrition prevalent in each region and made specific recommendations for how to tackle the problem. Platt's approach to nutrition was by no means narrow to begin with; his work in East Africa, for example, had been "planned to include a study of the relationship of the state of health and food intake to resources—to agricultural production in particular—as well as to other aspects of social and economic life."[121] But by the time he issued his report on the British West Indies, he portrayed the problem largely as one of specific nutrient deficiencies best addressed through specific nutrient substitution. Platt himself credited his experience during the war with motivating his change in perspective.[122] As joint secretary of the Scientific Food Policy Committee of the British War Cabinet, he had been instrumental in drawing up a "scientific food policy" that relied, first and foremost, on the "determination of the population's needs for health in terms of the more important nutrients." These nutrient requirements could then be translated into food needs in accordance with the available foodstuff and distributed equally among the population.

Platt proposed a similar approach for the colonies. His report on the British West Indies was guided by the idea of the "scientific food policy" he had established during the war. In a number of tables, he evaluated available foodstuffs and dietaries of the local population and compared them with "the nutrient food values taken as an immediate objective" by the First FAO conference.[123] This method allowed him to list the exact shortages of particular nutrients, which "served as a starting-point for planning immediate measures for improvement." In another table, he demonstrated "how the gaps can be filled," for example by the use of "long extraction flour" that had been "ennobled" with iron, calcium salt, and food yeast. The use of food yeast, he suggested, would "provide a supplement to the whole B complex instead of certain subcomponents only." He also evaluated the cheapness of such measures, using the cost of food yeast as a baseline. The use of skimmed milk solids instead of food yeasts ranked next to food yeast in cheapness but was still seven times more expensive." Pulses were fifteen times and fresh beef thirty-two times more expensive than food yeast. Yeast-ennobled flour would also be cheaper than the enriched flour used recently in the United States in a campaign spearheaded by commercial bakers (including the Wonder Bread Company).[124]

Platt's conception of nutritional policy and the endorsements of research on food yeast in the colonies by the LNHO and the FAO might well have been music to the ears of the Colonial Products Research Council, which had been seeking to find a new outlet for colonial industrial waste products like molasses. Food yeast would allow the Colonial Office to be seen to develop scientific infrastructure in the colonies while doing something against hunger in their territories. Food yeast was also a much cheaper intervention into colonial dietaries than economic or agricultural reform. Finally, food yeast experimentation was an arm of the same cutting-edge research current that investigated penicillin and other microorganism-derived products on the one hand, and the newly discovered "micronutrients" on the other. Promoting food yeast research in the colonies therefore aligned with Britain's colonial agenda to modernize its empire.

To put this strategy into practice, food yeast trials were soon conducted in several locations in the empire. Together, international organizations, the British Colonial Office, and local administrations in the colonies reimagined colonial territories as "living laboratories" full of poorly nourished experimental subjects.[125] At the Coonoor laboratories, Aykroyd cultivated yeast grown on a molasses medium using the yeast strain developed and manufactured by Thaysen at Teddington for a series of animal experiments.[126] He investigated "Food Yeast as a Supplement to a 'Poor European' Human Diet." Conforming to a typical characteristic of the "colonial laboratory," research parameters were defined by European scientific rather than local standards; the experiments sought to understand the effect of "adding dried food yeast" to a diet "modelled upon the poor European wartime basic dietary."[127] A few "modifications" to "suit Indian conditions," however, were made. Aykroyd found that the addition of yeast accelerated the growth rate of rats more than the addition of other protein sources, such as meat, milk, or fish. Food yeast, it seemed, was not merely a convenient and cheaper substitute to other sources of protein, but a superior preparation. "The addition of food yeast," Aykroyd concluded, "greatly improves the nutritive value" of a largely cereal-based diet.

Food yeast was therefore quickly put to trial in human subjects, both in Britain and in the colonies. In Britain, researchers undertook studies among airmen, "subjects living in Cambridge," in children's homes, and schools.[128] In the colonies, trials were conducted mostly in prisons, lunatic asylums, and institutions for the chronically ill. Platt played a significant role in coordinating the trials and in ensuring the supply of food yeast from the Colonial Office. In Trinidad, Platt engaged a physician who experimented with food yeast on the residents of a leper settlement and found that it increased his patients' appetites.[129] In Nigeria, he collaborated with physician William

Hughes who conducted experiments with food yeast on prisoners and lunatic asylum patients.[130]

To the patients and inmates, the experiments must have been sufficiently traumatic to induce them to try and "evade" the regime, in Hughes's words, and to make Hughes employ "much personal supervision," "checking" and "special remission[s] for good behavior and cooperation." Hughes also reported that two prisoners made formal complaints, reporting stomach-ache and diarrhea. The fact that Hughes compared yeast by mouth to riboflavin injections and that he arranged for his experimental subjects to be "put into a small block by themselves" gives an indication of the valid reasons (besides physical symptoms) for which patients and inmates might have feared the experiments. There is no indication that any form of consent was sought from either group. As such, the experiments with food yeast must be added to the long history of unethical human experimentation documented by historians in the "colonial laboratory."

To Hughes, the experiments signified a strengthened association between signs of "colonial malnutrition," in particular skin lesions which had been observed in "jails and institutions" in East Africa, Malaya, Sierra Leone, and Nigeria, with vitamin B_2 (riboflavin) deficiency.[131] That yeast, which was known to be rich in riboflavin, improved the lesions, suggested to him that "riboflavine deficiency is the outstanding clinical manifestation of tropical malnutrition in Lagos." He also concluded that a supplement of nine grams of food yeast daily would eliminate riboflavin deficiency (he had experimented with various doses) and recommended that a supplement of ten grams of food yeast daily could be "incorporated in the diet" of the "local population," supposedly "without offending local prejudice and cooking customs." Hughes made this recommendation without having been able to "work out an exact correlation between the dietary deficiency and the incidence and severity of symptoms." He found that it was still possible to "get an approximate idea of the daily supplement necessary for the general population" from his results.

Hughes's slippage in describing the biomedical and economic causes and treatments of nutritional deficiencies in the text might give us an indication as to why he pronounced this general recommendation for food yeast despite inconclusive evidence. "The adverse circumstances which determine the incidence of deficiency symptoms in these cases were identified most commonly as poverty, wasting disease . . ., pregnancy, and lactation," he declared. "A dosis of two teaspoonfuls of yeast daily for adults and children," he immediately continued in the next sentence, "appears to be quite satisfactory." Such a dose, he believed, would "be sufficient to cover all but the most extreme cases of poverty." At only "about 1/4 d. a day," he concluded, a sufficient daily dose of food yeast was "well within the means of the poorest classes."[132]

In India, human trials with food yeast were sponsored by the recently created Food Department. From 1945 to 1946, the department devised a scheme to investigate the effect of "the routine feeding of food yeast" on children's "growth and health."[133] In a communication to the Indian Research Fund Association, the Food Department's chief technical advisor pointed out that one hundred children aged between eight and fourteen years were "available as subjects for experiments" at an orphanage in Delhi.[134] The children's dietary habits ("completely vegetarian") were particularly suited to the experiments. Researchers divided the children into two groups and gave between a quarter to a half ounce of food yeast to one group with their regular meals of dal, bread, or vegetables. The other group received no food yeast. The researchers then compared the height, weight, and general condition of the two groups. They found that those who had received yeast had gained more weight. It is unlikely that the children were asked for consent or even informed about the experiment. One researcher consulted on the experiments advised that it was "desirable that the children should not know that they were being given any supplements."[135]

Trials in orphanages were also carried out in Madras.[136] The wardens of the orphanages, who had administered the yeast, had found the dose of one quarter ounce to be "unacceptable to the children" and had opted for a smaller dose. No "gastric or other disturbances" occurred under this regimen, but the experimenters also did not detect any growth or weight gain in the children. They explained this by pointing to the extremely poor basic diet the children received on a daily basis, which supposedly contributed to "suppressing the beneficent effects of yeast." Still, the wardens of the institutions, and allegedly some of the children, felt that "the yeast was doing them good, by improving their appetite and giving them a sense of well-being."

Food yeast trials in India spanned the transition toward the post-independence period. The FAO continued to be influential in Indian food yeast trials, supplying both experts and food yeast for the experiments. In 1952, the FAO supplied yeast and experts to a series of "consumer trials" in Uttar Pradesh.[137] Unlike previous trials, investigators made efforts to inform and seek consent from study participants, in this case inhabitants of a small village and students at a midwifery and health school. While the trials at the school were discontinued when participants developed gastrointestinal symptoms, the experiments among village inhabitants were completed and seemed to show an increase in appetite and an overall "better feeling" but no measurable gain in weight. When asked if they would continue to take yeast after the trial, given the option, however, nearly all participants replied in the negative.

Food yeast's promise thus outweighed its lack of practical use and verifiable efficacy. Interest in food yeast continued to be expressed among international health and development agencies over the coming years, including by the newly formed World Health Organization.[138] While this interest never amounted to a fully-fledged program of supplementary feeding, it set international health and development agencies firmly on the path toward the constituent-centric, geographically specific approach to hunger managed through nutritional consumer technologies that dominated the field from the 1960s.[139] Despite an overwhelming commitment to the biomedical universality of nutritional constituents among nutrition researchers, the experiments and programs involving food yeast in colonial, national, and international health settings contributed to cementing a conception of "tropical malnutrition" that required (and allowed) a distinct experimental and therapeutic approach.

CONCLUSION

In 1919, it would have been difficult to foresee the great divergence that yeast would undergo by the mid-twentieth century. Nothing about the scientific discussion seeking to illuminate yeast's protein and vitamin content, its role in growth, health, and disease, foreshadowed the discrepancy in mission, market, and meaning that would have emerged between the different yeast products discussed in this chapter by the late 1940s. That the yeast of the 1910s morphed into two such distinct types of wonder foods only three decades later attests to the contingent forces that shaped their trajectory in the United States and the British Empire, and shows the perseverance of racial, economic, and imperial divisions between particular kinds of eaters.

The story of Fleischmann's Yeast illustrates a number of important developments that continue to characterize present-day dietary supplements and nutraceuticals targeted at affluent consumers. Just as the success of contemporary products like omega-3-fatty acid capsules or probiotic yogurts cannot simply be explained with the "discovery" of omega-3-fatty-acids or probiotic yogurt cultures, the success of Yeast for Health was not just a consequence of "discoveries" in vitamin biochemistry. Instead, yeast's birth as a health food was the product of a complex relationship between nutrition science, medicine, and nutrition marketing. Fleischmann's Yeast shows the growing authority of science over food, but also the strategies employed by businesses and advertisers to comply with, utilize, or entirely sidestep such authority.

The success of Yeast for Health, this chapter has argued, lay primarily in how the Fleischmann Company and its advertising agencies manufactured cultures of consumer expertise that centered user experience over expert authority. They also exploited scientific dissent to prominent scientific theories that fit poorly with their advertising strategy. Rather than serve as yet another example of a product marketed through the power of science, then, Fleischmann's Yeast marks precisely the historical moment in which businesses and advertisers perfected crucial strategies to oppose scientific expertise and encourage consumer perspectives.

The story of how Fleischmann's Yeast became a health food, then, is even less a story of crafting a nutritional food in the laboratory and subsequently propelling it into the world through educational and promotional efforts than the previous case studies. The story of how Fleischmann's Yeast for Health was made *is* the story of its marketing. Rather than determining its scientific merit, the physiological mechanisms through which it acted on the body became part of the marketing experiment.

Food Yeast, by contrast, was the ancestor of a very different kind of twenty-first century wonder food. It was the product of a set of specific pressures on the British Empire to respond to colonial unrest, develop and modernize the colonies, and find long-term solutions to the sugar problem. As such, it was a highly historically specific by-product of British colonial policy in the 1930s and 1940s. At the same time, however, it resonated with interwar international health aspirations to sever ties with colonial medicine and create a more holistic approach to international health that was sufficiently aware of the economic and social determinants of health.

In this context, the excitement around a product like food yeast— nutritionally rich and cheap to produce—unfolded its own peculiar momentum and contributed to steer broadly intended nutritional ambitions to combat hunger and poverty increasingly toward narrow technical solutions, targeting specific nutritional deficiencies with specific magic bullets. As such, the story of food yeast contributes to our understanding of the enduring entanglement of contemporary global health with nutraceuticals and the narrowly conceived conceptions of food and famine associated with them.

Conclusion

TRANSPARENT MAN ON MAN-MADE LAND

"A VITAL STORY of human progress."

In giant letters, this slogan appeared above the entrance to the Wonder Bread building at the Chicago World's Fair of 1934.[1] Inside the building, visitors found "the story of scientific bread-making" with "automatic weighing, measuring and mixing of the ingredients," machines for kneading the dough, ovens with automatically regulated heat, "endless belts" transporting the breads out of the ovens and to the "slicing machines" and automatic wrapping stations where they were cut to convenience and packaged in Wonder Bread's characteristic balloon-adorned, moisture-resistant paper. A Wonder Sandwich Terrace completed the exhibit, where visitors could enjoy one of the many sweet and savory creations made with scientifically baked bread.

Just outside the Wonder Bread building was "the largest fountain ever constructed," extending 670 feet and emitting sixty-eight thousand gallons of water per minute (enough to provide a city of one hundred thousand inhabitants with water).[2] The fountain was named after the fair's overall motto: "A Century of Progress." The fair celebrated the past one hundred years of US technological, scientific, and commercial achievement, highlighting advances in transportation, engineering, medicine, agriculture, as well as food. The Science Pavilion, the "heart" of the exhibit according to the official guide, featured displays of oil-drilling, mining, a periodic table of chemical elements, water purification, the principles of heredity, tropical diseases, and a model of the "floating laboratory" presented to the Sudan government on the Nile.[3] A giant clock in the "Great Hall of Science" showed advancing geological periods, emphasizing the inevitable marching on of time and the earth's material transformation. The building itself stood

FIGURE 20. Wonder Bread at the 1934 Chicago World's Fair. The Janet A. Ginsburg Chicago Tribune Collection, Michigan State University Libraries.

on "man-made land"—only a few years earlier, a stream had been running freely through the area, which had then been drained in a spectacular engineering feat to make room for the exhibit. Nothing, not even the elements, could stand in the way of progress and of "man's advancing control over the forces of nature."[4]

A number of displays highlighted the gains in knowledge about how the human body works. A "Transparent Man," a life-size model of human anatomy made visible through a skin of "transparent cellon," formed the "outstandingly spectacular" centerpiece of the Medical Section.[5] As the visitor moved around the six-foot-tall statue, each organ was illuminated in turn resulting in a "spectacle of singular dramatic power" to reveal "the organism that is inside every human body." Special attention was given to food chemistry and digestion in the form of a "giant talking and gesturing robot." At ten feet tall, with a "transparent digestive tract," it was the "dramatic feature of the exhibit of physiological chemistry."[6] The robot regularly gave lectures on the chemistry of food in a theater down the hall and showed "food passing through his own stomach and intestines, and being digested."[7]

An entire section of the Science Building was dedicated to "Scientific Commercial Exhibits."[8] The overarching theme of the exhibition, according to the guide book, was also the "dependence of industrial advancement upon the pure sciences," and so the ground floor of the Hall of Science featured an "extensive series" of exhibits by "scientific manufacturers."[9] The displays illuminated "the uses of products in cooking, fireproofing, and building," from new techniques in welding to the "irradiation of milk to increase its vitamin D content." Pride of place was given to a modern drug store, which featured "drugs and chemical products," including "foods for infants and special invalid foods."

Even though the architectural commission of the exhibition had claimed not to "hark back to antique times," the past played a central role. The fair contrasted a "primitive" Native past with an advanced, scientific, and industrialized US-American modernity.[10] A poster of the exhibition displayed a figure in Native headdress labeled "1833" behind a Greco-Roman depiction of Lady Progress adorned by an eagle crown with the words "I Will" written across her forehead next to the year of the exhibition, 1933.[11] US progress, the poster suggested, was tied to determination, control, and Western European culture. The American continent's original inhabitants and their culture were a thing of the past. The medicine exhibition contrasted modern medical science and technologies with a display of "the antics of an Indian medicine man, practicing his primitive medicine."[12] The US Government Building of the exhibition featured a display of "primitive aborigines living and working as they did centuries ago," to contrast with "the immense spectacle of material achievement" in "the progress of man himself."[13]

A thought experiment described in the guidebook encouraged visitors to briefly immerse themselves in the past in order to appreciate the present state of progress. "You live roughly," wearing "crude dress," eating "foods that must be indigenous to the territory in which you live," with only "primitive medicines" or the "crude knowledge of a restricted man of medicine" available to cure any illness, the guidebook suggested. By contrast, in the present, the thought experiment continued, you "dine on foods in their original freshness and flavor, but grown leagues distant, and choose your foods by the scales and charts of science for health and strength."[14] And the future would hold even more discoveries and inventions that would quickly supersede the present in scientific achievement and technical mastery.

So went the vision of the world fair. Like the story told about Elmer Cline, Wonder Bread, and the balloon race, this was a tale with only tenuous ties to reality, created to conjure up an origin story that obscured more than it revealed. The world fair's narrative of progress left out the violence, dispossession, and erasure of Native cultures that had enabled the country's formation and expansion across the continent. It obscured the Native knowledge that had informed important aspects of scientific progress, including the development of nutritional products. It failed to acknowledge the economic and ecological exploitation of people and places that had enabled the country's prosperity. And it was blind to the irony that it was precisely such narratives of progress and primitivity that had sustained the continued commitment to extraction and erasure.

. . .

Wonder drugs might be a faint dream of the past: panaceas, bezoars, and philosopher's stones were the stuff of medieval alchemy or early modern quackery. Even the wondrous modern antibiotics have met their appropriate dose of pragmatism in the age of multi-drug-resistant tuberculosis and hospital-acquired infections. The enthusiasm for ever new *wonder foods*, however, seems undampened. From vitamin pills and probiotic yogurts to protein shakes and fortified breakfast cereals, nutritional products that promise to improve our health have become an almost unavoidable presence in many people's lives. In rich as well as poor countries, they float across TV screens, garnish magazine pages, and crowd the shelves of supermarkets and homes.

The reach of such products is remarkable. Few people have ever looked at government-issued nutritional guidelines, but many have held a product in their hands that claimed to contribute in some way to better nutrition and a better life. In the United States, 77 percent of the population consumed dietary supplements in 2019, and the global nutraceutical market is predicted to reach seven hundred billion by 2027.[15] Global health campaigns against malnutrition but also against chronic illnesses regularly revolve around concentrated nutraceuticals like Plumpy'nut (a peanut-based paste used as an emergency treatment for severe malnutrition). Wonder foods have taken over not only our health food aisles and pharmacy shelves but also our nutritional culture, our therapeutic imagination, and our humanitarian impulses.

Without a doubt, nutrition is one of the most pressing and complex challenges we face today. Our current system of global food production is a leading cause of climate change, while our dietary preferences as well as our beliefs about what constitutes healthy nutrition have a huge impact on how food is produced and consumed. This in turn affects our climate. Malnutrition accounts for more deaths than any other health-related issue worldwide, and leading WHO experts have declared both under-nutrition and obesity a "world health crisis."[16]

The development of highly specialized and commercialized nutritional products is certainly a valid strategy to tackle specific nutritional challenges. The history of such products is full of persistent dreams to improve health, eliminate hunger, ensure a stable food supply, and transform the world. Important scientific insights and technological improvements that few of us would like to live without were created along the way. The development of meat extracts like Gail Borden's meat biscuit gave us the bouillon cube, which forms part of a longer history of food preservation techniques that contributed to stabilizing and diversifying our diets. Benger's Food played an important role in the development of parenteral nutrition, while digestive enzyme substitution is a vital treatment for digestive organ insufficiency in pancreatic cancer, cystic fibrosis, celiac disease, and other conditions in which insufficient enzymes are produced by the body. Kellogg's health foods form part of the history of vegetarian meat substitute products which, under certain conditions, have the potential to contribute to planetary health. Research associated with vitamin preparations such as Fleischmann's Yeast was instrumental in identifying major nutritional deficiency diseases such as scurvy, pellagra, beriberi, and rickets, as well as finding effective treatments for them. Nutrient-compact, vitamin-rich products similar to food yeast continue to be used in global health efforts for acute cases of malnutrition where no other nourishment is available. And who would want to live without sliced bread?

The products in this book were also productive of crucial scientific insights. We now have a more accurate grasp of the role of various food components—proteins, carbohydrates, fats, vitamins—in our diets than we did two hundred years ago, and we understand the diseases that can develop if our food is deficient in particular macro- or micronutrients over a longer period of time. We also have a fuller grasp of the physiology of digestion, the role of individual enzymes, and their interplay with one another. The mechanisms of gastric secretion—a mixture of nerve impulses incited by the taste and smell of food, mechanical distension of the stomach, chemical irritation, and hormonal stimulation—have been further unraveled since the early twentieth century. There's every reason to be appreciative of these insights.

The trouble is that wonder foods have grabbed our attention and resources to such an extent that we have allowed them to dominate our thinking about nutrition, limiting our possible relationships with food and restricting the kinds of nutritional solutions we are capable of imagining. Masquerading as scientific progress, wonder foods have pulled the nutrition sciences and our shared nutritional culture along a narrow path. The nutritional modernity they may have achieved for those able to access and afford them has come at the expense of those for whom they were never envisaged. The stories of wonder foods told in this book help us understand how this situation came to be. They explain how and why commercial products became a celebrated means of tackling nutritional issues. They invite us to consider wonder foods as the historically particular, context-dependent phenomena that they are, rather than a self-evident and therefore immutable nutritional modernity. Wonder foods, this book has argued, are the specific outcome of imperial, market-driven, extractivist, and white supremacist imperatives that came to dominate how Western powers grappled with food.

Over the period explored in this book, nutritional expertise was formalized and gained a high degree of importance. Whereas knowledge about food in previous centuries had mattered primarily in medical, military, and religious contexts, food became a key concern of modern statecraft, a prized object of global trade, and a central challenge of empire in the nineteenth century. While everyday food production and preparation continued to be performed by women and workers of color, formal nutritional expertise was increasingly removed from kitchens, from the authority of women, indigenous peoples, and people of color, and even, to an extent, from the purview of physicians and nurses. Instead, white male experts subjected food to new investigative approaches that prized experimentation, measurement, specificity, and the tangible appeal of experimental apparatus. These experts attempted to make food legible within the latest scientific theories and techniques, applied chemical, physiological, evolutionary, and eugenic reasoning to food and eating bodies, and moved from individual dietetic consultations to population-wide nutritional interventions.

As the nutrition sciences expanded their grasp on nutritional knowledge over the course of the nineteenth and twentieth centuries, they did so within decidedly commercial contexts and economic frameworks of thought. The rise of the economic as a central category to think with shaped scientific knowledge production in general, and nutritional knowledge production in particular. While food undoubtedly continued to be embedded in religion, culture, morality, and pleasure, economic reasoning guided researchers in articulating their research questions and answers and shaped the ways in which consumers were invited to relate to the food they ate. Knowledge of food mattered more and more to political economy, to imperial governance, to the creation of national and individual wealth, and to consumer societies. Networks of economic and nutritional expertise overlapped to enable a cross-pollination of nutritional and economic ways of knowing food. Food, within these expert circles, became seen as a commodity, a commercial opportunity, a means to engineer populations and environments and eat oneself to civilization and whiteness.

The ability to consider the economic and commercial dimensions of food was itself regarded as a sign of development. Processing raw materials into refined goods, appropriating foodstuffs from across the world, turning "wasted" resources into wealth, and developing sophisticated and varied palates to appreciate the acquired products all signaled an advanced state of civilization in the minds of experts. Wonder foods were inseparably linked to the emergence of evolutionary, eugenic, and other chronological narratives about food, natural resources, and eaters, which overtook place-centric food cosmologies. Natural histories of food production and consumption replaced natural theologies of nourishment. Food, its nourishing power and distribution across the globe, was no longer an indicator of divine wisdom, but an imperfect arrangement in need of redistribution and optimization. Food became, at once, an indicator of progress and a means of achieving it. But the creation of narratives of modernity, as the Chicago exhibition demonstrated, was always dependent on tales of contrast with a racialized other past.

Along with commercial and economic ways of thinking about food came new conceptions of *nutritional value*. The development of wonder foods was shaped by a capitalist ethos prizing growth, accumulation, surplus value, and returns on investment; it was therefore inextricably linked to the appropriation and systematic devaluation of natural resources, indigenous and female knowledge, and racially minoritized, economically dispossessed groups. Imperialism, racial capitalism, and resource extractivism were not merely background noise in an otherwise pristine scientific experiment. A central insight of this book is that imperialist, racist, and extractivist thinking permeated the very heart of nutritional scientific activity and shaped the nutritional mechanisms through which wonder foods were imagined to act on bodies. Wonder foods, in other words, were not merely commercial applications of nutritional scientific "discoveries" such as nutrients, food groups, digestive enzymes, and vitamins. Instead, the cultural impulse to create condensed nourishment, to extract and accumulate nutritional value, to economize digestive labor and maximize digestive efficiency, and to incentivize bodily function preceded, and shaped, scientific theories and technical achievements.

Wonder foods also created new possibilities of imagining and inhabiting the eating and digesting body. Through their materiality, visual cues, labels, and promotional lore, nutritional products conveyed economic metaphors and scientific concepts that continue to shape our relationships to food today. We can suspect our bodily compositions to be incomplete without the "recommended daily intake" of certain nutrients, and we might seek to improve our sleep, energy levels, immunity, and mental alertness through an extra dose of magnesium, vitamin C, or omega-3 fatty acids. We can deem our physiological functions insufficient or under-stimulated because we ate the wrong foods, or not enough of the right ones. And we are constantly reminded of our responsibility to keep well, while being offered the illusion of control over our own health. Producers of wonder foods have long known to harness this impulse to their own advantage. In order to sidestep formal expertise and external regulation, they have encouraged consumers to trust "alternative" forms of evaluation that center user-driven, experiential, testimonial, tacit, and sensorial ways of knowing good food. When it comes to nutrition, most of us still like to hear that we can trust our gut.

Wonder foods—miraculous, superlative, "more-than-foods"—are merely the most extreme manifestation of a much more profound shift in our relationship to *all* food. We parse every encounter with food—from broccoli to burgers—for its function, its value, its effect. We think of food in terms of its content of health-bringing, stimulating, energy-inducing potential—or its "junk." The economic turn has not only transformed the way we work, but the way we eat. Our nutritional culture is no longer primarily characterized by a quest for religious redemption but evolves around accumulation—of wealth, of function, of health, of energy, of productivity. Our nutritional culture has come to evolve centrally around products.

Understanding the history of wonder foods allows us to view our current relationship to food as neither inevitable nor immutable; we got here through a very specific and contingent historical path. It was a path that involved the racist-imperialist philosophies of nineteenth century food experts who pitted waste against efficiency and modernity against primitivity. It relied on evolutionary tales of development and the propensity to contrast, map, and chronicle foods and eaters. It was shaped by late nineteenth- and early twentieth-century aversions to civilization and anxieties about racial degeneration and economic regression. It was determined by late-colonial anxieties about the industrial self-sufficiency of imperial territories. It was a path informed by the increasingly close relationship between science and commerce.

While they might have dazzled with promises of brighter food futures, wonder foods have repeatedly failed to address the deeper challenges underlying poor nutrition. Nutrition is a powerful indicator of social inequality, and poor nutrition perpetuates social divides. Food insecurity is associated with lower nutrient intake and higher rates of obesity, while supermarkets with more nutritious food choices tend to be concentrated in comparably affluent neighborhoods. Meanwhile, nutraceuticals for undernutrition are welcomed by global health organizations and local governments as quick fixes to reduce disease prevalence rates, but this often comes at the expense of long-term investment in nutritious local foods, which, in turn, exacerbates the dependence of undernourished communities on nutritional supplements and international aid. There is every reason to remain hopeful about scientifically grounded, technologically innovative solutions to broad structural problems like nutrition. But, as with balloons and the gas needed to make them fly, beneath many a spectacular, colorful innovation often lies a tired story of mundane resource scarcity and the tragic banality of basic needs.

. . .

If the story of wonder foods is a contingent path, there are alternative ways forward. Having learned to think about food in a particular way, we can learn differently. Fortunately, a growing number of scholars in the nutrition sciences, in food studies, and in indigenous studies have already begun to show us how.

Within the nutrition sciences, the fixation on single food constituents and their effect on the body has long obscured other ways of studying food. A focus on distinct food components and their quantity as the seat of specific functions, augmentable by degree, continued to dominate nutritional thinking long after alternative approaches had been articulated. The compatibility of constituent-centric approaches with nineteenth-century imperial fantasies, economic trends, and quantitative-experimental scientific cultures partly explains their durability. The enthusiasm over vitamins and their role in deficiency diseases cemented the power of constituent-centric approaches in the twentieth century. This view was so compelling that while minimum requirements for nutrients and calories were defined by the 1940s, attempts to determine maximum daily doses of nutrients never gained the same momentum.[17] Hypervitaminoses continue to be underestimated and misdiagnosed, and regulation of supplements in the United States does not specify a maximum concentration of key ingredients, as long as the recommended daily dose is printed on the label.[18] And nutritional health in populations has long been studied as a relationship between individual consumption of certain nutrients and the prevalence of metabolic diseases.[19] Wonder foods have tempted us to configure nutritional value and agency around a narrow set of molecules according to a highly individualistic mold.

But nutritional thinking outside the molecular and individualistic box is slowly emerging. In the late 1980s, researchers began to consider what they call the food matrix, each food's "bulk" or physical surroundings within which nutrients are embedded. Initially a concern of food technologists interested in texture, the food matrix has also been shown to affect the nutritional properties of a food. Alterations of the matrix have been linked to changes in the so-called bio-availability of nutrients (the degree to which nutrients can be absorbed and used in the body), to their digestion in the gastrointestinal tract, and even to the degree of satiety felt after eating particular foods.[20] Researchers have also paid increasing attention to so-called nutrient-nutrient interactions, the effects that nutrients can have on one another.[21] For example, certain proteins can affect the function of iron, vitamin A, and vitamin D, while omega-3-fatty acids interact with vitamin E. A radically different approach to understanding nutrition has developed within microbiome research, which examines how changes in the microbial flora of the gut affect nutrition and the development of dietary disease.[22] This research connects concerns about the physiology of digestion and the content of food with the dynamic relationship between human bodies and their environment.[23] Rather than a unidirectional assessment of nutrients' effects, research on food and the eating body is moving steadily toward what historian and STS scholar Hannah Landecker has called a "biology of the in between."[24]

Not only the content of nutritional scientific research requires rethinking, but also the broader political frameworks enabling nutritional knowledge production and regulation. As Marion Nestle has shown, much of nutrition science continues to be sponsored by the food industry.[25] Food industry and agricultural interests shape official dietary guidelines, the apparent objective standards to which consumers are supposed to gear their eating.[26] In the United States, to this day there is no independent government agency dedicated to food outside of the fragmented oversight provided by the Food and Drug Administration, the United States Department of Agriculture, and the Federal Trade Commission, which all regulate different aspects of food. Historians Gabriel Rosenberg and Jan Dutkiewicz have recently called for the establishment of a 'Ministry of Food' in the United States.[27] Such an agency, they suggest, could "maintain a just, healthy, and sustainable food system" without being mired in the conflicts of interest governing existing regulatory bodies. Whether through a Ministry of Food or a comparable structure, putting political will behind the idea that matters of food and nutrition are vital concerns deserving serious consideration in themselves and not just as an afterthought of agricultural policy or corporate interests will be crucial to guaranteeing better nutritional research and better nutrition.

While independent research on the nutritional properties of foods and their effects on individuals and populations is important, it still operates within the same product-centric paradigm that shaped generations of wonder foods. A focus on unraveling the nutritional profile of particular foods tends to result either in recommendations aimed at individuals to eat more or less of a given food or attempts to hold food companies accountable for the impacts of their products. But even this often comes down to better nutrition only for those who can access and afford better food. Meanwhile, access to healthy food remains profoundly unequal, and the inequality maps onto racial and socioeconomic lines.[28] While new nutritional discoveries about individual foodstuffs will no doubt emerge, we might invest more in implementing the nutritional knowledge we already possess in a just and sustainable way.

The long history of nutritional research into food's nutritious content is paralleled by a long history of food activism primarily concerned with what's in our food. Food activists and food movements such as Slow Food at different times campaigned against chemical food additives, pesticides, antibiotics, and GMOs.[29] While issues of environmental sustainability have received some consideration within these (predominantly white) concerns, very little attention has been paid to the labor conditions under which foods are produced.[30] A product-centric nutritional consumer activism without concern for the welfare of those who produce food is a short-sighted exercise. The grievances raised by workers at the Kellogg company who went on strike between October and December 2021 attest to the stark disconnect between some companies' health claims about their products and their lack of commitment to their workers' well-being. When we talk about healthy food, we should absolutely talk about healthy consumption. But we should talk much more than we do about healthy production.

Taken to the extreme, a hyper-focused concern with nutritional products together with a fixation on nutritional "hacks" like wonder foods as preferred solutions to nutritional challenges can amount to a myopic, even self-centered relationship to food. Modern-day wonder foods like Soylent, a meal replacement product supposedly guaranteeing complete nutrition, are at the center of a transhumanism movement that seeks to enhance human capabilities through technological interventions. The tenets of this movement stay within the boundaries of a productivist neoliberalism. Soylent has been explicitly promoted as a tool to maximize productivity by minimizing time spent preparing, eating, and even enjoying food. Eating, for transhumanists and biohackers, is nothing but a nuisance, a distraction to be eliminated for greater output. The promise of productivity through nutrition is not entirely to be dismissed. Many of us surely would not object to gaining more alertness, energy, and vitality by simply changing our diets or taking the right supplements. The trouble is that so much of food discourse has come to equate "healthy nutrition" with foods and nutritional products that bring alertness, vitality, and productivity to the individual eater.

Substantially changing our relationship to food will require expanding our definitions of healthy nutrition and broadening our methods for gaining knowledge about food. Challenging transactional, proprietary, and epistemologically narrow approaches to food, advocates of indigenous food sovereignty have articulated a relationship to food grounded in community ownership that integrates traditional food knowledge, considers environmental sustainability, and seeks to eliminate food-related health inequities.[31] In her book *Braiding Sweetgrass*, mother, scientist, decorated professor, and enrolled member of the Citizen Potawatomi Nation Robin Wall Kimmerer proposes that we expand Western scientific approaches to food by cultivating a relationship of gratitude toward the natural world and remember the reciprocity that is at the basis of the ecological unity connecting humans and other living beings.[32] Reciprocity resides, for example, in the growth patterns of the so-called Three Sisters, the main agricultural products of many indigenous communities: corn, beans, and squash. These three crops are grown in close proximity and complement each other agriculturally, nutritionally, and culturally. Their growing patterns mutually benefit one another, their nutrients form a nutritionally balanced meal, and their colors and stories harmonize and resonate.

To Kimmerer, the generosity inherent in the Three Sisters and the natural world more broadly is "simultaneously a moral and a material imperative" in a world where the "well-being of one is linked to the well-being of all." While the earth's resources are generously given and wisely interconnected, they are also finite. The earth's generosity demands that we uphold our end of the "pact of mutual responsibility" by not seeking to possess, hoard, or squander her gifts. The forces described in this book have driven many of us to relate to and know food precisely through an impulse to extract, accumulate, and exploit. Perhaps it is time we stop chasing this particular hot air balloon and let it fade into the horizon.

ACKNOWLEDGMENTS

At the end of a decade of researching and writing this book, what remains most strongly in my mind is the generosity and kindness of my mentors and colleagues in the intellectual communities I was privileged to be a part of. They have shaped this book, and I owe them a debt of gratitude that cannot fully be accounted for in these pages.

Three places in particular have informed this book. At the History of Science Department at Harvard University, I found a generous and vibrant community of gracious and inspiring scholars who patiently guided my intellectual trajectory. My first debt of gratitude is to Allan Brandt, who has invested immeasurable amounts of knowledge, kindness, patience, and encouragement in this book and in my development as a scholar. Steven Shapin enriched my thinking on the history of food and knowledge through his incomparable intellect, boundless generosity, and delicious lunches. Sarah Richardson's intellectual rigor and thoughtfulness held my work up to a higher standard, for which I am deeply grateful. Emma Rothschild has enlarged my historical horizons through her vast knowledge of the history of economic life, and I am lucky to have profited from her mentorship. Janet Browne also supported this book at the dissertation prospectus stage and provided valuable feedback on my work. My scholarship has been profoundly influenced by Jeremy Greene, my first advisor at Harvard, whose infinite knowledge, inspired scholarship, and dedication to the field of history of medicine continue to amaze me. I am also grateful to David Jones for his valuable support and mentorship, and his kind interest in my work; the generals field in the history of medicine I read with him and Jeremy has been an important source of inspiration for this book. I am lucky to have been mentored by Charles Rosenberg, whose scholarship was one of the reasons I entered the field of history of medicine. He provided valuable advice on this project. Sophia Roosth is an exceptionally generous scholar whose work formed and stretched my thinking. I am privileged to have benefitted from her vast cross-disciplinary knowledge and her insightful reading of my work. Katharine

Park, whose scholarship had a profound effect on me when I first entered the field, commented on early iterations of this project. I am also grateful to Shigehisa Kuriyama, whose scholarship and creativity have been transformative forces in my career, and who kindly provided comments on this project at the dissertation prospectus stage. Stephanie Dick, whose generosity and collegiality have few parallels, provided valuable feedback on my writing numerous times, including when she was in the middle of moving house. Toward the end of my time at Harvard, I was privileged to meet Gabriela Soto-Laveaga, Victor Seow, Hannah Marcus, and Evan Hepler-Smith who also took a kind interest in my work and offered thoughtful suggestions. This book would not exist without the graduate student community at Harvard. My colleagues Leena Akhtar, Cara Fallon, Paolo Savoia, Laura Lee Schmidt, Kristen Friedman, Anouska Bhattacharya, Colleen Lanier-Christensen, Hannah Conway, Allyssa Metzger, Yvan Prkachin, He Bian, Joelle Abi-Rached, Deirdre Moore, Yan Liu, James Bergman, Wythe Marschall, Miriam Rich, Alyssa Botelho, Jacob Moses, Kit Heintzman, as well as Lan Li and Lucas Mueller (who I hope will forgive me for lumping them in with the Harvard crowd) challenged my thinking and provided support and community. I am deeply grateful to them. I had the privilege of working with outstanding students during my time at Harvard, some of whom have become colleagues. They have inspired my work and helped me become a better teacher and scholar. I am particularly grateful to Daniel Gross, Nicole Bassoff, Alona Bach, Jessica Barzilay, Qing Qing Miao, Sean Kinyon, and Sufia Mehmood. I also thank Elizabeth Lunbeck, Linda Schneider, Allie Belser, Deborah Valdovinos, and Sarah Champlin-Scharff for their untiring efforts to create department community and to support graduate students in the program.

This book also owes its existence in no small part to the food studies community of the Culinaria Research Centre at the University of Toronto, where I spent some of my happiest and intellectually formative years. Words are inadequate to do justice to the intellectual generosity, dedication to mentorship, and culinary skills of my postdoc mentor Daniel Bender. I am deeply grateful to him, not only for how he supported me and this book, but also for his dedication to the field of food studies in general, particularly to its early career scholars. During one of the most crucial stages of development of this book, my Culinaria colleagues Jo Sharma, Jeffrey Pilcher, Donna Gabaccia, Ken MacDonald, Josée Johnston, Shyon Baumann, Kathy Burke, Valeria Mantilla-Morales, Koby Song-Nichols, Janita Van Dyk, Sarah Elton, Joel Dickau, Rick Halpern, Béatrice Lego, and Kelsey Kilgore lent their generous intellects and warm support to this project and to my professional development. I am also grateful to the History of Science Community at the University of Toronto, especially to Rebecca Woods, Marga Vicedo, and Mark Solovey, for their kind engagement with my work and for the community they provided at the department. I found a supportive and inspiring community in my Gastronomica colleagues Daniel Bender, Jessica Carbone, Simone Cinotto, James

Farrer, Melissa Fuster, Paula J. Johnson, Josée Johnston, Eric C. Rath, Krishnendu Ray, Jaclyn Rohel, Signe Rousseau, Amy Trubek, Robert Valgenti, and Helen Zoe Veit. Their creativity and expertise shaped this book in no small measure.

The final stages of this book were completed at the University of Zurich. I am deeply grateful for the support and intellectual community I have found here in Switzerland. Flurin Condrau has been an inspiring interlocutor and generous mentor. I am very grateful to my colleagues Yvan Prkachin, Sebastian Fonseca, Leander Diener, Manuel Merkofer, Sarah Scheidmantel, Julia Engelschalt, Beat Bächi, Martina Sochin-Delia, Ryan Whitacre, Gudrun Kling, and Raphael Christen for their support and community.

Beyond these places, this book was informed by the generosity and knowledge of the broader scholarly communities in the histories of science, medicine, food studies, and beyond. A number of generous individuals read parts of the book in progress and provided valuable advice in conversations. My profound thanks go to Lan Li, Gyorgy Scrinis, and Krishnendu Ray for their deep engagement with this project at various stages of its development. I am also grateful to Janina Wellmann, Carin Berkowitz, Justin Rivest, Roksana Filipowska, Andreas Weber, Elena Conis, Donna Bilak, Roger Eardley-Pryor, Eli Anders, Julia Cummiskey, Tripp Rebrovick, Robert Aronowitz, Projit Mukherjee, Heidi Voskuhl, Benjamin Cohen, Anna Zeide, Mookie Kideckel, Sally Sheard, Lucas Richert, Susan Lederer, Walter Johnson, Naomi Rogers, and Rakesh Khurana for their kind input on my work. My profound thanks go to the members of the writing group on food at the Radcliffe Institute of Advanced Study organized by Julie Guthman, which brought together a formidable cast of my intellectual heroes, including Alexander Blanchette, Susanne Freidberg, Wythe Marschall, and Allison-Marie Loconto. Many of the better ideas in this book are probably owed to their thoughtful engagement with my work.

Parts of the book in progress were discussed at colloquia, including at the School of Pharmacy at the University of Wisconsin–Madison, the STS Department at Tufts University, the Department of Social Studies of Medicine at McGill University, the Culinaria Research Centre at the University of Toronto, the History of Science Department at the University of Toronto, the STS Program at Harvard University, and the History of Medicine Working Group at Harvard University. I also presented early drafts of chapters at conferences and received valuable feedback, including at the American Association for the History of Medicine, the History of Science Society, the European Association for the History of Medicine and Health, the Society for the Social History of Medicine, the British Society for the History of Science, the Joint Atlantic Seminar for the History of Medicine, the American Society for Environmental History, the Oxford Symposium on Food and Cookery, the Amsterdam Symposium on the History of Food, and the Graduate Association for Food Studies.

This book is severely indebted to the expertise of librarians and archivists at the Dolph Briscoe Center for American History at the University of Texas, the Manchester Museum of Science and Industry, the Foyle Special Collections Library at King's College London, the Daughters of the Republic of Texas Library, the John W. Hartman Center for Sales, Advertising & Marketing History at Duke University, the Bentley Historical Library at the University of Michigan, the Michigan State University Archives and Historical Collections, the Medical Historical Library at the College of Physicians, and the National Archives of India. I am particularly grateful to Joshua Larkin Rowley, Beth Lander, Jan Hicks, Adam Ray, and Jennie Russell. There is a special place in heaven reserved for people like Robbie Danielson at the B.L. Fisher Library, Asbury Theological Seminary, Wilmore, Kentucky, who found a particularly hard-to-locate but very important source and emailed it to me—free of charge. I am also thankful to the library and archive staff who supplied me with digitized photographs for the book, especially as they did so under extremely difficult circumstances during a pandemic.

The research for this project was generously supported by a John Furr Fellowship at the Hartman Center for Sales, Advertising and Marketing History at the David M. Rubenstein Rare Book & Manuscript Library at Duke University, a Radcliffe Institute for Advanced Study Graduate Student Fellowship, a Chemical Heritage Foundation (Science History Institute) Haas Dissertation Fellowship, a Harvard GSAS Pre-Dissertation Fellowship, and a Harvard University Presidential Scholarship.

The writing of this book profited in no small measure from the Firefly Creative Writing community in Toronto, in particular the expertise of Britt Smith and the participants of a multi-week intensive writing course in which I was fortunate to workshop sections of this book. I am also deeply indebted to Megan Pugh, who provided invaluable developmental editing services for this project. I am in awe of her deep knowledge, clarity, and creativity.

I am profoundly grateful to my editor at the University of California Press, Kate Marshall, for her faith in my project and for her expert guidance through the daunting process of publishing an academic monograph as a first-time author. I also thank Enrique Ochoa-Kaup for his invaluable support throughout the publishing process. My series editor, Darra Goldstein, gave valuable suggestions that greatly improved the book. I was extremely lucky to benefit from the expertise and thoughtfulness of what might well have been the two most generous peer reviewers in the history of peer review. Their insight, care, and humor, during a pandemic no less, have shaped the manuscript into an infinitely superior document from when it was first submitted. I am also deeply grateful to the anonymous faculty reader for their generous reading of my work and for providing valuable additional suggestions. My colleague and friend Yvan Prkachin helped me navigate the thicket of permission forms and copyright clauses and assisted me in no small measure in locating images for the book. Glynnis Koike designed the cover of my dreams. My frighteningly talented and infinitely generous friend Bircan Tulga at Black Edge Productions donated his time and expertise to supply the author photo.

My friends have carried me through the challenging and transformative process of writing this book. A long and unshaking friendship connects me to my dear friend Connie Leupold who has been a rock throughout this process. There is no one I would have rather wrestled the trolls of medical school, grad school, and life in general with. I am moved, inspired, and filled with gratitude by the unwavering friendship of Nele, Christine, Suzan, Anthony, Camille, Chris, Anya, Sophie, Bircan, Sharon, Jason, Ilaria, and Alek. I am eternally grateful to them for their support, their kindness, and their patience, and for not letting something as trivial as an ocean come between our friendship. My dear friend and intellectual role model Meg Luxton was an invaluable companion and intellectual interlocutor during one of the most crucial stages of working on this book. She read the entire manuscript front to back at the draft stage and provided thoughtful comments and much needed encouragement, not to mention stimulating conversation and delicious food. Few influences on my work and life have been as profound as that of my brilliant friend, colleague, mentor, kindred spirit, and coconspirator in all things medicine and history, Kate Womersley. Conversations with Kate are an intellectual feast, and one of my greatest sources of inspiration. Over the years, Kate has repeatedly lent her sharp intellect, creative capacity, exceptional editorial skills, and overall brilliance to my work, and has made me a better writer, thinker, and person as a result of it. In the final stages of this project, she read nearly every word of the manuscript at incredible speed and provided generous, thoughtful, and thoroughly helpful comments. I am also deeply grateful to Lukas Engelmann for his friendship and mentorship during the years, and for his thoughtful and generous engagement with my work. This book would not exist without the support of this my extended family.

Finally, my family, to whom I dedicate this book. My brother Johannes is my dearest friend, my most faithful cheerleader, and my greatest role model. His boundless energy, creativity, joy, and genius inspire me every day. This book simply would not have seen the light without his unwavering faith in his sister. My beloved parents, Ingrid and Gotthard, are my anchor and my rock. Their unconditional love has carried me through life and is the source of all my achievements. They inspire me through their zest for life, their courage, and the unflinching dedication with which they constantly rediscover themselves and the world around them. They gave me roots and wings. I carry them in my heart wherever I am.

NOTES

INTRODUCTION

1. "Six Huge Gas Bags Fly the Skies for Prize Cup," *Indianapolis Star*, June 6, 1909.

2. Carl Hunt, "Making Consumers out of Competing Housewives: An Interview with E. L. Cline," *Printer's Ink* 87, no. 6 (May 14, 1914): 17–24.

3. "Lining Up the Salesmen," *Associated Advertising* 6 (1915): 66–67; Hunt, "Making Consumers out of Competing Housewives."

4. I. L. Miller, "Enforcement of the Indiana Bread Law," in *Weights and Measures Seventeenth Annual Conference*, ed. Department of Commerce (Washington, DC: Government Printing Office, 1924), 40–47.

5. "Wonder What?," *Indianapolis Star*, May 18, 1921; "Wonder?," *Indianapolis Star*, May 19, 1921; "Wonder," *Indianapolis Star*, May 21, 1921.

6. "Taggart's Wonder Bread," *Indianapolis Star*, May 23, 1921.

7. Molly Wade McGrath, *Top Sellers, U.S.A.: Success Stories behind America's Best-Selling Products from Alka-Seltzer to Zippo* (New York: William Morrow, 1983), 130; Janice Jorgensen, *Encyclopedia of Consumer Brands* (Detroit: St. James Press, 1994), 644–46; Evan Morris, *From Altoids to Zima: The Surprising Stories Behind 125 Famous Brand Names* (New York: Simon and Schuster, 2004), 81; Tim Carman, "Wonder Bread: 90 Years of Spiritual Vacuousness?," *Washington Post*, March 18, 2011; Dan Myers, "5 Things You Didn't Know about Wonder Bread," *ABC News*, March 6, 2015; Alexander Theroux, *Einstein's Beets* (Seattle: Fantagraphics Books, 2017), 229; "Wonder Bread: Our Story," Wonder Bread, 2019, https://www.wonder bread.com/about-us.

8. *The Wonder Bread Cookbook* (Berkeley, CA: Ten Speed Press, 2007), 2.

9. "These Men Will Represent U.S. in Big Balloon Race," *Lake County Times*, September 1, 1921.

10. "Six Huge Gas Bags Fly the Skies for Prize Cup"; "Throngs Packed the Grounds," *Cincinnati Inquirer*, June 6, 1909; "Throngs Watch Balloons Start in Great Race," *Nashville Tennessean*, June 5, 1909.

11. "Balloon Races Facing Gas Ban," *Indiana Daily Times*, August 7, 1920; "No Gas for Balloon Race," *Aircraft Journal*, August 23, 1920, 8.

12. "No Gas for Balloon Race."

13. *Official Guide Book of the World's Fair of 1934* (Chicago: Cuneo Press, 1934), 63.

14. "Dramatic Story of the $6,000,000 Bread," *Chicago Daily Tribune*, March 31, 1929.

15. *The Wonder Bread Cookbook*, 5.

16. Aaron Bobrow-Strain, *White Bread: A Social History of the Store-Bought Loaf* (Boston: Beacon Press, 2012), 118–25; Andrew F. Smith, *Food in America: The Past, Present, and Future of Food, Farming, and the Family Meal*, vol. 1 (Santa Barbara: ABC-CLIO, 2017), 20.

17. On racist imaginaries of nourishment, see Kyla Wazana Tompkins, *Racial Indigestion: Eating Bodies in the 19th Century* (New York: New York University Press, 2012), 53–88; Sebastián Gil-Riaño and Sarah E. Tracy, "Developing Constipation: Dietary Fiber, Western Disease, and Industrial Carbohydrates," *Global Food History* 2, no. 2 (July 2, 2016): 179–209; Aaron Bobrow-Strain, "White Bread Biopolitics: Purity, Health, and the Triumph of Industrial Baking," in *Geographies of Race and Food: Fields, Bodies, Markets*, ed. Rachel Slocum and Arun Saldanha (Oxon: Routledge, 2016), 265–90; Ina Zweiniger-Bargielowska, "'Not a Complete Food for Man': The Controversy about White versus Wholemeal Bread in Interwar Britain," in *Setting Nutritional Standards: Theory, Policies, Practices*, ed. Elizabeth Neswald, David F. Smith, and Ulrike Thoms (Rochester, NY: University of Rochester Press, 2017), 142–64; Hiʻilei Julia Hobart and Stephanie Maroney, "On Racial Constitutions and Digestive Therapeutics," *Food, Culture & Society* 22, no. 5 (October 20, 2019): 576–94.

18. Famously, this segregation of food production prompted Martin Luther King to call for a boycott of Wonder Bread (and other brands) in 1968. Bobrow-Strain, *White Bread*, 168.

19. "Vital Women," *Los Angeles Times*, April 25, 1937. On gendered food advertising, see, for example, Carol J. Adams, *The Sexual Politics of Meat: A Feminist-Vegetarian Critical Theory* (New York: Continuum, 1990); Sherrie A. Inness, ed., *Kitchen Culture in America: Popular Representations of Food, Gender, and Race* (Philadelphia: University of Pennsylvania Press, 2001); Katherine J. Parkin, *Food Is Love: Advertising and Gender Roles in Modern America* (Philadelphia: University of Pennsylvania Press, 2006); Emily J. H. Contois, *Diners, Dudes, and Diets: How Gender and Power Collide in Food Media and Culture* (Chapel Hill: University of North Carolina Press, 2020).

20. Kat Anderson, *Tending the Wild: Native American Knowledge and the Management of California's Natural Resources* (Berkeley: University of California Press, 2005), 96–99; Thomas D. Finger, "Tulare Lake and the Past Future of Food," in *Acquired Tastes: Stories about the Origins of Modern Food*, ed. Benjamin R. Cohen, Michael S. Kideckel, and Anna Zeide (Cambridge, MA: MIT Press, 2021), 17–34.

21. Harriet Friedmann, "Feeding the Empire: The Pathologies of Globalized Agriculture," *Socialist Register* 41 (2005): 124–43; Chris Otter, "The British Nutrition Transition and Its Histories," *History Compass* 10, no. 11 (2012): 812–25.

22. For scholarly accounts of these specific contemporary and historical categories, see for example Mark Lawrence and John Germov, "Future Food: The Politics of Functional Foods and Health Claims," in *A Sociology of Food and Nutrition: The Social Appetite*, ed. John Germov and Lauren Williams, 2nd ed. (South Melbourne, Australia: Oxford University Press, 2004), 119–47; Michael Ackerman, "Interpreting the 'Newer Knowledge of Nutrition': Science, Interests, and Values in the Making of Dietary Advice in the United States, 1915–1965" (PhD dissertation, University of Virginia, 2005); Mark Nichter and Jennifer Thompson, "For My Wellness, Not Just My Illness: North Americans' Use of Dietary Supplements," *Culture, Medicine and Psychiatry* 30, no. 2 (2006); Emma Spary, *Feeding France: New Sciences of Food, 1760–1815* (Cambridge: Cambridge University Press, 2014), 125–66; John P. Swann, "The History of Efforts to Regulate Dietary Supplements in the USA," *Drug Testing and Analysis* 8, nos. 3–4 (2016): 271–82; Alice Street, "Food as Pharma: Marketing Nutraceuticals to India's Rural Poor," *Critical Public Health* 25, no. 3 (May 27, 2015): 361–72; Stephen J. Pintauro, *The Regulation of Dietary Supplements: A Historical Analysis* (Boca Raton, FL: CRC Press, 2018); Richard Wilk and Emma McDonell, eds., *Critical Approaches to Superfoods* (New York: Bloomsbury Publishing, 2020); Lesley Steinitz, "Transforming Pig's Wash into Health Food: The Construction of Skimmed Milk Protein Powders," *Global Food History*, December 29, 2021, 1–34.

23. For scholarly attempts to historicize and critically examine the food-medicine boundary, see for example Mikko Jauho and Mari Niva, "Lay Understandings of Functional Foods as Hybrids of Food and Medicine," *Food, Culture & Society* 16, no. 1 (March 1, 2013): 43–63; Juliana Adelman and Lisa Haushofer, "Introduction: Food as Medicine, Medicine as Food," *Journal of the History of Medicine and Allied Sciences* 73, no. 2 (April 1, 2018): 127–34, https://doi.org/10.1093/jhmas/jry010; Xaq Frohlich, "The Rise (and Fall) of the Food-Drug Line: Classification, Gatekeepers, and Spatial Mediation in Regulating US Food and Health Markets," in *Risk on the Table: Food Production, Health, and the Environment*, ed. Angela N. H. Creager and Jean-Paul Gaudillière (New York: Berghahn Books, 2021), 297–329.

24. On early modern dietetic theories, see Ken Albala, *Eating Right in the Renaissance* (Berkeley: University of California Press, 2002); Steven Shapin, "How to Eat Like a Gentleman: Dietetics and Ethics in Early Modern England," in *An Anglo-American Tradition of Self-Help Medicine and Hygiene*, ed. Charles E. Rosenberg (Baltimore: Johns Hopkins University Press, 2003), 21–58; Emma Spary, *Eating the Enlightenment: Food and the Sciences in Paris* (Chicago: University of Chicago Press, 2012), 17–50.

25. Alice Adams Proctor, "Science Perfects a Vastly Better Bread," *Chicago Daily Tribune*, May 5, 1929; Alice Adams Proctor, *The Wonder Sandwich Book* (New York: Continental Baking Company, 1928); Alice Adams Proctor, *Wonder Sandwich Suggestions* (New York: Bakeries Service Corporation, 1930).

26. Here, I draw on the vast scholarship on the relationship between scientific objects and knowledge production. For some key texts, see Steven Shapin and Simon Schaffer, *Leviathan and the Air-Pump: Hobbes, Boyle, and the Experimental Life* (Princeton, NJ: Princeton University Press, 1985); Simon Schaffer, "Glass Works: Newton's Prisms and the Uses of Experiment," in *The Uses of Experiment: Studies in the Natural Sciences*, ed. David Gooding, Trevor Pinch, and Simon Schaffer (Cambridge: Cambridge University Press, 1989), 67–104; Peter Galison, *Image and Logic: A Material Culture of Microphysics* (Chicago: University of Chicago Press, 1997); Hans-Jörg Rheinberger, *Toward a History of Epistemic Things: Synthesizing Proteins in the Test Tube*, Writing Science (Stanford, CA: Stanford University Press, 1997); Bruno Latour, *Reassembling the Social: An Introduction to Actor-Network-Theory* (Oxford: Oxford University Press, 2005); Lorraine Daston, *Things That Talk: Object Lessons from Art and Science* (New York: Zone Books, 2007); Karin Knorr Cetina, *Epistemic Cultures: How the Sciences Make Knowledge* (Cambridge, MA: Harvard University Press, 2009); Stephanie Dick, "After Math: (Re)Configuring Minds, Proof, and Computing in the Postwar United States" (PhD dissertation, Harvard University, 2015); Sophia Roosth, *Synthetic: How Life Got Made* (Chicago: University of Chicago Press, 2017).

27. Lorraine Daston and Katharine Park, *Wonders and the Order of Nature, 1150–1750* (Cambridge, MA: Zone Books, 1998), 20.

28. Allan Brandt, *No Magic Bullet: A Social History of Venereal Disease in the United States Since 1880* (New York: Oxford University Press, 1987); Jeremy Greene, *Prescribing by Numbers: Drugs and the Definition of Disease* (Baltimore: Johns Hopkins University Press, 2007); Elizabeth Siegel Watkins, *The Estrogen Elixir: A History of Hormone Replacement Therapy in America* (Baltimore: Johns Hopkins University Press, 2007); Robert Bud, *Penicillin: Triumph and Tragedy* (Oxford: Oxford University Press, 2007); Bruno J. Strasser, "Magic Bullets and Wonder Pills: Making Drugs and Diseases in the Twentieth Century," *Historical Studies in the Natural Sciences* 38, no. 2 (May 1, 2008): 303–12; David Herzberg, *Happy Pills in America: From Miltown to Prozac* (Baltimore: Johns Hopkins University Press, 2010); Scott Podolsky, *The Antibiotic Era: Reform, Resistance, and the Pursuit of a Rational Therapeutics* (Baltimore: Johns Hopkins University Press, 2015).

29. This literature is too vast to adequately cover here, but for a few key texts, see Rima Apple, *Mothers and Medicine: A Social History of Infant Feeding, 1890–1950* (Madison: University of Wisconsin Press, 1987); Harvey Levenstein, *Revolution at the Table: The Transformation of the American Diet* (New York: Oxford University Press, 1988); Rima Apple, *Vitamania: Vitamins in American Culture* (New Brunswick, NJ: Rutgers University Press, 1996); Marion Nestle, *Food Politics: How the Food Industry Influences Nutrition and Health* (Berkeley: University of California Press, 2002); Nick Cullather, "The Foreign Policy of the Calorie," *The American Historical Review* 112, no. 2 (2007): 337–64; Julie Guthman, *Weighing In: Obesity, Food Justice, and the Limits of Capitalism* (Berkeley: University of California Press, 2011); Hannah Landecker, "Food as Exposure: Nutritional Epigenetics and the New Metabolism," *Biosocieties* 6, no. 2 (June 2011): 167–94; Spary, *Eating the*

Enlightenment; Gyorgy Scrinis, *Nutritionism: The Science and Politics of Dietary Advice* (New York: Columbia University Press, 2013); Spary, *Feeding France*; Ian Mosby, *Food Will Win the War: The Politics, Culture, and Science of Food on Canada's Home Front* (Vancouver: University of British Columbia Press, 2014); Elizabeth Neswald, David F. Smith, and Ulrike Thoms, eds., *Setting Nutritional Standards: Theory, Policies, Practices* (Rochester, NY: University of Rochester Press, 2017); Corinna Treitel, *Eating Nature in Modern Germany* (Cambridge: Cambridge University Press, 2017).

30. For products as commercial vehicles for nutritional scientific knowledge, see Rima Apple, "'Advertised by Our Loving Friends': The Infant Formula Industry and the Creation of New Pharmaceutical Markets, 1870–1910," *Journal of the History of Medicine and Allied Sciences* 41, no. 1 (January 1, 1986): 3–23; Apple, *Vitamania*; Sally Horrocks, "Consuming Science: Science, Technology and Food in Britain, 1870–1939" (PhD dissertation, University of Manchester, 1993); Paul Weindling, "The Role of International Organizations in Setting Nutritional Standards in the 1920s and 1930s," in *The Science and Culture of Nutrition, 1840–1940*, ed. Andrew Cunningham and Harmke Kamminga (Amsterdam: Rodopi, 1995), 319–32, also especially chapters by Sally Horrocks, Mark Finlay, and Rima Apple; Ackerman, "Interpreting the 'Newer Knowledge of Nutrition'"; Margaret Barnett, "Fletcherism: The Chew-Chew Fad of the Edwardian Era," in *Nutrition in Britain: Science, Scientists and Politics in the Twentieth Century*, ed. David Smith (London: Routledge, 2013), 6–28; Anna Zeide, *Canned: The Rise and Fall of Consumer Confidence in the American Food Industry* (Oakland: University of California Press, 2018). See also James Secord, "Knowledge in Transit," *Isis* 95, no. 4 (2004): 654–72.

31. Naomi Aronson, "Fuel for the Human Machine: The Industrialization of Eating in America" (PhD dissertation, Brandeis University, 1978); Susanne Freidberg, *Fresh* (Cambridge, MA: Harvard University Press, 2009); Spary, *Eating the Enlightenment*; Spary, *Feeding France*; Zeide, *Canned*; Julie Guthman, *Wilted: Pathogens, Chemicals, and the Fragile Future of the Strawberry Industry* (Oakland: University of California Press, 2019); Joshua Specht, *Red Meat Republic: A Hoof-to-Table History of How Beef Changed America* (Princeton, NJ: Princeton University Press, 2019).

32. Steven L. Kaplan and Sophus A. Reinert, eds., *The Economic Turn: Recasting Political Economy in Enlightenment Europe* (London: Anthem Press, 2019).

33. Steven L. Kaplan and Sophus A. Reinert, "The Economic Turn in Enlightenment Europe," in *The Economic Turn: Recasting Political Economy in Enlightenment Europe*, ed. Steven L. Kaplan and Sophus A. Reinert (London: Anthem Press, 2019), 6.

34. Kaplan and Reinert, 7.

35. I draw on recent histories of economic life, concerned with "human participation in the production, exchange, and consumption of goods," and on histories of capitalism that approach economic regimes as forms of knowing and organizing the world. William H. Sewell, "A Strange Career: The Historical Study of Economic Life," *History and Theory* 49, no. 4 (December 1, 2010): 146; for histories of economic life, see Jeremy Adelman, *Republic of Capital: Buenos Aires and the Legal*

Transformation of the Atlantic World (Stanford, CA: Stanford University Press, 2002); Jeffrey Sklansky, *The Soul's Economy: Market Society and Selfhood in American Thought, 1820–1920* (Chapel Hill: University of North Carolina Press, 2002); Emma Rothschild, "Isolation and Economic Life in Eighteenth-Century France," *American Historical Review* 119, no. 4 (October 1, 2014): 1055–82; Alexia M. Yates, *Selling Paris: Property and Commercial Culture in the Fin-de-Siècle Capital* (Cambridge, MA: Harvard University Press, 2015); Erika Vause, *In the Red and in the Black: Debt, Dishonor, and the Law in France between Revolutions* (Charlottesville: University of Virginia Press, 2018); for histories of capitalism and knowledge production, see Basil S. Yamey, "Accounting and the Rise of Capitalism: Further Notes on a Theme by Sombart," *Journal of Accounting Research* 2, no. 2 (1964): 117–36; William Cronon, *Nature's Metropolis: Chicago and the Great West* (New York: W. W. Norton, 1991); Mary Poovey, *A History of the Modern Fact: Problems of Knowledge in the Sciences of Wealth and Society* (Chicago: University of Chicago Press, 1998); Warwick Funnell and Jeffrey Robertson, *Accounting by the First Public Company: The Pursuit of Supremacy* (London: Routledge, 2013); Miranda Joseph, *Debt to Society: Accounting for Life Under Capitalism* (Minneapolis: University of Minnesota Press, 2014).

36. Aronson, "Fuel for the Human Machine the Industrialization of Eating in America"; Landecker, "Food as Exposure"; Tompkins, *Racial Indigestion*; Spary, *Eating the Enlightenment*; Spary, *Feeding France*; Steven Shapin, "'You Are What You Eat': Historical Changes in Ideas about Food and Identity," *Historical Research* 87, no. 236 (2014): 1–16; Street, "Food as Pharma"; Nina Mackert, "Feeding Productive Bodies: Calories, Nutritional Values, and Ability in the Progressive-Era US," in *Histories of Productivity: Genealogical Perspectives on the Body and Modern Economy*, ed. Peter-Paul Bänziger and Mischa Suter (New York: Routledge, 2016), 117–35.

37. Gyorgy Scrinis, "On the Ideology of Nutritionism," *Gastronomica: The Journal of Critical Food Studies* 8, no. 1 (February 1, 2008): 39–48; Scrinis, *Nutritionism*.

38. Cedric J. Robinson, *Black Marxism: The Making of the Black Radical Tradition* (Chapel Hill: University of North Carolina Press, 1983), 2.

CHAPTER 1. "FOCUSSED FLESH"

1. William Mumford Baker, *A Year Worth Living: A Story of a Place and a People One Cannot Afford Not to Know* (Boston: Lee and Shepard, 1887).

2. Baker was preempted by S. L. Goodale, *A Brief Sketch of Gail Borden, and His Relations to Some Forms of Concentrated Food* (Portland, ME: Thurston, 1872).

3. Joe B. Frantz, *Gail Borden: Dairyman to a Nation* (Norman: University of Oklahoma Press, 1951), vii; Clarence Wharton, *Gail Borden, Pioneer* (San Antonio: Naylor, 1941); George Kienzle, *The Story of Gail Borden: The Birth of an Industry* (New York: Priv. Print., 1947); this strand of storytelling continues today, see for example Charles W. Carey, "Borden, Gail, Jr.," in *American Inventors, Entrepreneurs, and Business Visionaries* (New York: Infobase Publishing, 2002), 35–36.

4. Andrew F. Smith, *Eating History: 30 Turning Points in the Making of American Cuisine* (New York: Columbia University Press, 2009), 67–73; Zeide, *Canned*, 10–40.

5. Carolyn Hughes Crowley, "The Man Who Invented Elsie, the Borden Cow," *Smithsonian Magazine*, August 31, 1999.

6. George Colpitts, *Pemmican Empire: Food, Trade, and the Last Bison Hunts in the North American Plains, 1780–1882* (Cambridge: Cambridge University Press, 2014); Sue Shephard, *Pickled, Potted, and Canned: How the Art and Science of Food Preserving Changed the World* (New York: Simon and Schuster, 2006).

7. Borden did not leave a record of his journey to St. Louis. The following passage is speculation; the description of St. Louis in 1850 is taken from Frederick Piercy, *Route from Liverpool to Great Salt Lake Valley*, ed. James Linforth (Los Angeles: Westernlore Press, 1855), 55–57; George Conclin, *Conclin's New River Guide; or, A Gazetteer of All the Towns on the Western Waters* (Cincinnati, OH: H.S. & J. Applegate, 1850), 80–81; "Commerce of St. Louis," *The Western Journal, and Civilian*, January 1851; Elihu H. Shepard, *The Early History of St. Louis and Missouri* (St. Louis: Southwestern Book and Publishing Company, 1870).

8. Walter Johnson, *The Broken Heart of America: St. Louis and the Violent History of the United States* (New York: Basic Books, 2020), 143–44.

9. Frantz, *Gail Borden*, 15–64, 129–43, 154–56.

10. Donald Meinig, *The Shaping of America: A Geographical Perspective on 500 Years of History*, vol. 2 (New Haven, CT: Yale University Press, 1993), 135–44.

11. Borden's tax returns from 1846 to 1850 list him as the owner of five or six enslaved people. He also employed German laborers and a German engineer. Frantz Papers, Box 3J244, 6470, 1846–50.

12. Laura E. Gómez, *Manifest Destinies: The Making of the Mexican American Race* (New York: New York University Press, 2008), 15–21.

13. Reginald Horsman, *Race and Manifest Destiny: The Origins of American Racial Anglo-Saxonism* (Cambridge, MA: Harvard University Press, 2009), 229–48.

14. Frantz, *Gail Borden*, 64–71.

15. Frantz, 84–128; Goodale, *A Brief Sketch of Gail Borden*, 4–5.

16. Gail Borden Jr., Quintana, Texas, to J. Pinckney Henderson and Henry Smith, draft, May 23, 1837, Gail Borden Papers, Col. 874, Folder 1 (Correspondence), Daughters of the Republic of Texas Library.

17. On Ashbel Smith, see Elizabeth Silverthorne, *Ashbel Smith of Texas: Pioneer, Patriot, Statesman, 1805–1886* (College Station: Texas A&M University Press, 1982).

18. For the fashion of American medical migration to Europe between 1810 and 1860, see John Harley Warner, *Against the Spirit of System: The French Impulse in Nineteenth-Century American Medicine* (Baltimore: Johns Hopkins University Press, 2003).

19. Silverthorne, *Ashbel Smith of Texas*, 72.

20. Ashbel Smith, *An Oration Pronounced before the Connecticut Alpha of the Phi Beta Kappa at Yale College, New Haven, August 15, 1849* (New Haven, CT: B.L. Hamlen, 1849), 26.

21. Ashbel Smith, *An Address Delivered in the City of Galveston on the 22d of February, 1848, the Anniversary of the Birth Day of Washington and of the Battle of Buena Vista by Ashbel Smith* (Galveston: W. Richardson, 1848), 11–12; Smith, *An Oration*, 27–28.

22. "England and Texas," *Niles' National Register*, April 13, 1844.

23. Ashbel Smith, *An Account of the Yellow Fever Which Appeared in the City of Galveston, Republic of Texas in the Autumn of 1839 : With Cases and Dissections* (Galveston, TX: Hamilton Stuart, 1839), http://archive.org/details/2572008R.nlm.nih.gov.

24. Wharton, *Gail Borden, Pioneer*, 155–56.

25. No formal contract of their arrangement survives, but in February 1848 (around the time Borden claimed to have begun experimenting on the meat biscuit) Smith wrote to his father to request five hundred dollars in order to enter into a business partnership. His father disapproved vehemently but still raised the money. "Moses Smith, Hartford, to Ashbel Smith, Galveston, February 15, 1848," Frantz Papers, Box 3J245, Literary Productions 1851–53.

26. Silverthorne, *Ashbel Smith of Texas*, 120, 195.

27. Walter Johnson, *River of Dark Dreams* (Cambridge, MA: Harvard University Press, 2013), 46–72.

28. Johnson, 176–208.

29. Frantz, *Gail Borden*, 160.

30. "The Rohan Potato," *The Gardener's Magazine and Register of Rural & Domestic Improvement*, 1840.

31. Johnson, *River of Dark Dreams*, 18–45.

32. Scrinis, "On the Ideology of Nutritionism"; Scrinis, *Nutritionism*.

33. Michael Pollan, *In Defense of Food: An Eater's Manifesto* (London: Penguin, 2008), 17–82; see also Jessica J. Mudry, *Measured Meals: Nutrition in America* (Albany: State University New York Press, 2009).

34. Ranjani R. Starr, "Too Little, Too Late: Ineffective Regulation of Dietary Supplements in the United States," *American Journal of Public Health* 105, no. 3 (March 2015): 478–85.

35. Shapin, "'You Are What You Eat.'"

36. Spary, *Feeding France*, 89–124; Mikuláš Teich, "Circulation, Transformation, Conservation of Matter and the Balancing of the Biological World in the Eighteenth Century," *Ambix* 29, no. 1 (1982): 17–28.

37. Bruce T. Moran, *Distilling Knowledge: Alchemy, Chemistry, and the Scientific Revolution* (Cambridge, MA: Harvard University Press, 2005), 8–36.

38. Frederic Holmes, *Eighteenth-Century Chemistry as an Investigative Enterprise* (Berkeley: Office for History of Science and Technology, University of California at Berkeley, 1989), 62.

39. Moran, *Distilling Knowledge*, 17–20.

40. Spary, *Eating the Enlightenment*, 205; Jennifer J. Davis, *Defining Culinary Authority: The Transformation of Cooking in France, 1650–1830* (Baton Rouge: Louisiana State University Press, 2013), 27–28.

41. Spary, *Feeding France*, 101–15.

42. The rupture between qualitative premodern and quantitative modern modes of analysis and evaluation in science in general, and in chemistry and dietetics in particular, has been overstated. Nevertheless, changes in matter analysis that were concerned with questions of quantity rather than quality were crucial in the imperial context in which Borden's biscuit was made and impacted conceptions of food and the eating body. For an illuminating discussion of quantitative versus qualitative methods in chymistry/chemistry, see William R. Newman and Lawrence M. Principe, *Alchemy Tried in the Fire: Starkey, Boyle, and the Fate of Helmontian Chymistry* (Chicago: University of Chicago Press, 2002), 118–19.

43. Albala, *Eating Right in the Renaissance*, 63–66; Spary, *Feeding France*, 93.

44. For examples, see Louis Lémery, *A Treatise of All Sorts of Foods* (London: T. Osborne, 1745); Francis de Valangin, *A Treatise on Diet; or, The Management of Human Life* (London: J. & W. Oliver, 1768); Anthony Willich, *Lectures on Diet and Regimen* (London: Longman and Rees, 1799).

45. Shapin, "You Are What You Eat"; Spary, *Feeding France*, 235–67.

46. John Coveney, *Food, Morals and Meaning: The Pleasure and Anxiety of Eating*, 2nd ed. (Oxon: Routledge, 2006), 59; Mudry, *Measured Meals*; Charlotte Biltekoff, *Eating Right in America: The Cultural Politics of Food and Health* (Durham, NC: Duke University Press, 2013), 13–44.

47. I am overstating the shift from alchemical qualitative essences to constituent-centric views of nutrition. Corpuscular theories of matter were, in fact, also articulated by alchemists and influenced Robert Boyle's corpuscular theory of matter. But as the meat biscuit shows, notions of essence in nutrition long outlasted ideas of corpusculism in elite chemistry. William R. Newman, *Atoms and Alchemy: Chymistry and the Experimental Origins of the Scientific Revolution* (Chicago: University of Chicago Press, 2006).

48. Holmes, *Eighteenth-Century Chemistry*.

49. Londa Schiebinger, *Plants and Empire* (Cambridge, MA: Harvard University Press, 2004); Londa Schiebinger, "Prospecting for Drugs: European Naturalists in the West Indies," in *Colonial Botany: Science, Commerce, and Politics in the Early Modern World*, ed. Londa Schiebinger and Claudia Swan (Philadelphia: University of Pennsylvania Press, 2005), 119–33.

50. Lissa Roberts, "The Death of the Sensuous Chemist: The 'New' Chemistry and the Transformation of Sensuous Technology," *Studies in History and Philosophy of Science* 26, no. 4 (1995): 503–29; Holmes, *Eighteenth-Century Chemistry*, 61–83.

51. Frederic Holmes, "Analysis by Fire and Solvent Extractions: The Metamorphosis of a Tradition," *Isis* 62, no. 2 (Summer 1971): 128–48.

52. Ursula Klein, "Origin of the Concept Chemical Compound," *Science in Context* 7, no. 2 (1994): 163–204; Spary, *Feeding France*, 89–91.

53. William Prout, "On the Ultimate Composition of Simple Alimentary Substances," *Philosophical Transactions of the Royal Society of London* 117 (1827): 355–88; Barbara Orland, "The Invention of Nutrients: William Prout, Digestion

and Alimentary Substances in the 1820s," *Food and History* 8, no. 1 (January 1, 2010): 149–68.

54. François Magendie, "Mémoire sur les propriétés nutritives des substances qui ne contiennent pas d'azote," *Annales de Chimie et de Physique* 3 (September 1816): 72.

55. Justus Liebig, *Chemische Untersuchung über das Fleisch und seine Zubereitung zum Nahrungsmittel* (Heidelberg: C. F. Winter, 1847); Mark R. Finlay, "Early Marketing of the Theory of Nutrition: The Science and Culture of Liebig's Extract of Meat," in *The Science and Culture of Nutrition, 1840–1940*, ed. Harmke Kamminga and Andrew Cunningham (Amsterdam: Rodopi, 1995), 48–74; William H. Brock, *Justus Von Liebig: The Chemical Gatekeeper* (Cambridge: Cambridge University Press, 2002), 215–49.

56. On the debate about Liebig's extract of meat, see Arthur Hill Hassall, "On the Nutritive Value of Liebig's Extract of Beef, Beef-Tea, and of Wine," *Lancet*, July 8, 1865, 49–50, 386–87, 441–43, 469, 486, 547, 579–80, 633, 651, 717.

57. Baker, *A Year Worth Living*, 106.

58. Frantz, *Gail Borden*, 201.

59. Anderson, *Tending the Wild*, 261.

60. Pekka Hämäläinen, *The Comanche Empire* (New Haven, CT: Yale University Press, 2008), 288–90; David La Vere, *The Texas Indians* (College Station: Texas A&M University Press, 2004), 33–35.

61. Colpitts, *Pemmican Empire*, 58–99.

62. Gail Borden and Ashbel Smith, *Letter of Gail Borden, Jr., to Dr. Ashbel Smith, Setting Forth an Important Invention in the Preparation of a New Article of Food, Termed Meat Biscuit* (Galveston: Gibson & Cherry, 1850), 1–2.

63. Borden and Smith, 2; Spary, *Feeding France*, 204–11.

64. Gray (and Liebig, see below) was brought to Borden's attention by the patent agency Borden consulted. Whether he had any knowledge of their work before he made the meat biscuit is therefore unclear. Borden and Smith, *Letter of Gail Borden*, 2; Samuel Frederick Gray, *The Operative Chemist: Being a Practical Display of the Arts and Manufactures Which Depend Upon Chemical Principles* (London: Hurst, Chance, & Co., 1828), 850.

65. Borden and Smith, *Letter of Gail Borden*, 2.

66. Borden and Smith, 4.

67. Borden and Smith, 1.

68. Borden and Smith, 6.

69. Kara W. Swanson, "Authoring an Invention: Patent Production in the Nineteenth-Century United States," in *Making and Unmaking Intellectual Property: Creative Production in Legal and Cultural Perspective*, ed. Mario Biagioli, Peter Jaszi, and Martha Woodmansee (Chicago: University of Chicago Press, 2011), 41–54.

70. *Scientific American* 2, no. 1 (September 26, 1846): 1.

71. "Portable Soup Bread," *Scientific American* 5, no. 11 (December 1849): 84.

72. Borden and Smith, *Letter of Gail Borden*, 2.

73. Gail Borden, Preparation of portable soup-bread, US7066 A (Galveston, Texas, issued February 5, 1850), http://www.google.com/patents/US7066.

74. The pamphlet consists of a letter Borden supposedly wrote to Smith about his invention, which was almost certainly written specifically for promotional purposes, and likely with Smith's help, and a letter of endorsement written by Smith to the American Association for the Advancement of Science. Borden had both letters reprinted as a pamphlet. Borden and Smith, *Letter of Gail Borden*.

75. Borden and Smith, 7.

76. Borden and Smith, 5.

77. Borden and Smith, 7.

78. Borden and Smith, 8.

79. On the construction of the "hostile Indian," see Gary B. Nash, "The Image of the Indian in the Southern Colonial Mind," *The William and Mary Quarterly* 29, no. 2 (1972): 198–230; Robert H. Keller, "Hostile Language: Bias in Historical Writing about American Indian Resistance," *Journal of American Culture* 9, no. 4 (1986): 9–23.

80. Borden and Smith, *Letter of Gail Borden*, 8.

81. Rodrigo Lazo, *Writing to Cuba: Filibustering and Cuban Exiles in the United States* (Chapel Hill: University of North Carolina Press, 2006), 76.

82. Borden and Smith, *Letter of Gail Borden*, 6–7.

83. Borden and Smith, 6.

84. Borden and Smith, 8.

85. Mauro Boianovsky, "Humboldt and the Economists on Natural Resources, Institutions and Underdevelopment (1752–1859)," *European Journal of the History of Economic Thought* 20, no. 1 (2013): 58–88.

86. Alexander von Humboldt, *Political Essay on the Kingdom of New Spain*, 4 vols. (London: Longman, Hurst, Rees, Orme, and Brown, 1814); Boianovsky, "Humboldt and the Economists on Natural Resources."

87. Tompkins, *Racial Indigestion*, 72.

88. Henry Charles Carey, *The Harmony of Interests, Agricultural, Manufacturing, and Commercial* (Philadelphia: J. S. Skinner, 1851), 100.

89. Carey, 46.

90. Henry Charles Carey, *The Past, the Present, and the Future* (Philadelphia: Carey & Hart, 1848), 443.

91. Smith, *An Address Delivered in the City of Galveston*, 13.

92. Smith, 14.

93. Smith, 11–12.

94. Ashbel Smith, "Manufactures for the South—Gail Borden's Meat Biscuit Factory, Texas," *Debow's Review*, May 1851.

95. Smith, 589.

96. Smith, 590.

97. Smith, 589.

98. *The Military Laws of the United States* (Washington, DC: US Government Printing Office, 1917), 278–81. Before the advent of mass consumerism, corporate consumption through institutions like the military, the navy, and hospitals was the most important form of consumption for entrepreneurs especially of food and proprietary drugs. See Justin Rivest, "Secret Remedies and the Rise of Pharmaceutical Monopolies in France during the First Global Age" (Baltimore, PhD dissertation, Johns Hopkins University, 2016); Frank Trentmann, ed., "Introduction," in *The Oxford Handbook of the History of Consumption* (Oxford: Oxford University Press, 2012), 16–17.

99. Thomas T. Smith, *The US Army and the Texas Frontier Economy, 1845—1900* (College Station: Texas A&M University Press, 1999); Robert W. Frazer, *Forts and Supplies: The Role of the Army in the Economy of the Southwest, 1846–1861* (Albuquerque: University of New Mexico Press, 1983).

100. A. B. Eaton to Geo. Gibson, May 30, 1850, Frantz Papers, Box 3J245, Literary Productions 1851–53.

101. Eaton to Gibson, May 30, 1850.

102. E. V. Sumner to Major A. B. Eaton, May 14, 1850, Records of the Quartermaster General, War Department, the National Archives, Washington, D.C.," in Frantz Papers, Box 3J245, Literary Productions 1851–53.

103. Eaton to Gibson, May 30, 1850.

104. Uli Haller, "Tod, John Grant, Sr.," Handbook of Texas Online, June 15, 2010, https://tshaonline.org/handbook/online/articles/ft005.

105. John G. Tod to Charles M. Conrad, October 7, 1850, Frantz Papers, Box 3J245, Literary Productions 1851–53.

106. Tod to Conrad, October 7, 1850.

107. C. M. Conrad, secretary of war, October 31, 1850, Frantz Papers, Box 3J245, Literary Productions 1851–53.

108. Gail Borden to Ashbel Smith, 30 October 1850, Box 2G223, Ashbel Smith Papers, 1823–1926, Dolph Briscoe Center for American History, University of Texas at Austin.

109. John G. Tod to Charles M. Conrad, Washington D.C., February 25, 1851, Frantz Papers, Box 3J245, Folder Letters 1850, Literary Productions 1851–53.

110. Gail Borden to Ashbel Smith, 30 October 1850 and 25 November 1850, Box 2G223, Ashbel Smith Papers.

111. C. M. Conrad to John G. Tod, March 13, 1851, Frantz Papers, Box 3J245, Literary Productions 1851–53.

112. Orders No 4, W. J. Hardee, June 13, 1851, Frantz Papers, Box 3J245, Literary Productions 1851–53.

113. H. W. Merrill, W. J. Newton, L. Guild, G. H. Stewart, H. F. De Lano, and L. M. Walker to Head Quarters 8th Department, June 21, 1851, Frantz Papers, Box 3J245, Literary Productions 1851–53.

114. Frantz, *Gail Borden*, 220.

115. Merrill et al. to Head Quarters 8th Department, June 21, 1851.

1. T. Bazley to Ashbel Smith, 19 June 1851; John Wilson to Ashbel Smith, undated; Box 2G223, Ashbel Smith Papers.

2. Ashbel Smith, Reminiscences on the Great Council Exhibition, Box 3J245, Literary Productions 1851–53, Frantz Papers.

3. John Wilson to Ashbel Smith, 24 June 1851; W. Crossman to Ashbel Smith, 27 June 1851 and 5 July 1851; Box 2G223, Ashbel Smith Papers.

4. Joseph Nash, Louis Haghe, and David Roberts, *Dickinsons' Comprehensive Pictures of the Great Exhibition of 1851* (London: Dickinson Brothers, 1854).

5. Ashbel Smith to Sam Houston, 9 May 1851, Ashbel Smith Papers, Box 3J245, Literary Productions 1851–53, Frantz Papers.

6. Nash et al., *Dickinsons' Comprehensive Pictures of the Great Exhibition of 1851*.

7. Gail Borden to Ashbel Smith, 23 April 1851, Letters 1851, Box 2G223, Ashbel Smith Papers.

8. Jeffrey Auerbach, *The Great Exhibition of 1851: A Nation on Display* (New Haven, CT: Yale University Press, 1999), 10.

9. *Reports by the Juries on the Subjects in the Thirty Classes into Which the Exhibition Was Divided* (London: Clowes and Sons, 1852), 51.

10. Chris Otter, *Diet for a Large Planet: Industrial Britain, Food Systems, and World Ecology* (Chicago: University of Chicago Press, 2020), 4.

11. Charles Dickens, *The Mudfog Papers* (New York: Henry Holt, 1880), 73–74.

12. Richard Tames, *Economy and Society in Nineteenth Century Britain* (Routledge, 2013), 21; Chris Cook, *The Routledge Companion to Britain in the Nineteenth Century, 1815–1914* (London: Routledge, 2005), 198.

13. John Burnett, *Plenty and Want: A Social History of Food in England from 1815 to the Present Day* (Edinburgh: Nelson, 1966); Leslie A. Williams, *Daniel O'Connell, the British Press and the Irish Famine: Killing Remarks* (New York: Routledge, 2003); John Bohstedt, *The Politics of Provisions: Food Riots, Moral Economy, and Market Transition in England, C. 1550–1850* (London: Ashgate, 2010); James Vernon, *Hunger: A Modern History* (Cambridge, MA: Harvard University Press, 2007); Boyd Hilton, *The Age of Atonement: The Influence of Evangelicalism on Social and Economic Thought, 1785–1865* (Oxford: Clarendon Press, 1988), 73–114.

14. David Lambert and Alan Lester, eds., *Colonial Lives across the British Empire: Imperial Careering in the Long Nineteenth Century* (Cambridge: Cambridge University Press, 2006); Thomas Martin Devine and David Dickson, eds., *Ireland and Scotland, 1600–1850: Parallels and Contrasts in Economic and Social Development* (Edinburgh: Donald, 1983), 12; Eric Richards, "Scotland and the Uses of the Atlantic Empire," in *Strangers within the Realm: Cultural Margins of the First British Empire*, ed. Bernard Bailyn and Philip D. Morgan (Chapel Hill: University of North Carolina Press, 2012), 67–114; Emma Rothschild, *The Inner Life of Empires: An Eighteenth-Century History* (Princeton, NJ: Princeton University Press, 2011).

15. The report played a role in the repeal of the Corn Laws. *Copy of the Report of Dr Playfair and Mr Lindley on the Present State of the Irish Potato Crop, and on the Prospect of the Approaching Scarcity* (London: Clowes and Sons, 1846); Christine Kinealy, *This Great Calamity: The Great Irish Famine: The Irish Famine 1845–52* (Dublin: Gill & Macmillan Ltd, 1994), 34–35.

16. *Reports by the Juries*, 51, 590.

17. Auerbach, *The Great Exhibition of 1851*, 70–75, 92–94.

18. *Catalogue of the Collection of Animal Products* (London: Clowes and Sons, 1858); on Simmonds, see "Obituary. Peter Lund Simmonds, F.L.S.," *Journal of the Society of Arts* 45, no. 2343 (October 15, 1897): 1150; David Greysmith, "Simmonds, Peter Lund (1814–1897)," in *Oxford Dictionary of National Biography* (Oxford: Oxford University Press, 2004), http://www.oxforddnb.com.ezp-prod1.hul.harvard.edu/view/article/41011.

19. Simmonds's major published work on waste was Peter Lund Simmonds, *Waste Products and Undeveloped Substances; or, Hints for Enterprise in Neglected Fields* (London: R. Hardwicke, 1862) with subsequent editions in 1873 and 1876; his speeches on waste utilization include Peter Lund Simmonds, "On Some Undeveloped and Unappreciated Articles of Raw Produce from Different Parts of the World," *Journal of the Society of Arts* 2, no. 106 (December 1, 1854): 33–42; Peter Lund Simmonds, "On the Utilization of Waste Substances," *Journal of the Royal Society of Arts* 7, no. 325 (February 11, 1859): 175–88; Peter Lund Simmonds, "On the Useful Application of Waste Products and Undeveloped Substances," *Journal of the Royal Society of Arts* 17, no. 846 (February 5, 1869): 171–81; for a succinct analysis of Simmonds and waste, see Timothy Cooper, "Peter Lund Simmonds and the Political Ecology of 'Waste Utilisation' in Victorian Britain," *Technology and Culture* 52, no. 1 (January 2011): 21–44.

20. Matthew Paskins, "Sentimental Industry: The Society of Arts and the Encouragement of Public Useful Knowledge, 1754–1848" (London, PhD dissertation, University College London, 2014); on the early history of the Society, see also Max Louis Kent, "The British Enlightenment and the Spirit of the Industrial Revolution: The Society for the Encouragement of Arts, Manufactures and Commerce (1754–1815)" (PhD dissertation, University of California, 2007).

21. "Subjects for Premiums," *Journal of the Society of Arts* 1 (December 15, 1852): 39–43; "List of Subjects for Premiums," *Journal of the Society of Arts* 1 (December 10, 1852): 26–28.

22. R. H. Horne, "Dust; or Ugliness Redeemed," ed. Charles Dickens, *Household Words* 1, no. 16 (July 13, 1850): 379–84.

23. Horne, 380.

24. Horne, "Dust; or Ugliness Redeemed."

25. Henry Mayhew, *London Labour and the London Poor* (London: Griffin, Bone and Co., 1851), 166–81.

26. Though it has been interpreted as such; see Pierre Desrochers, "Victorian Pioneers of Corporate Sustainability," *Business History Review* 83, no. 4 (2009): 703–29.

27. Simon Werrett, *Thrifty Science: Making the Most of Materials in the History of Experiment* (Chicago: Chicago University Press, 2019), 15–41.

28. Cooper, "Peter Lund Simmonds"; Erland Marald, "Everything Circulates: Agricultural Chemistry and Recycling Theories in the Second Half of the Nineteenth Century," *Environment and History* 8, no. 1 (2002): 65–84.

29. Edwin Lankester, *The Uses of Animals in Relation to the Industry of Man; Being a Course of Lectures Delivered at the South Kensington Museum* (London: Hardwicke, 1860), 11.

30. Werrett, *Thrifty Science*, 181–87.

31. Charles Babbage, *On the Economy of Machinery and Manufactures*, 1st ed. (London: Charles Knight, 1832), 6.

32. Babbage, 10.

33. Charles Babbage, *On the Economy of Machinery and Manufactures*, 4th ed. (London: Charles Knight, 1835), 393–96.

34. Simmonds, "On Some Undeveloped and Unappreciated Articles."

35. Lyon Playfair, "The Chemical Principles Involved in the Manufactures of the Exhibition as Indicating the Necessity of Industrial Instruction," in *Lectures on the Results of the Great Exhibition of 1851* (London: G. Barclay, 1852), 159–66.

36. John Joseph Mechi, "Fourth Paper on British Agriculture with Some Account of His Own Operations at Tiptree Hall Farm," *Journal of the Royal Society of Arts* 3, no. 107 (December 8, 1854): 49–50.

37. Playfair, "The Chemical Principles Involved in the Manufactures of the Exhibition," 162–63.

38. Lankester, *The Uses of Animals in Relation to the Industry of Man*.

39. Ann Christie, "'Nothing of Intrinsic Value': The Scientific Collections at the Bethnal Green Museum," *V&A Online Journal*, no. 3 (Spring 2011); Pierre Desrochers, "Promoting Corporate Environmental Sustainability in the Victorian Era: The Bethnal Green Museum Permanent Waste Exhibit (1875–1928)," *V&A Online Journal*, no. 3 (Spring 2011); Desrochers, "Victorian Pioneers of Corporate Sustainability."

40. Edward Solly, "On the Mutual Relations of Trade and Manufactures," *Journal of the Society of Arts* 3, no. 131 (May 25, 1855): 487–94; Edwin Lankester, *A Guide to the Food Collection in the South Kensington Museum* (London: Eyre and Spottiswoode, 1860), 1.

41. Solly, "On the Mutual Relations of Trade and Manufactures."

42. Solly, 494; *Catalogue of the Collection of Animal Products*, 1.

43. Lankester, *A Guide to the Food Collection in the South Kensington Museum*, 1.

44. Edwin Lankester, *Vegetable Substances Used for the Food of Man* (London: Charles Knight, 1832), 5.

45. Alexander von Humboldt, *Essai politique sur le royaume de la Nouvelle-Espagne*, vol. 2 (Paris: F. Schoell, 1811).

46. Lankester, *Vegetable Substances*, 150; William Jacob, *Tracts Relating to the Corn Trade and Corn Laws* (London: John Murray, 1828), 169–71.

47. Spary, *Feeding France*, 89–124.

48. Lankester, *Vegetable Substances*, 160.

49. On Humphry Davy, see Jan Golinski, *The Experimental Self: Humphry Davy and the Making of a Man of Science* (Chicago: University of Chicago Press, 2016).

50. Humphry Davy, *Elements of Agricultural Chemistry* (London: Longman, Hurst, Rees, Orme, and Brown, 1813), 10.

51. Davy, 10.

52. Lankester, *Vegetable Substances*, 150.

53. Justus Liebig, *Organic Chemistry in Its Applications to Agriculture and Physiology*, trans. Lyon Playfair (London: Taylor and Walton, 1840); Lyon Playfair, *On the Food of Man in Relation to His Useful Work* (Edinburgh: Edmonston and Douglas, 1865).

54. Justus Liebig, *Familiar Letters on Chemistry: And Its Relation to Commerce, Physiology, and Agriculture*, trans. John Gardner (Philadelphia: Taylor and Walton, 1843); Brock, *Justus Von Liebig*.

55. On attempts to reconcile newer conceptions of nourishment with older animal-vegetable hierarchies, see Alan David Krinsky, "Let Them Eat Horsemeat: Science, Philanthropy, State, and the Search for Complete Nutrition in Nineteenth-Century France" (PhD dissertation, University of Wisconsin, Madison, 2001), 71–82.

56. Jonathan Pereira, *A Treatise on Food and Diet* (New York: J. & H.G. Langley, 1843).

57. Edward Smith, "On Private and Public Dietaries," Journal of the Society of Arts 12, no. 587 (February 19, 1864): 212; see also Edward Smith, *Dietaries for the Inmates of Workhouses. Report to the President of the Poor Law Board.* (London: Eyre and Spottiswoode, 1866); "Workhouse Dietaries," in *Accounts and Papers of the House of Commons*, vol. 60, 1867.

58. *Reports by the Juries*, 67.

59. John Lindley, "Substances Used as Food, Illustrated by the Great Exhibition," in *Lectures on the Results of the Great Exhibition of 1851* (London: G. Barclay, 1852), 223–24.

60. Lindley, 225; *Reports by the Juries*, 65–67.

61. Lindley, 226.

62. William Bridges Adams, "What Is Food," *Journal of the Society of Arts*, September 7, 1855, 695–96.

63. Auerbach, *The Great Exhibition of 1851*, 100.

64. Simmonds, "On Some Undeveloped and Unappreciated Articles"; Simmonds, "On the Utilization of Waste Substances"; Simmonds, *Waste Products and Undeveloped Substances*; Simmonds, "On the Useful Application of Waste Products and Undeveloped Substances."

65. Simmonds, "On Some Undeveloped and Unappreciated Articles."

66. Lindley, "Substances Used as Food, Illustrated by the Great Exhibition," 212.

67. Lindley, 212.

68. Lindley, 218–19.

69. Lindley, 219–20.

70. *Substances Used as Food, as Exemplified in the Great Exhibition* (London: Society for Promoting Christian Knowledge, 1854), 72.

71. Gail Borden and Ashbel Smith, *Letter of Gail Borden, Jr., to Dr. Ashbel Smith, Setting Forth an Important Invention in the Preparation of a New Article of Food, Termed Meat Biscuit* (Galveston: Gibson & Cherry, 1850), 8.

72. *Reports by the Juries*, 155.

73. Lindley, "Substances Used as Food, Illustrated by the Great Exhibition," 225.

74. *Official Descriptive and Illustrated Catalogue of the Great Exhibition of the Works of Industry of All Nations, 1851*, vol. 3 (London: Clowes and Sons, 1851), 1466.

75. Auerbach, *The Great Exhibition of 1851*, 92; Steve Edwards, "The Accumulation of Knowledge or, William Whewell's Eye," in *The Great Exhibition of 1851: New Interdisciplinary Essays*, ed. Louise Purbrick (Manchester: Manchester University Press, 2001), 26–52.

76. Auerbach, *The Great Exhibition of 1851*, 101.

77. Peter Lund Simmonds, *The Commercial Products of the Vegetable Kingdom* (London: T. F. A. Day, 1854), 4.

78. Simmonds, *Waste Products and Undeveloped Substances*, 4; Simmonds, "On Some Undeveloped and Unappreciated Articles," 34.

79. Simmonds, "On Some Undeveloped and Unappreciated Articles," 41.

80. Simmonds, 33.

81. Simmonds, 46. As Rebecca Woods has shown, however, the aspiration to feed large parts of the British population on concentrated, preserved meat products was largely thwarted by the lack of appetite British consumers seemed to have for such products. Woods, Rebecca J. H. "The Shape of Meat: Preserving Animal Flesh in Victorian Britain." *Osiris* 35 (August 2020): 123–41.

82. Simmonds, 33.

83. Pratik Chakrabarti, *Inscriptions of Nature: Geology and the Naturalization of Antiquity* (Baltimore: Johns Hopkins University Press, 2020).

84. Lankester, *Vegetable Substances*, 196.

85. Lankester, 85–86.

86. Lankester, 102.

87. Playfair, "The Chemical Principles Involved in the Manufactures of the Exhibition," 165.

88. Lankester, *Vegetable Substances*, 86.

89. Paul Young, "The Cooking Animal: Economic Man at the Great Exhibition," *Victorian Literature and Culture* 36, no. 2 (January 1, 2008): 569–86.

90. Lankester, *Vegetable Substances*, 85–86.

91. Lankester, 2.

92. Fredrik Albritton Jonsson, *Enlightenment's Frontier: The Scottish Highlands and the Origins of Environmentalism* (New Haven, CT: Yale University Press, 2013).

93. Lankester, *Vegetable Substances*, 171.

94. Reports by the Juries, 65.

1. Louisa Down to Benger's Food Ltd. Manchester, 8 January 1912, Letter Number 635, YA2005.84.195, Copies of testimonials 1911–1917, Archive of Benger's Food Ltd, Science and Industry Museum, Manchester. The following passage is based on Louisa Down's letter, with some passages lifted verbatim.

2. Though Pepsi's company website declares that pepsin was never an ingredient in Pepsi-Cola, an early twentieth-century visitor to the Pepsi-Cola plant observed the addition of pepsin during the production process. Pepsin was also a regular ingredient in many soda beverage recipes listed in pharmacy soda fountain recipe books at the time. "The Coast and the Coastal Plains," *National Magazine*, 1911; George H. Dubelle, *Dubelle's Famous Formulas for Soda Fountain Beverages* (New York: Spon & Chamberlain, 1901); George H. Dubelle, *Soda Fountain Beverages: A Practical Receipt Book for Druggists, Chemists, Confectioners and Venders of Soda Water* (New York: Spon & Chamberlain, 1905); The Soda Fountain, *The Dispenser Soda Water Guide: A Collection of Over 1300 Formulas for the Soda Fountain, to Which Has Been Added Numerous Hints and Suggestions for Plant Equipment and Operation, Refrigeration, the Manufacture of Ice Cream, Etc., Etc.* (New York: D.O. Haynes & Company, 1909).

3. Mary Terrall, *Catching Nature in the Act: Réaumur and the Practice of Natural History in the Eighteenth Century* (Chicago: University of Chicago Press, 2014), 161–64; René Antoine Ferchault de Réaumur, "Sur la digestion des oiseaux," *Histoire de l'Académie Royale des Sciences*, 1752, 266–307; 461–96.

4. Terrall, *Catching Nature in the Act*, 162.

5. Réaumur, "Sur la digestion des oiseaux."

6. Réaumur, 483–84.

7. Spary, *Eating the Enlightenment*, 43–48; Jessica Riskin, "The Defecating Duck, or, the Ambiguous Origins of Artificial Life," *Critical Inquiry* 29, no. 4 (June 1, 2003): 599–633; Frederic Holmes, *Claude Bernard and Animal Chemistry: The Emergence of a Scientist* (Cambridge, MA: Harvard University Press, 1974), 141–43.

8. Riskin, "The Defecating Duck."

9. William Beaumont, *Experiments and Observations on the Gastric Juice, and the Physiology of Digestion* (Plattsburgh, NY: Allen, 1833).

10. Johann Nepomuk Eberle, *Physiologie der Verdauung nach Versuchen auf natürlichem und künstlichem Wege* (Würzburg: Etlinger, 1834), 74–104.

11. Eberle, 104.

12. Johannes Müller and Theodor Schwann, "Versuche über die künstliche Verdauung des geronnenen Eiweisses," *Archiv für Anatomie, Physiologie und wissenschaftliche Medicin*, 1836, 66–89; Theodor Schwann, "Ueber das Wesen des Verdauungsprocesses," *Archiv Für Anatomie, Physiologie und Wissenschaftliche Medicin*, 1836, 90–138; Eberle, *Physiologie der Verdauung nach Versuchen auf natürlichem und künstlichem Wege*.

13. Ohad Parnes, "From Agents to Cells: Theodor Schwann's Research Notes of the Years 1835–1838," in *Reworking the Bench: Research Notebooks in the History of*

Science, ed. F. L. Holmes, J. Renn, and Hans-Jörg Rheinberger (Dordrecht: Kluwer, 2003), 119–39.

14. Schwann, "Ueber das Wesen," 110.

15. Schwann, 110; Parnes, "From Agents to Cells"; Holmes, *Claude Bernard and Animal Chemistry*, 160–72.

16. Gabriel Valentin, "Einige Resultate der im Sommer des gegenwärtigen Jahres zu Breslau über künstliche Verdauung angestellten Versuche," *Notizen aus dem Gebiete der Natur- und Heilkunde* 50, no. 14 (October 1836): 210–11.

17. August Vogel, "Über das Verdauungsprincip, Pepsin," *Münchener Gelehrte Anzeigen*, 1842, 717–19, 721–26.

18. *Amtlicher Bericht über die 18. Versammlung deutscher Naturforscher und Ärzte zu Erlangen im September 1840* (Braunschweig: Friedrich Vieweg, 1842), 129; Vogel, "Über das Verdauungsprincip, Pepsin," 725.

19. Vogel, "Über das Verdauungsprincip, Pepsin," 725.

20. Vogel, 725.

21. Lucien Corvisart, "De l'emploi des poudres nutrimentives (pepsine acidifiée),ressources qu'elles offrent à la médicine pratique," *Bulletin Général de Thérapeutique Médicale, Chirurgicale, Obstétricale et Pharmaceutique* 47 (1854): 320.

22. Corvisart, "De l'emploi des poudres nutrimentives."

23. Corvisart.

24. "The Lancet General Advertiser," *The Lancet*, April 4, 1857.

25. Julius Clarus, *Handbuch der speciellen Arzneimittellehre* (Leipzig: Otto Wigand, 1860), 329–30.

26. Clarus, 329–30.

27. Herrmann Hager, "Ueber Pepsin, seine Darstellung, Wirkung, und Dispensation," *Pharmazeutische Zentralhalle für Deutschland* 11, no. 7 and 8 (1870): 53–54 and 59–61.

28. Hager uses the German word *Köchinnen* which is unequivocally female.

29. "Lancashire and Cheshire Branch: Intermediate Meeting," *British Medical Journal*, May 17, 1879, 756–57.

30. William Roberts, "Observations on the Digestive Ferments and Their Therapeutical Uses," *British Medical Journal* 2, no. 983 and 984 (November 1, 1879): 683.

31. Robert Hampson, "The Condition and Prospects of Pharmacy in Its Relation to the Medical Profession," *Pharmaceutical Journal* 11, no. 7 (January 1870): 404–8.

32. Hampson, 408.

33. Frederick Baden Benger, "On the Pharmaceutical Applications of Glycerine," *American Journal of Pharmacy* 34 (1865): 61–67.

34. Frederick Baden Benger, "Note on the Condition in Which Salicylic Acid Is Excreted by Patients," *Pharmaceutical Journal and Transactions* 7 (September 30, 1876): 282–83.

35. Benjamin R. Cohen, *Pure Adulteration: Cheating on Nature in the Age of Manufactured Food* (Chicago: University of Chicago Press, 2019); Deborah Blum, *The Poison Squad: One Chemist's Single-Minded Crusade for Food Safety at the Turn of the Twentieth Century* (New York: Penguin, 2018).

36. The nature of pepsin as a purely proteolytic ferment or a simultaneously proteolytic and milk-curdling ferment was long debated. The research was difficult because the powers of pepsin depend on the presence of hydrochloric acid as well as pH and temperature. In addition, researchers often used the extracts of different animal stomachs (some of which contained chymosin, a milk-curdling enzyme, and some of which did not) interchangeably. I cite Benger's research not because he achieved insights that we today consider true but to show that he was participating in scientific activity on a par with physiologists, using the same methods and pursuing the same questions as physiologists. His interest went beyond practical concerns of pharmacy, and his results were cited in discussions of the mechanisms of digestive physiology.

37. Though it is clear Benger and Roberts worked together, and that a female relative played a major role particularly in the development of the culinary preparations, we only have Roberts's record of the results of their research. Besides crediting Benger with the preparation of the ferment products used during research, Roberts acknowledged Benger for having rendered him "invaluable aid throughout" the investigations with digestive ferments "by his skill as a practical pharmaceutist and his aptitude for experimental work." An apprentice at Paine's and Benger's firm later confirmed that Benger was conducting "certain experimental work" at Benger's laboratory while Roberts "was practically a daily visitor to the laboratory." He also insisted that "the knowledge acquired of the digestive ferments during the course of the work done for Dr. William Roberts suggested to Mr. Benger the preparation now known as Benger's Food." All the experimental work in connection with Benger's Food and the "digestive liquors" preceding it, according to the assistant, was done in Benger's laboratory in Manchester. Besides a brief mention by Roberts in his Lumleian lectures, there is no further reference to the contribution of the female relative. Roberts, "Observations on the Digestive Ferments and Their Therapeutical Uses," 725; A. E. H. Blackburn, "Origins of Benger's Food," *Pharmaceutical Journal and Pharmacist* 34 (April 27, 1912): 562; William Roberts, "The Lumleian Lectures on the Digestive Ferments, and the Preparation and Use of Artificially Digested Food: Lecture III," *British Medical Journal* 1, no. 1009 and 1010 (1880): 649.

38. Roberts, "Observations on the Digestive Ferments and Their Therapeutical Uses," 683.

39. Roberts, 683.

40. John Richardson & Co., "Peptocolos," *London Medical Record* 7 (December 15, 1879): Advertisements; "Messrs. Savory & Moore Beg to Invite the Attention of the Medical Profession," *Medical Times and Gazette*, May 29, 1875.

41. Roberts, "Observations on the Digestive Ferments and Their Therapeutical Uses," 684.

42. William Roberts, "The Lumleian Lectures on the Digestive Ferments, and the Preparation and Use of Artificially Digested Food: Lecture I," *British Medical Journal* 1, no. 1006 (April 10, 1880): 543.

43. Roberts, "Observations on the Digestive Ferments and Their Therapeutical Uses," 685.

44. "Benger's Preparations of the Natural Digestive Ferments," *The Lancet*, December 13, 1879.

45. "Benger's Preparations of the Natural Digestive Ferments," in *Yearbook of Pharmacy* (London: J. & A. Churchill, 1880), 630.

46. Roberts, "Observations on the Digestive Ferments and Their Therapeutical Uses," 685.

47. Roberts, 724.

48. Benjamin Ward Richardson, "On Thrift in Relation to Food," *Journal of the Society of Arts*, March 19, 1880, 383–85.

49. Benjamin Ward Richardson, "The Skeleton in the National Cupboard," *Asclepiad* 3 (1886): 218.

50. Richardson, "On Thrift in Relation to Food."

51. Richardson, 385.

52. Richardson, "On Thrift in Relation to Food."

53. Beverly Lemire, *The Business of Everyday Life: Gender, Practice and Social Politics in England, c. 1600–1900* (Manchester: Manchester University Press, 2005), 142–59.

54. This is most clearly articulated in Samuel Smiles, *Workmen's Earnings, Strikes, and Savings* (London: J. Murray, 1862); Samuel Smiles, *Thrift* (London: Murray, 1875); see also the anonymously written *Low Wages; or, Thrift and Good Management* (London: S. W. Partridge, 1863); on Samuel Smiles and the development of his views on thrift, see Kenneth Fielden, "Samuel Smiles and Self-Help," *Victorian Studies* 12, no. 2 (1968): 155–76.

55. "A Self-Help Society," *Chambers's Journal of Popular Literature, Science and Arts* 4, no. 932 (November 5, 1881): 705.

56. Linda Colley, *Britons: Forging the Nation, 1707–1837* (New Haven, CT: Yale University Press, 2009), 5.

57. Leone Levi, "Thrift the Virtue," *Thrift: A Monthly Journal of Social Progress and Reform* 1, no. 1 (January 1882): 4.

58. Leone Levi, *Work and Pay; or, Principles of Industrial Economy* (London: Strahan and Company, 1877).

59. "Introduction," *Thrift: A Monthly Journal of Social Progress and Reform* 1, no. 1 (January 1882): 1.

60. Levi, *Work and Pay*, 111.

61. "Reception by H.R.H. the Prince of Wales, K.G., of the International Juries," in *The Health Exhibition Literature*, vol. 18 (London: Clowes and Sons, 1884), 6–10.

62. "Reception of the International Juries," 11–12.

63. *The Health Exhibition Literature*, vol. 18 (London: Clowes and Sons, 1884), 14.

64. Benjamin Ward Richardson, *Hygeia: A City of Health* (London: Macmillan, 1876).

65. George Vivian Poore, "Our Duty in Relation to Health," in *The Health Exhibition Literature*, vol. 7 (London: William Clowes, 1884), 8.

66. Poore, 3–4.

67. May Yates, "Bread Reform," *Thrift: A Monthly Journal of Social Progress and Reform* 1, no. 1 (January 1882): 11.

68. Yates.

69. Henry Law, "Thrift: An Address to the Working Classes," *Journal of the Royal Sanitary Institute* 9 (1888): 464.

70. Levi, *Work and Pay*, 104.

71. Levi, 105.

72. Smith, *Dietaries for the Inmates of Workhouses*, 33.

73. Smith, 35.

74. According to the floorplans of the exhibition. *Health Exhibition Literature*, 18:99–100.

75. *Health Exhibition Literature*, 18:203, 241, 288.

76. *Health Exhibition Literature*, 18:46, 488.

77. *The Health Exhibition Literature*, vol. 19 (London: Clowes and Sons, 1884), 13; Jessup Whitehead, "The Bouillons-Duvals System," in *The Steward's Handbook and Guide to Party Catering* (Chicago: J. Anderson, 1889), 96–98; "Duval Dinners," *Coffee Public-House News and Temperance Hotel Journal*, January 1, 1886.

78. *The Health Exhibition Literature*, 19:18.

79. Albala, *Eating Right in the Renaissance*, 56–62.

80. Roberts, "Lumleian Lectures III," 647.

81. Phebe Lankester, *The National Thrift Reader* (London: Allman and Son, 1880), 90.

82. Lankester, 90.

83. Benjamin Ward Richardson, "Woman as a Sanitary Reformer," in *Report of the Fourth Congress of the Sanitary Institute of Great Britain*, ed. Henry Burdett and F. de Chaumont (Office of the Institute, 1880), 2:183–202; quotation on 188.

84. Smiles, *Thrift*, 281–82.

85. Arthur Gamgee, "Physiology of Digestion and the Digestive Organs," in *The Health Exhibition Literature. Volume IV: Health in Diet* (London: Clowes and Sons, 1884), 1–162; Arthur Gamgee, "The Digestive Ferments and the Chemical Processes of Digestion," in *The Health Exhibition Literature. Volume VI: Health in Diet* (London: Clowes and Sons, 1884), 1–36; Septimus Berdmore, "The Principles of Cooking," in *The Health Exhibition Literature. Volume IV: Health in Diet* (London: Clowes and Sons, 1884), 163–250; Alexander Winter Blythe, "Diet in Relation to Health and Work," in *The Health Exhibition Literature. Volume IV: Health in Diet* (London: Clowes and Sons, 1884), 251–354.

86. Blythe, "Diet in Relation to Health," 286.

87. Blythe, 287; Theodor Bischoff and Karl von Voit, *Die Gesetze der Ernährung des Fleischfressers durch neue Untersuchungen* (Leipzig: Winter, 1860); Ernst Bischoff, "Versuche über die Ernährung mit Brod," *Zeitschrift für Biologie* 5 (1869): 452–75; Hugo Weiske, "Untersuchungen über die Verdaulichkeit der Cellulose beim Menschen," *Zeitschrift für Biologie* 6 (1870): 456–66; Gustav Meyer, "Ernährungsversuche mit Brod am Hund und Menschen," *Zeitschrift für Biologie* 7 (1871):

1–48; Max Rubner, "Ueber die Ausnützung einiger Nahrungsmittel im Darmcanale des Menschen," *Zeitschrift für Biologie* 15 (1879): 115–202.

88. Blythe, "Diet in Relation to Health," 287.

89. Blythe, 288.

90. Gamgee, "Physiology of Digestion," 109; 133–35.

91. Gamgee, "The Digestive Ferments," 3.

92. Gamgee, 18–19.

93. Gamgee, 31.

94. Gamgee, 32.

95. Gamgee, 32–33.

96. "Leube-Rosenthal Improved Meat Solution," *Archives of Medicine: A Bi-Monthly Journal Devoted to Original Communications on Medicine, Surgery, and Their Special Branches* 12, no. 3 (1885): 1.

97. *Health Exhibition Literature*, 18:202.

98. "Mellin's Food for Infants and Invalids," *British Medical Journal* 1185 (September 15, 1883): Advertisements; *Health Exhibition Literature*, 18:201.

99. Lucien Corvisart, *Étude sur les aliments et les nutriments et sur la méthode nutrimentive dans les cas de vice de sécrétion de l'estomac* (Paris: Labé, 1854), 8.

100. Lucien Corvisart, "Recherches ayant pour but d'administrer aux malades qui ne digèrent point, des aliments tout digérés par le suc gastrique des animaux," *Comptes Rendus Hebdomadaires des Séances de l'Académie des Sciences* 35 (1852): 331.

101. Corvisart, 331.

102. William Marcet, *On a New Process for Preparing Meat for Weak Stomachs* (London: J. Churchill, 1867).

103. Marcet, 16.

104. Frederick William Pavy, *A Treatise on the Function of Digestion: Its Disorders, and Their Treatment* (London: Churchill, 1867), 214.

105. Pavy, 215.

106. William Roberts, "On Some New Articles of Peptonised Food Prepared by the Pancreatic Method," in *Transactions of the International Medical Congress, Seventh Session, Held in London, August 2d to 9th, 1881* (London: J.W. Kolckmann, 1881), 518.

107. Roberts, 518–19.

108. Roberts, 518.

109. Roberts, "Lumleian Lectures III," 649.

110. "A Descriptive List of Benger's Preparations of the Natural Digestive Ferments" (Bodleian Library, Oxford University, John Johnson Collection, 1889), http://gateway.proquest.com/openurl?url_ver=Z39.88-2004&res_dat=xri:jjohnson:&rft_dat=xri:jjohnson:rec:20090605102612kg.

111. Roberts, "On Some New Articles of Peptonised Food," 519.

112. Roberts, "Lumleian Lectures III," 647.

113. Pavy, *A Treatise on the Function of Digestion*, 217.

114. Roberts, "On Some New Articles of Peptonised Food," 518.

115. Roberts, "Lumleian Lectures III," 649.

116. William Roberts, *On the Digestive Ferments and the Preparation and Use of Artificially Digested Food: Being the Lumleian Lectures for the Year 1880* (London: Smith, Elder, 1881), 61.

117. Roberts, 61.

118. William Roberts, "Address in Therapeutics," *British Medical Journal* 1 (August 1, 1885): 192.

119. Roberts, 192.

120. "Fifty-Third Annual Meeting of the British Medical Association," *British Medical Journal* 2 (September 5, 1885): 452; Roberts, "Address in Therapeutics," 192.

121. James Wallace Anderson, *Lectures on Medical Nursing: Delivered in the Royal Infirmary, Glasgow* (Glasgow: James Maclehose, 1883), 208–10; Charles Egerton Fitz-Gerald, *Lectures on Physiology, Hygiene, Etc. for Hospital and Home Nursing* (London: George Bell & Sons, 1892), 85; Laurence Humphry, *A Manual of Nursing* (Philadelphia: P. Blakiston, Son, & Company, 1894), 242; E. M. Worsnop, *The Nurse's Handbook of Cookery: A Help in Sickness and Convalescence* (London: Black, 1897), 96–100; James Kenneth Watson, *A Handbook for Nurses* (London: The Scientific Press, 1899), 83–84.

122. Worsnop, *The Nurse's Handbook of Cookery*, 96–100.

123. Anderson, *Lectures on Medical Nursing*, 208–10; Fitz-Gerald, *Lectures on Physiology, Hygiene, Etc. for Hospital and Home Nursing*, 86; For example, Humphry, *A Manual of Nursing*, 242; Watson, *A Handbook for Nurses*, 83–84; Marion Greenwood Bidder and Florence Baddeley, *Domestic Economy in Theory and Practice: A Text-Book for Teachers and Students in Training* (Cambridge: Cambridge University Press, 1901), 192.

124. "Savory & Moore's Peptoniser," *Medical Press and Circular*, October 3, 1883; *Health Exhibition Literature*, 18:201.

125. W. H. Spencer, "On Giving Rest to the Digestive Organs by the Use of Peptonised Food," *Bristol Medico-Chirurgical Journal* 2 (1884): 39.

126. Roberts, "Lumleian Lectures 1," 540.

127. "Benger's Self-Digestive Food," *Truth* 17 (January 15, 1885): 116; "A Descriptive List of Benger's Preparations," 6; "For Indigestion—Benger's Food," *Canadian Nurse* 8, no. 10 (October 1912): 581.

128. Anson Rabinbach, *The Human Motor: Energy, Fatigue, and the Origins of Modernity* (Berkeley: University of California Press, 1990), 136.

129. Benger's Food Limited, *Benger's Food and How to Use It* (Manchester: Taylor, Garnett, Evans & Co., 1907), Homeopathy Pamphlets vol. 250, no. 7, Cage, Historical Medical Library, College of Physicians of Philadelphia.

130. "Benger's Food," *The Strand Magazine* 38 (1909): 59.

131. *Health Exhibition Literature*, 18:58.

132. Roberts, "Address in Therapeutics," 188.

133. Roberts, 188–89.

1. John Harvey Kellogg, "Health Observations among American Aborigines," *Good Health* 24 (1889): 3–5, 36–38, 67–69, 102–3.

2. Kellogg, 3.

3. Kellogg, 37.

4. Kellogg, 37.

5. Kellogg.

6. Brian C. Wilson, *Dr. John Harvey Kellogg and the Religion of Biologic Living* (Bloomington: Indiana University Press, 2014).

7. Ellen H. Richards, *The Cost of Shelter* (New York: Wiley, 1905), 12.

8. Charles Rosenberg, "Pathologies of Progress: The Idea of Civilization as Risk," *Bulletin of the History of Medicine* 72, no. 4 (1998): 714–30.

9. Stephen Nissenbaum, *Sex, Diet, and Debility in Jacksonian America: Sylvester Graham and Health Reform*, American Society and Culture (London: Greenwood Press, 1980), 17–19.

10. On John Harvey Kellogg, see Wilson, *Biologic Living*; Howard Markel, *The Kelloggs: The Battling Brothers of Battle Creek* (New York: Pantheon Books, 2017); Richard Schwarz, *John Harvey Kellogg, M.D.: Pioneering Health Reformer* (Hagerstown, MD: Review and Herald Pub. Association, 2006).

11. Wilson, *Biologic Living*, 35–37.

12. Wilson, 30–61.

13. According to Schwarz, the Sanitarium provided between five thousand and ten thousand dollars' worth of free services to poor people in the first fifteen years after Kellogg took over. Later, a separate charity hospital and a free dispensary were added. Schwarz, *John Harvey Kellogg, M.D.*, 2006, 298–99.

14. Wilson, *Biologic Living*, 44–50.

15. Schwarz, *John Harvey Kellogg, M.D.*, 2006, 418–19.

16. "Food Experiments," Collection 13, Box 5, John Harvey Kellogg Papers, Michigan State University Archives and Historical Collections, East Lansing, Michigan (hereafter JHKP-MSU).

17. "Appeal from the Circuit Court of the United States for the Southern District of New York," *Official Gazette of the United States Patent Office* 92, no. 8 (August 21, 1900): 1620–22.

18. Ella Eaton Kellogg, *Science in the Kitchen* (Battle Creek: Health Publishing Company, 1892), 3.

19. Kellogg, 3.

20. Kellogg, 3; Ella Eaton Kellogg, *Healthful Cookery: A Collection of Choice Recipes for Preparing Foods, with Special Reference to Health* (Battle Creek: Modern Medicine Publishing Company, 1904), 5–6; on Ella Kellogg's central contribution to Sanitarium food, see Adam Shprintzen, "Ella Eaton Kellogg's Protose: Fake Meat and the Gender Politics That Made American Vegetarianism Modern," in *Acquired Tastes: Stories about the Origins of Modern Food*, ed. Benjamin R. Cohen, Michael S. Kideckel, and Anna Zeide (Cambridge, MA: MIT Press, 2021), 219–34.

21. Kellogg, *Healthful Cookery*, 5.

22. Unsigned Note, "Hotel Metropole, Paris, April 9," JHKP-MSU 13, 5, Note 5.

23. While only a few instances of Ella Kellogg's feedback are preserved in the archives, there are a number of notes in which John Harvey Kellogg provides feedback on the use of foods in cooking, so it is likely that Ella Kellogg often communicated orally with her husband, who then passed on her comments in writing to the food department.

24. Ella Eaton Kellogg to William Keith Kellogg, February 26, 1906, JHKP-MSU, Collection 13, Box 5 (Food experiments), Folder 9, Notes 25–26.

25. William Keith Kellogg to Arthur Kellogg, September 20, 1901, JHKP-MSU, Collection 13, Box 5 (Food experiments), Folder 6, Note 26.

26. "Food Experiments," Collection 13, Box 5, JHKP-MSU.

27. Daniel E. Bender, *American Abyss: Savagery and Civilization in the Age of Industry* (Ithaca, NY: Cornell University Press, 2009), 15–39.

28. Bender, 40–68; Alexandra Minna Stern, *Eugenic Nation: Faults and Frontiers of Better Breeding in Modern America* (Berkeley: University of California Press, 2005).

29. Bender, *American Abyss*, 69–98.

30. Sylvester Graham, *Lectures on the Science of Human Life* (Boston: Marsh, Capen, Lyon & Webb, 1839), 112.

31. Graham, 11.

32. John Harvey Kellogg, "Needed—A New Human Race," in *Proceedings of the First National Conference on Race Betterment* (Battle Creek: Gage, 1914), 438.

33. Sylvester Graham, *A Treatise on Bread, and Bread-Making* (Boston: Light & Stearns, 1837), 20.

34. Graham, 40–41.

35. Battle Creek Sanitarium, *Battle Creek Sanitarium Health Foods*, Pamphlets and handbills ca. 1895–1925, Medical Trade Ephemera, Cage, MHLCPP, ca. 1893, 3.

36. Battle Creek Sanitarium, 1.

37. Graham, *Lectures*, 130.

38. John Harvey Kellogg, *Plain Facts for Old and Young* (Burlington, IA: Segner & Condit, 1881).

39. Graham, *A Treatise on Bread, and Bread-Making*, 35.

40. Graham, 34.

41. Nissenbaum, *Sex, Diet, and Debility in Jacksonian America*, 17–19.

42. Graham, *A Treatise on Bread, and Bread-Making*, 34.

43. Tompkins, *Racial Indigestion*, 53–88.

44. Kellogg, "Health Observations," 3.

45. Kellogg, 36.

46. Kellogg, 5.

47. Kellogg describes that key to convincing the sisters to help him was a copy of his book on domestic medicine, which one of the sisters kept in her office and which the sisters allegedly relied on entirely in the management of disease outbreaks at the school. Kellogg, 5.

48. Kellogg, 36.

49. Ian Mosby, "Administering Colonial Science: Nutrition Research and Human Biomedical Experimentation in Aboriginal Communities and Residential Schools, 1942–1952," *Histoire Sociale/Social History* 46, no. 1 (2013): 145–72.

50. Kellogg, "Health Observations," 67.

51. Kellogg, 68.

52. Kellogg, 69.

53. "A Mild Return to Savagery," *Battle Creek Idea*, March 1914.

54. Kellogg, "Health Observations," 69.

55. "The Maltine Manufacturing Company," in *New York's Great Industries* (New York and Chicago: Historical Publishing Company, 1885), 308; "Malt-Diastase Co.," *Dietetic and Hygienic Gazette*, October 1897; "News," *American Druggist and Pharmaceutical Record* 27, no. 8 (October 25, 1895): 265; "Fairchild Brothers & Foster," in *Illustrated New York: The Metropolis of To-Day* (New York: International Publishing Company, 1888), 194–95.

56. "Peptenzyme," *Philadelphia Polyclinic* 4, no. 52 (December 28, 1895): ii.

57. Russell H. Chittenden, "On the Ferments Contained in the Juice of the Pineapple (Ananassa Sativa), Together with Some Observations on the Composition and Proteolytic Action of the Juice," *Transactions of the Connecticut Academy of Arts and Sciences* 8 (1888): 281–309; Russell H. Chittenden, "Papoid-Digestion," *Transactions of the Connecticut Academy of Arts and Sciences* 9, no. 1 (1892): 298–332.

58. "Pine-Apple Juice as Digestion Helper," *Medical Mirror* 8 (May 1897): 246–49; "Dygestiv," *Dietetic and Hygienic Gazette* 21, no. 3 (March 1905): 188; Bell and Company, Papayans, MHLCPP, Cage, Medical Trade Ephemera; Johnson and Johnson, Papoid Digestive Tablets, Cage, Medical Trade Ephemera.

59. For a detailed account of Taroena and the racist-imperialist logic to which it pertained, see Hobart and Maroney, "On Racial Constitutions and Digestive Therapeutics.".

60. The Taro Food Company, *An Illustrated History of Taroena, the Hawaiian Health Food* (Danbury, CT: The Taro Food Company, 1900), MHLCPP, Cage, Homeopathy Pamphlets Vol. 178, no. 15.

61. The Taro Food Company, *An Illustrated History of Taroena*, 1.

62. The Taro Food Company, 12.

63. "The Tuber Food," *Trained Nurse and Hospital Review* 34, no. 6 (1905): Advertisements.

64. The Sanitas Health Food Company, "Something Good to Eat," *Bulletin of the American Medical Temperance Association* 2, no. 4 (April 1895): Advertisements.

65. Battle Creek Sanitarium, *Battle Creek Sanitarium Health Foods*, 9.

66. Battle Creek Sanitarium, 10; "Granola, a Healthful Food," *The Bacteriological World and Modern Medicine* 1 (1891): Advertisements, 14.

67. "Granola, a Healthful Food."

68. Nicholas Bauch, *A Geography of Digestion: Biotechnology and the Kellogg Cereal Enterprise* (Berkeley: University of California Press, 2016), 79–80; Richard W.

Schwarz, *John Harvey Kellogg, M.D.: Pioneering Health Reformer* (Nashville, TN: Southern Publishing Association, 1970), 277–78.

69. Battle Creek Sanitarium, *Battle Creek Sanitarium Health Foods*, 10.

70. Battle Creek Sanitarium, 17.

71. Battle Creek Sanitarium, 17.

72. Schwarz, *John Harvey Kellogg, M.D.*, 1970, 276–83; Bauch, *A Geography of Digestion: Biotechnology and the Kellogg Cereal Enterprise*, 77–101.

73. Kellogg, "Health Observations," 103.

74. Battle Creek Sanitarium, *Battle Creek Sanitarium Health Foods*, 3–7.

75. Kellogg, *Science in the Kitchen*, 148–49.

76. Battle Creek Sanitarium, *Undigested Cereals the Cause of American Dyspepsia* (Pamphlets and handbills, ca.1895–1925, Cage, Medical Trade Ephemera, MHLCPP, n.d.).

77. Bauch, *A Geography of Digestion: Biotechnology and the Kellogg Cereal Enterprise*, 92.

78. Battle Creek Sanitarium, *Undigested Cereals the Cause of American Dyspepsia*.

79. *Undigested Cereals*.

80. *Undigested Cereals*.

81. "A Fruit and Nut Diet," *Good Health* 35 (1900): 373–76.

82. Battle Creek Sanitarium, *Battle Creek Sanitarium Health Foods*, 4.

83. Battle Creek Sanitarium, 11.

84. William Keith Kellogg to Arthur Kellogg, December 12, 1899, JHKP-MSU, Collection 13, Box 5 (Food experiments), Folder 2, Note 77.

85. John Harvey Kellogg to William Keith Kellogg, September 28, 1898, JHKP-MSU, Collection 13, Box 5 (Food experiments), Folder 1, Notes 10–11.

86. John Harvey Kellogg, *First Book in Physiology and Hygiene* (New York: American Book Company, 1888), 35.

87. John Harvey Kellogg, Flaked cereals and process of preparing same, United States US558393A, issued April 14, 1896, https://patents.google.com/patent/US558393A/en.

88. Kellogg.

89. The Sanitas Health Food Company, "Something Good to Eat."

90. John C. Hemmeter, "The Use and Abuse of Digestive Ferments," *Medical News* 80 (June 7, 1902): 1073–76.

91. "Scientific Slaughtering," *Scientific American*, January 20, 1894, 37. This article appeared originally in *Drover's Magazine*, and was reprinted in trade journals such as *Ice and Refrigeration*, *Industrial Refrigeration*, and *American Soap Journal and Manufacturing Chemist*; for pharmacists' fears of competition through the packinghouses, see "The Digestive Ferment Market," *The Bulletin of Pharmacy* 5, no. 9 (September 1891): 397.

92. John Harvey Kellogg, *Methods of Precision in the Investigation of Disorders of Digestion* (Battle Creek, MI: Modern Medicine Publishing Company, 1893), 5.

93. J. U. Lloyd, "Pepsin," *The Eclectic Medical Journal* 37 (1877): 497–99.

94. Frank Woodbury, "On the Digestive Ferment of the Carica Papaya in Gastro-Intestinal Disorders," *New York Medical Journal* 56 (July 30, 1892): 115–18.

95. "The Be-Gum of Spearmint," *The Fra: For Philistines and Roycrofters* 11 (1913): 48b–48c and preparations in author's private collection.

96. Dubelle, *Dubelle's Famous Formulas for Soda Fountain*, 45–46; Dubelle, *Soda Fountain Beverages*, 37–40; The Soda Fountain, *The Dispenser Soda Water Guide*, 35, 40–41, 43, 63, 71, 92–94, 103, 105, 121–22.

97. "Pepsin Tonic: A New Soda Drink," *Practical Druggist and Spatula* 24 (August 1908): 466; "The Passing of Pepsin," *Practical Druggist and Spatula* 24 (August 1908): 466.

98. This had been a concern voiced since at least the 1880s, including by William Roberts. Roberts, *On the Digestive Ferments and the Preparation and Use of Artificially Digested Food.*

99. "Editor's Table: The Conflict of Modern Society," *Appletons' Popular Science Monthly* 53 (1898): 840–42.

100. John F. Cowan, "Predigested Tommy," *The Christian Endeavor World* 19, no. 22 (March 2, 1905): 438

101. Cowan.

102. Lilian M. Heath, *The Red Telephone; or, Tricks of the Temper Exposed; Being Messages from the Under-World of Sin and How They Are Answered: A Book Portraying the Grave Dangers Found in the Various Walks of Life* (Chicago: W. R. Vansant, 1905), 5.

103. Heath, 100.

104. "Editor's Table: The Conflict of Modern Society."

105. Walter T. K. Nugent, *The Tolerant Populists: Kansas, Populism and Nativism* (Chicago: University of Chicago Press, 1963), 60.

106. N. B. Ashby, *The Riddle of the Sphinx* (Des Moines, IA: Industrial Publishing Company, 1890), 310, 373.

107. Herbert Spencer, *The Principles of Ethics*, vol. 2 (New York: Appleton, 1898), 376–94.

108. Alexander Johnson, "The Ethical Basis of Charity," *Open Court* 2, no. 10 (May 3, 1888): 927.

109. Johnson, 927.

110. Bender, *American Abyss.*

111. Ashby, *The Riddle of the Sphinx*, 21.

112. Ashby, 211–12.

113. Frederick Ludwig Hoffman, *Race Traits and Tendencies of the American Negro* (New York: Macmillan Company for the American Economic Association, 1896).

114. Hoffman, 326–29; see also Beatrix Hoffman, *The Wages of Sickness: The Politics of Health Insurance in Progressive America* (Chapel Hill: University of North Carolina Press, 2001), 57–67.

115. John Harvey Kellogg, "Cold Philosophy," *Medical Missionary* 3, no. 8 (August 1893): 178–79.

116. John Harvey Kellogg, "City Medical Missions," *Medical Missionary* 8 (1898): 138.

117. Kellogg, "Health Observations," 5.

118. John Harvey Kellogg, *The Living Temple* (Battle Creek, MI: Good Health Publishing Company, 1903), 106–7.

119. John Harvey Kellogg, *The Stomach: Its Disorders, and How to Cure Them* (Battle Creek, MI: Modern Medicine Publishing Company, 1896), 262.

120. Kellogg, 38.

121. Kellogg, 39.

122. John Harvey Kellogg, "What Is the Matter with the American Stomach?," *Modern Medicine and Bacteriological Review* 5 (March 1896): 25–30, 53–58, 72–78.

123. Kellogg.

124. Pavlov and Kellogg corresponded for several years; Kellogg visited Pavlov in 1907, kept an enlarged photograph of Pavlov in his office, and even hired one of Pavlov's former students, Vladimir Boldyrev, to erect a Pavlovian physiological laboratory in the Sanitarium. Pavlov returned the visit in 1923 and even spent some time as a patient in the Sanitarium. Daniel P. Todes, *Ivan Pavlov: A Russian Life in Science* (Oxford: Oxford University Press, 2014), 316–17, 456–57; Markel, *The Kelloggs*, 114–16, 186.

125. Michael Vincent O'Shea and John Harvey Kellogg, *The Body in Health*, vol. 3 (New York: Macmillan, 1915), 58–73.

126. O'Shea and Kellogg, 3:58–59.

127. O'Shea and Kellogg, 3:63.

128. O'Shea and Kellogg, 3:71.

129. John Harvey Kellogg, "The Battle Creek Sanitarium Diet List" (Pamphlets and handbills ca. 1895–1925, Medical Trade Ephemera, Cage, HMLCCP, 1916), 26.

130. Kellogg, 20–21.

131. This was a direct challenge to the remote, personal God of Seventh-day Adventism, and ultimately led to Kellogg's split from the church. Wilson, *Biologic Living*, 62–105; Schwarz, *John Harvey Kellogg, M.D.*, 1970, 184–86; Markel, *The Kelloggs*, 168–69.

132. Kellogg, *The Living Temple*, 84.

133. Paradoxically, one of Ellen White's testimonies provided the inspiration for Kellogg's conception of a divine stimulating presence in the material world. Wilson, *Biologic Living*, 71–74.

134. Kellogg, *The Living Temple*, 66.

135. "Pure Grape Juice," *Modern Medicine and Bacteriological Review* 1, no. 4 (February 1892): Advertisements 3.

136. Kellogg, "The Battle Creek Sanitarium Diet List," 36.

137. John Harvey Kellogg, "Pan-Peptogen," *Modern Medicine and Bacteriological Review* 11, no. 1 (1902): Back Cover.

138. Sanitas Nut Food Company, *Sanitas Nut Preparations and Specialities* (Battle Creek, MI: Review and Herald Publishing Company, 1898).

139. John Harvey Kellogg, "Fat and Blood," *Modern Medicine and Bacteriological Review* 4 (September 1895): 234.

140. Kellogg, *The Stomach: Its Disorders, and How to Cure Them*, 229.

141. Kellogg, "Fat and Blood."

142. John Harvey Kellogg, "A Last Word about Digestion," *Dietetic and Hygienic Gazette* 18 (1902): 148–51.

143. Reed & Carnrick, "Peptenzyme a Perfect Digestant," *St. Louis Clinique: A Monthly Journal of Clinical Medicine and Surgery* 11, no. 10 (October 1898): 565.

144. "Carnrick's Liquid Peptonoids," *Australasian Medical Gazette* 21 (December 20, 1902): xliii.

145. "Proteinol," *Saint Louis Medical and Surgical Journal* 63 (1892): 11.

146. G. W. Carnrick & Co., "Secretogen: A Natural Stimulus to the Outpouring of the Digestive Secretions" (Homeopathy Pamphlets vol. 239, pamphlet 47, Cage, HMLCPP, Philadelphia, 1900).

147. Laboratories of Applied Physiology of France, American Branch, "Hepptine," *American Medicine* 17, no. 9 (September 1911): 6; Laboratories of Applied Physiology of France, American Branch, "Gastro-Enteritis and Dyspepsia of Children: Clinical Observations" (Homeopathy Pamphlets vol. 250, pamphlet 11, Cage, HMLCPP, 1905); Todes, *Pavlov's Physiology Factory*, 259–88.

148. "7 Reasons Why Papoid Is Superior to Pepsin," *Saint Louis Medical and Surgical Journal* 63, no. 6 (December 1892): Advertisements.

149. John Harvey Kellogg, "Biennial Report of the Medical Superintendent of the Battle Creek Sanitarium," *Bacteriological World and Modern Medicine* 1 (1891): 112.

150. Kellogg, 112.

151. On the raced and classed construction of the consumer in the early twentieth-century breakfast cereal industry, see Michael S. Kideckel, "The Search for the Average Consumer: Breakfast Cereal and the Industrialization of the American Food Supply," in *Acquired Tastes: Stories about the Origins of Modern Food*, ed. Benjamin R. Cohen, Michael S. Kideckel, and Anna Zeide (Cambridge, MA: MIT Press, 2021), 117–32.

152. Race Betterment Foundation, *Proceedings of the First National Conference on Race Betterment* (Battle Creek, MI: Gage, 1914), 554–89.

153. Kellogg, "Needed—A New Human Race."

154. Kellogg, 436.

155. Kellogg, 448–49.

156. Kellogg, 446.

157. Kellogg, *The Living Temple*, 108.

CHAPTER 5. THE BREWER, THE BAKER, AND THE HEALTH FOOD MAKER

1. Philip B. Hawk, Clarence A. Smith, and Ralph C. Holder, "Baker's Yeast as Food for Man," *American Journal of Physiology* 48 (1919): 199–210.

2. Philip B. Hawk, Hamilton R. Fishback, and Olaf Bergeim, "Compressed Yeast as Food for the Growing Organism," *American Journal of Physiology*, 1919, 211–20.

3. Thomas B. Osborne and Lafayette B. Mendel, "The Nutritive Value of Yeast Protein," *Journal of Biological Chemistry* 38 (1919): 223–27.

4. Hawk, Smith, and Holder, "Baker's Yeast as Food for Man," 199; Osborne and Mendel, "The Nutritive Value of Yeast Protein," 223.

5. "Yeast in a New Role," *Journal of the American Medical Association* 66, no. 18 (April 29, 1916): 1390–91.

6. Catherine Price, *Vitamania: How Vitamins Revolutionized the Way We Think about Food* (New York: Penguin, 2016), 42–46.

7. "Good Health Through Yeast," *National Labor Digest* 1 (1919): 36.

8. "Good Health Through Yeast."

9. Levenstein, *Revolution at the Table*, 153–59; James Whorton, *Inner Hygiene: Constipation and the Pursuit of Health in Modern Society* (New York: Oxford University Press, 2000), 170–72; Catherine Price, "The Healing Power of Compressed Yeast," *Distillations Magazine*, Fall 2015.

10. Apple, *Vitamania: Vitamins in American Culture*; Ackerman, "Interpreting the 'Newer Knowledge of Nutrition'"; Price, *Vitamania*.

11. Christiaan Klieger, *The Fleischmann Yeast Family*, Images of America (Charleston, SC: Arcadia, 2004), 64.

12. Michael Worboys, "The Discovery of Colonial Malnutrition between the Wars," in *Imperial Medicine and Indigenous Societies*, ed. David Arnold (Manchester: Manchester University Press, 1988), 208–25.

13. Street, "Food as Pharma."

14. See for example Emil Braun, *Perfection in Baking* (Urica, NY: J. Braun, 1893).

15. Eleanor Kirk, *Choice Recipes: How to Use Fleischmann's Compressed Yeast* (New York: Jourgensen, 1889); other examples of recipe collections contrasting Fleischmann's Yeast with the unreliability of homemade yeast include Braun, *Perfection in Baking*, 53; and Jane Putnam Chauven, *The Columbian Cook Book: Containing Reliable Rules for Plain and Fancy Cooking* (St. Paul, MN: J.W. Cunningham, 1892), 5.

16. Helen Campbell, "Our Daily Bread," *Good Housekeeping*, November 14, 1885, 8.

17. Wilbur Olin Atwater, *Foods: Nutritive Value and Cost* (Washington: Government Printing Office, 1894), 4.

18. *American Food Journal* (March 1915), 2.

19. Cohen, *Pure Adulteration*; Blum, *The Poison Squad*.

20. Clayton A. Coppin and Jack C. High, *The Politics of Purity: Harvey Washington Wiley and the Origins of Federal Food Policy* (Ann Arbor: University of Michigan Press, 1999), 72.

21. "Keeping Faith with Food Officials," *American Food Journal* (March 1915), 122.

22. *American Food Journal*, between January and July 1912.

23. Helen Veit, *Modern Food, Moral Food: Self-Control, Science, and the Rise of Modern American Eating in the Early Twentieth Century* (Chapel Hill: University of North Carolina Press, 2013).

24. *American Food Journal* (July 1918).

25. *American Food Journal* (April 1918).

26. Brian J. McCabe, *No Place Like Home: Wealth, Community and the Politics of Homeownership* (Oxford: Oxford University Press, 2016), 24–26.

27. Cindy R. Lobel, *Urban Appetites: Food and Culture in Nineteenth-Century New York* (Chicago: University of Chicago Press, 2014), 106–8.

28. Andrew P. Haley, *Turning the Tables: Restaurants and the Rise of the American Middle Class, 1880–1920* (Chapel Hill: University of North Carolina Press, 2011), 71–72.

29. C. P. Russell, "Advertising in New Fields When the Initial Market Becomes Smaller," *Printers' Ink* 61, no. 4 (April 22, 1920): 4.

30. Philip B. Hawk, "The Use of Baker's Yeast in Diseases of the Skin and of the Gastro-Intestinal Tract," *Journal of the American Medical Association* 69, no. 15 (October 13, 1917): 1243–47.

31. For example, The Fleischmann Company, "Used in All Tests," *West Virginia Medical Journal* 13 (October 1918): xvi; The Fleischmann Company, "Rich in Vitamins," *Illinois Medical Journal* 35, no. 2 (February 1919): 23; The Fleischmann Company, "Scientific Precisions," *Illinois Medical Journal* 35, no. 5 (March 1919): 23.

32. Klieger, *The Fleischmann Yeast Family*, 64; Price, "The Healing Power of Compressed Yeast."

33. "Spending a Million to Sell a Three Cent Product," *Advertising & Selling Magazine*, September 17, 1921.

34. Ward Gedney, "Getting a New Rise Out of the Yeast Cake," *Advertising & Selling* 30, no. 20 (November 6, 1920): 5–6; Russell, "Advertising in New Fields When the Initial Market Becomes Smaller."

35. Joseph M. Gabriel, *Medical Monopoly: Intellectual Property Rights and the Origins of the Modern Pharmaceutical Industry* (Chicago: University of Chicago Press, 2014), 195–96, 214–17.

36. "Our Advertisers," *Texas State Journal of Medicine* 14, no. 10 (February 1919): 321.

37. On the history of intracellular enzymes and their importance for the formation of biochemistry, see Robert E. Kohler, "The Enzyme Theory and the Origin of Biochemistry," *Isis* 64, no. 2 (1973): 181–96.

38. Eduard Buchner, "Alkoholische Gährung ohne Hefezellen (Vorläufige Mitteilung)," *Berichte der Deutschen Chemischen Gesellschaft* 30 (January 1897): 117–24.

39. Philip B. Hawk, *Practical Physiological Chemistry: A Book Designed for Use in Courses in Practical Physiological Chemistry in Schools of Medicine and of Science*, 3rd ed. (Philadelphia: P. Blakiston's Son, 1910), 2.

40. Martin E. Rehfuss, Olaf Bergheim, and Philip B. Hawk, "The Question of the Residuum Found in the Empty Stomach," *Journal of the American Medical Association* 63, no. 1 (July 4, 1914): 11; Martin E. Rehfuss, "A New Method of Gastric

Testing, with a Description of a Method for the Fractional Testing of the Gastric Juice," *American Journal of the Medical Sciences* 147, no. 6 (June 1914): 848–55.

41. Rehfuss, Bergheim, and Hawk, "The Question of the Residuum Found in the Empty Stomach."

42. Philip B. Hawk, *Practical Physiological Chemistry: A Book Designed for Use in Courses in Practical Physiological Chemistry in Schools of Medicine and of Science*, 5th ed. (Philadelphia: P. Blakiston's Son & Company, 1916), 148–51.

43. Whorton, *Inner Hygiene*, 22–28; Bauch, *A Geography of Digestion*, 53–55.

44. Philip B. Hawk, "What We Eat and What Happens to It," *Ladies Home Journal*, February 1918, 44, and April 1918, 59.

45. Hawk, "The Use of Baker's Yeast in Diseases of the Skin and of the Gastro-Intestinal Tract," 1243.

46. Louis-Anne-Jean Brocq, "La levure de bière dans la furonculose," *La Presse médicale* 7, no. 8 (January 28, 1899): 45–47.

47. Hawk, "The Use of Baker's Yeast in Diseases of the Skin and of the Gastro-Intestinal Tract," 1244.

48. John R. Murlin and Henry A. Mattill, "The Laxative Action of Yeast," *American Journal of Physiology* 64, no. 1 (March 1, 1923): 76; Hawk was also accused of improper scientific methods in another case, printed, ironically, in *JAMA*: "Susto-Nee Vinol Powder: The Conception and Birth of a Nostrum," *Journal of the American Medical Association* 79, no. 2 (October 28, 1922): 1538–39.

49. Hawk, "The Use of Baker's Yeast in Diseases of the Skin and of the Gastro-Intestinal Tract," 1247.

50. The Fleischmann Company, "Used in All Tests," xvi.

51. "Yeast—Living or 'Killed,'" *Illinois Medical Journal* 35, no. 4 (April 1919), 23.

52. The Fleischmann Company, "Scientific Precision,", 23; The Fleischmann Company, "Yeast Dosage," *Illinois Medical Journal* 35, no. 5 (May 1919), 25.

53. The Fleischmann Company, "Rich in Vitamins,"23.

54. "The Treatment of Constipation, with Remarks on the Yeast Treatment of Some Gastro-Intestinal Disorders," *West Virginia Medical Journal* 13 (February 1919): 290–92.

55. "Some Facts about Yeast," *West Virginia Medical Journal* 13 (August 1918): 53–56.

56. For example, the article "Some facts about years appeared in the *West Virginia Medical Journal* 13 (August 1918), 53–56, and in the *American Journal of Clinical Medicine* 25, 11 (November 1918), 863–64.

57. "Is your appetite uncertain—is your digestion impaired?" (December 2, 1921) 35 mm Microfilms, Reel 26-2, JWT Archives, "Made to grow or stunted at will," undated, 35 mm Microfilms, Reel 26-1, JWT Archives.

58. Research Department, "Analysis of Fleischmann's Foil Sales 1922–23," May 1923, 16 mm Microfilms, Reel 55-1, JWT Archives.

59. Department of Information Records, "Fleischmann's Yeast for Health National Campaign 1924," Information Center Records, Box 2 (Accounts), Folder 6 (Prizes, Contests 1923–1934).

60. Roy W. Johnson, "When a Consumer Contest Is Profitable and When It Isn't," *Printers' Ink* 96, no. 6 (August 10, 1916): 3–10.

61. R. L. Burdick, "Are Contests Successful To-Day?," *Printers' Ink* 112 (September 9, 1920): 73.

62. Fleischmann Publicity Story for *Editor and Publisher*, "The Story of the Fleischmann 'Yeast for Health Contest,' Information Center Records, Box 2 (Accounts), Folder 6 (Prizes, Contests 1923–1934).

63. Statistical Department, "The Fleischmann Yeast Investigation (Questionnaire by mail)," July 1923, 16 mm Microfilms, Reel 55-1, JWT Archives, 1.

64. Fleischmann Publicity Story for *Editor and Publisher*, "The Story of the Fleischmann 'Yeast for Health Contest,'" undated, Information Center Records, Box 2 (Accounts), Folder 6 (Prizes, Contests 1923–1934), 1.

65. "The Greatest Health Contest Ever Held," *New York Tribune*, July 15, 1923.

66. "Memo to: Miss Stocking, Mr Leffingwell, The Fleischmann Company— Yeast for Health Contest Analysis," September 15, 1923, Information Center Records, Box 2 (Accounts), Folder 6 (Prizes, Contests 1923–1934), JWT Archives.

67. "You know such people," and "People you might know," 1925, 35 mm Microfilm Proofs, Reel 27-7, JWT Archives; "They might be your neighbors," 35 mm Microfilm Proofs, Reel 27-9, JWT Archives, 38.

68. 35 mm Microfilms, Reel 27-7, JWT Archives.

69. "Fleischmann's Yeast for Health Investigation among men and women readers of *N.Y. Times* and *N.Y. Herald-Tribune*," March 11 1927, 16 mm, 55-2, JWT Archives, pp. 3–4 (hereafter NYT Investigation).

70. NYT Investigation, 2.

71. NYT Investigation, 2–3.

72. NYT Investigation, 2–3.

73. NYT Investigation, 2–3.

74. NYT Investigation, 3.

75. NYT Investigation, 3.

76. "My friend's spectacular recovery convinced me," 1928, 35 mm Microfilms, Reel 27-18, JWT Archives, 10.

77. "Stop work they told me–but I had to struggle on," 1928, 35 mm Microfilms, Reel 27-18, JWT Archives, 5.

78. "Such Symptoms as these are warnings," 1928, 35 mm Microfilms, Reel 27-18, JWT Archives, 2.

79. "First a headache–then a heartache," 1928, 35 mm Microfilms, Reel 27-18, JWT Archives, 59.

80. NYT Investigation, 3.

81. NYT Investigation, 4.

82. Sabine Clarke, *Science at the End of Empire: Experts and the Development of the British Caribbean, 1940–62* (Manchester: Manchester University Press, 2018), 22–23.

83. Clarke, 25.

84. Clarke, 26–31.

85. Clarke, 41–43.

86. A. C. Thaysen, "Food Yeast: Its Nutritive Value and Its Production From Empire Sources," *Journal of the Royal Society of Arts* 93, no. 4693 (1945): 354.

87. Thaysen, 354.

88. Thaysen, 353.

89. Osborne and Mendel, "The Nutritive Value of Yeast Protein"; Thaysen, "Food Yeast," 354.

90. Thaysen, "Food Yeast," 356.

91. Thaysen, 354.

92. Thaysen, 356.

93. Thaysen, 357.

94. Thaysen, 358.

95. Thaysen, 359.

96. Thaysen, 356.

97. Medical Research Council Accessory Food Factors Committee, *Food Yeast: A Survey of Its Nutritive Value*, 1945, 4.

98. Clarke, *Science at the End of Empire*, 120.

99. Thaysen, "Food Yeast," 359.

100. Ackerman, "Interpreting the 'Newer Knowledge of Nutrition'"; Iris Borowy, "International Social Medicine between the Wars: Positioning a Volatile Concept," *Hygiea Internationalis* 6, no. 2 (July 2007): 13–35.

101. Randall M. Packard, *A History of Global Health: Interventions into the Lives of Other Peoples* (Baltimore: Johns Hopkins University Press, 2016), 62–88.

102. Kenneth J. Carpenter, "The Work of Wallace Aykroyd: International Nutritionist and Author," *Journal of Nutrition* 137, no. 4 (April 1, 2007): 873–78.

103. Etienne Burnet and Wallace Ruddell Aykroyd, "Nutrition and Public Health," *Quarterly Bulletin of the Health Organization of the League of Nation* 4, no. 2 (1935): 323–474.

104. League of Nations, *Final Report of the Mixed Committee of the League of Nations on the Relation of Nutrition to Health, Agriculture and Economic Policy* (Geneva: League of Nations, 1937).

105. League of Nations, 63–64.

106. Technical Commission on Nutrition, "Report by the Technical Commission on Nutrition on the Work of Its Third Session," *Bulletin of the Health Organisation of the League of Nations* 7 (1938): 460–502.

107. Technical Commission on Nutrition, "Report by a Special Committee Which Met in Geneva from August 22nd to 24th 1938," *Bulletin of the Health Organisation of the League of Nations* 7 (1938): 666–76.

108. Technical Commission on Nutrition, 666–76.

109 Vernon, *Hunger*, 146.

110. Vernon, 106–8, 147–48.

111. *United Nations Conference on Food and Agriculture, Hot Springs, Virginia, May 18–June 3, 1943: Final Act and Section Reports* (Washington, DC: Government Printing Office, 1943).

112. *United Nations Conference on Food and Agriculture*, 35.

113. *United Nations Conference on Food and Agriculture*, 37.

114. Maria Letícia Galluzzi Bizzo, "Postponing Equality: From Colonial to International Nutritional Standards, 1932–1950," in *Health and Difference: Rendering Human Variation in Colonial Engagements*, ed. Alexandra Widmer and Veronika Lipphardt (New York: Berghahn, 2016), 129–48.

115. *United Nations Conference on Food and Agriculture*, 47.

116. Worboys, "The Discovery of Colonial Malnutrition between the Wars."

117. Economic Advisory Council, Committee on Nutrition in the Colonial Empire, *Nutrition in the Colonial Empire* (London: His Majesty's Stationary Office, 1939).

118. Economic Advisory Council, Committee on Nutrition in the Colonial Empire, 38.

119. Economic Advisory Council, Committee on Nutrition in the Colonial Empire, 68.

120. Veronica Berry and Celia Petty, eds., *The Nyasaland Survey Papers, 1938–1943: Agriculture, Food and Health* (London: Academy Books, 1992); Benjamin Stanley Platt, *Nutrition in the British West Indies.* (London: His Majesty's Stationary Office, 1946); Cynthia Brantley, *Feeding Families: African Realities and British Ideas of Nutrition and Development in Early Colonial Africa* (Portsmouth, NH: Heinemann, 2002).

121. Platt, *Nutrition in the British West Indies.*, 1.

122. Benjamin Stanley Platt, "Aspects of Nutritional Research," *British Medical Bulletin* 2, nos. 10–11 (January 1, 1944): 204–7.

123. Platt, *Nutrition in the British West Indies.*, 5.

124. Platt, 6.

125. On the colony as laboratory, see Warwick Anderson, *Colonial Pathologies: American Tropical Medicine, Race, and Hygiene in the Philippines* (Durham, NC: Duke University Press, 2006); Helen Tilley, *Africa as a Living Laboratory: Empire, Development, and the Problem of Scientific Knowledge, 1870–1950* (Chicago: University of Chicago Press, 2011); on nutrition research specifically, see Vernon, *Hunger*, 105–6.

126. Accessory Food Factors Committee, *Food Yeast*, 11.

127. Accessory Food Factors Committee, 13.

128. Accessory Food Factors Committee, 12–14.

129. Accessory Food Factors Committee, 14–15.

130. William Hughes, "Food Yeast in Tropical Malnutrition," *The Lancet* 247, no. 6399 (April 20, 1946): 569–72.

131. Hughes, 571.

132. Hughes, 571.

133. Indian Research Fund Association, "Feeding Trials with Food Yeast," 1945, PR_000002822725, 23/63/45-R, National Archives of India.

134. B. C. Guha to Secretary, Indian Research Fund Association, February 23, 1946, "Feeding Trials with Food Yeast," 1945, PR_000002822725, 23/63/45-R, National Archives of India.

135. Dr. K. P. Basu to The Secretary, Governing Body & Scientific Advisory Board, Indian Research Fund Association, March 14, 1946, "Feeding Trials with Food Yeast," 1945, PR_000002822725, 23/63/45-R, National Archives of India.

136. "Final Report of the Consumer Trials with Food Yeast," July 30, 1954, "Assistance from F.A.O. of the United Nations by way of experts & Supply of 250 Kg. of Food Yeast to the government of India," 1952, PR_000001673909, Progs., Nos. 42-16, National Archives of India.

137. "Consumer Trials with Food Yeast in Uttar Pradesh," April 4, 1954, "Assistance from F.A.O. of the United Nations by way of experts & Supply of 250 Kg. of Food Yeast to the government of India," 1952, PR_000001673909, Progs., Nos. 42-16, National Archives of India.

138. Executive Board, World Health Organization, "Collaboration Between WHO and FAO on Nutrition," January 14, 1949, 9.

139. Aya Hirata Kimura, "Who Defines Babies' 'Needs'? The Scientization of Baby Food in Indonesia," *Social Politics: International Studies in Gender, State & Society* 15, no. 2 (July 1, 2008): 232–60; Peter Redfield, "Bioexpectations: Life Technologies as Humanitarian Goods," *Public Culture* 24, no. 1 (66) (January 1, 2012): 157–84; Aya Hirata Kimura, *Hidden Hunger: Gender and the Politics of Smarter Foods* (Ithaca, NY: Cornell University Press, 2013); Street, "Food as Pharma"; Tom Scott-Smith, *On an Empty Stomach: Two Hundred Years of Hunger Relief* (Ithaca, NY: Cornell University Press, 2020).

CONCLUSION

1. *Official Guide Book of the World's Fair of 1934* (Chicago: Cuneo Press, 1934), 63.

2. *Official Guide Book of the World's Fair,* 61.

3. *Official Guide Book of the World's Fair,* 26–47.

4. *Official Guide Book of the World's Fair,* 27.

5. *Official Guide Book of the World's Fair,* 42.

6. *Official Guide Book of the World's Fair,* 39.

7. *Official Guide Book of the World's Fair,* 39.

8. *Official Guide Book of the World's Fair,* 44–45.

9. *Official Guide Book of the World's Fair,* 29, 44.

10. Amy Laura Hall, "Whose Progress? The Language of Global Health," *Journal of Medicine and Philosophy* 31, no. 3 (June 2006): 285–304.

11. Hall, 290; George Petty, *Century of Progress Poster,* COP_17_0023_00000_049, 1933, 1933, Century of Progress records, Special Collections and University Archives, University of Illinois at Chicago Library, https://collections.carli.illinois.edu/digital/collection/uic_cop/id/1508/.

12. *Official Guide Book of the Fair, 1933* (Chicago: A Century of progress, 1933), 40.

13. *Official Guide Book of the World's Fair,* 16.

14. *Official Guide Book of the Fair, 1933*, 13–14.

15. Council for Responsible Nutrition, "Dietary Supplement Use Reaches All Time High," September 30, 2019, https://www.crnusa.org/newsroom/dietary -supplement-use-reaches-all-time-high.

16. World Health Organization, "Malnutrition Is a World Health Crisis," September 26, 2019, https://www.who.int/news/item/26-09-2019-malnutrition-is-a -world-health-crisis.

17. Suzanne P Murphy et al., "History of Nutrition: The Long Road Leading to the Dietary Reference Intakes for the United States and Canada," *Advances in Nutrition* 7, no. 1 (January 7, 2016): 157–68.

18. Peter N. Taylor and J. Stephen Davies, "A Review of the Growing Risk of Vitamin D Toxicity from Inappropriate Practice," *British Journal of Clinical Pharmacology* 84, no. 6 (June 2018): 1121–27; Starr, "Too Little, Too Late."

19. The focus on singular nutrients and the repercussions of this focus have been most succinctly articulated by Gyorgy Scrinis, *Nutritionism: The Science and Politics of Dietary Advice* (New York: Columbia University Press, 2013).

20. Sylvie L. Turgeon and Laurie-Eve Rioux, "Food Matrix Impact on Macronutrients Nutritional Properties," *Food Hydrocolloids, 25 years of Advances in Food Hydrocolloid Research*, 25, no. 8 (December 1, 2011): 1915–24; José Miguel Aguilera, "The Food Matrix: Implications in Processing, Nutrition and Health," *Critical Reviews in Food Science and Nutrition* 59, no. 22 (December 16, 2019): 3612–29.

21. C. E. Bodwell and John W. Erdman, eds., *Nutrient Interactions* (New York: CRC Press, 1988); K. S. Kubena and D. N. McMurray, "Nutrition and the Immune System: A Review of Nutrient-Nutrient Interactions," *Journal of the American Dietetic Association* 96, no. 11 (November 1996): 1156–64; Emilie Combet and Stuart R. Gray, "Nutrient-Nutrient Interactions: Competition, Bioavailability, Mechanism and Function in Health and Diseases," *Proceedings of the Nutrition Society* 78, no. 1 (February 2019): 1–3.

22. Dirk Hadrich, "Microbiome Research Is Becoming the Key to Better Understanding Health and Nutrition," *Frontiers in Genetics* 9, no. 212 (2018): 1–10, https://doi.org/10.3389/fgene.2018.00212.

23. Political scientist Tripp Rebrovick has rightly argued that this "eco-dietetics" constitutes a new discursive formation in Western dietetics. Tripp Rebrovick, "The Politics of Diet: 'Eco-Dietetics,' Neoliberalism, and the History of Dietetic Discourses," *Political Research Quarterly* 68, no. 4 (December 1, 2015): 678–89.

24. Hannah Landecker, "Food as Exposure: Nutritional Epigenetics and the New Metabolism," *Biosocieties* 6, no. 2 (June 2011): 167–94.

25. Marion Nestle, *Unsavory Truth: How Food Companies Skew the Science of What We Eat* (New York: Basic Books, 2018).

26. Marion Nestle, *Food Politics: How the Food Industry Influences Nutrition and Health* (Berkeley: University of California Press, 2002).

27. Gabriel N. Rosenberg and Jan Dutkiewicz, "Abolish the Department of Agriculture," *New Republic*, December 27, 2021, https://newrepublic.com/article /164874/abolish-department-agriculture.

28. Anthony Ryan Hatch, *Blood Sugar: Racial Pharmacology and Food Justice in Black America* (Minneapolis: University of Minnesota Press, 2016); Chin Jou, *Supersizing Urban America: How Inner Cities Got Fast Food with Government Help* (Chicago: University of Chicago Press, 2017); Ashanté M. Reese, *Black Food Geographies: Race, Self-Reliance, and Food Access in Washington* (Chapel Hill: University of North Carolina Press, 2019); Marcia Chatelain, *Franchise: The Golden Arches in Black America* (New York: Liveright, 2020).

29. Cohen, *Pure Adulteration*; Alison Alkon and Julie Guthman, eds., *The New Food Activism: Opposition, Cooperation, and Collective Action* (Oakland: University of California Press, 2017).

30. Julie Guthman, "Neoliberalism and the Making of Food Politics in California," *Geoforum*, Rethinking Economy, 39, no. 3 (May 1, 2008): 1171–83; Margaret Gray, *Labor and the Locavore: The Making of a Comprehensive Food Ethic* (Berkeley: University of California Press), 2013; Sarah Besky and Sandy Brown, "Looking for Work: Placing Labor in Food Studies," *Labor* 12, nos. 1–2 (May 1, 2015): 19–43; Hanna Goldberg and Laura-Anne Minkoff-Zern, "Teaching Labor in Food Studies: Challenging Consumer-Based Approaches to Social Change through Student Research Community Partnerships," *Food, Culture & Society* 0, no. 0 (August 11, 2021): 1–17.

31. Tara L Maudrie et al., "A Scoping Review of the Use of Indigenous Food Sovereignty Principles for Intervention and Future Directions," *Current Developments in Nutrition* 5, no. 7 (July 1, 2021): 1–22.

32. Robin Wall Kimmerer, *Braiding Sweetgrass: Indigenous Wisdom, Scientific Knowledge and the Teachings of Plants* (Minneapolis, MN: Milkweed Editions, 2015).

BIBLIOGRAPHY

ARCHIVES

Ashbel Smith Papers, Gail Borden Jr. Papers, and Joe B. Frantz Papers, Dolph Briscoe
  Center for American History, University of Texas, Austin.
Benger's Food Ltd. Archives, Museum of Science and Industry, Manchester.
Gail Borden Papers, Daughters of the Republic of Texas Library, the Alamo, San
  Antonio.
J. Walter Thompson Company Collection, John W. Hartman Center for Sales,
  Advertising & Marketing History, Rubenstein Library, Duke University, Dur-
  ham, NC.
John Harvey Kellogg Papers, Bentley Historical Library, University of Michigan,
  Ann Arbor.
John Harvey Kellogg Papers, Michigan State University Archives and Historical Col-
  lections, East Lansing.
Medical Historical Library, College of Physicians, Philadelphia (MHLCPP).
National Archives of India.

PUBLISHED PRIMARY SOURCES

Accessory Food Factors Committee, Medical Research Council. *Food Yeast: A Survey
  of Its Nutritive Value*, 1945.
Adams, William Bridges. "What Is Food." *Journal of the Society of Arts*, September
  7, 1855, 695–96.
*Amtlicher Bericht über die 18. Versammlung deutscher Naturforscher und Ärzte zu
  Erlangen im September 1840*. Braunschweig: Friedrich Vieweg, 1842.
Anderson, James Wallace. *Lectures on Medical Nursing: Delivered in the Royal Infir-
  mary, Glasgow*. Glasgow: James Maclehose, 1883.

"Appeal from the Circuit Court of the United States for the Southern District of New York." *Official Gazette of the United States Patent Office* 92, no. 8 (August 21, 1900): 1620–22.

Ashby, N. B. *The Riddle of the Sphinx*. Des Moines, IA: Industrial Publishing Company, 1890.

Atwater, Wilbur Olin. *Foods: Nutritive Value and Cost*. Washington, DC: Government Printing Office, 1894.

Babbage, Charles. *On the Economy of Machinery and Manufactures*. 1st ed. London: Charles Knight, 1832.

———. *On the Economy of Machinery and Manufactures*. 4th ed. London: Charles Knight, 1835.

Baker, William Mumford. *A Year Worth Living: A Story of a Place and a People One Cannot Afford Not to Know*. Boston: Lee and Shepard, 1887.

"Balloon Races Facing Gas Ban." *Indiana Daily Times*, August 7, 1920.

Battle Creek Sanitarium. *Undigested Cereals the Cause of American Dyspepsia*. Pamphlets and handbills, ca.1895–1925, Cage, Medical Trade Ephemera, MHLCPP, n.d.

Beaumont, William. *Experiments and Observations on the Gastric Juice, and the Physiology of Digestion*. Plattsburgh, NY: Allen, 1833.

"The Be-Gum of Spearmint." *The Fra: For Philistines and Roycrofters* 11 (1913): 48b–48c.

Benger, Frederick Baden. "Note on the Condition in Which Salicylic Acid Is Excreted by Patients." *The Pharmaceutical Journal and Transactions* 7 (September 30, 1876): 282–83.

———. "On the Pharmaceutical Applications of Glycerine." *American Journal of Pharmacy* 34 (1865): 61–67.

"Benger's Food." *The Strand Magazine* 38 (1909): 59.

"Benger's Preparations of the Natural Digestive Ferments." *The Lancet*, December 13, 1879.

"Benger's Preparations of the Natural Digestive Ferments." In *Yearbook of Pharmacy*, 630. London: J. & A. Churchill, 1880.

"Benger's Self-Digestive Food." *Truth* 17 (January 15, 1885): 116.

Berdmore, Septimus. "The Principles of Cooking." In *The Health Exhibition Literature. Volume IV: Health in Diet*, 163–250. London: Clowes and Sons, 1884.

Bidder, Marion Greenwood, and Florence Baddeley. *Domestic Economy in Theory and Practice: A Text-Book for Teachers and Students in Training*. Cambridge: Cambridge University Press, 1901.

Bischoff, Ernst. "Versuche über die Ernährung mit Brod." *Zeitschrift für Biologie* 5 (1869): 452–75.

Bischoff, Theodor, and Karl von Voit. *Die Gesetze der Ernährung des Fleischfressers durch neue Untersuchungen*. Leipzig: Winter, 1860.

Blackburn, A. E. H. "Origins of Benger's Food." *The Pharmaceutical Journal and Pharmacist* 34 (April 27, 1912): 562.

Blythe, Alexander Winter. "Diet in Relation to Health and Work." In *The Health Exhibition Literature. Volume IV: Health in Diet*, 251–354. London: Clowes and Sons, 1884.

Borden, Gail. Preparation of portable soup-bread. US7066 A. Galveston, Texas, issued February 5, 1850. http://www.google.com/patents/US7066.

Borden, Gail, and Ashbel Smith. *Letter of Gail Borden, Jr., to Dr. Ashbel Smith, Setting Forth an Important Invention in the Preparation of a New Article of Food, Termed Meat Biscuit*. Galveston, TX: Gibson & Cherry, 1850.

Braun, Emil. *Perfection in Baking*. Urica, NY: J. Braun, 1893.

Adams, William Bridges. "What Is Food." *Journal of the Society of Arts*, September 7, 1855, 695–96.

Brocq, Louis-Anne-Jean. "La levure de bière dans la furonculose." *La Presse Médicale* 7, no. 8 (January 28, 1899): 45–47.

Buchner, Eduard. "Alkoholische Gährung ohne Hefezellen (Vorläufige Mitteilung)." *Berichte der Deutschen Chemischen Gesellschaft* 30 (January 1897): 117–24.

Burdick, R. L. "Are Contests Successful To-Day?" *Printers' Ink* 112 (September 9, 1920): 73–80.

Burnet, Etienne, and Wallace Ruddell Aykroyd. "Nutrition and Public Health." *Quarterly Bulletin of the Health Organization of the League of Nation* 4, no. 2 (1935): 323–474.

Campbell, Helen. "Our Daily Bread." *Good Housekeeping*, November 14, 1885.

Carey, Henry Charles. *The Harmony of Interests, Agricultural, Manufacturing, and Commercial*. Philadelphia: J. S. Skinner, 1851.

———. *The Past, the Present, and the Future*. Philadelphia: Carey & Hart, 1848.

"Carnrick's Liquid Peptonoids." *Australasian Medical Gazette* 21 (December 20, 1902): xliii.

Catalogue of the Collection of Animal Products. London: Clowes and Sons, 1858.

Chauven, Jane Putnam. *The Columbian Cook Book: Containing Reliable Rules for Plain and Fancy Cooking*. St. Paul, MN: J.W. Cunningham, 1892.

Chittenden, Russell H. "On the Ferments Contained in the Juice of the Pineapple (*Ananassa sativa*), Together with Some Observations on the Composition and Proteolytic Action of the Juice." *Transactions of the Connecticut Academy of Arts and Sciences* 8 (1888): 281–309.

———. "Papoid-Digestion." *Transactions of the Connecticut Academy of Arts and Sciences* 9, no. 1 (1892): 298–332.

Clarus, Julius. *Handbuch der speciellen Arzneimittellehre*. Leipzig: Otto Wigand, 1860.

"The Coast and the Coastal Plains." *National Magazine*, 1911.

"Commerce of St. Louis." *Western Journal and Civilian*, January 1851.

Conclin, George. *Conclin's New River Guide; or, A Gazetteer of All the Towns on the Western Waters*. Cincinnati, OH: H.S. & J. Applegate, 1850.

Copy of the Report of Dr Playfair and Mr Lindley on the Present State of the Irish Potato Crop, and on the Prospect of the Approaching Scarcity. London: Clowes and Sons, 1846.

Corvisart, Lucien. "De l'emploi des poudres nutrimentives (pepsine acidifiée), ressources qu'elles offrent à la médicine pratique." *Bulletin Général de Thérapeutique Médicale, Chirurgicale, Obstétricale et Pharmaceutique* 47 (1854): 320–30.

———. *Étude sur les aliments et les nutriments et sur la méthode nutrimentive dans les cas de vice de secrétion de l'estomac.* Paris: Labé, 1854.

———. "Recherches ayant pour but d'administrer aux malades qui ne digèrent point, des aliments tout digérés par le suc gastrique des animaux." *Comptes Rendus Hebdomadaires des Séances de l'Académie des Sciences* 35 (1852): 244–48, 330–32.

Cowan, John F. "Predigested Tommy." *Christian Endeavor World* 19, no. 22 (March 2, 1905): 433, 438.

Davy, Humphry. *Elements of Agricultural Chemistry.* London: Longman, Hurst, Rees, Orme, and Brown, 1813.

"A Descriptive List of Benger's Preparations of the Natural Digestive Ferments." Bodleian Library, Oxford University, John Johnson Collection, 1889. http://gateway.proquest.com/openurl?url_ver=Z39.88-2004&res_dat=xri:jjohnson:&rft_dat=xri:jjohnson:rec:20090605102612kg.

Dickens, Charles. *The Mudfog Papers.* New York: Henry Holt, 1880.

"Dramatic Story of the $6,000,000 Bread." *Chicago Daily Tribune.* March 31, 1929.

Dubelle, George H. *Dubelle's Famous Formulas for Soda Fountain Beverages.* New York: Spon & Chamberlain, 1901.

———. *Soda Fountain Beverages: A Practical Receipt Book for Druggists, Chemists, Confectioners and Venders of Soda Water.* New York: Spon & Chamberlain, 1905.

"Duval Dinners." *The Coffee Public-House News and Temperance Hotel Journal*, January 1, 1886.

"Dygestiv." *Dietetic and Hygienic Gazette* 21, no. 3 (March 1905): 188.

Eberle, Johann Nepomuk. *Physiologie der Verdauung nach Versuchen auf natürlichem und künstlichem Wege.* Würzburg: Etlinger, 1834.

Economic Advisory Council, Committee on Nutrition in the Colonial Empire. *Nutrition in the Colonial Empire.* London: His Majesty's Stationary Office, 1939.

"Editor's Table: The Conflict of Modern Society." *Appletons' Popular Science Monthly* 53 (1898): 840–42.

"England and Texas." *Niles' National Register*, April 13, 1844.

Executive Board, World Health Organization. "Collaboration between WHO and FAO on Nutrition," January 14, 1949.

"Fairchild Brothers & Foster." In *Illustrated New York: The Metropolis of To-Day*, 194–95. New York: International Publishing Company, 1888.

"Fifty-Third Annual Meeting of the British Medical Association." *British Medical Journal* 2 (September 5, 1885).

Fitz-Gerald, Charles Egerton. *Lectures on Physiology, Hygiene, Etc. for Hospital and Home Nursing.* London: George Bell & Sons, 1892.

The Fleischmann Company. "Rich in Vitamins." *Illinois Medical Journal* 35, no. 2 (February 1919): 23.

———. "Scientific Precision." *Illinois Medical Journal* 35, no. 5 (March 1919): 23.

———. "Used in All Tests." *West Virginia Medical Journal* 13 (October 1918): xvi.

———. "Yeast Dosage." *Illinois Medical Journal* 35, no. 5 (May 1919): 25.

———. "Yeast—Living or 'Killed.'" *Illinois Medical Journal* 35, no. 4 (April 1919): 23.

"For Indigestion—Benger's Food." *Canadian Nurse* 8, no. 10 (October 1912): 581.

Frantz, Joe B. *Gail Borden: Dairyman to a Nation.* Norman: University of Oklahoma Press, 1951.

"A Fruit and Nut Diet." *Good Health* 35 (1900): 373–76.

Gamgee, Arthur. "The Digestive Ferments and the Chemical Processes of Digestion." In *The Health Exhibition Literature. Volume VI: Health in Diet,* 1–36. London: Clowes and Sons, 1884.

———. "Physiology of Digestion and the Digestive Organs." In *The Health Exhibition Literature. Volume IV: Health in Diet,* 1–162. London: Clowes and Sons, 1884.

Gedney, Ward. "Getting a New Rise out of the Yeast Cake." *Advertising & Selling* 30, no. 20 (November 6, 1920): 5–6.

"Good Health through Yeast." *National Labor Digest* 1 (1919): 36.

Goodale, S. L. *A Brief Sketch of Gail Borden, and His Relations to Some Forms of Concentrated Food.* Portland, ME: Thurston, 1872.

Graham, Sylvester. *A Treatise on Bread, and Bread-Making.* Boston: Light & Stearns, 1837.

———. *Lectures on the Science of Human Life.* Boston: Marsh, Capen, Lyon & Webb, 1839.

"Granola, a Healthful Food." *The Bacteriological World and Modern Medicine* 1 (1891): Advertisements, 14.

Gray, Samuel Frederick. *The Operative Chemist: Being a Practical Display of the Arts and Manufactures Which Depend Upon Chemical Principles.* London: Hurst, Chance, & Co., 1828.

"The Greatest Health Contest Ever Held." *New York Tribune,* July 15, 1923.

Hager, Herrmann. "Ueber Pepsin, seine Darstellung, Wirkung, und Dispensation." *Pharmazeutische Zentralhalle für Deutschland* 11, no. 7 and 8 (1870): 53–54 and 59–61.

Hampson, Robert. "The Condition and Prospects of Pharmacy in Its Relation to the Medical Profession." *Pharmaceutical Journal* 11, no. 7 (January 1870): 404–8.

Hassall, Arthur Hill. "On the Nutritive Value of Liebig's Extract of Beef, Beef-Tea, and of Wine." *Lancet,* July 8, 1865, 49–50.

Hawk, Philip B. *Practical Physiological Chemistry: A Book Designed for Use in Courses in Practical Physiological Chemistry in Schools of Medicine and of Science.* 3rd ed. Philadelphia: P. Blakiston's Son, 1910.

———. *Practical Physiological Chemistry: A Book Designed for Use in Courses in Practical Physiological Chemistry in Schools of Medicine and of Science.* 5th ed. Philadelphia: P. Blakiston's Son & Company, 1916.

———. "The Use of Baker's' Yeast in Diseases of the Skin and of the Gastro-Intestinal Tract." *Journal of the American Medical Association* 69, no. 15 (October 13, 1917): 1243–47.

———. "What We Eat and What Happens to It." *Ladies Home Journal*, February 1918, April 1918.

Hawk, Philip B., Hamilton R. Fishback, and Olaf Bergeim. "Compressed Yeast as Food for the Growing Organism." *American Journal of Physiology*, 1919, 211–20.

Hawk, Philip B., Clarence A. Smith, and Ralph C. Holder. "Baker's Yeast as Food for Man." *American Journal of Physiology* 48 (1919): 199–210.

The Health Exhibition Literature. Vol. 18. London: Clowes and Sons, 1884.

The Health Exhibition Literature. Vol. 19. London: Clowes and Sons, 1884.

Heath, Lilian M. *The Red Telephone; or, Tricks of the Temper Exposed; Being Messages from the Under-World of Sin and How They Are Answered: A Book Portraying the Grave Dangers Found in the Various Walks of Life.* Chicago: W. R. Vansant, 1905.

Hemmeter, John C. "The Use and Abuse of Digestive Ferments." *The Medical News* 80 (June 7, 1902): 1073–76.

Hoffman, Frederick Ludwig. *Race Traits and Tendencies of the American Negro.* New York: Macmillan Company for the American Economic Association, 1896.

Horne, R. H. "Dust; or Ugliness Redeemed." Edited by Charles Dickens. *Household Words* 1, no. 16 (July 13, 1850): 379–84.

Hughes, William. "Food Yeast in Tropical Malnutrition." *The Lancet* 247, no. 6399 (April 20, 1946): 569–72.

Humboldt, Alexander von. *Essai politique sur le royaume de la Nouvelle-Espagne.* Vol. 2. Paris: F. Schoell, 1811.

———. *Political Essay on the Kingdom of New Spain.* 4 vols. London: Longman, Hurst, Rees, Orme, and Brown, 1814.

Humphry, Laurence. *A Manual of Nursing.* Philadelphia: P. Blakiston, Son, & Company, 1894.

Hunt, Carl. "Making Consumers out of Competing Housewives: An Interview with E. L. Cline." *Printer's Ink* 87, no. 6 (May 14, 1914): 17–24.

"Introduction." *Thrift: A Monthly Journal of Social Progress and Reform* 1, no. 1 (January 1882): 1.

Jacob, William. *Tracts Relating to the Corn Trade and Corn Laws.* London: John Murray, 1828.

John Richardson & Co. "Peptocolos." *London Medical Record* 7 (December 15, 1879): Advertisements.

Johnson, Alexander. "The Ethical Basis of Charity." *Open Court* 2, no. 10 (May 3, 1888): 927–30.

Johnson, Roy W. "When a Consumer Contest Is Profitable and When It Isn't." *Printers' Ink* 96, no. 6 (August 10, 1916): 3–10.

Kellogg, Ella Eaton. *Healthful Cookery: A Collection of Choice Recipes for Preparing Foods, with Special Reference to Health.* Battle Creek, MI: Modern Medicine Publishing Company, 1904.

———. *Science in the Kitchen.* Battle Creek, MI: Health Publishing Company, 1892.

Kellogg, John Harvey. "Biennial Report of the Medical Superintendent of the Battle Creek Sanitarium." *Bacteriological World and Modern Medicine* 1 (1891): 73–76, 110–13, 143–48, 183–86.

———. "City Medical Missions." *The Medical Missionary* 8 (1898): 74–82, 104–8, 136–41, 167–71.

———. "Cold Philosophy." *Medical Missionary* 3, no. 8 (August 1893): 178–79.

———. "Fat and Blood." *Modern Medicine and Bacteriological Review* 4 (September 1895): 234.

———. *First Book in Physiology and Hygiene*. New York: American Book Company, 1888.

———. Flaked cereals and process of preparing same. United States US558393A, issued April 14, 1896. https://patents.google.com/patent/US558393A/en.

———. "Health Observations among American Aborigines." *Good Health* 24 (1889): 3–5, 36–38, 67–69, 102–3.

———. "A Last Word about Digestion." *Dietetic and Hygienic Gazette* 18 (1902): 148–51.

———. *The Living Temple*. Battle Creek, MI: Good Health Publishing Company, 1903.

———. *Methods of Precision in the Investigation of Disorders of Digestion*. Battle Creek, MI: Modern Medicine Publishing Company, 1893.

———. "Needed—A New Human Race." In *Proceedings of the First National Conference on Race Betterment*, 431–56. Battle Creek: Gage, 1914.

———. "Pan-Peptogen." *Modern Medicine and Bacteriological Review* 11, no. 1 (1902): Back Cover.

———. *Plain Facts for Old and Young*. Burlington, IA: Segner & Condit, 1881.

———. *The Stomach: Its Disorders, and How to Cure Them*. Battle Creek, MI: Modern Medicine Publishing Company, 1896.

———. "What Is the Matter with the American Stomach?" *Modern Medicine and Bacteriological Review* 5 (March 1896): 25–30, 53–58, 72–78.

Kirk, Eleanor. *Choice Recipes: How to Use Fleischmann's Compressed Yeast*. New York: Jourgensen, 1889.

Laboratories of Applied Physiology of France, American Branch. "Hepptine." *American Medicine* 17, no. 9 (September 1911): 6.

"Lancashire and Cheshire Branch: Intermediate Meeting." *British Medical Journal*, May 17, 1879, 756–57.

"The Lancet General Advertiser." *The Lancet*, April 4, 1857.

Lankester, Edwin. *A Guide to the Food Collection in the South Kensington Museum*. London: Eyre and Spottiswoode, 1860.

———. *The Uses of Animals in Relation to the Industry of Man; Being a Course of Lectures Delivered at the South Kensington Museum*. London: Hardwicke, 1860.

———. *Vegetable Substances Used for the Food of Man*. London: Charles Knight, 1832.

Lankester, Phebe. *The National Thrift Reader*. London: Allman and Son, 1880.

Law, Henry. "Thrift: An Address to the Working Classes." *Journal of the Royal Sanitary Institute* 9 (1888): 459–68.

League of Nations. *Final Report of the Mixed Committee of the League of Nations on the Relation of Nutrition to Health, Agriculture and Economic Policy*. Geneva: League of Nations, 1937.

Lémery, Louis. *A Treatise of All Sorts of Foods*. London: T. Osborne, 1745.

"Leube-Rosenthal Improved Meat Solution." *Archives of Medicine: A Bi-Monthly Journal Devoted to Original Communications on Medicine, Surgery, and Their Special Branches* 12, no. 3 (1885): 1.

Levi, Leone. "Thrift the Virtue." *Thrift: A Monthly Journal of Social Progress and Reform* 1, no. 1 (January 1882): 4.

———. *Work and Pay; or, Principles of Industrial Economy*. London: Strahan and Company, 1877.

Liebig, Justus. *Chemische Untersuchung über das Fleisch und seine Zubereitung zum Nahrungsmittel*. Heidelberg: C. F. Winter, 1847.

———. *Familiar Letters on Chemistry: And Its Relation to Commerce, Physiology, and Agriculture*. Translated by John Gardner. Philadelphia: Taylor and Walton, 1843.

———. *Organic Chemistry in Its Applications to Agriculture and Physiology*. Translated by Lyon Playfair. London: Taylor and Walton, 1840.

Lindley, John. "Substances Used as Food, Illustrated by the Great Exhibition." In *Lectures on the Results of the Great Exhibition of 1851*, 209–42. London: G. Barclay, 1852.

"Lining Up the Salesmen." *Associated Advertising*. 6 (1915): 66–67.

"List of Subjects for Premiums." *Journal of the Society of Arts* 1 (December 10, 1852): 26–28.

Lloyd, J. U. "Pepsin." *Eclectic Medical Journal* 37 (1877): 497–99.

Low Wages; or, Thrift and Good Management. London: S. W. Partridge, 1863.

Magendie, François. "Mémoire sur les propriétés nutritives des substances qui ne contiennent pas d'azote." *Annales de Chimie et de Physique* 3 (September 1816): 66–77.

"Malt-Diastase Co." *Dietetic and Hygienic Gazette*, October 1897.

"The Maltine Manufacturing Company." In *New York's Great Industries*, 308. New York: Historical Publishing Company, 1885.

Marcet, William. *On a New Process for Preparing Meat for Weak Stomachs*. London: J. Churchill, 1867.

Mayhew, Henry. *London Labour and the London Poor*. London: Griffin, Bone and Co., 1851.

Mechi, John Joseph. "Fourth Paper on British Agriculture with Some Account of His Own Operations at Tiptree Hall Farm." *Journal of the Royal Society of Arts* 3, no. 107 (December 8, 1854): 49–58.

"Mellin's Food for Infants and Invalids." *British Medical Journal* 1185 (September 15, 1883): Advertisements.

"Messrs. Savory & Moore Beg to Invite the Attention of the Medical Profession." *Medical Times and Gazette*, May 29, 1875.

Meyer, Gustav. "Ernährungsversuche mit Brod am Hund und Menschen." *Zeitschrift für Biologie* 7 (1871): 1–48.

"A Mild Return to Savagery." *Battle Creek Idea*, March 1914.

The Military Laws of the United States. Washington: US Government Printing Office, 1917.

Miller, I. L. "Enforcement of the Indiana Bread Law." In *Weights and Measures Seventeenth Annual Conference*, edited by Department of Commerce, 40–47. Washington, DC: Government Printing Office, 1924.

Müller, Johannes, and Theodor Schwann. "Versuche über die künstliche Verdauung des geronnenen Eiweisses." *Archiv für Anatomie, Physiologie und wissenschaftliche Medicin*, 1836, 66–89.

Murlin, John R., and Henry A. Mattill. "The Laxative Action of Yeast." *American Journal of Physiology* 64, no. 1 (March 1, 1923): 75–96.

Nash, Joseph, Louis Haghe, and David Roberts. *Dickinsons' Comprehensive Pictures of the Great Exhibition of 1851*. London: Dickinson Brothers, 1854.

"News." *American Druggist and Pharmaceutical Record* 27, no. 8 (October 25, 1895): 265.

"No Gas for Balloon Race." *Aircraft Journal*, August 23, 1920, 8.

"Obituary. Peter Lund Simmonds, F.L.S." *Journal of the Society of Arts* 45, no. 2343 (October 15, 1897): 1150.

Official Descriptive and Illustrated Catalogue of the Great Exhibition of the Works of Industry of All Nations, 1851. Vol. 3. London: Clowes and Sons, 1851.

Official Guide Book of the Fair, 1933. Chicago: A Century of Progress, 1933.

Official Guide Book of the World's Fair of 1934. Chicago: Cuneo Press, 1934.

Osborne, Thomas B., and Lafayette B. Mendel. "The Nutritive Value of Yeast Protein." *Journal of Biological Chemistry* 38 (1919): 223–27.

O'Shea, Michael Vincent, and John Harvey Kellogg. *The Body in Health*. Vol. 3. New York: Macmillan, 1915.

"Our Advertisers." *Texas State Journal of Medicine* 14, no. 10 (February 1919): 321.

"The Passing of Pepsin." *Practical Druggist and Spatula* 24 (August 1908): 466.

Pavy, Frederick William. *A Treatise on the Function of Digestion: Its Disorders, and Their Treatment*. London: Churchill, 1867.

"Pepsin Tonic: A New Soda Drink." *Practical Druggist and Spatula* 24 (August 1908): 466.

"Peptenzyme." *Philadelphia Polyclinic* 4, no. 52 (December 28, 1895): ii.

Pereira, Jonathan. *A Treatise on Food and Diet*. New York: J. & H.G. Langley, 1843.

Petty, George. *Century of Progress Poster, COP_17_0023_00000_049*. 1933. Century of Progress records, Special Collections and University Archives, University of Illinois at Chicago Library. https://collections.carli.illinois.edu/digital/collection /uic_cop/id/1508/.

Piercy, Frederick. *Route from Liverpool to Great Salt Lake Valley*. Edited by James Linforth. Los Angeles: Westernlore Press, 1855.

"Pine-Apple Juice as Digestion Helper." *Medical Mirror* 8 (May 1897): 246–49.

Platt, Benjamin Stanley. "Aspects of Nutritional Research." *British Medical Bulletin* 2, no. 10–11 (January 1, 1944): 204–7.

———. *Nutrition in the British West Indies*. London: His Majesty's Stationary Office, 1946.

Playfair, Lyon. "The Chemical Principles Involved in the Manufactures of the Exhibition as Indicating the Necessity of Industrial Instruction." In *Lectures on the Results of the Great Exhibition of 1851*, 159–208. London: G. Barclay, 1852.

———. *On the Food of Man in Relation to His Useful Work*. Edinburgh: Edmonston and Douglas, 1865.

Poore, George Vivian. "Our Duty in Relation to Health." In *The Health Exhibition Literature*, 7:1–83. London: William Clowes, 1884.

Poovey, Mary. *A History of the Modern Fact: Problems of Knowledge in the Sciences of Wealth and Society*. Chicago: University of Chicago Press, 1998.

"Portable Soup Bread." *Scientific American* 5, no. 11 (December 1849): 84.

Proctor, Alice Adams. "Science Perfects a Vastly Better Bread." *Chicago Daily Tribune*, May 5, 1929.

———. *The Wonder Sandwich Book*. New York: Continental Baking Company, 1928.

———. *Wonder Sandwich Suggestions*. New York: Bakeries Service Corporation, 1930.

"Proteinol." *Saint Louis Medical and Surgical Journal* 63 (1892): 11.

Prout, William. "On the Ultimate Composition of Simple Alimentary Substances." *Philosophical Transactions of the Royal Society of London* 117 (1827): 355–88.

"Pure Grape Juice." *Modern Medicine and Bacteriological Review* 1, no. 4 (February 1892): Advertisements 3.

Race Betterment Foundation. *Proceedings of the First National Conference on Race Betterment*. Battle Creek, MI: Gage, 1914.

Réaumur, René Antoine Ferchault de. "Sur la digestion des oiseaux." *Histoire de l'Académie Royale des Sciences*, 1752, 266–307; 461–96.

"Reception by H.R.H. the Prince of Wales, K.G., of the International Juries." In *The Health Exhibition Literature*, 18:3–28. London: Clowes and Sons, 1884.

Redfield, Peter. "Bioexpectations: Life Technologies as Humanitarian Goods." *Public Culture* 24, no. 1 (66) (January 1, 2012): 157–84.

Reed & Carnrick. "Peptenzyme A Perfect Digestant." *St. Louis Clinique: A Monthly Journal of Clinical Medicine and Surgery* 11, no. 10 (October 1898): 565.

Rehfuss, Martin E. "A New Method of Gastric Testing, with a Description of a Method for the Fractional Testing of the Gastric Juice." *American Journal of the Medical Sciences* 147, no. 6 (June 1914): 848–55.

Rehfuss, Martin E., Olaf Bergheim, and Philip B. Hawk. "The Question of the Residuum Found in the Empty Stomach." *Journal of the American Medical Association* 63, no. 1 (July 4, 1914): 11–13.

Reports by the Juries on the Subjects in the Thirty Classes into Which the Exhibition Was Divided. London: Clowes and Sons, 1852.

Richards, Ellen H. *The Cost of Shelter*. New York: Wiley, 1905.

Richardson, Benjamin Ward. *Hygeia: A City of Health*. London: Macmillan, 1876.

———. "On Thrift in Relation to Food." *Journal of the Society of Arts*, March 19, 1880, 383–85.

———. "The Skeleton in the National Cupboard." *The Asclepiad* 3 (1886): 217–30.

———. "Woman as a Sanitary Reformer." In *Report of the Fourth Congress of the Sanitary Institute of Great Britain*, edited by Henry Burdett and F. de Chaumont: 2:183–202. Office of the Institute, 1880.

Roberts, William. "Address in Therapeutics." *British Medical Journal* 1 (August 1, 1885): 188–92.

———. "The Lumleian Lectures on the Digestive Ferments, and the Preparation and Use of Artificially Digested Food: Lecture I." *British Medical Journal* 1, no. 1006 (April 10, 1880): 539–44.

———. "The Lumleian Lectures on the Digestive Ferments, and the Preparation and Use of Artificially Digested Food: Lecture III." *British Medical Journal* 1, no. 1009 and 1010 (1880): 647–49; 683–85.

———. "Observations on the Digestive Ferments and Their Therapeutical Uses." *British Medical Journal* 2, no. 983 and 984 (November 1, 1879): 683–85, 724–25.

———. "On Some New Articles of Peptonised Food Prepared by the Pancreatic Method." In *Transactions of the International Medical Congress, Seventh Session, Held in London, August 2d to 9th, 1881*, 517–19. London: J.W. Kolckmann, 1881.

———. *On the Digestive Ferments and the Preparation and Use of Artificially Digested Food: Being the Lumleian Lectures for the Year 1880*. London: Smith, Elder, 1881.

"The Rohan Potato." *The Gardener's Magazine and Register of Rural & Domestic Improvement*, 1840.

Rubner, Max. "Ueber die Ausnützung einiger Nahrungsmittel im Darmcanale des Menschen." *Zeitschrift für Biologie* 15 (1879): 115–202.

Russell, C. P. "Advertising in New Fields When the Initial Market Becomes Smaller." *Printers' Ink* 61, no. 4 (April 22, 1920): 3–12.

The Sanitas Health Food Company. "Something Good to Eat." *Bulletin of the American Medical Temperance Association* 2, no. 4 (April 1895): Advertisements.

Sanitas Nut Food Company. *Sanitas Nut Preparations and Specialities*. Battle Creek, MI: Review and Herald Publishing Company, 1898.

"Savory & Moore's Peptoniser." *Medical Press and Circular*, October 3, 1883.

Schwann, Theodor. "Ueber das Wesen des Verdauungsprocesses." *Archiv Für Anatomie, Physiologie Und Wissenschaftliche Medicin*, 1836, 90–138.

"Scientific Slaughtering." *Scientific American*, January 20, 1894.

"A Self-Help Society." *Chambers's Journal of Popular Literature, Science and Arts* 4, no. 932 (November 5, 1881): 705–8.

"7 Reasons Why Papoid Is Superior to Pepsin." *Saint Louis Medical and Surgical Journal* 63, no. 6 (December 1892): Advertisements.

Shepard, Elihu H. *The Early History of St. Louis and Missouri*. St. Louis: Southwestern Book and Publishing Company, 1870.

Simmonds, Peter Lund. *The Commercial Products of the Vegetable Kingdom*. London: T. F. A. Day, 1854.

———. "On Some Undeveloped and Unappreciated Articles of Raw Produce from Different Parts of the World." *Journal of the Society of Arts* 2, no. 106 (December 1, 1854): 33–42.

———. "On the Useful Application of Waste Products and Undeveloped Substances." *Journal of the Royal Society of Arts* 17, no. 846 (February 5, 1869): 171–81.

———. "On the Utilization of Waste Substances." *Journal of the Royal Society of Arts* 7, no. 325 (February 11, 1859): 175–88.

———. *Waste Products and Undeveloped Substances; or, Hints for Enterprise in Neglected Fields*. London: R. Hardwicke, 1862.

"Six Huge Gas Bags Fly the Skies for Prize Cup." *Indianapolis Star*, June 6, 1909.

Smiles, Samuel. *Thrift*. London: Murray, 1875.

———. *Workmen's Earnings, Strikes, and Savings*. London: J. Murray, 1862.

Smith, Ashbel. *An Account of the Yellow Fever Which Appeared in the City of Galveston, Republic of Texas in the Autumn of 1839 : With Cases and Dissections*. Galveston: Hamilton Stuart, 1839. http://archive.org/details/2572008R.nlm.nih.gov" http://archive.org/details/2572008R.nlm.nih.gov.

———. *An Address Delivered in the City of Galveston on the 22d of February, 1848, the Anniversary of the Birth Day of Washington and of the Battle of Buena Vista by Ashbel Smith*. Galveston: W. Richardson, 1848.

———. "Manufactures for the South—Gail Borden's Meat Biscuit Factory, Texas." *Debow's Review*, May 1851.

———. *An Oration Pronounced before the Connecticut Alpha of the Phi Beta Kappa at Yale College, New Haven, August 15, 1849*. New Haven, CT: B.L. Hamlen, 1849.

Smith, Edward. *Dietaries for the Inmates of Workhouses. Report to the President of the Poor Law Board*. London: Eyre and Spottiswoode, 1866.

———. "On Private and Public Dietaries." *Journal of the Society of Arts* 12, no. 587 (February 19, 1864): 212–24.

The Soda Fountain. *The Dispenser Soda Water Guide: A Collection of Over 1300 Formulas for the Soda Fountain, to Which Has Been Added Numerous Hints and Suggestions for Plant Equipment and Operation, Refrigeration, the Manufacture of Ice Cream, Etc., Etc*. New York: D.O. Haynes & Company, 1909.

Solly, Edward. "On the Mutual Relations of Trade and Manufactures." *Journal of the Society of Arts* 3, no. 131 (May 25, 1855): 487–94.

"Some Facts about Yeast." *West Virginia Medical Journal* 13 (August 1918): 53–56.

Spencer, Herbert. *The Principles of Ethics*. Vol. II. New York: Appleton, 1898.

Spencer, W. H. "On Giving Rest to the Digestive Organs by the Use of Peptonised Food." *Bristol Medico-Chirurgical Journal* 2 (1884): 32–72.

"Spending a Million to Sell a Three Cent Product." *Advertising & Selling Magazine*, September 17, 1921.

"Subjects for Premiums." *Journal of the Society of Arts* 1 (December 15, 1852): 39–43.

Substances Used as Food, as Exemplified in the Great Exhibition. London: Society for Promoting Christian Knowledge, 1854.

"Susto-Nee Vinol Powder: The Conception and Birth of a Nostrum." *Journal of the American Medical Association* 79, no. 2 (October 28, 1922): 1538–39.

"Taggart's Wonder Bread." *Indianapolis Star*, May 23, 1921.

Tames, Richard. *Economy and Society in Nineteenth Century Britain*. London: Routledge, 2013.

Technical Commission on Nutrition. "Report by a Special Committee Which Met in Geneva from August 22nd to 24th 1938." *Bulletin of the Health Organisation of the League of Nations* 7 (1938): 666–76.

———. "Report by the Technical Commission on Nutrition on the Work of Its Third Session." *Bulletin of the Health Organisation of the League of Nations* 7 (1938): 460–502.

Thaysen, A. C. "Food Yeast: Its Nutritive Value and Its Production from Empire Sources." *Journal of the Royal Society of Arts* 93, no. 4693 (1945): 353–64.

"These Men Will Represent U.S. in Big Balloon Race." *Lake County Times*, September 1, 1921.

"Throngs Packed the Grounds." *Cincinnati Inquirer*, June 6, 1909.

"Throngs Watch Balloons Start in Great Race." *Nashville Tennessean*, June 5, 1909.

"The Treatment of Constipation, with Remarks on the Yeast Treatment of Some Gastro-Intestinal Disorders." *West Virginia Medical Journal* 13 (February 1919): 290–92.

"The Tuber Food." *Trained Nurse and Hospital Review* 34, no. 6 (1905): Advertisements.

United Nations Conference on Food and Agriculture, Hot Springs, Virginia, May 18–June 3, 1943: Final Act and Section Reports. Washington, DC: Government Printing Office, 1943.

Valangin, Francis de. *A Treatise on Diet; or, The Management of Human Life*. London: J. & W. Oliver, 1768.

Valentin, Gabriel. "Einige Resultate der im Sommer des gegenwärtigen Jahres zu Breslau über künstliche Verdauung angestellten Versuche." *Notizen aus dem Gebiete der Natur- und Heilkunde* 50, no. 14 (October 1836): 210–11.

"Vital Women." *Los Angeles Times*, April 25, 1937.

Vogel, August. "Über das Verdauungsprincip, Pepsin." *Münchener Gelehrte Anzeigen*, 1842, 717–19, 721–26.

Watson, James Kenneth. *A Handbook for Nurses*. London: The Scientific Press, 1899.

Weiske, Hugo. "Untersuchungen über die Verdaulichkeit der Cellulose beim Menschen." *Zeitschrift für Biologie* 6 (1870): 456–66.

Wharton, Clarence. *Gail Borden, Pioneer*. San Antonio: Naylor, 1941.

Whitehead, Jessup. "The Bouillons-Duvals System." In *The Steward's Handbook and Guide to Party Catering*, 96–98. Chicago: J. Anderson, 1889.

Willich, Anthony. *Lectures on Diet and Regimen*. London: Longman and Rees, 1799.

"Wonder?" *Indianapolis Star*, May 19, 1921.

"Wonder." *Indianapolis Star*, May 21, 1921.

Wonder Bread. "Wonder Bread: Our Story," 2019. https://www.wonderbread.com/about-us.

"Wonder What?" *Indianapolis Star*, May 18, 1921.

Woodbury, Frank. "On the Digestive Ferment of the Carica Papaya in Gastro-Intestinal Disorders." *New York Medical Journal* 56 (July 30, 1892): 115–18.

"Workhouse Dietaries." In *Accounts and Papers of the House of Commons*, Vol. 60, 1867.

Worsnop, E. M. *The Nurse's Handbook of Cookery: A Help in Sickness and Convalescence*. London: Black, 1897.

Yates, May. "Bread Reform." *Thrift: A Monthly Journal of Social Progress and Reform* 1, no. 1 (January 1882): 11.

"Yeast in a New Role." *Journal of the American Medical Association* 66, no. 18 (April 29, 1916): 1390–91.

Ackerman, Michael. "Interpreting the 'Newer Knowledge of Nutrition': Science, Interests, and Values in the Making of Dietary Advice in the United States, 1915–1965." PhD dissertation, University of Virginia, 2005.

Adams, Carol J. *The Sexual Politics of Meat: A Feminist-Vegetarian Critical Theory*. New York: Continuum, 1990.

Adelman, Jeremy. *Republic of Capital: Buenos Aires and the Legal Transformation of the Atlantic World*. Stanford, CA: Stanford University Press, 2002.

Adelman, Juliana, and Lisa Haushofer. "Introduction: Food as Medicine, Medicine as Food." *Journal of the History of Medicine and Allied Sciences* 73, no. 2 (April 1, 2018): 127–34, https://doi.org/10.1093/jhmas/jry010.

Aguilera, José Miguel. "The Food Matrix: Implications in Processing, Nutrition and Health." *Critical Reviews in Food Science and Nutrition* 59, no. 22 (December 16, 2019): 3612–29.

Albala, Ken. *Eating Right in the Renaissance*. Berkeley: University of California Press, 2002.

Alkon, Alison, and Julie Guthman, eds. *The New Food Activism: Opposition, Cooperation, and Collective Action*. Oakland: University of California Press, 2017.

Anderson, Kat. *Tending the Wild: Native American Knowledge and the Management of California's Natural Resources*. Berkeley: University of California Press, 2005.

Anderson, Warwick. *Colonial Pathologies: American Tropical Medicine, Race, and Hygiene in the Philippines*. Durham, NC: Duke University Press, 2006.

Apple, Rima. "'Advertised by Our Loving Friends': The Infant Formula Industry and the Creation of New Pharmaceutical Markets, 1870–1910." *Journal of the History of Medicine and Allied Sciences* 41, no. 1 (January 1, 1986): 3–23.

———. *Mothers and Medicine: A Social History of Infant Feeding, 1890–1950*. Madison: University of Wisconsin Press, 1987.

———. *Vitamania: Vitamins in American Culture*. New Brunswick, NJ: Rutgers University Press, 1996.

Aronson, Naomi. "Fuel for the Human Machine the Industrialization of Eating in America." PhD dissertation, Brandeis University, 1978.

Auerbach, Jeffrey. *The Great Exhibition of 1851: A Nation on Display*. New Haven, CT: Yale University Press, 1999.

Barnett, Margaret. "Fletcherism: The Chew-Chew Fad of the Edwardian Era." In *Nutrition in Britain: Science, Scientists and Politics in the Twentieth Century*, edited by David Smith, 6–28. London: Routledge, 2013.

Bauch, Nicholas. *A Geography of Digestion: Biotechnology and the Kellogg Cereal Enterprise*. Berkeley: University of California Press, 2016.

Bender, Daniel E. *American Abyss: Savagery and Civilization in the Age of Industry*. Ithaca, NY: Cornell University Press, 2009.

Berry, Veronica, and Celia Petty, eds. *The Nyasaland Survey Papers, 1938–1943: Agriculture, Food and Health*. London: Academy Books, 1992.

Besky, Sarah, and Sandy Brown. "Looking for Work: Placing Labor in Food Studies." *Labor* 12, no. 1–2 (May 1, 2015): 19–43.

Biltekoff, Charlotte. *Eating Right in America: The Cultural Politics of Food and Health*. Durham, NC: Duke University Press, 2013.

Blum, Deborah. *The Poison Squad: One Chemist's Single-Minded Crusade for Food Safety at the Turn of the Twentieth Century*. New York: Penguin, 2018.

Bobrow-Strain, Aaron. *White Bread: A Social History of the Store-Bought Loaf*. Boston: Beacon Press, 2012.

———. "White Bread Biopolitics: Purity, Health, and the Triumph of Industrial Baking." In *Geographies of Race and Food: Fields, Bodies, Markets*, edited by Rachel Slocum and Arun Saldanha, 265–90. Oxon: Routledge, 2016.

Bodwell, C. E., and John W. Erdman, eds. *Nutrient Interactions*. New York: CRC Press, 1988.

Bohstedt, John. *The Politics of Provisions: Food Riots, Moral Economy, and Market Transition in England, C. 1550–1850*. London: Ashgate, 2010.

Boianovsky, Mauro. "Humboldt and the Economists on Natural Resources, Institutions and Underdevelopment (1752–1859)." *European Journal of the History of Economic Thought* 20, no. 1 (2013): 58–88.

Borowy, Iris. "International Social Medicine between the Wars: Positioning a Volatile Concept." *Hygiea Internationalis* 6, no. 2 (July 2007): 13–35.

Brandt, Allan. *No Magic Bullet: A Social History of Venereal Disease in the United States Since 1880*. New York: Oxford University Press, 1987.

Brantley, Cynthia. *Feeding Families: African Realities and British Ideas of Nutrition and Development in Early Colonial Africa*. Portsmouth, NH: Heinemann, 2002.

Brock, William H. *Justus Von Liebig: The Chemical Gatekeeper*. Cambridge: Cambridge University Press, 2002.

Bud, Robert. *Penicillin: Triumph and Tragedy*. Oxford: Oxford University Press, 2007.

Burnett, John. *Plenty and Want: A Social History of Food in England from 1815 to the Present Day*. Edinburgh: Nelson, 1966.

Carey, Charles W. "Borden, Gail, Jr." In *American Inventors, Entrepreneurs, and Business Visionaries*, 35–36. New York: Infobase Publishing, 2002.

Carman, Tim. "Wonder Bread: 90 Years of Spiritual Vacuousness?" *Washington Post*, March 18, 2011.

Carpenter, Kenneth J. "The Work of Wallace Aykroyd: International Nutritionist and Author." *Journal of Nutrition* 137, no. 4 (April 1, 2007): 873–78.

Cetina, Karin Knorr. *Epistemic Cultures: How the Sciences Make Knowledge*. Cambridge, MA: Harvard University Press, 2009.

Chakrabarti, Pratik. *Inscriptions of Nature: Geology and the Naturalization of Antiquity*. Baltimore: Johns Hopkins University Press, 2020.

Chatelain, Marcia. *Franchise: The Golden Arches in Black America*. New York: Liveright, 2020.

Christie, Ann. "'Nothing of Intrinsic Value': The Scientific Collections at the Bethnal Green Museum." *V&A Online Journal*, no. 3 (Spring 2011).

Clarke, Sabine. *Science at the End of Empire: Experts and the Development of the British Caribbean, 1940–62.* Manchester: Manchester University Press, 2018.

Cohen, Benjamin R. *Pure Adulteration: Cheating on Nature in the Age of Manufactured Food.* Chicago: University of Chicago Press, 2019.

Colley, Linda. *Britons: Forging the Nation, 1707–1837.* New Haven, CT: Yale University Press, 2009.

Colpitts, George. *Pemmican Empire: Food, Trade, and the Last Bison Hunts in the North American Plains, 1780–1882.* Cambridge: Cambridge University Press, 2014.

Combet, Emilie, and Stuart R. Gray. "Nutrient-Nutrient Interactions: Competition, Bioavailability, Mechanism and Function in Health and Diseases." *Proceedings of the Nutrition Society* 78, no. 1 (February 2019): 1–3.

Contois, Emily J. H. *Diners, Dudes, and Diets: How Gender and Power Collide in Food Media and Culture.* Chapel Hill: University of North Carolina Press, 2020.

Cook, Chris. *The Routledge Companion to Britain in the Nineteenth Century, 1815–1914.* London: Routledge, 2005.

Cooper, Timothy. "Peter Lund Simmonds and the Political Ecology of 'Waste Utilisation' in Victorian Britain." *Technology and Culture* 52, no. 1 (January 2011): 21–44.

Coppin, Clayton A., and Jack C. High. *The Politics of Purity: Harvey Washington Wiley and the Origins of Federal Food Policy.* Ann Arbor: University of Michigan Press, 1999.

Council for Responsible Nutrition. "Dietary Supplement Use Reaches All Time High," September 30, 2019. https://www.crnusa.org/newsroom/dietary-supplement-use-reaches-all-time-high.

Coveney, John. *Food, Morals and Meaning: The Pleasure and Anxiety of Eating.* 2nd ed. Oxon: Routledge, 2006.

Cronon, William. *Nature's Metropolis: Chicago and the Great West.* New York: W. W. Norton, 1991.

Crowley, Carolyn Hughes. "The Man Who Invented Elsie, the Borden Cow." *Smithsonian Magazine,* August 31, 1999.

Cullather, Nick. "The Foreign Policy of the Calorie." *American Historical Review* 112, no. 2 (2007): 337–64.

Daston, Lorraine. *Things That Talk: Object Lessons from Art and Science.* New York: Zone Books, 2007.

Daston, Lorraine, and Katharine Park. *Wonders and the Order of Nature, 1150–1750.* Cambridge, MA: Zone Books, 1998.

Davis, Jennifer J. *Defining Culinary Authority: The Transformation of Cooking in France, 1650–1830.* Baton Rouge: Louisiana State University Press, 2013.

Desrochers, Pierre. "Promoting Corporate Environmental Sustainability in the Victorian Era: The Bethnal Green Museum Permanent Waste Exhibit (1875–1928)." *V&A Online Journal,* no. 3 (Spring 2011).

———. "Victorian Pioneers of Corporate Sustainability." *Business History Review* 83, no. 4 (2009): 703–29.

Devine, Thomas Martin, and David Dickson, eds. *Ireland and Scotland, 1600–1850: Parallels and Contrasts in Economic and Social Development.* Edinburgh: Donald, 1983.

Dick, Stephanie. "After Math: (Re)Configuring Minds, Proof, and Computing in the Postwar United States." PhD dissertation, Harvard University, 2015.

Edwards, Steve. "The Accumulation of Knowledge or, William Whewell's Eye." In *The Great Exhibition of 1851: New Interdisciplinary Essays*, edited by Louise Purbrick, 26–52. Manchester: Manchester University Press, 2001.

Fielden, Kenneth. "Samuel Smiles and Self-Help." *Victorian Studies* 12, no. 2 (1968): 155–76.

Finger, Thomas D. "Tulare Lake and the Past Future of Food." In *Acquired Tastes: Stories about the Origins of Modern Food*, edited by Benjamin R. Cohen, Michael S. Kideckel, and Anna Zeide, 17–34. Cambridge, MA: MIT Press, 2021.

Finlay, Mark R. "Early Marketing of the Theory of Nutrition: The Science and Culture of Liebig's Extract of Meat." In *The Science and Culture of Nutrition, 1840–1940*, edited by Harmke Kamminga and Andrew Cunningham, 48–74. Amsterdam: Rodopi, 1995.

Frazer, Robert W. *Forts and Supplies: The Role of the Army in the Economy of the Southwest, 1846–1861.* Albuquerque: University of New Mexico Press, 1983. .

Freidberg, Susanne. *Fresh*. Cambridge, MA: Harvard University Press, 2009.

Friedmann, Harriet. "Feeding the Empire: The Pathologies of Globalized Agriculture." *Socialist Register* 41 (2005): 124–43.

Frohlich, Xaq. "The Rise (and Fall) of the Food-Drug Line: Classification, Gatekeepers, and Spatial Mediation in Regulating US Food and Health Markets." In *Risk on the Table: Food Production, Health, and the Environment*, edited by Angela N. H. Creager and Jean-Paul Gaudillière, 297–329. New York: Berghahn Books, 2021.

Funnell, Warwick, and Jeffrey Robertson. *Accounting by the First Public Company: The Pursuit of Supremacy.* London: Routledge, 2013.

Gabriel, Joseph M. *Medical Monopoly: Intellectual Property Rights and the Origins of the Modern Pharmaceutical Industry.* Chicago: University of Chicago Press, 2014.

Galison, Peter. *Image and Logic: A Material Culture of Microphysics.* Chicago: University of Chicago Press, 1997.

Galluzzi Bizzo, Maria Letícia. "Postponing Equality: From Colonial to International Nutritional Standards, 1932–1950." In *Health and Difference: Rendering Human Variation in Colonial Engagements*, edited by Alexandra Widmer and Veronika Lipphardt, 129–48. New York: Berghahn, 2016.

Gil-Riaño, Sebastián, and Sarah E. Tracy. "Developing Constipation: Dietary Fiber, Western Disease, and Industrial Carbohydrates." *Global Food History* 2, no. 2 (July 2, 2016): 179–209.

Goldberg, Hanna, and Laura-Anne Minkoff-Zern. "Teaching Labor in Food Studies: Challenging Consumer-Based Approaches to Social Change through Student Research Community Partnerships." *Food, Culture & Society* 0, no. 0 (August 11, 2021): 1–17.

Golinski, Jan. *The Experimental Self: Humphry Davy and the Making of a Man of Science*. Chicago: University of Chicago Press, 2016.

Gómez, Laura E. *Manifest Destinies: The Making of the Mexican American Race*. New York: New York University Press, 2008.

Gray, Margaret. *Labor and the Locavore: The Making of a Comprehensive Food Ethic*. Berkeley: University of California Press, 2013.

Greene, Jeremy. *Prescribing by Numbers: Drugs and the Definition of Disease*. Baltimore: Johns Hopkins University Press, 2007.

Greysmith, David. "Simmonds, Peter Lund (1814–1897)." In *Oxford Dictionary of National Biography*. Oxford: Oxford University Press, 2004. http://www.oxforddnb.com.ezp-prod1.hul.harvard.edu/view/article/41011.

Guthman, Julie. "Neoliberalism and the Making of Food Politics in California." *Geoforum*, Rethinking Economy, 39, no. 3 (May 1, 2008): 1171–83.

———. *Weighing In: Obesity, Food Justice, and the Limits of Capitalism*. Berkeley: University of California Press, 2011.

———. *Wilted: Pathogens, Chemicals, and the Fragile Future of the Strawberry Industry*. Berkeley: University of California Press, 2019.

Hadrich, Dirk. "Microbiome Research Is Becoming the Key to Better Understanding Health and Nutrition." *Frontiers in Genetics* 9, no. 212 (2018): 1–10. https://doi.org/10.3389/fgene.2018.00212.

Haley, Andrew P. *Turning the Tables: Restaurants and the Rise of the American Middle Class, 1880–1920*. Chapel Hill: University of North Carolina Press, 2011.

Hall, Amy Laura. "Whose Progress? The Language of Global Health." *Journal of Medicine and Philosophy* 31, no. 3 (June 2006): 285–304.

Haller, Uli. "Tod, John Grant, Sr." Handbook of Texas Online, June 15, 2010. https://tshaonline.org/handbook/online/articles/fto05.

Hämäläinen, Pekka. *The Comanche Empire*. New Haven, CT: Yale University Press, 2008.

Hatch, Anthony Ryan. *Blood Sugar: Racial Pharmacology and Food Justice in Black America*. Minneapolis: University of Minnesota Press, 2016.

Haushofer, Lisa. "Between Food and Medicine: Artificial Digestion, Sickness, and the Case of Benger's Food." *Journal of the History of Medicine and Allied Sciences* 73, no. 2 (April 1, 2018): 168–87.

Herzberg, David. *Happy Pills in America: From Miltown to Prozac*. Baltimore: Johns Hopkins University Press, 2010.

Hilton, Boyd. *The Age of Atonement: The Influence of Evangelicalism on Social and Economic Thought, 1785–1865*. Oxford: Clarendon Press, 1988.

Hobart, Hiʻilei Julia, and Stephanie Maroney. "On Racial Constitutions and Digestive Therapeutics." *Food, Culture & Society* 22, no. 5 (October 20, 2019): 576–94.

Hoffman, Beatrix. *The Wages of Sickness: The Politics of Health Insurance in Progressive America*. Chapel Hill: University of North Carolina Press, 2001.

Holmes, Frederic. "Analysis by Fire and Solvent Extractions: The Metamorphosis of a Tradition." *Isis* 62, no. 2 (Summer 1971): 128–48.

———. *Claude Bernard and Animal Chemistry: The Emergence of a Scientist.* Cambridge, MA: Harvard University Press, 1974.

———. *Eighteenth-Century Chemistry as an Investigative Enterprise.* Berkeley: Office for History of Science and Technology, University of California at Berkeley, 1989.

Horrocks, Sally. "Consuming Science: Science, Technology and Food in Britain, 1870–1939." PhD dissertation, University of Manchester, 1993.

Horsman, Reginald. *Race and Manifest Destiny: The Origins of American Racial Anglo-Saxonism.* Cambridge, MA: Harvard University Press, 2009.

Inness, Sherrie A., ed. *Kitchen Culture in America: Popular Representations of Food, Gender, and Race.* Philadelphia: University of Pennsylvania Press, 2001.

Jauho, Mikko, and Mari Niva. "Lay Understandings of Functional Foods as Hybrids of Food and Medicine." *Food, Culture & Society* 16, no. 1 (March 1, 2013): 43–63.

Johnson, Walter. *The Broken Heart of America: St. Louis and the Violent History of the United States.* New York: Basic Books, 2020.

———. *River of Dark Dreams.* Cambridge, MA: Harvard University Press, 2013.

Jonsson, Fredrik Albritton. *Enlightenment's Frontier: The Scottish Highlands and the Origins of Environmentalism.* New Haven, CT: Yale University Press, 2013.

Jorgensen, Janice. *Encyclopedia of Consumer Brands.* Detroit: St. James Press, 1994.

Joseph, Miranda. *Debt to Society: Accounting for Life under Capitalism.* Minneapolis: University of Minnesota Press, 2014.

Jou, Chin. *Supersizing Urban America: How Inner Cities Got Fast Food with Government Help.* Chicago: University of Chicago Press, 2017.

Kaplan, Steven L., and Sophus A. Reinert. "The Economic Turn in Enlightenment Europe." In *The Economic Turn: Recasting Political Economy in Enlightenment Europe*, edited by Steven L. Kaplan and Sophus A. Reinert, 1–33. London: Anthem Press, 2019.

———, eds. *The Economic Turn: Recasting Political Economy in Enlightenment Europe.* London: Anthem Press, 2019.

Keller, Robert H. "Hostile Language: Bias in Historical Writing about American Indian Resistance." *Journal of American Culture* 9, no. 4 (1986): 9–23.

Kent, Max Louis. "The British Enlightenment and the Spirit of the Industrial Revolution: The Society for the Encouragement of Arts, Manufactures and Commerce (1754–1815)." PhD dissertation, University of California, 2007.

Kideckel, Michael S. "The Search for the Average Consumer: Breakfast Cereal and the Industrialization of the American Food Supply." In *Acquired Tastes: Stories about the Origins of Modern Food*, edited by Benjamin R. Cohen, Michael S. Kideckel, and Anna Zeide, 117–32. Cambridge, MA: MIT Press, 2021.

Kienzle, George. *The Story of Gail Borden: The Birth of an Industry.* New York: Priv. Print., 1947.

Kimmerer, Robin Wall. *Braiding Sweetgrass: Indigenous Wisdom, Scientific Knowledge and the Teachings of Plants.* Minneapolis, MN: Milkweed Editions, 2015.

Kimura, Aya Hirata. *Hidden Hunger: Gender and the Politics of Smarter Foods.* Ithaca, NY: Cornell University Press, 2013.

———. "Who Defines Babies' 'Needs'? The Scientization of Baby Food in Indonesia." *Social Politics: International Studies in Gender, State & Society* 15, no. 2 (July 1, 2008): 232–60.

Kinealy, Christine. *This Great Calamity: The Great Irish Famine: The Irish Famine 1845–52*. Dublin: Gill & Macmillan Ltd, 1994.

Klein, Ursula. "Origin of the Concept Chemical Compound." *Science in Context* 7, no. 2 (1994): 163–204.

Klieger, Christiaan. *The Fleischmann Yeast Family*. Images of America. Charleston, SC: Arcadia, 2004.

Kohler, Robert E. "The Enzyme Theory and the Origin of Biochemistry." *Isis* 64, no. 2 (1973): 181–96.

Krinsky, Alan David. "Let Them Eat Horsemeat: Science, Philanthropy, State, and the Search for Complete Nutrition in Nineteenth-Century France." PhD dissertation, University of Wisconsin, Madison, 2001.

Kubena, K. S., and D. N. McMurray. "Nutrition and the Immune System: A Review of Nutrient-Nutrient Interactions." *Journal of the American Dietetic Association* 96, no. 11 (November 1996): 1156–64.

Lambert, David, and Alan Lester, eds. *Colonial Lives across the British Empire: Imperial Careering in the Long Nineteenth Century*. Cambridge: Cambridge University Press, 2006.

Landecker, Hannah. "Food as Exposure: Nutritional Epigenetics and the New Metabolism." *Biosocieties* 6, no. 2 (June 2011): 167–94.

Latour, Bruno. *Reassembling the Social: An Introduction to Actor-Network-Theory*. Oxford: Oxford University Press, 2005.

La Vere, David. *The Texas Indians*. College Station: Texas A&M University Press, 2004.

Lawrence, Mark, and John Germov. "Future Food: The Politics of Functional Foods and Health Claims." In *A Sociology of Food and Nutrition: The Social Appetite*, edited by John Germov and Lauren Williams, 2nd ed., 119–47. South Melbourne, Australia: Oxford University Press, 2004.

Lazo, Rodrigo. *Writing to Cuba: Filibustering and Cuban Exiles in the United States*. Chapel Hill: University of North Carolina Press, 2006.

Lemire, Beverly. *The Business of Everyday Life: Gender, Practice and Social Politics in England, C. 1600–1900*. Manchester: Manchester University Press, 2005.

Levenstein, Harvey. *Revolution at the Table: The Transformation of the American Diet*. New York: Oxford University Press, 1988.

Lobel, Cindy R. *Urban Appetites: Food and Culture in Nineteenth-Century New York*. Chicago: University of Chicago Press, 2014.

Mackert, Nina. "Feeding Productive Bodies: Calories, Nutritional Values, and Ability in the Progressive-Era US." In *Histories of Productivity: Genealogical Perspectives on the Body and Modern Economy*, edited by Peter-Paul Bänziger and Mischa Suter, 117–35. New York: Routledge, 2016.

Marald, Erland. "Everything Circulates: Agricultural Chemistry and Recycling Theories in the Second Half of the Nineteenth Century." *Environment and History* 8, no. 1 (2002): 65–84.

Markel, Howard. *The Kelloggs: The Battling Brothers of Battle Creek*. New York: Pantheon Books, 2017.

Maudrie, Tara L., Uriyoán Colón-Ramos, Kaitlyn M. Harper, Brittany W. Jock, and Joel Gittelsohn. "A Scoping Review of the Use of Indigenous Food Sovereignty Principles for Intervention and Future Directions." *Current Developments in Nutrition* 5, no. 7 (July 1, 2021): 1–22.

McCabe, Brian J. *No Place Like Home: Wealth, Community and the Politics of Homeownership*. Oxford: Oxford University Press, 2016.

McGrath, Molly Wade. *Top Sellers, U.S.A.: Success Stories behind America's Best-Selling Products from Alka-Seltzer to Zippo*. New York: William Morrow, 1983.

Meinig, Donald. *The Shaping of America: A Geographical Perspective on 500 Years of History*. Vol. 2. 3 vols. New Haven, CT: Yale University Press, 1993.

Moran, Bruce T. *Distilling Knowledge: Alchemy, Chemistry, and the Scientific Revolution*. Cambridge, MA: Harvard University Press, 2005.

Morris, Evan. *From Altoids to Zima: The Surprising Stories Behind 125 Famous Brand Names*. New York: Simon and Schuster, 2004.

Mosby, Ian. "Administering Colonial Science: Nutrition Research and Human Biomedical Experimentation in Aboriginal Communities and Residential Schools, 1942–1952." *Histoire Sociale/Social History* 46, no. 1 (2013): 145–72.

———. *Food Will Win the War: The Politics, Culture, and Science of Food on Canada's Home Front*. Vancouver: University of British Columbia Press, 2014.

Mudry, Jessica J. *Measured Meals: Nutrition in America*. Albany: State University of New York Press, 2009.

Murphy, Suzanne P., Allison A. Yates, Stephanie A. Atkinson, Susan I. Barr, and Johanna Dwyer. "History of Nutrition: The Long Road Leading to the Dietary Reference Intakes for the United States and Canada." *Advances in Nutrition* 7, no. 1 (January 7, 2016): 157–68.

Myers, Dan. "5 Things You Didn't Know about Wonder Bread." *ABC News*, March 6, 2015.

Nash, Gary B. "The Image of the Indian in the Southern Colonial Mind." *William and Mary Quarterly* 29, no. 2 (1972): 198–230.

Nestle, Marion. *Food Politics: How the Food Industry Influences Nutrition and Health*. Berkeley: University of California Press, 2002.

———. *Unsavory Truth: How Food Companies Skew the Science of What We Eat*. New York: Basic Books, 2018.

Neswald, Elizabeth, David F. Smith, and Ulrike Thoms, eds. *Setting Nutritional Standards: Theory, Policies, Practices*. Rochester, NY: University of Rochester Press, 2017.

Newman, William R. *Atoms and Alchemy: Chymistry and the Experimental Origins of the Scientific Revolution*. Chicago: University of Chicago Press, 2006.

Newman, William R., and Lawrence M. Principe. *Alchemy Tried in the Fire: Starkey, Boyle, and the Fate of Helmontian Chymistry*. Chicago: University of Chicago Press, 2002.

Nichter, Mark, and Jennifer Thompson. "For My Wellness, Not Just My Illness: North Americans' Use of Dietary Supplements." *Culture, Medicine and Psychiatry* 30, no. 2 (2006).

Nissenbaum, Stephen. *Sex, Diet, and Debility in Jacksonian America: Sylvester Graham and Health Reform.* American Society and Culture. London: Greenwood Press, 1980.

Nugent, Walter T. K. *The Tolerant Populists: Kansas, Populism and Nativism.* Chicago: University of Chicago Press, 1963.

Orland, Barbara. "The Invention of Nutrients: William Prout, Digestion and Alimentary Substances in the 1820s." *Food and History* 8, no. 1 (January 1, 2010): 149–68.

Otter, Chris. *Diet for a Large Planet: Industrial Britain, Food Systems, and World Ecology.* Chicago: University of Chicago Press, 2020.

———. "The British Nutrition Transition and Its Histories." *History Compass* 10, no. 11 (2012): 812–25.

Packard, Randall M. *A History of Global Health: Interventions into the Lives of Other Peoples.* Baltimore: Johns Hopkins University Press, 2016.

Parkin, Katherine J. *Food Is Love: Advertising and Gender Roles in Modern America.* Philadelphia: University of Pennsylvania Press, 2006.

Parnes, Ohad. "From Agents to Cells: Theodor Schwann's Research Notes of the Years 1835–1838." In *Reworking the Bench: Research Notebooks in the History of Science*, edited by F. L. Holmes, J. Renn, and Hans-Jörg Rheinberger, 119–39. Dordrecht: Kluwer, 2003.

Paskins, Matthew. "Sentimental Industry: The Society of Arts and the Encouragement of Public Useful Knowledge, 1754–1848." PhD diss., University College London, 2014.

Pintauro, Stephen J. *The Regulation of Dietary Supplements: A Historical Analysis.* Boca Raton, FL: CRC Press, 2018.

Podolsky, Scott. *The Antibiotic Era: Reform, Resistance, and the Pursuit of a Rational Therapeutics.* Baltimore: Johns Hopkins University Press, 2015.

Pollan, Michael. *In Defense of Food: An Eater's Manifesto.* London: Penguin, 2008.

Price, Catherine. "The Healing Power of Compressed Yeast." *Distillations Magazine,* Fall 2015.

———. *Vitamania: How Vitamins Revolutionized the Way We Think about Food.* New York: Penguin, 2016.

Rabinbach, Anson. *The Human Motor: Energy, Fatigue, and the Origins of Modernity.* Berkeley: University of California Press, 1990.

Rebrovick, Tripp. "The Politics of Diet: 'Eco-Dietetics,' Neoliberalism, and the History of Dietetic Discourses." *Political Research Quarterly* 68, no. 4 (December 1, 2015): 678–89.

Reese, Ashanté M. *Black Food Geographies: Race, Self-Reliance, and Food Access in Washington.* Chapel Hill: University of North Carolina Press, 2019.

Rheinberger, Hans-Jörg. *Toward a History of Epistemic Things: Synthesizing Proteins in the Test Tube.* Writing Science. Stanford, CA: Stanford University Press, 1997.

Richards, Eric. "Scotland and the Uses of the Atlantic Empire." In *Strangers within the Realm: Cultural Margins of the First British Empire*, edited by Bernard Bailyn and Philip D. Morgan, 67–114. Chapel Hill: University of North Carolina Press, 2012.

Riskin, Jessica. "The Defecating Duck, or, the Ambiguous Origins of Artificial Life." *Critical Inquiry* 29, no. 4 (June 1, 2003): 599–633.

Rivest, Justin. "Secret Remedies and the Rise of Pharmaceutical Monopolies in France during the First Global Age." PhD Dissertation, Johns Hopkins University, 2016.

Roberts, Lissa. "The Death of the Sensuous Chemist: The 'New' Chemistry and the Transformation of Sensuous Technology." *Studies in History and Philosophy of Science* 26, no. 4 (1995): 503–29.

Robinson, Cedric J. *Black Marxism: The Making of the Black Radical Tradition*. University of North Carolina Press, 1983.

Roosth, Sophia. *Synthetic: How Life Got Made*. Chicago: University of Chicago Press, 2017.

Rosenberg, Charles. "Pathologies of Progress: The Idea of Civilization as Risk." *Bulletin of the History of Medicine* 72, no. 4 (1998): 714–30.

Rosenberg, Gabriel N., and Jan Dutkiewicz. "Abolish the Department of Agriculture." *New Republic*, December 27, 2021. https://newrepublic.com/article/164874/abolish-department-agriculture.

Rothschild, Emma. *The Inner Life of Empires: An Eighteenth-Century History*. Princeton, NJ: Princeton University Press, 2011.

———. "Isolation and Economic Life in Eighteenth-Century France." *American Historical Review* 119, no. 4 (October 1, 2014): 1055–82.

Schaffer, Simon. "Glass Works: Newton's Prisms and the Uses of Experiment." In *The Uses of Experiment: Studies in the Natural Sciences*, edited by David Gooding, Trevor Pinch, and Simon Schaffer, 67–104. Cambridge: Cambridge University Press, 1989.

Schiebinger, Londa. *Plants and Empire*. Cambridge, MA: Harvard University Press, 2004.

———. "Prospecting for Drugs: European Naturalists in the West Indies." In *Colonial Botany: Science, Commerce, and Politics in the Early Modern World*, edited by Londa Schiebinger and Claudia Swan, 119–33. Philadelphia: University of Pennsylvania Press, 2005.

Schwarz, Richard. *John Harvey Kellogg, M.D.: Pioneering Health Reformer*. Nashville, TN: Southern Publishing Association, 1970.

———. *John Harvey Kellogg, M.D.: Pioneering Health Reformer*. Hagerstown, MD: Review and Herald Pub. Association, 2006.

Scott-Smith, Tom. *On an Empty Stomach: Two Hundred Years of Hunger Relief*. Ithaca, NY: Cornell University Press, 2020.

Scrinis, Gyorgy. *Nutritionism: "On the Ideology of Nutritionism."* *Gastronomica: The Journal of Critical Food Studies* 8, no. 1 (February 1, 2008): 39–48.

———. *The Science and Politics of Dietary Advice*. New York: Columbia University Press, 2013.

Secord, James. "Knowledge in Transit." *Isis* 95, no. 4 (2004): 654–72.

Sewell, William H. "A Strange Career: The Historical Study of Economic Life." *History and Theory* 49, no. 4 (December 1, 2010): 146–66.

Shapin, Steven. "How to Eat Like a Gentleman: Dietetics and Ethics in Early Modern England." In *An Anglo-American Tradition of Self-Help Medicine and Hygiene*, edited by Charles E. Rosenberg, 21–58. Baltimore: Johns Hopkins University Press, 2003.

———. "'You Are What You Eat': Historical Changes in Ideas about Food and Identity." *Historical Research* 87, no. 236 (2014): 1–16.

Shapin, Steven, and Simon Schaffer. *Leviathan and the Air-Pump: Hobbes, Boyle, and the Experimental Life*. Princeton, NJ: Princeton University Press, 1985.

Shephard, Sue. *Pickled, Potted, and Canned: How the Art and Science of Food Preserving Changed the World*. New York: Simon and Schuster, 2006.

Shprintzen, Adam. "Ella Eaton Kellogg's Protose: Fake Meat and the Gender Politics That Made American Vegetarianism Modern." In *Acquired Tastes: Stories about the Origins of Modern Food*, edited by Benjamin R. Cohen, Michael S. Kideckel, and Anna Zeide, 219–34. Cambridge, MA: MIT Press, 2021.

Silverthorne, Elizabeth. *Ashbel Smith of Texas: Pioneer, Patriot, Statesman, 1805–1886*. College Station: Texas A&M University Press, 1982.

Sklansky, Jeffrey. *The Soul's Economy: Market Society and Selfhood in American Thought, 1820–1920*. Chapel Hill: University of North Carolina Press, 2002.

Smith, Andrew F. *Eating History: 30 Turning Points in the Making of American Cuisine*. New York: Columbia University Press, 2009.

———. *Food in America: The Past, Present, and Future of Food, Farming, and the Family Meal*. Vol. 1. 3 vols. Santa Barbara: ABC-CLIO, 2017.

Smith, Thomas T. *The US Army and the Texas Frontier Economy, 1845–1900*. College Station: Texas A&M University Press, 1999.

Spary, Emma. *Eating the Enlightenment: Food and the Sciences in Paris*. Chicago: University of Chicago Press, 2012.

———. *Feeding France: New Sciences of Food, 1760–1815*. Cambridge: Cambridge University Press, 2014.

Specht, Joshua. *Red Meat Republic: A Hoof-to-Table History of How Beef Changed America*. Princeton. NJ: Princeton University Press, 2019.

Starr, Ranjani R. "Too Little, Too Late: Ineffective Regulation of Dietary Supplements in the United States." *American Journal of Public Health* 105, no. 3 (March 2015): 478–85.

Steinitz, Lesley. "Transforming Pig's Wash into Health Food: The Construction of Skimmed Milk Protein Powders." *Global Food History*, December 29, 2021, 1–34.

Stern, Alexandra Minna. *Eugenic Nation: Faults and Frontiers of Better Breeding in Modern America*. Berkeley: University of California Press, 2005.

Strasser, Bruno J. "Magic Bullets and Wonder Pills: Making Drugs and Diseases in the Twentieth Century." *Historical Studies in the Natural Sciences* 38, no. 2 (May 1, 2008): 303–12.

Street, Alice. "Food as Pharma: Marketing Nutraceuticals to India's Rural Poor." *Critical Public Health* 25, no. 3 (May 27, 2015): 361–72.

Swann, John P. "The History of Efforts to Regulate Dietary Supplements in the USA." *Drug Testing and Analysis* 8, nos. 3–4 (2016): 271–82.

Swanson, Kara W. "Authoring an Invention: Patent Production in the Nineteenth-Century United States." In *Making and Unmaking Intellectual Property: Creative Production in Legal and Cultural Perspective*, edited by Mario Biagioli, Peter Jaszi, and Martha Woodmansee, 41–54. Chicago: University of Chicago Press, 2011.

Taylor, Peter N., and J. Stephen Davies. "A Review of the Growing Risk of Vitamin D Toxicity from Inappropriate Practice." *British Journal of Clinical Pharmacology* 84, no. 6 (June 2018): 1121–27.

Teich, Mikuláš. "Circulation, Transformation, Conservation of Matter and the Balancing of the Biological World in the Eighteenth Century." *Ambix* 29, no. 1 (1982): 17–28.

Terrall, Mary. *Catching Nature in the Act: Réaumur and the Practice of Natural History in the Eighteenth Century*. Chicago: University of Chicago Press, 2014.

Theroux, Alexander. *Einstein's Beets*. Seattle: Fantagraphics Books, 2017.

Tilley, Helen. *Africa as a Living Laboratory: Empire, Development, and the Problem of Scientific Knowledge, 1870–1950*. Chicago: University of Chicago Press, 2011.

Todes, Daniel P. *Ivan Pavlov: A Russian Life in Science*. Oxford: Oxford University Press, 2014.

———. *Pavlov's Physiology Factory: Experiment, Interpretation, Laboratory Enterprise*. Baltimore: Johns Hopkins University Press, 2002.

Tompkins, Kyla Wazana. *Racial Indigestion: Eating Bodies in the 19th Century*. New York: New York University Press, 2012.

Treitel, Corinna. *Eating Nature in Modern Germany*. Cambridge: Cambridge University Press, 2017.

Trentmann, Frank, ed. "Introduction." In *The Oxford Handbook of the History of Consumption*, 1–19. Oxford: Oxford University Press, 2012.

Turgeon, Sylvie L., and Laurie-Eve Rioux. "Food Matrix Impact on Macronutrients Nutritional Properties." *Food Hydrocolloids*, 25 years of Advances in Food Hydrocolloid Research, 25, no. 8 (December 1, 2011): 1915–24.

Vause, Erika. *In the Red and in the Black: Debt, Dishonor, and the Law in France between Revolutions*. Charlottesville: University of Virginia Press, 2018.

Veit, Helen. *Modern Food, Moral Food: Self-Control, Science, and the Rise of Modern American Eating in the Early Twentieth Century*. Chapel Hill: University of North Carolina Press, 2013.

Vernon, James. *Hunger: A Modern History*. Cambridge, MA: Harvard University Press, 2007.

Warner, John Harley. *Against the Spirit of System: The French Impulse in Nineteenth-Century American Medicine*. Baltimore: Johns Hopkins University Press, 2003.

Watkins, Elizabeth Siegel. *The Estrogen Elixir: A History of Hormone Replacement Therapy in America*. Baltimore: Johns Hopkins University Press, 2007.

Weindling, Paul. "The Role of International Organizations in Setting Nutritional Standards in the 1920s and 1930s." In *The Science and Culture of Nutrition, 1840–1940*, edited by Andrew Cunningham and Harmke Kamminga, 319–32. Amsterdam: Rodopi, 1995.

Werrett, Simon. *Thrifty Science: Making the Most of Materials in the History of Experiment*. Chicago: Chicago University Press, 2019.

Whorton, James. *Inner Hygiene: Constipation and the Pursuit of Health in Modern Society*. New York: Oxford University Press, 2000.

Wilk, Richard, and Emma McDonell, eds. *Critical Approaches to Superfoods*. New York: Bloomsbury Publishing, 2020.

Williams, Leslie A. *Daniel O'Connell, the British Press and the Irish Famine: Killing Remarks*. New York: Routledge, 2003.

Wilson, Brian C. *Dr. John Harvey Kellogg and the Religion of Biologic Living*. Bloomington: Indiana University Press, 2014.

The Wonder Bread Cookbook. Berkeley, CA: Ten Speed Press, 2007.

Woods, Rebecca J. H. "The Shape of Meat: Preserving Animal Flesh in Victorian Britain." *Osiris* 35 (August 2020): 123–41.

Worboys, Michael. "The Discovery of Colonial Malnutrition between the Wars." In *Imperial Medicine and Indigenous Societies*, edited by David Arnold, 208–25. Manchester: Manchester University Press, 1988.

World Health Organization. "Malnutrition Is a World Health Crisis," September 26, 2019. https://www.who.int/news/item/26-09-2019-malnutrition-is-a-world-health-crisis.

Yamey, Basil S. "Accounting and the Rise of Capitalism: Further Notes on a Theme by Sombart." *Journal of Accounting Research* 2, no. 2 (1964): 117–36.

Yates, Alexia M. *Selling Paris: Property and Commercial Culture in the Fin-de-Siècle Capital*. Cambridge, MA: Harvard University Press, 2015.

Young, Paul. "The Cooking Animal: Economic Man at the Great Exhibition." *Victorian Literature and Culture* 36, no. 2 (January 1, 2008): 569–86.

Zeide, Anna. *Canned: The Rise and Fall of Consumer Confidence in the American Food Industry*. Oakland: University of California Press, 2018.

Zweiniger-Bargielowska, Ina. "'Not a Complete Food for Man': The Controversy about White versus Wholemeal Bread in Interwar Britain." In *Setting Nutritional Standards: Theory, Policies, Practices*, edited by Elizabeth Neswald, David F. Smith, and Ulrike Thoms, 142–64. Rochester, NY: University of Rochester Press, 2017.

INDEX

abattoir. *See* slaughterhouse
advertising, 1–5, 7–9, 15, 18–19, 33–36, 79–80, 86, 104–6, 110, 123*fig.*, 124, 127, 130, 142–44, 148–65, 178, 186; essay contests, 159–61, 160*fig.;* testimonial, 72, 122, 158–65. *See also* Donovan and Armstrong Company; J. Walter Thompson Company; yeast
agriculture, 5, 23, 35–38, 45, 55–58, 61–63, 67, 110, 135–36, 169, 171, 179
alchemy, 25–26
American Food Journal, 151
appetite, 66–67, 93, 104, 112, 117, 119–20, 138–46, 174, 176–77. *See also* taste
artificial digestion. *See* artificially digested foods; digestive ferments
artificially digested foods, 72–74, 84, 98–108, 104*fig.*, 111, 120–30, 128*fig.*, 130*fig. See also* digestive ferments
Ashby, N. B., 135–36
Atwater, Wilbur, 150–51
Austin, Stephen F., 21
autointoxication, 155, 163
Aykroyd, Wallace R., 169–70, 174

Babbage, Charles, 53–54
bacteriology, 155, 168, 174
baking, 1–3, 148–52. *See also* yeast
Battle Creek Sanitarium, 109–10, 112–15, 113*fig.*, 122–23, 141, 144. *See also* Kellogg, John Harvey
Bauch, Nicholas, 126
Beaumont, William, 77, 93

Bender, Daniel, 115, 136
Benger, Frederick Baden, 72, 81–86, 98, 100–104, 218nn36,37
Benger's Food, 14, 71–75, 73*fig.*, 14, 81, 90, 98–108, 105*fig.*, 183; company letters, 72; preparation of, 72; promotion of, 72, 74. *See also* artificially digested foods
beriberi. *See* malnutrition
blood cakes. *See* Brocchieri's Blood Cakes
body, 6, 8, 25, 28, 58, 69, 74, 82, 92–94, 97, 100, 104, 106, 132, 140–42, 154–55, 178, 181, 186
Borden, Gail, 13, 18, 20–22, 28–44, 45–46, 183; condensed milk, 18, 68–69; food experiments, 23
Boudault, Charles-Pierre, 79–80
Braun, Lundy, 119
bread, 47, 72, 97, 101, 116–19, 126–27, 129, 148, 150–51, 160, 179; national fortification campaign of, 4–5. *See also* Wonder Bread
breakfast cereal, 14; flaked, 123–29; Granola, 120–23, 127, 142, 123*fig.*; Granose, 123–24, 126–27, 142–43; Gofio, 122–23
British Colonial Office, 149, 165, 167–69, 172, 174
British Economic Advisory Council, 172
British Pharmaceutical Society, 82
Brocchieri's Blood Cakes, 60
Bromose, 142–43

canned food, 18
carbohydrates, 24, 171–72, 184

Carey, Henry Charles, 36
cereal. *See* breakfast cereal
Chakrabarti, Pratik, 65
chemistry, 25–28, 43, 55, 58, 66, 76–78, 99–101, 107, 181; physiological chemistry, 152–54, 181
Chicago World's Fair, 4, 12, 179–82, 180*fig.*, 185
Chittenden, Russell, 121
Clarke, Sabine, 165
climate, 29, 34, 37, 42, 67, 183
Colley, Linda, 91
Colonial Development and Welfare Act, 165, 168–69
colonial malnutrition. *See* malnutrition
Colonial Products Research Council, 165, 174,
concentrated foods, 13, 19, 23, 27–29, 40, 42–44, 64, 68, 107, 116–18, 122, 183; pemmican, 29; pinole, 28–29. *See also* Gail Borden's meat biscuit
Conrad, Charles Magill, 39–40
consumer. *See* consumption
consumption, 13, 72, 74, 118, 129, 133–38, 144, 146, 149, 154, 158–65, 167, 170, 176–78, 185–86; consumer activism, 190; corporate consumption, 19, 38, 46, 68–69, 210n98
cookery, 8, 25–26, 28, 34–35, 81, 93–97, 100, 102–3, 107, 114, 119, 122, 124–27
Coonoor Nutrition Research Laboratories, 169–70, 174
Corn Laws, 48, 57
Corvisart, Lucien, 79, 99–100
cost-nutritiousness, 14, 56, 59, 63, 68, 89, 92–93, 102, 149, 151, 173
Cowan, John F., 133

Darby, Stephen, 72, 100
Daston, Lorraine, 8
Davenport, Charles, 144
Davy, Humphry, 58
Dewey, Annie, 144
Dewey, Melvin, 144
dextrin, 85–86, 99, 101–2, 126–29, 139, 142–43. *See also* digestive ferments
diastase, 72, 84–86, 121, 154. *See also* digestive ferments

Dickens, Charles, 47–48, 53
dietary supplements, 7, 183. *See also* wonder foods
dietetics. *See* early modern dietetics
digestibility, 4, 7, 10, 14, 26, 74, 89, 93–94, 96–97, 99, 102, 106–7, 116, 120–22, 124, 126–27, 129, 140, 150–51, 155, 157
digestion, 13–14, 54, 74, 78, 112, 181; cookery as preparation of, 96, 100, 122; diseases of, 79–87, 152, 155, 159, 162–64; fistula experiments of, 77; physiology of, 10, 14, 72, 75–81, 83–84, 94, 97–98, 120, 122, 126, 138–44, 184, 189; pre-19th century conceptions of, 26, 76; as work, 106, 132, 139, 158, 186. *See also* artificially digested foods; dextrin; digestive ferments; pepsin; peptogenic foods
digestive enzymes. *See* digestive ferments
digestive ferments, 72–74, 77–88, 90, 94, 96–106, 104*fig.*, 120–30, 132–35, 154, 184; commercial products of, 72–73, 73*fig.*, 78–82, 80*fig.*, 84, 87*fig.*, 98–99, 120–32, 123*fig.*, 132*fig.*; research on, 72–82, 84–88, 90, 94, 97–98, 139–40, 142–43, 154. *See also* artificially digested foods; Benger's Food; dextrin; digestion; pepsin; peptogenic foods
distillation analysis, 25
domestic economy, 103, 150
Donovan and Armstrong Company, 157
dust heaps, 51–53
Dutkiewicz, Jan, 189
dyspepsia. *See* digestion

early modern dietetics, 24–26, 29–31, 43, 57, 207nn42,47
Eaton, A. B., 38–39
Eberle, Johann, 77–78
economic development, 19, 33, 35–38, 46–48, 51, 54, 65–68, 117–18, 165, 167–68, 172, 177, 185, 187
economic life, 88, 92–97, 105–8, 133–38, 150–52, 173, 203n35. *See also* economic thought
economic thought, 9–11, 35–38, 48, 50–51, 53–56, 115, 117–18, 133–38, 149, 152, 169, 172–75, 185. *See also* economic life
economic turn, 9–10

laboratory, 11, 82, 84, 86, 90, 97, 102, 104, 114, 127, 153; colonial, 172–77. *See also* physiology; chemistry
Ladies Home Journal, 155
Landecker, Hannah, 189
Lankester, Edwin, 49–50, 53, 55–59, 65–69
League of Nations Health Organization, 149, 168–73
Levi, Leon, 91, 93
Liebig, Justus von, 28, 31–32, 58, 69, 102
Lindley, John, 49, 61, 61–63

Magendie, François, 27
malnutrition, 9, 15, 149, 167, 169–72, 183, 187; beriberi, 24, 172, 183; colonial, 172–77; pellagra, 172, 183; rickets, 183; scurvy, 24, 183; tropical, 172–77. *See also* hunger
malted foods. *See* maltose
Malthus, Thomas, 48
maltose, 72, 74, 85, 99, 102–3, 121, 126, 129, 142–43. *See also* digestive ferments
Manifest Destiny, 19, 23, 33–38, 44
marketing. *See* advertising
McCollum, Elmer, 169
meat biscuit. *See* Gail Borden's meat biscuit
meatpackers, 130
medicinal foods, 7, 12. *See also* wonder foods
Mellanby, Edward, 169
metate, 110, 124
Mexican-American War, 21–22, 36, 38, 40–41
Mexican Cession, 21
military, 13, 19–20, 22–23, 33–44, 59, 68–69, 184
Montesquieu, 35
Mottershead Company, 82–83, 101
Mudfog Society, 47–48, 70
Müller, Johannes, 77–78

National Health, 75, 92–96, 107
National Thrift Society, 90–91
Native genocide, 5, 13, 19, 34–35, 38–44
Native knowledge, 28–29, 111, 115–20, 120–30, 146, 182, 190–91
Nestle, Marion, 189
nitrogen, 27–28, 58–60, 69, 101, 142, 148, 170

nutraceuticals, 7, 183. *See also* wonder foods
nutrients. *See* food constituents
nutritional growth mentality, 7, 9–11, 23, 24, 28, 31–32, 43–44, 54, 56–60, 93, 172–73, 186–87, 190
nutritionism, 10, 24
nutritiousness, 7, 13, 24–26, 29–33, 43–44, 56–60, 99–100, 140–41, 148, 158, 187, 190. *See also* cost-nutritiousness

osmazome, 99; Warriner's Osmazome, 60, 64

Paget, James, 92
Paine, Standen, 83
pancreatic extract. *See* pancreatic ferments
pancreatic ferments, 72, 82, 84–86, 87*fig.*, 98, 100–103, 121, 130. *See also* digestive ferments
Park, Katharine, 8
patents, 31–33, 43
Pavlov, Ivan, 139–40, 143, 228n124
Pavy, William, 100, 102
pellagra. *See* malnutrition
Pepsi-Cola. *See* pepsin
pepsin, 72, 74, 78–85, 98–100, 103, 106, 121, 130–32, 139, 142, 154, 218n36; Boudault's, 80–81, 80*fig.*; in Pepsi-Cola, 74, 132, 216n2; as remedy, 78–79
peptogenic foods, 14–15, 111, 138–46
peptogens. *See* peptogenic foods
peptone, 85–86, 101–6, 130, 132–33, 139, 142–43, 145. *See also* digestive ferments
peptonization. *See* peptone
Pereira, Jonathan, 59
pharmacy, 27, 79, 82, 83, 130, 132; Council on Pharmacy and Chemistry, 153–54; experimental, 83; Pharmacy Act of 1868, 82
physiology, 83–84, 111–12; Christian, 112; of consumption, 112, 139, 144–46; experimental, 75–77, 83–84; of subsistence, 112, 117. *See also* artificial digestion; chemistry: physiological chemistry; digestion
Platt, Benjamin S., 172–74
Playfair, Lyon, 49–50, 54–56, 58–60, 63, 66–69

pneumography, 118–19
Pollan, Michael, 24
poor house dietaries. *See* institutional dietaries
poverty, 5, 9, 11, 35, 47–48, 53, 59, 66, 70, 74, 91–93, 135–37, 148–49, 168–69, 172, 175–76, 178
predigestion. *See* artificially digested foods; digestive ferments
Price, Catherine, 152
prison dietaries. *See* institutional dietaries
processed foods, 20, 46, 63–64. *See also* Gail Borden's meat biscuit
protective foods, 7, 12. *See also* wonder foods
protein, 24, 83–86, 101–3, 139, 143, 147, 149, 152, 166–77, 184, 188. *See also* nitrogen
Prout, William, 27
public health, 4, 11, 49, 74–75, 88, 90, 92, 96, 102, 106, 169, 171
Pure Food and Drug Act, 15, 151, 154

Quechan, 109–12, 118–20, 124, 126, 129, 137–38

Rabinbach, Anson, 104
racial capitalism, 11, 12, 186
Réaumur, René Antoine Ferchault de, 75–77
regulation, 15, 48, 57, 82, 151, 154, 165, 168–69, 186, 188–89
Reinert, Sophus, 9
religion, 6, 8, 26, 53, 91, 110–13, 126, 135, 137, 139, 141–42, 145–46, 184–85, 187
resource abundance, 20, 35, 68, 165
Richardson, Benjamin Ward, 88–90, 92, 96, 99
rickets. *See* malnutrition
Roberts, William, 72, 81–88, 96, 98, 100–107
Robinson, Cedric, 11
Roosevelt, Franklin, 171
Rosenberg, Gabriel, 189

sanitary science. *See* public health
Schiff, Moritz, 139
Schwann, Theodor, 77–78
Scrinis, Gyorgy, 10, 24

scurvy. *See* malnutrition
self-digestive foods. *See* artificially digested foods
Sharpey, William, 83
Simmonds, Peter Lund, 50, 54, 56, 61, 64–65, 69
skin disease, 8, 152, 155–57, 159, 164, 175
slaughterhouse, 59–60, 92
slavery, 21–23, 37, 48, 119, 137
Slow Food, 190
Smiles, Samuel, 91, 97
Smith, Adam, 35
Smith, Ashbel, 19, 22, 31, 34–38, 40, 45–47, 49; food experiments, 16–18, 23; medicine, 22. *See also* Gail Borden's meat biscuit
Smith, Edward, 59, 93–94
Society for the Encouragement of Arts, Commerce and Manufacture, 50–51, 55, 59–60, 69, 88–89
Society of Arts. *See* Society for the Encouragement of Arts, Commerce and Manufacture
soda fountains, 131–32. *See also* Pepsi-Cola
solvent analysis, 27–28
solvent extraction. *See* solvent analysis
Soylent, 190
Spary, Emma, 25
special foods, 7, 12. *See also* wonder foods
Spencer, Herbert, 135, 137
Starling, Ernest, 139, 143
stimulation, 7, 100, 116–18, 139–44, 143, 145, 158
St. Louis, 20, 23, 38
St. Martin, Alexis, 77, 93
subsistence office, 38
sugar, 23, 27, 35, 58, 64, 85–86, 101–2, 127, 129, 165–66, 168, 171, 174, 178; substitution, 48; Sugar Duties Act, 48
Sumner, E. V., 39–40
superfoods, 7. *See also* wonder foods

Taroena, 121–22. *See also* artificially digested foods; digestive ferments
taste, 59–60, 66–67, 69, 102, 112, 127–29, 139–41, 184. *See also* appetite
Texas, 20–23, 35, 38, 40, 63
Thaysen, Aage Christian, 166–68, 174

Thrift Society. *See* National Thrift Society
thrift, 5, 13, 74, 88–94, 96–97, 99, 106, 107, 150
Tod, John G., 39–40
tropical malnutrition. *See* malnutrition

United States Department of Agriculture, 151, 154, 189

Vegetarian Society, 95
vegetarianism, 89, 95, 112, 116, 130, 172, 176, 183
Vernon, James, 48, 170
vitamins, 10, 15, 24, 147–49, 152–53, 155, 157–58, 166–72, 175, 177–78, 181–84, 186, 188

war, 4, 48, 68, 148, 151, 166, 173–74. *See also* Mexican-American War
waste, 13, 46–47, 50–57, 52*fig.*, 59–65, 69–70, 88, 148, 150–51, 165–66, 168, 174, 185, 187

Werrett, Simon, 53
white supremacy, 4, 6, 11, 15, 22–23, 40, 43–44, 184
White, Ellen, 112–13
Wonder Bread, 1–5, 7–8, 12, 173, 179–80, 180*fig.*, 182
wonder foods, 182–87; categories, 7, 12; definition, 6–9
Worboys, Michael, 172
World Health Organization, 177, 183

Yeast for Health campaign. *See* yeast
yeast, 154–56; baker's, 147–48, 150, 152, 156–57, 166–67; brewer's, 147–49, 156, 166; Colonial Food Yeast Company, 168; Fleischmann's Yeast, 15, 148, 150–65, 160*fig.*, 177–78, 183; food yeast, 15, 149, 165–78, 183; Torula utilis, 166–67; Yeast for Health campaign, 15, 149, 150–52, 157–65, 160*fig.*

Founded in 1893,
UNIVERSITY OF CALIFORNIA PRESS
publishes bold, progressive books and journals
on topics in the arts, humanities, social sciences,
and natural sciences—with a focus on social
justice issues—that inspire thought and action
among readers worldwide.

The UC PRESS FOUNDATION
raises funds to uphold the press's vital role
as an independent, nonprofit publisher, and
receives philanthropic support from a wide
range of individuals and institutions—and from
committed readers like you. To learn more, visit
ucpress.edu/supportus.